TAKING SIDES

Clashing Views on Controversial

Issues in
Special Education

SECOND EDITION

Selected, Edited, and with Introductions by

MaryAnn Byrnes
University of Massachusetts–Boston

McGraw-Hill/Dushkin
A Division of The McGraw-Hill Companies

Photo Acknowledgment
Cover image: D. Berry/PhotoLink/Getty Images

Cover Acknowledgment
Maggie Nickles

Manufactured in the United States of America

Second Edition

123456789DOCDOC987654

Library of Congress Cataloging-in-Publication Data
Main entry under title:
Taking Sides: clashing views on controversial issues in special education /selected, edited, and with introductions by MaryAnn Byrnes.—2nd ed.
Includes bibliographical references and index.
1. Special education. I. Byrnes, MaryAnn, ed. II. Series.
371.9
0-07-304399-0
ISSN: 1537-0739

Printed on Recycled Paper

Preface

Special education is full of questions, emotions and opinions. Public responsibility for the education of children with disabilities is a relatively new endeavor that is still forging its identity and boundaries. Sometimes it seems that just as one set of issues is resolved, such as the creation of a range of services in public schools, a host of new challenges arises to take its place. Other issues, such as appropriate funding and inclusion, seem to defy resolution, despite long and thoughtful deliberation. Through *Taking Sides: Clashing Views on Controversial Issues in Special Education*, I invite you to consider some of the currently active issues in this volatile field.

A few basic principles guided the choice of selections for this book. Each reading needed to represent a widely held point of view on the question at hand. Other opinions surely exist, but the ones presented needed to be broadly held. Each had to employ solid reasoning; its position could not be easily refuted because of faulty logic. Finally, each selection, along with references for additional study, needed to be interesting to read. If an article did not captivate my attention, I did not want to include it.

Taking Sides: Clashing Views on Controversial Issues in Special Education has two major goals. First, to introduce key questions in special education, so that readers can learn about the field from authors who have thought long and carefully about educational policy and practice. Second, to stimulate thinking and discussion, so that readers can explore possibilities and debate the consequences of positions and actions. I hope you will find yourselves engaged and enlivened by the discussions these topics stimulate. Most of all, I trust your thinking will contribute to constructive solutions to puzzles which demand careful thinking and care about all our children.

This book includes 20 issues, addressing active debates in the field. I have grouped the issues into three parts. Part 1, Special Education and Society introduces questions of social policy and practice. Part 2, Inclusion, highlights varied perspectives on this controversial philosophy. And Part 3, Issues about Disabilities, presents critical considerations about specific disabilities and treatments.

Each issue is framed as a question and begins with an *introduction*, designed to set the stage for discussion. Two readings, presenting contrasting points of view, come next. Each issue closes with a *postscript*, which summarizes the expressed points of view, suggests other points of view and provides additional readings on the topic at hand. The *introductions* and *postscripts* also feature questions to stimulate your thinking as you weigh the topic at hand and its relationship to schools. Each question represents challenges to be resolved in the policy and practice of educating children with disabilities.

To expand your own thinking, you may want to reference the *On the Internet* pages that precede each section. These contain a sampling of Internet site addresses (URLs) that present varied points of view as well as links to related sites and bibliographies for further study.

The YES and NO positions on every issue express strongly held opinions. You may agree or disagree with the authors, or you may find your own view lies somewhere in between. You will likely identify additional perspectives as you study the issues more thoroughly. You will certainly find connections between issues. Perhaps class discussions will lead you to formulate a new and completely different response to the issue question. Doubtless, as you continue in your professional and personal life, your ideas will change and develop. What is critical as you read this book is to reflect on positions, options and emotions so you can decide what you think and use your opinion to guide your actions and decisions.

A word to the instructor   An *Instructor's Manual with Test Questions* (multiple choice and essay) is available through Dushkin/McGraw Hill for the instructor using *Taking Sides* in the classroom. Also available is *Using Taking Sides in the Classroom*, a general guidebook which presents strategies and examples of using the pro-con method in classroom settings. Faculty members using this text also have access to an online version of *Using Taking Sides in the Classroom* and a correspondence service, located at http://www.dushkin.com/usingts/.

Taking Sides: Clashing Views on Controversial Issues in Special Education is only one title in the *Taking Sides* series. The table of contents for any of the other titles can be found at the *Taking Sides* website at http://www.dushkin.com/takingsides/.

Changes to this edition   This 2nd Edition includes 3 completely new issues: *Can Brain Scans Unravel the Mystery of Learning Disabilities* (Issue 14); *Are There Scientifically Effective Treatments for Autism?* (Issue 18); and *Do Accommodations Enable Student Success?* (Issue 19). Three issues have been reframed and have new articles: *Is Eliminating Overrepresentation Beyond the Scope of Public Schools?* (Issue 2); *Are School Choice Options Open to Students with Disabilities?* (Issue 4); and *Do Students with Disabilities Threaten Effective School Discipline?* (Issue 6). Issue 15, *Is Attention Deficit (Hyperactivity) Disorder Overdiagnosed?* has two new selections. In all, there are 14 new selections.

Acknowledgements   So long as I have been in education, spirited debate about "the right thing to do" has been part of life. So long as we keep children in mind, debating possibilities is exhilarating. First, and most importantly, I thank the children, educators and parents who framed the questions and taught me almost anything is possible—not always easy, but possible. I have appreciated the gentle thoughtfulness of Nichole Altman, stepping into the *Taking Sides* family and all the efforts of supporting staff at McGraw-Hill/Dushkin. And, of course, Joe.

MaryAnn Byrnes
University of Massachusetts–Boston

Contents In Brief

Contents

Scot Danforth, a member of the School of Education of the University of Missouri–St. Louis, argues that America's trust in science has led to the creation of an array of artificial terms, such as *mental retardation*, that devalue individuals, have no basis in reality, and blunt the voices of those to whom they are applied. James M. Kauffman, a professor of education at the University of Virginia, cautions readers not to be overly distracted by criticism and asserts that special education is a relatively young profession that uses accepted research practices and self-reflection to generate reliable common knowledge of effective instructional strategies for students with disabilities who were previously excluded from schools.

M. Suzanne Donovan and Christopher Cross, researchers representing the findings of a National Research Council study on minority students in special and gifted education, believe overrepresentation issues are complex and not easily resolvable. While teachers can make a difference, environmental factors and poverty have a large impact and require interventions beyond schools. Daniel J. Losen and Gary Orfield, both policy experts, present the results of research commissioned by the Civil Rights Project of Harvard University. While agreeing with some of the NRC recommendations, these findings suggest that patterns will change with stricter enforcement of federal and state regulations.

Issue 3. Do Funding Formulas Make Special Education Too Expensive? 57

Teresa S. Jordan, an associate professor at the University of Las Vegas–Nevada; Carolyn A. Weiner, president of Syndactics, Inc.; and K. Forbis Jordan, a professor emeritus at Arizona State University, contend that the number of students identified as disabled is increasing at an excessive rate because of funding systems that encourage overidentification and discourage flexible, creative, inclusive school programming. Sheldon Berman, a school superintendent, and his colleagues maintain that districts have been careful and conservative in identifying children with disabilities but that enrollment and costs are increasing primarily because of the increased numbers of children with more significant disabilities.

Issue 4. Does School Choice Open Doors for Students with Disabilities? 82

Lewis M. Andrews, executive director for the Yankee Institute for Public Policy, reviewing the experiences of a number of countries with considerable school choice experience, maintains that children with disabilities will find unexpected opportunities in choiice-sponsored schools. Barbara Miner, a freelance writer and former managing editor of *Rethinking Schools*, exploring experiences with the pioneering Milwaukee voucher system, discusses exclusionary policies and practices that limit access for students with disabilities.

Issue 5. Does Society Have the Capacity to Prevent Emotional/Behavioral Disabilities? 100

Hill M. Walker and Jeffrey R. Sprague, educational researchers at the University of Oregon's Institute on Violence and Destructive Behavior, describe the path that leads from exposure to risk factors to destructive outcomes. They argue that society must recommit itself to raising children safely, and they advocate strong collaborative arrangements between schools, families, and communities. James M. Kauffman, a professor of education at the University of Virginia, states that experts know what needs to be done to prevent emotional and behavioral disorders but that society as a whole has invented many reasons not to make prevention a reality.

Kay S. Hymowitz, a regular contributing editor to *The City Journal* (published by The Manhattan Institute), cities inclusive educational programming for students with disabilities and the legal limitations of IDEA97 as primary contributors to the destruction of effective discipline in today's schools. James A. Taylor and Richard A. Baker, Jr., president and vice-president of Edleaders.com, respectively, believe that school administrators who design and implement an effective disciplinary code that applies to all students, including those with disabilities, can create a more orderly environment for everyone.

The National Council on Disability (NCD), an independent federal agency dedicated to promoting policies, programs, practices, and procedures that guarantee equal opportunity and empowerment for all individuals with disabilities, found that all 50 U.S. states are out of compliance with special education law, a condition that the council argues must be remedied by increased federal attention. Frederick M. Hess, an assistant professor of education and government, and Frederick J. Brigham, an assistant professor of education, both at the University of Virginia, maintain that increased federal monitoring will only deepen the separation between general and special education, drawing resources away from true educational excellence for all.

significant cognitive disabilities does not provide appropriate preparation for successful life following school.

Harlan Lane, a faculty member at Northeastern University; Robert Hoffmeister, director of the Deaf Studies Program at Boston University; and Ben Bahan, a deaf scholar in American Sign Language linguistics, value residential schools as rich cultural resources that enable Deaf children to participate fully in the educational experience. Tom Bertling, who acquired a severe hearing loss at age 5 and attended a residential school for the deaf after third grade, favors the use of sign language in social situations but views residential schools as segregated enclaves designed to preserve the Deaf culture rather than to develop adults who can contribute fully to society.

Rex Knowles, a retired college professor, and Trudy Knowles, an assistant professor of elementary education, argue that federal mandates for all students to master the same curriculum fail to consider students' individual differences and needs. Jerry Jesness, a special education teacher, stresses that students who complete school without learning the basics will be ill-equipped to succeed as adults and that any program that avoids teaching these essentials fails to address the long-term needs of students.

Michael F. Giangreco, a research associate professor specializing in inclusive education, and his colleagues assert that untrained teacher assistants spend too much time closely attached to individual students, often hindering the involvement of certified teachers and nondisabled peers. Susan Unok Marks, Carl Schrader, and Mark Levine, of the

Behavioral Counseling and Research Center in San Rafael, California, find that professionally trained classroom teachers are often less prepared than some assistants to work with children in inclusive settings and that, unprepared to supervise assistants, they use this lack of knowledge to avoid teaching children with disabilities.

PART 3   ISSUES ABOUT DISABILITIES   261

Sally and Bennett Shaywitz, codirectors of the National Institute of Child Health and Human Development–Yale Center for the Study of Learning and Attention, and Yale University professors, summarize their recent research findings suggesting that advances in medicine, together with reading research, can virtually eliminate reading disabilites. Gerald Coles, an educational psychologist and former member of the Robert Wood Johnson Medical School, University of Medicine and Dentistry of New Jersey, contests the claim that meurological procedures can identify reading disabilities and identify the methods to help children read.

Arthur Allen, reporter for *The Washington Post*, believes ADHD exists, but thinks too many children are given this diagnosis, masking other conditions (or simply normal behavior), and resulting in the prescribing of drugs that do more harm than good. Dr. Russell Barkley, director of psychology and a professor at the University of Massachusetts Medical Center, addresses several current beliefs about ADHD and amintains it is, in fact, under-diagnosed and undertreated in today's children.

Lawrence H. Diller, a pediatrician and family therapist, asserts that the use of stimulants on children has risen to epidemic proportions, occasioned by competitive social pressures for ever more effective functioning in school and at work. Larry S. Goldman, a faculty member of the Pritzker School of Medicine at the University of Chicago, and his colleagues review 20 years of medical literature regarding the diagnosis of attention deficit hyperactivity disorder and the use of stimulants. They conclude that the condition is not being overdiagnosed or misdiagnosed and that medications are not being overprescribed or overused.

Thomas Balkany, Annelle V. Hodges, and Kenneth W. Goodman, of the University of Miami, argue that the Deaf community actively works to dissuade families from choosing cochlear implants for their children, preferring to have the decision made by Deaf individuals as a way to perpetuate the existence of a separate culture. The authors maintain that parents must decide whether or not their children receive cochlear implants, based on each child's best interest. The National Association of the Deaf (NAD), an education and advocacy organization committed to supporting the deaf and the hard of hearing, uses its updated position paper on cochlear implants to express concern that medical professionals will dissuade parents from considering the positive benefits of the Deaf community and choose, instead, a medical procedure that is not yet proven.

James B. Adams, a professor at Arizona State University; Stephen M. Edelson, director of the Center for the Study of Autism; Temple Grandin, an associate professor at Colorado State University; and Bernard Rimland, director of the Autism Research Institute (ARI), recommend to parents of young children with autism an array of effective treatment options, many of them biomedically based. The Committee on Educational Interventions for Children with Autism, chaired by Catherine Lord, director of the University of Michigan's Autism and Communication Disorders Center, summarizes its examination of research studies of educational treatments for children with autism, finding little consistent evidence to support the efficacy claims made by proponents.

James M. Kauffman, a faculty member at the University of Virginia, along with Kathleen McGee and Michele Brigham, both special education teachers, maintains that special education has pursued its goal of normalization to an extreme. The emphasis has shifted from increasing competence to perpetuating disabilities through the unwise use of accomodations. MaryAnn Byrnes, a University of Massachusetts–Boston faculty member, former special education administrator, and editor of this *Taking Sides*, argues that relevant accommodations are necessary to ensure that people with disabilities have a fair chance to demonstrate what they know and can do.

Martha L. Thurlow, director of the National Center on Educational Outcomes, and David R. Johnson, director of the Institute on Community Integration, both at the University of Minnesota, assert that high-stakes testing may hold many benefits for students with disabilities, especially if the tests are carefully designed and implemented. Pixie J. Holbrook, a special education teacher and consultant, maintains that high-stakes testing marks children with disabilities as worthless failures, ignores their accomplishments and positive attributes, and seriously limits their range of possibilities in adult life.

Introduction

MaryAnn Byrnes

I introduce ... a bill ... to insure equal opportunities for the handicapped by prohibiting needless discrimination in programs receiving federal financial assistance.... The time has come when we can no longer tolerate the invisibility of the handicapped in America.... These people have the right to live, to work to the best of their ability—to know the dignity to which every human being is entitled. But too often we keep children whom we regard as 'different' or a 'disturbing influence' out of our schools and community altogether.... Where is the cost-effectiveness in consigning them to ... 'terminal' care in an institution?

—Senator Hubert H. Humphrey (D-Minnesota), January 20, 1972, on introducing to Congress a bill mandating education for children with disabilities (as quoted in "Back to School on Civil Rights," National Council on Disability, 2000)

Unfortunately, this bill promises more than the federal government can deliver, and its good intentions could be thwarted by the many unwise provisions it contains.... Even the strongest supporters of this measure know as well as I that they are falsely raising the expectations of the groups affected by claiming authorization levels which are excessive and unrealistic.... [This bill also contains a] vast array of detailed complex and costly administrative requirements which would unnecessarily assert federal control over traditional state and local government functions.

— President Gerald Ford, November 29, 1975, upon signing federal legislation to mandate education for children with disabilities (as quoted in *Congress and the Nation, IV*)

Special education was born of controversy. Controversy about who belongs in schools and how far schools need to stretch to meet student needs. The debate continues.

When was the first time you saw someone with a disability? Think hard about your school experience. What do you remember? Compare your recollections with those of someone one generation older—and one younger. The differences will be startling.

Chances are you remember The Room. Usually it was in the basement of the school. Hardly anyone went into The Room. Hardly anyone came out. The kids in The Room never seemed to be part of recess or plays or lunch or gym. The teachers were invisible, too. Sometimes the windows of The Room were covered with paper. Usually the shades were drawn. Kids in your class whispered about The Room, but no one really knew what happened "in there."

Likely, the students who went to school in The Room were older, bigger, and not as smart as most of the other kids in the school. They had few books to learn from and rarely studied any but the most basic academic tasks. No one really knew what happened to the kids in The Room once they left elementary school. There never seemed to be a Room at high school. Hard as it is to believe, those who made it to the inside of The Room may have been the lucky ones.

Less than 30 years ago, if you were the parent of a child with a disability, your local school had the option to tell you that your child was not welcome—that there was no place in the school for your child. The choices were few—you could teach your child at home (or just have him spend his days there); you could try to find a space in a kind school run by dedicated religious people; or you could have your child "put away" in a faceless institution for life. Try looking at Burton Blatt and Fred Kaplan's *Christmas in Purgatory: A Photographic Essay on Mental Retardation* (Human Policy Press, 1974) for a view of some of the worst options.

I remember The Room in the elementary schools I attended, but I never knew much about its students. I remember the Catholic school for girls with Down syndrome where I volunteered as a Girl Scout. The residents learned cooking and sewing while I was getting ready for high school and college. I never saw the girls outside the school and do not know what they did when they grew into adults.

I also remember the boys who sat in the back row of my classes and tried to avoid the teachers' attention. The teachers hoped that these boys would just be quiet and behave. The boys dropped out of school as soon as they could.

Many years later, in the early 1970s, I moved from being a fourth grade teacher to a special education teacher because I was intrigued with unlocking the puzzles that made learning so hard for some of my students. One of my early jobs was as a teacher in an updated version of The Room. It was my first experience in a small district. The day before school began, all the teachers and their students were listed in the local newspaper, along with the bus routes. I eagerly looked for my name, but instead of Mrs. Byrnes, I read "Emotionally Disturbed Classroom." For the entire time I worked at that school, I was the "emotionally disturbed teacher."

Times had changed a little since I attended school. My classroom was on the main floor, next door to the third grade; we had academic books to use; and we had lunch and recess with everyone else. But we were still different. Each day, my students and I needed to leave our room from 11:30 to 1:30 so that it could be used by the gym teacher while the gym was being turned into the cafeteria. Since there were only 10 of us, it seemed to be an easy solution to have us without a classroom space. No one seemed to care where we went or what we did during that time. Plenty of people were surprised to see us camp out in the library tackling "real" school work.

In contrast, I think about the schools of today. Children with learning problems that might be significant enough to be disabilities are the focus of concentrated attention. Trained professionals and researchers strive to understand disabilities and to address them with specific teaching methods and approaches. Parents and teachers actively consider ways to adapt instruction. Program options seem limitless. Many children with disabilities now grow into adults who hold jobs and contribute to society instead of spending their lives in isolation at home, in institutions, or on the streets.

Despite this progress, I still know schools in which students with disabilities are separated into sections of the school where no one else ever goes. There are still districts where no one thinks to include students with disabilities when counting up the number of new math books that need to be ordered. And once formal schooling ends, there are still many young adults who sit at home without jobs because there is no guaranteed support.

Has the promise of special education been met or exceeded? Has society done too much or not enough? Despite what feels like progress, arguments about special education continue. Many of them are included in this book.

As you consider the issues ahead, think about the people with disabilities you first remember. How would their lives have been changed by today's special education? What could be done to help them be more productive citizens? How have the dreams of Hubert Humphrey and the cautions of Gerald Ford been realized?

Recent History and Legal Foundations

The history of special education in American public schools is short and defined by legislation. Private or religious schools have long offered specialized options for students who are blind or deaf or who have mental retardation. Until the last quarter of the twentieth century, public options were largely limited to residential institutions and a few "Opportunity Classes" in public schools.

Following the civil rights struggles of the 1960s came the realization that another significant segment of children in the United States—those with disabilities—were not being afforded a quality education. Although a few states instituted their own policies and regulations regarding the education of children with disabilities, districts could still refuse to enroll children with disabilities.

Successful court cases in individual states establishing the right of children with disabilities to be educated led to the 1975 passage of federal Public Law 94-142, which requires every public school district to deliver a free and appropriate education to all children with disabilities. Renamed the Individuals with Disabilities Education Act (IDEA) in its 1990 and 1997 reauthorizations, the regulations connected to these laws form the foundation of special education for every state that receives funds from IDEA. In addition, individual states have constructed local legislation to clarify federal language or to extend commitments beyond the federal standard.

Even if districts chose not to seek federal funds and thereby sidestep IDEA regulations, the education of students with disabilities would be covered by other legislation. Section 504 of the Rehabilitation Act of 1973 is a civil rights statute prohibiting organizations that receive federal funds from discriminating against any individual based on a disability that substantially limits a major life activity. Reasonable accommodations must be implemented so that individuals with disabilities have equal access to the activities of such organizations. Curb cuts, lowered water fountains, and signs in Braille all came to be in response to Section 504. Since all school districts receive federal funds, Section 504 forbids the exclusion of students with disabilities, although it does not address education with the detail of IDEA.

The Americans with Disabilities Act (ADA), which was passed in 1990, expands the protections of Section 504 to the private sector. The ADA forbids businesses, governmental agencies, and public accommodations (other than churches or private clubs) from discriminating against any individual who has a disability that substantially limits a major life activity. The ADA carries the same responsibility for accommodations as Section 504 and impacts the practices of almost every employer. One of the most recently decided ADA cases established the right of golfer Casey Martin to use a cart as an accommodation during PGA Tour events so that his physical condition does not prevent him from competing.

Many people say that the elements of these laws are vague and undefined. Terms are interpreted differently across the states, and businesses struggle with the range of accommodations and the meaning of "reasonable." Clarity is often achieved through the resolution of legal challenges, some of which have reached the Supreme Court. Because of the continually changing natures of disabilities and society, a single court decision can radically alter the obligations of an employer.

The ground shifts for schools as well. For example, as you proceed through the readings in this book, you will encounter the debate between "least restrictive environment" and "free appropriate public education." Each term is critical to the development of a school's special education program, but each is also fluid in meaning. Federal law does not provide solid definitions that can be used with precision. Schools do their best to apply these terms to individual children with widely varying needs. As with businesses and the ADA, court cases about individual children continue to define what is "restrictive" and what is "appropriate."

Essential Terms and Concepts

Special education has its own unique vocabulary and terms, just as any other field. Being familiar with the concepts discussed below will increase your understanding of the issues ahead.

Disabilities.   All federal laws refer to the following list of disabilities: autism, deaf-blindness, deafness, developmental delay, emotional disturbance, hearing impairment, mental retardation, orthopedic impairment, other health impairment, specific learning disability, speech or language impairment, traumatic brain injury, and visual impairment. Autism and traumatic brain injury are recent additions to the list because their occurrence has increased. State laws frequently amplify the federal definitions of each disability with particular diagnostic criteria, satisfied through the administration of appropriate assessment tools in the child's dominant language. It is important to note that this list of disabilities does not include children who need instructional assistance solely because of language differences, cultural differences, or lack of instruction. In order for a child to be eligible for special education, the school's educational team must determine that a disability exists.

Federal definition of a child who is eligible for special education.   According   to IDEA, this is a child with a disability who is not making effective progress in school because of that disability and who requires specially designed instruction or related services in order to make progress in school. Federal legislation applies to individuals from birth to either the receipt of a high school diploma or age 22. In most states, public schools are charged with educational responsibility beginning on a child's third birthday.

Individual education program (IEP).   IDEA requires each child's educational team, including parents, to meet at least annually to formulate this agreement, which describes the education of a child with a disability. The IEP outlines the impact of the student's disability, current educational status, necessary accommodations, the nature and amount of services to be provided to the child, and the goals and objectives that are the targets for each year. Services cannot be delivered—nor can they be ended—without a parent-approved IEP. Parents who disagree with evaluations or services have the right to seek redress through an administrative hearing or a legal suit. All educators are bound to abide by the terms of an approved IEP.

Related services.   These supportive, noneducational services permit a child with a disability to participate in special education. Related services can include, but are not limited to, transportation, various therapies, mobility instruction, social work, and medical services for diagnostic or evaluation purposes.

Free appropriate public education (FAPE).   This cornerstone of IDEA guarantees that special education and related services are provided at no cost to parents. The word appropriate, which has never been clearly defined, is the source of much controversy and litigation.

Least restrictive environment (LRE).   Another key element of IDEA, this phrase refers to each school's responsibility to ensure that "to the maximum extent appropriate, children with disabilities... are educated with children who are nondisabled; and that... removal from the regular educational environment occurs only if the nature or severity of the disability is such that education in regular classes with the use of supplementary aids and services cannot be achieved satisfactorily" (IDEA, Section 300.550). Here, too, different interpretations of many undefined terms can lead to disagreement and litigation.

Continuum of services.   Special education services take many forms and happen in many places. Inside the classroom, these can range from consulting with a teacher on the format of a test to team teaching a special educator and an English teacher. Outside the general education classroom, specialized instruction might be delivered to small groups of children with disabilities. A few children are taught in separate classes or schools (day, residential, or hospital) that enroll children with disabilities only. The entire spectrum of options, the continuum of services, must be considered when designing individualized special education programs.

Inclusion. This term may be one of the first that comes to mind when special education is mentioned. Surprisingly, the word *inclusion* does not appear in any federal legislation. Its meaning differs across states, across districts, and even within schools, and it can change from year to year. Defining and applying this term has resulted in dedication as well as confusion, frustration as well as opportunity, creativity as well as litigation. The common element in all definitions involves increasing the participation of children with disabilities in general education classes.

Differing Orientations

Underlying the controversies in *Taking Sides: Clashing Views on Controversial Issues in Special Education* are three separate perspectives, each of which affects the way in which people envision a solid special education program. Although disagreements cannot always be reduced to one of these, it is likely that people who support differing sides of an issue question will also be on opposite sides of the following dynamics.

Medical or Educational Model?

The medical model of special education views disabilities as conditions that can be improved, remedied, remediated, or perhaps prevented. Medical model adherents seek a specific treatment or therapy to address the physical, psychological, or cognitive issues that result in school problems. Those who follow an educational model aim to address the impact of a disability on school performance directly. Proponents focus on improving educational success by teaching individual skills or employing particular strategies that sidestep the areas of difficulty. Is it wiser to deliver occupational therapy to increase the handwriting skills of a child with cerebral palsy or to teach the child how to use voice-activated software to enable his or her words to become print?

Special Need or Disability?

The federal list of disabilities does not mention children who need instructional assistance solely due to language differences, cultural differences, poverty, or lack of instruction. Neither does it include students who are gifted and talented. Yet children in each of these groups may not have their needs met in a standard classroom without extra attention. In addition, almost everyone can remember struggling with learning at one point in life. Despite these hurdles, special education does not help children who are covered by any of these descriptions unless those children also have disabilities. Special education is about the education of children who have disabilities rather than those who struggle. This delineation causes controversy. If we know children whose lives put them at risk for failure, should we wait until that failure occurs before we give them help, or should we expand special education to include them? If we expand special education by including these children, are we helping them or burdening them with a stigmatizing label?

Regular or Special Responsibilities?

Thirty years ago, millions of children with disabilities were excluded from school. Federal laws mandated their education, which initially occurred mostly in specialized locations by specialized teachers. Seeing these students grow, teachers and parents began to seek out special education services. In many districts, special education ceased being a stigma and became a desired and protected resource, particularly when budget stress increased class sizes. As the number of children receiving services increased, resistance rose to the expansion and costs of special education and to its separation from the overall school curriculum. This backlash resulted in tighter definitions that restricted services to those who are truly disabled and increased expectations that classroom teachers would assume responsibility for a wider range of children. Has the aura surrounding special education deluded people into thinking that there is a special magic to this part of education, or will legislators, teachers, and parents be frustrated by the limits to which one teacher's attention can stretch?

Understanding Controversy

Precisely because the issues surrounding special education are so powerful and the stakes for children are so high, it is vital that we engage actively in their resolution. To achieve this end, it is essential to recognize differences and collaborate to find common ground.

Disagreements About Applying the Law

Parents and teachers must come to agreement about the best way to meet the needs of a child with a disability. Honorable people may be equally committed to the goal of a free appropriate public education in the least restrictive environment but differ on the definition and application of these terms. Although few people would argue about the meaning of *free*, some parents and teachers prefer focused instruction in small groups of children with similar learning needs, while other parents and educators feel that the letter and spirit of the law can only be met when all children (regardless of individual need) are taught within the general education classroom all day. Two children may be very similar but have dramatically different special education programs because the preferences and reasoning of their educational teams differ dramatically. Since each child is unique and can only experience one option at a time, it is impossible to know which choice will lead to the best outcome. In fact, the "best" option may change as the child grows and develops.

Sometimes the differing interpretations of parents and teachers can result in heated arguments. The keys to coming to a consensus in this difference (as with all others) are listening, learning, and being open to new information and different perspectives. Equally important is evaluating each source of information and each course of action in a measured, careful way, even if it differs dramatically from what you feel is right. Often, putting yourself in the other person's place helps. Ask yourself, What would I do if this were my child? What would I do if I were the teacher?

As with most issues regarding children, the best solution is achieved when the adults involved put their attitudes, emotions, and pride aside to understand what the other person wants and why he or she wants it.

Disagreements About Interpreting Facts and Figures

While some of the issues in *Taking Sides* address decision making about individual children, others require the interpretation of objective facts. Analyzing these controversies requires a different approach.

For example, educators and legislators often argue about the significant increase in special education numbers and costs. While this is a debate that deserves examination, it is also one that highlights the importance of evaluating information carefully. The meaning of seemingly objective facts can change depending on the context that is used for interpretation.

Consider the following statement: "Student enrollment in special education programs increased from 3.6 million in 1976–77 to 6 million in 1996–97. During that same time, the total student population increased by only 4.4%" (Center for Special Education Finance [CSEF], *Resource*, Winter, 1999–2000).

A truly alarming increase. What a terrible situation! Truly, this is a system running amok. The number of children in special education has doubled while the number of children in schools has barely increased at all. There must be a way to slow this trend. At this rate there will not be any money to buy new books to meet new standards. Perhaps the law is poorly written. Perhaps districts are not evaluated closely enough. Perhaps parents are too unreasonable and administrators too ready to provide any service requested.

Or is it? Additional information might change the interpretation. The cited enrollment statistics begin with 1976, the first year after federal law mandated a free appropriate public education for all children with disabilities. In 1973 the Senate Labor and Public Welfare Committee documented "more than seven million deaf, blind, retarded, speech-impaired, emotionally disturbed or otherwise handicapped children in the United States ... only 40 per cent were receiving an adequate education, and many were not in school at all" (*Congress and the Nation, IV*, 1973).

Millions of children with disabilities were not in school in 1976, so their addition to the rolls made a big bump. Many children were in institutions, which declined in size and scope as school doors opened. Many children became identified as having disabilities and entered the special education count—do the statistics subtract them from the "total student population"?

Searching out background information about statistics or seemingly objective facts can change your interpretation of their meaning and, with it, your position on the issue. Bringing to light the assumptions made by others may do the same.

Some believe that special education enrollments have risen due to the creation of "invisible disabilities" invented by those looking for a cause or an excuse for poor performance or any other way to get extra help for their children. Others contend that science is becoming more adept at understanding learning and behavior. In doing so, research identifies real reasons to explain why some students struggle and productive strategies to facilitate learning.

Some maintain that society has become looser and more permissive. Drugs and alcohol are more readily available. Also, children are not supervised the way they used to be and are influenced heavily by exposure to media representations of violent behavior. Others point to statistics on poverty, one-parent homes, three-job parents, and the disintegration of family and community supports to explain the increasing numbers of students who push the limits of courtesy, tolerance, and the law.

Some are proud that medicine is making remarkable strides, sustaining one-pound babies and victims of tragic accidents or chronic illnesses who live to come to school ready to learn. Others are concerned that these miracles of life require extensive support and extraordinary methods that are beyond the scope of schools.

Each point of view puts a different spin on the analysis of enrollment figures in special education. The interpretation you choose to accept depends on the argument you find most compelling. Careful deliberation of all information helps you formulate your own opinion.

Being Aware of Bias

We all bring to every discussion our own background and inclinations. We cannot help but apply these to the issues in this book. In fact, individual experiences may very well lead to creative options that change the course of a debate. As you begin to tackle your first issue, I offer the following reflections, gathered from students, parents, and colleagues.

Acknowledge and be mindful of your own experiences.   If you or a family member has encountered special education (or a lack of it), you will have formed strong opinions about its worth. If you have not had direct experience, your community's media coverage of special education may have shaped your thoughts. Recognize the impact of your experience, and consider its influence as you debate the issues.

Be cautious of solutions that claim to apply equally to every situation.   Two children with Down syndrome can be as different from each other as two "typical" seventh-grade children. Urban and suburban elementary schools pose very different sets of possibilities and limitations. Appropriate strategies in kindergarten transfer poorly to 10th grade. Ideas can usually be adapted but rarely be duplicated.

Think of possibilities rather than limitations.   It is easy to say, "That can't be done," and be constrained by what you have already observed. Creative solutions emerge from asking, "How can it be done?"

Consider the impact of roles, motivations, and perspectives.   Teachers come to their work because they want to help children grow and learn. Special education professionals believe in their ability to help children conquer the limitations of their disabilities and become productive learners and adults. Parents seek educators who are dedicated to helping children reach their potential. District administrators serve two masters. First, they believe in the power of education and want to clear financial and legal hurdles so that teachers can do their job as well as possible. Second, they understand that they are entrusted with the finite resources of a community and need to be answerable for their decisions in a way that will sustain the confidence of the citizens. Finally, legislators are committed to ensuring equal treatment and benefits for their constituents, whose lives span a wide range of circumstances.

Each of these roles demands responsibility and accountability. The tasks of each role shape opinions and decisions. The outlook of people inhabiting each role can lead to widely different perspectives, powerful arguments, and creative solutions. Consider the background of each of the authors as you evaluate their points of view. What in their backgrounds leads them to their opposite conclusions?

Final Words

As you read the selections in this book and discuss them with your colleagues, your challenge is to sort through competing arguments and information to form your own opinions about the education of children with disabilities. Perhaps you will have the opportunity to apply your point of view to an issue within your community or school. Perhaps you will discover practices in those schools that will change your opinion on an issue.

Controversies in special education are likely to endure. The topics will change, but there will always be argument about the right thing to do for children who seem to need so much. You might be tempted to search for global answers. You might find yourself frustrated by limited options. Or you might come to a unique solution that works perfectly for your district and your school.

As a special education administrator, especially in the spring, I often woke up in the middle of the night with a seemingly irresolvable problem running and running and running through my brain. Usually, it involved balancing competing views of how to help a child. None of the options seemed totally satisfactory. A wise friend suggested I let go of the feeling that I needed to solve the problem alone and, instead, ask others to discuss together the pros and cons of each avenue. This suggestion has always served me well as I struggled over issues of doing the right thing for children. I hope the issues in *Taking Sides* keep you thinking at night and that my friend's suggestion helps you come to your own resolutions whenever you think about educating children with disabilities.

On the Internet . . .

National Institute of Mental Health

A branch of the National Institutes of Health, the National Institute of Mental Health (NIMH) is focused on generating and disseminating information regarding mental health conditions. This site contains information regarding the full range of behavioral disorders and conditions as well as up-to-date research information related to their existence, causes, and treatment.

http://www.nimh.nih.gov

Center for Special Education Finance

Established in 1992, the Center for Special Education Finance (CSEF) addresses fiscal and policy questions related to the delivery and support of special education services in the United States. This Web site provides access to CSEF publications, studies, and research activities.

http://csef.air.org

Center for Education Reform

This Web site is the home base for the Center for Education Reform (CER), a national, independent, nonprofit advocacy organization committed to education reform. The Web site contains information about school choice options and charter schools as well as a range of other efforts for changing schools.

http://www.edreform.com/index.html

OSEP Technical Assistance Center on Positive Behavioral Interventions and Supports

This federally funded technical assistance center maintains an extensive Web site dedicated to informing educators and school systems about an array of school-wide behavioral interventions. Examples of positive practice are available for use with families, entire schools, classrooms and individuals. The Web site includes links to practicing schools, a newsletter and online information and supports.

http://www.pbis.org

Thomas B. Fordham Foundation

Affiliated with the Manhattan Institute for Policy Research, the Thomas B. Fordham Foundation supports research, publications, and action projects, with a special interest in education reform. This site contains a link to Rethinking Education for a New Century, a compilation of thought-provoking essays about the status of special education in today's schools.

http://www.eexcellence.net/foundation/global/index.cfm

PART 1

Special Education and Society

It seemed simple enough in the beginning. All students have a right to education. No excuses for not educating a child would be acceptable. Unfortunately, schools needed to be compelled by force of law to enroll all students. Once federal and state laws ensured enrollment, the boundaries of required services were interpreted as frequently by the words of litigation as by the decisions of educators. Opportunities for some are interpreted as limitations for others. As medicine becomes more sophisticated, disabilities become more complex. As budgets strain, the limitations of the commitment to educate all become increasingly contentious. As society changes, the definition of acceptable behavior evolves. The spirit and the letter of the law are not always clear, but remain the source of heated discussion.

- Is Special Education an Illegitimate Profession?
- Is Eliminating Overrepresentation Beyond the Scope of Public Schools?
- Do Funding Formulas Make Special Education Too Expensive?
- Does School Choice Open Doors for Students with Disabilities?
- Does Society Have the Capacity to Prevent Emotional/Behavioral Disabilities?
- Do Students with Disabilities Threaten Effective School Discipline?
- Will More Federal Oversight Result in Better Special Education?
- Should One-on-One Nursing Care Be Part of Special Education?

ISSUE 1

Is Special Education an Illegitimate Profession?

YES: Scot Danforth, from "On What Basis Hope? Modern Progress and Postmodern Possibilities," *Mental Retardation* (April 1997)

NO: James M. Kauffman, from "Commentary: Today's Special Education and Its Messages for Tomorrow," *The Journal of Special Education* (vol. 32, no. 4, 1999)

ISSUE SUMMARY

YES: Scot Danforth, a member of the School of Education of the University of Missouri–St. Louis, argues that America's trust in science has led to the creation of an array of artificial terms, such as *mental retardation*, that devalue individuals, have no basis in reality, and blunt the voices of those to whom they are applied.

NO: James M. Kauffman, a professor of education at the University of Virginia, cautions readers not to be overly distracted by criticism and asserts that special education is a relatively young profession that uses accepted research practices and self-reflection to generate reliable common knowledge of effective instructional strategies for students with disabilities who were previously excluded from schools.

T hirteen categories of disabilities are contained in the Individuals with Disabilities Education Act Amendments of 1997 (IDEA97). To be eligible for special education, a child must be identified as having one of these disabilities. In fact, many teachers fret over the length of time it takes to identify a disability and to secure the special services needed to help a child progress in school. IDEA97 contains several sections dealing with the assessment of disabilities, as well as other sections addressing the avenues that parents can follow if they disagree with the decisions made by the school.

Special education law was developed to require schools to teach children who had been excluded as being "uneducable." In the last 30 years, definitions of disabilities have increased in sophistication. Teachers and researchers have struggled to identify and refine the practices that are most effective in increasing the academic achievement of children found to have disabilities.

During the same 30 years, the philosophies of postmodernism and cultural relativity gained prominence. First applied to fields such as psychology, sociology, and the arts, these theories decry the single version of history or reality often depicted by powerful, Eurocentric, white men who are out of touch with the breadth of human experience. Within the philosophy of postmodernism, previously mute voices—including those supporting feminism, alternative sexual orientations and life styles, and ethnic and racial identity—gain volume, power, and influence.

Instead of a single narrative defining "the way things are," postmodernists substitute myriad individual stories, supporting the idea that truth is based uniquely within the individual. Only when all the stories are heard—when no individuals are suppressed or oppressed because they are not part of a powerful elite—will society truly include everyone.

Applied to education, postmodernism connects with constructivist theories of learning and multicultural education, both of which place a high value on the experience of individuals as the foundation for learning. When postmodernism encounters special education, the very existence of disabilities is called into question.

In the following selection, Scot Danforth acknowledges that everyone involved in the field of special education cherishes the hope of improving the lives of children with disabilities. He offers, however, two very different versions of hope—one based on the "project of progressive social science devoted to the comprehension and correction" of disabilities, the other on the possibility that people limited by labels will speak out and, perhaps, overcome the tyranny of these disabling categories, which Danforth feels artificially sort children and silence their voices.

In the second selection, James M. Kauffman, in reflecting on the past and future of special education, expresses concern that critics of special education have forgotten the strides made during the last 30 years, focusing on shortcomings rather than accomplishments in this relatively new field. Providing examples of the empowerment that science has brought to those who were previously excluded from society and finding benefits in shared knowledge, Kauffman values the rigor of the scientific process, which builds on objective facts rather than unsubstantiated fads.

Danforth is concerned that overreliance on scientific verification of educational methodologies limits the range of possibilities for every child. Kauffman worries that without careful scrutiny, valuable learning time for a vulnerable child can be wasted.

As you read these selections, consider the opposing views. Has "acceptable learning" been defined so narrowly that labels are sought to separate those who vary even slightly? Or has scientific analysis been used to refine our understanding of intellectual development and the best practices that support it? Where is the boundary between a limiting stereotype and a descriptive term?

Scot Danforth

 **YES**

On What Basis Hope? Modern Progress and Postmodern Possibilities

Special education and hope seem to go hand in hand. Common sense tells us that individuals could not work to improve the lives of students with mental retardation without carrying and embodying hope in their professional practice. Despite the powerful and assumed role of hope in special education, it is an unexamined aspect of work in this professional field. My purpose in this paper is to provide a deep analysis of the philosophical and historical bases of hope in special education. I describe two separate and conflicting modes of hope: the modern version of hope as a project of progressive social science devoted to the comprehension and correction of mental retardation and other disability conditions, and a postmodern version of hope as an ongoing critique of the scientific ground and language by which individuals are habitually and casually devalued with disabling terms and identities such as "mental retardation." Although the modern version of hope promises a steady climb toward more enlightened findings and facts about mental retardation and services, for the postmodern mode claims that a critical dialogue is necessary, wherein professionals, parents, and, of course, labeled persons may confront, contest, and perhaps overturn the standard mental retardation construct.

Modern discourse in special education emerges from an American historical myth of scientific progress, what Gergen called "the grand narrative of modernism." This explanatory story extends from the Enlightenment rationalism of this nation's founding fathers to present day mainstream social science research to some faith-held, extrapolated future date when scientific knowledge and technological practice peak at a mastery of all necessary variables. This totalizing narrative links the revolutionary birth and subsequent political, economic, and moral rise of this democratic civilization with the deliberate advancement of science, industry, and technology. In the 20th century, this grand narrative of progress may be seen in the growth of interventionist social sciences (e.g., sociology, psychology, education, social work) and the many allied human service professions that ground their practices in these empirical research knowledges.

What does modernism mean for special education philosophy in the field of mental retardation? Modernist special educators hold that the profession should follow the lead of empirical social science to describe accurately the reality of mental retardation and identify the modes of intervention best suited to those conditions. From this perspective, hope lies in the gradual, scientific production of improved approximations of "truth" and the development of intervention technologies, practices, programs, and instruments "that work" according to the truth-clarifying research. Progress, the scientific development of increasingly accurate representations of human living and more powerful interventions to positively adjust that living, and the hope of helping special education students are taken to be conceptually and morally conjoined.

In stark and critical contrast, the postmodern professional concepts and practices of hope break from the modern tradition of progressive empiricism. Postmodern practices found hope not on the production of generalized, context-free facts about mental retardation and interventions but on the creation of human relationships and conversations in which "mental retardation" as a standard and overriding definition of self can be contested and more positive personal identities, roles, and activities constructed.

Proponents of postmodern positions critique modern empiricism and propose alternative possibilities for action. Postmodernists find the historical myth of scientific progress to be a socially constructed story of uncertain truth value, a narrative that relies on the naive assumption that human knowledge and ability are flowing in continuous motion through time toward perfection or eternal betterment. Lacking a transhistorical perspective from which to evaluate the truth value of modernism, postmodern scholars critique the sociopolitical effects of that narrative, finding it to be a dominating story with profound moral and political implications in the lives of the children served by special education programs. To postmodern special educators, the most notable result of modernism is not scientific progress but the reification of mental retardation as a "real" or "objective" phenomenon of human limitation and stigma in specific lives. Mental retardation, as fashioned in scientific discourse and daily practice, is perpetuated as a natural and unreproachable state, a ready and waiting deficient identity. From this critical analysis, new directions of hope allow us to ask: If the activities of modernist social scientists are not moving professional knowledge, practice, and hope for the improvement of children's lives forward, then how shall professionals, students, and families forge new forms of hope in special education? ...

Modernism: Hope as Scientific Progress

Gergen noted that the:

> *grand narrative* of modernism ... is a story told by Western culture to itself about its journey through time, a story that makes this journey both intelligible and gratifying. The grand narrative is one of continuous upward movement—improvement, conquest, achievement—toward some goal. Science furnishes the guiding metaphor. Had science not demonstrated the capacity to defy gravity, extend the lifespan, harness human energies, and

carry voice and image through the stratosphere? Because of individual's capacities for reason and observation, as expressed in our scientific attitude, utopias were now within our grasp.

The dominant discourse among special educators in the field of mental retardation claims the value of modernist research to discover the pieces to the mental retardation puzzle and to find "what works" in practice with children and parents. The ultimate goal is to objectively unveil the approaches and tactics that can be confirmed to produce positive effects in the education and treatment of children with mental retardation. These "best practice" approaches, it is commonly stated, should then be generalized, encapsulated in standard form, and dispensed for use by professionals throughout the nation.

Professionals, family members, and students who pioneer pathways that are not supported by scientific knowledge, including those involved in inclusion programs and facilitated communication, are criticized by modernist special educators as promulgating "long-odds approaches ... [that] foster unrealistic hopes against formidable odds." From this vantage point, professional and nonprofessional activities that are supported by social science research are valued as contributions to a reality-based hope for concrete improvements in the education of "exceptional" students. Such hope is viewed as "realistic" or "truthful," unswayed by the power of overhyped fads and irrational emotional currents. In contrast, those innovations and developments not sanctioned by modernist social science are viewed as lacking a basis in reality. They are spirited "fanaticism," the long-shot pipedreams and tomfoolery of persons lacking the reason of empirical science....

How have modernist special educators arrived at such a faith in the progress of social science? How has hope for the improvement of the lives of persons called "disabled" come to be viewed as inherently dependent on the progress of social science knowledge? ...

American Myth of Scientific Progress

Perhaps in America, as in no other Western country, the idea of progress has played the most powerful role in guiding and unifying a national sense of identity, history, and purpose. A New World burst forth from the political fervor of the Enlightenment to launch a uniquely American brand of progressive mentality. This American idea of progress, as it has developed through a wide range of intellectual ideas and popular movements over the past 2 centuries, has enabled citizens to create great unity in common interpretations of a victorious civilization rising up an ever-improving road. Stretching from the rationalism of the founding fathers to the current incarnation of progress in the professional application of modernist social science knowledge as redemption for a variety of social ills, this road brings us notably to our special education profession as intervention for the "social problem" of students with mental retardation. Although the central cultural meaning of progress was recast in varying forms and lights over those many decades, it remained ever closely tied to both modern science and a nationalistic, optimistic American identity....

Modernism and Interventionist Social Science

As the 20th century dawned, it became clear to many that the practical application of natural science knowledge had brought a particular kind of progress, a
proliferation of an urbanized, industrial, and technological culture. America
had its factories, bridges, tall buildings, and enormous cities. Yet, the apparent
fall-out of this capitalistic/technological expansion was a variety of social ills,
including school failure, delinquency, crime, and poverty. The cure for these
social ills and the hope for social progress became entrusted to the imitator of
natural science: the new, developing social sciences and the social science professions. An experimental science of humanity and society would be unleashed
to intervene in spaces of imperfection and weakness, suffering and disorder.

No depiction of the development of modern social science would prove
adequate to the task of explaining the common philosophical ground behind
the geometric growth of the fields of psychology, social work, education, and
special education in this century. My analysis, therefore, is limited to the
career of one of the early creators of interventionist social science, Lester
Frank Ward, a man who may rightfully be called the father of American sociology. Although it would be a foolish stretch to claim that special education
science was born of sociology, a brief analysis of Ward's philosophy of an
interventionist social science provides great insight into modernist special
education assumptions about the necessary and powerful role of empirical
knowledge in relation to hopeful professional practice. Ward's extension of
natural science principles into the nascent field of sociology demonstrates
both the attempt of social science to imitate the obvious successes of the natural sciences and the continuing narrative of progress newly imbedded in the
hope to heal American society.

Lester Frank Ward developed a science of human, social living based
within the principles and evident success of natural science, growing from a
specific interpretation of the work of [Charles] Darwin. Although many
claimed that society evolved in a manner analogous to biological evolution,
relying on haphazard advancement via probability, Ward disagreed. He theorized two distinct forms of evolution: (a) the Darwinian mode of genetic or
natural evolution that described the random and slow progression of nature
to more perfect forms and (b) a conscious, intentional mode of social evolution in which people applied his scientific knowledge to push social improvement along at an increased pace. Because humans may understand the
operations of evolutionary development in the social sphere, they should
then intervene to artificially boost the natural process, making social progress
more efficient and less time-consuming.

The power to know the truths of Nature ... had gradually become the
power to know the truths of Society. A rational social science would accurately
describe human, social activity just as an earlier natural science had unlocked
the laws of physical motion. Notably, as manifested in Ward's interventionist
sociology, the modern social sciences combined the task of knowing truths
with the related mission of affecting social change. A constantly improving
comprehension of individual activity and social problems—a gradual but

steady piecing together the pieces of the puzzle—would place the new social science in the most hopeful position of all: the cultural and historical place of redemptive power. Human problems could be solved through the faithful application of an interventionist brand of modern social science.

Birth of Special Education as Interventionist Social Science

Where does the early development of special education fit in with this development of an interventionist, modern social science? More specifically, what was the connection between this social science and the work of early professionals and the development of early institutions in the field of mental retardation?

Space limitations in this paper demand that I address this issue in direct and brief fashion. The work of Henry Goddard in the first 2 decades of the 20th century provides us with a useful glimpse at the role of modern social science (namely, measurement psychology) in the growth of mental retardation as a construct and a legitimate professional field.

Conducting research at the Training School at Vineland with institutionalized, "mentally deficient" persons, Goddard was one of the first American psychologists to import and apply the intelligence testing instruments of Binet and Simon. The intelligence test allowed specialists to "objectively" classify persons along a graded scale, to separate the "normal" from the mentally deficient, and to classify the mentally deficient within ranges of intellectual deficit.

Goddard's application of intelligence testing to the identification and categorization of mentally deficient persons was important for two reasons. First, the importation of the mathematical schemes of measurement from natural sciences provided a dramatic boost of legitimacy to the fields of psychology and early special education. These disciplines and professions accessed a source of tremendous power and credibility within Western society through alliance with the assumed accuracy, progressive motion, and morality of modern science. It is not surprising that Goddard's utilization of intelligence testing at Vineland quickly led to his rise as a leading psychologist in the field of mental deficiency and Vineland as the preeminent research and early special education teacher training site.

The second reason that Goddard's use of cognitive measurement was important involves the theorized relation between mental deficiency, immorality, and a range of early 20th century social problems. Trent described Goddard, his professional colleagues at institutions for the "feebleminded," and the public at-large as subscribing to a general fear of "the menace of feebleminded." In both popular and the scientific publications, social vices such as criminality, alcohol abuse, unemployment, and sexual promiscuity were linked to mental deficiency.

... Specifically, mentally deficient persons, due to their pathology, were the purveyors of social vices. In accordance with prominent scientific thought at the time, feeblemindedness was assumed to be genetically inherited. As

Goddard fully explained in his famous study of the Kallikak family, immorality was being passed on from one feebleminded generation to the next.

Perhaps the greatest insight into the early development of special education as a scientific practice based in intelligence testing can be gleaned from an analysis of the connection between modern social science and the hope to cure America of social vices in Goddard's work. Through the use of intelligence testing, Goddard claimed to have discovered a new class of feebleminded persons whom he called "morons." This group was undoubtedly the most dangerous of the feebleminded menace. Morons, according to Goddard, had the physical characteristics of "normal" persons and the intelligence of high-range mental deficients. In essence, Goddard claimed that there was an entire group of feebleminded persons who remained undetected, who had intermixed with the normal population, and passed by appearance for normal. Given the propensity of the feebleminded to commit acts of social misconduct, the existence of this class of morons in the general population was a frightening prospect. Evil was hidden among the population, but who could say where? (Or, more accurately, who?)

Goddard and his colleagues at Vineland proposed that intelligence tests be used to identify the "immoral element" for purposes of exclusion and population control. He and many professional leaders at that time advocated that the feebleminded be completely isolated from the mainstream in residential institutions. In addition, he joined the then-popular eugenics movement, supporting the surgical termination of the reproductive capacities of mentally deficient persons. Through exclusion and eugenics, Goddard believed that feeblemindedness could be wiped out through scientific intervention, thus solving the vast array of American social problems and ensuring the continued progress of this society.

At the recent crest of this wave of modern progress rises present-day special education, a field devoted to the practical improvement of the lives of a specific group of children commonly viewed as social or educational failures. Proponents of the centrality of modern social science to special education continue the story of a progressing science in relation to the hopeful mission of helping students with mental retardation and their families. From this modernist perspective, professional hope must rest on a faith in the grand narrative of scientific progress led by special education researchers.

But what if one, in agreement with philosophers Nietzsche and Foucault, holds no faith in the modernist story of progress? What if one does not believe that social science provides gradually improving pictures of social reality? What if the certain and upward motion of modern progress is viewed as neither certain nor upward-moving? Postmodern philosophers in many academic fields, including education and special education, are posing these and other critical questions about the truthfulness of the modernist account.

Postmodernism and Hope in Special Education

... A postmodern philosophy of special education asserts that the current governing story, the guiding scheme of modern social science, no longer provides a valuable basis for hope and unity in the struggle to educate children described as "mentally retarded." Postmodernists typically eschew any universal guiding story as deceptive and totalizing, providing not generalizable or useful facts but a harmful privileging of some knowledges and vocabularies over others of lesser sociocultural power. In brief, the modernist grand narrative cannot be determined to be objectively true. Its maintenance and re-creation in daily practice relies on the faith and actions of persons who believe in the American myth of historical progress. Postmodernists claim that adherence to this historical tale by professionals, students, and families perpetuates the belief that certain persons in society have a deficit condition called "mental retardation" that requires professional intervention and institutional control. As a result, postmodern educators encourage a professional shift from the primary explanatory story of modern social science to a pluralistic, conversational arena in which a multitude of smaller, nongeneralizable stories may be told by the diversity of participants in special education.

In the place of the dominating grand narrative, postmodernism supports a patchwork quilt of many stories, a provisional and ever-changing fabric honoring diverse cultural traditions and multiple versions of "the way it is." A place of many legitimate stories is an arena of dialogue and possibility, allowing individuals and groups to claim their voices, call out their own identities, and forge paths of action that need not comply with the scientific dictates of truth. The scientific goal of progressively finding and describing truth is thus replaced by the moral and political goals of supporting human freedom and community.

Postmodern special educators contend that the hope of educating and supporting children considered to have disabilities can no longer be fueled and conceptualized through the modern social science story, that "insuperable obstacles to this story's coming true" have indeed arisen. Scientific truth is in trouble.

Modern Truth in Crisis

... A number of movements described as postmodern or poststructural have struck at the very core of modern academic disciplines, contesting and undermining the underlying assumption that an objective world is knowable and may be established through the workings of a neutral, rational science. Gergen, in his analysis of the academic upheaval, stated:

> Most of the cherished beliefs that undergird the traditional goals of research and teaching are in eclipse. Some consider the demise of traditional assumptions to be an event little short of catastrophe, to part with the longstanding ideals of truth and understanding is to invite chaos, first in the academic world and then in society generally. Others feel an innervating sense that history is at a turning point, that a new and exciting era is in the making.

This "catastrophe" or "turning point," depending on one's perspective, is evident through much of academia as postmodern concepts have swept into writings in numerous disciplines, including anthropology, history, psychology, sociology, philosophy, and education. The intellectual stir in opposition to the domination of the modernist scientific project is rising in many bubbling caldrons.

Not surprisingly, the knowledge base of special education is the subject of similar doubt and critique from postmodern perspectives. Skrtic described special education as one of a group of professions based in modern social science that has suffered a crisis of legitimacy since the 1960s. This crisis gained initial impetus from Kuhn's analysis of the social and paradigmatic nature of science.

Kuhn's analysis removed scientific activity from the realm of cold rationality and redefined it in terms of social negotiations among perspective-bearing human actors. The truth-producing capabilities of science, according to Kuhn, do not depend on the strict performance of dry and neutral procedures but flex and change within the social and political interactions of scientists. What is held to produce the theoretical ground of authorized research in a given scientific field is a matter of social agreement among those scientists who have the status and reputation that allow them to declare certain theories and hypotheses to be better than alternatives.

... Often, modernist researchers have no or little awareness of how their paradigmatic assumptions form a field of assumed truths that greatly determines what aspects of living will be called "data," what data will be collected, how that data will be symbolized and manipulated, and what hypotheses will ultimately be supported by the inquiry. Parallel to [Sigmund] Freud's assertion that the hidden weavings of unconscious mental activity influence and determine behavior for reasons beyond conscious awareness, modernist researchers' unacknowledged paradigmatic framework surreptitiously provides the structural limitations, linguistic make-up, and conceptual substance of the knowledge they claim to "find" in the external world.

The alternative postmodernism should not be viewed as laying claim to a "better" paradigm; a new process holier than the modern, mechanistic way of constructing meaning; a more "truthful" outline for delineating "what is the case." Instead, we should understand postmodernism as a mode of critical vigilance maintaining that no means of describing reality holds universal privilege over alternatives. All descriptions are viewed as limited and partial, confined and influenced by the linguistic and sociohistorical contexts from which persons speak and write. They are understood to be contingent on the sociocultural context, the language community of the speaker, the knower's paradigmatic predisposition, and the historical situation in which the representation occurs.

Truth, Power, and Special Education

The greatest danger of modern social science, from a postmodern position, concerns the overwhelming authority generally accorded to both the modernist account and the bearers of that account. Knowledge and power are interrelated, integrated socially and institutionally. Each depends on and is supported by the other. The danger of modernism is tyranny in mundane forms, proceeding from what Foucault described as the "general politics of truth," the regime of power running through the social procedures and mechanisms creating truth and manifested within the applications of truth in social practice. What is made true applies power in the lives of those who are the objects of the truth.

For example, in special education, a series of "objective" and psychometric descriptions of a student can justify a mental retardation diagnosis and extrusion to a special education classroom. A child's social identity is quickly refashioned from "normal" status to debilitated learner through procedures of truth and power, processes whose credibility relies on modernist claims of "value-free," rational operation in depicting an "objective truth." The diagnosis makes up merely one moment of the powerful drama by which a person's social identity is constructed in stigmatized form. The on-going services provided by professionals and institutions continue this devaluation project by further reifying the mental retardation status in the life of the diagnosed and treated individual.

If, as the postmodernists contend, adherence to modernist grand narrative cannot be supported by claims to truthfulness or factuality, and if this history produces not so much hope as the social control of persons considered "abnormal," then special educators may choose to view special education science and disability as historical and bureaucratic artifacts of an international special education that may be questioned and contested on local levels. This practical contestation may bring about opportunities for the making of new stories, nongeneralizable tales of local identity generating valuable meaning for individuals and small educational communities. Students "disabled" by modernism may be re-defined or re-interpreted in terms and priorities that do not include disability concepts and descriptions.

As the hope generated by the myth of social science progress has faltered, space for the making of new versions of hope may arise in special education work with students considered to have mental retardation. Professionals may join with "persons who have disabilities" in their struggle to overturn disability constructs and roles in their own lives. Professionals can ally themselves with labeled persons, their families, and loved ones in efforts to transform social constructions of deficiency and incompetence into relationship-based and self based understandings of personal power and efficacy. ...

Postmodern philosophers propose that the sources of hope in the field of mental retardation services erupt from precisely those mouths and writing (or typing) hands that do not speak the language of science. Beyond, under, and beside the booming voice of science, that discourse attempting to conform the activities of many to the truth declarations of few, are voices of hope. These are the contributions of parents, students, family members, front-line practitioners, and program directors. Where the modern quest of a uniform knowledge that informs and limits practice has failed; where the science-prescribed methods to be used with students of a certain label or diagnosis are set aside as irrelevant intrusions on the local task of figuring out what to do and how to do it; where the many partners in the Individual Educational Plan (IEP) and educational planning process no longer depend on the promised progress of research to find a better way; in all these and other spaces where a more equal and open dialogue may be developed between practitioners, parents, and students, the hope of postscientific forms of knowledge abounds. The small stories and the soft voices so often devalued and silenced as subjective and biased, unscientific and unknowing, may become genuine and full participants in conversations about pressing matters in the day-to-day education of students labeled as having mental retardation.

Hope in Discourse Beyond Science

... The most important conversations occur in schools and homes, where labeled students, family members, friends, and professionals create practices and relationships far from the gaze of researchers and professional authors. These spaces offer the greatest opportunities for the cultivation of hope beyond modern science, for the arrangement of services in which the individuals involved can place their faith and trust. Small groups of 3, 5, 10, or 12 persons devoted to the well-being of an individual labeled as having mental retardation have the opportunity to set aside scientific talk and disability constructs in favor of language and relationships that value the labeled individual. Within such local circles, the stigmatizing identity of mental retardation may be tossed out and replaced with understandings that seek to protect labeled persons from stigma and devaluation. This reconstructive and relational task disavows universal concepts of progress for the sake of hope.

NO

James M. Kauffman

Today's Special Education and Its Messages for Tomorrow

Characterizing today's special education is in many ways a dangerous undertaking. It is risky because no particular view is likely to be entirely accurate, and there is much diversity of opinion among special educators on nearly every issue. Furthermore, prognostication may make the forecaster look foolish. Had I been asked 20 years ago, or even 10, to guess what the future held, I would not have forecast the developments that have occurred in our field. I am thus acutely aware that my commentary about the meaning of today's special education for the future may be inaccurate and that in 10 or 20 years, or in even fewer, I will be embarrassed by my lack of understanding and foresight. However, in all candor, I am not very happy with most of what I see in our field today. I think we are in a period of considerable upset and danger, and our future could look rather bleak depending on how we respond to current pressures. Consequently, I offer a series of cautions about our present course.

The one sentence or metaphor that I believe best characterizes special education today is this: We are a middle-aged profession going through a profound identity crisis that includes self-destructive behavior. I refer here to the middle age of our profession's evolution, of course, not to the middle age of its members. Some might think that my characterization of special education merely reflects my own middle age or struggle with personal identity. Be that as it may, I offer more specific observations of our present-day characteristics and what they portend. Although there are exceptions, including individuals and pockets of our professional culture, I think the majority in our field could be said to have the following attributes: They are (a) ignorant of our history, (b) apologetic for existing, (c) preoccupied with image, (d) lost in space, (e) unrealistic in expectations, (f) unprepared to focus on teaching and learning, (g) unaware of sociopolitical drift, (h) mesmerized by postmodern/deconstructivist inanities, (i) an easy target for scam artists, and (j) immobilized by anticipation of systemic transformation.

Each of these 10 attributes has implications for our future, and I discuss [five of them] briefly. Because I am not single-mindedly negative and pessimistic about our field today, I conclude with a brief commentary on some positive characteristics that merit attention.

From *The Journal of Special Education*, 1999, pp. 244-254. Copyright © 1999 by PRO-ED, Inc. Reprinted by permission.

Apologetic for Existing

... [M]y impression is that some of our colleagues today see our very existence in public education as both unfortunate and avoidable. Their line of argument seems to be roughly as follows: If we had done our job as we should have, then we would quickly have worked ourselves out of business. Perhaps we should just quit special education now. The only reason we exist is that general education is flawed and we are evil co-conspirators, maintaining harmful domination over those we label as needing so-called special education. If we reform education in the right way, there will be no more need for labels or so-called special services because education will be a seamless and flexible web of indistinguishable supports for all students. We do not really belong in public education; we were grafted on as an ugly appendage when general education was weak and needed us to help maintain a stratified society by giving privilege to high performers and keeping the so-called disabled powerless.

... We are at a curious juncture in our profession's development a point at which the value of science in special education policy and practice is being attacked by those—including some special educators—who believe that special education has become an evil empire (see Walker et al., in press, for a discussion of such issues in behavioral disorders). Brantlinger, for example, uses concepts of postmodern, deconstructivist philosophy to condemn the presumed power of special education "traditionalists," which she sees as coercive of the powerless—those who, like herself, seek to transform education so that special education is unnecessary. If Brantlinger and others who condemn special education acquire the power of "voice" they feel they are now denied, it will be interesting to see not only whether they then loathe their own dominance but also whether students with disabilities benefit and what language, if any, is used to describe the students we now say have disabilities. Perhaps some prefer the role of victim and the pretense that difference and disability can be acknowledged without labels.

People who are apologetic about their very existence often self-destruct. They may accomplish their own demise in a variety of ways, including their imagined transformation to a new level of existence. If we are going to survive as a viable professional field, then I think we are going to need to change the way we view our legitimacy in public education and develop a sense of self-worth and pride in what we do. I would like to see us become unapologetic about our function, our identity, our distinctiveness, our visibility. I hope we can become unafraid to suggest that students *can* be better off for their contact with us, actually helped more than harmed by our services, including services delivered outside general education when that is appropriate. But many in our field today are preoccupied with an image as antisegregationist to the near exclusion of concern for our substance. ...

Unrealistic in Expectations

Today there is great unhappiness with special education and its outcomes, and unhappiness with general education, too. Rightfully so. Certainly, I agree that we need to improve outcomes. But what will happen if special education really works and general education does, too? That is, what would we expect to happen to the distribution of outcomes and our students' relative position in that curve if both special education and general education worked the way we think they should? What some reformers seem to be suggesting is that we should expect all children to be successful by a common standard—that is, that we should have the same high standards and expectations for all students and include all students in the same curriculum and assessment procedures, as if by some magic participation therein defines success. In the February 23, 1998, issue of *The New Yorker*, cartoonist Jack Ziegler depicted a California business executive exhorting a subordinate, "Damn it, Henderson, New York is *still* three hours ahead of us. Get on that!" Just as ludicrous would have been an educator saying, "Damn it, Kauffman, some students are *still* two standard deviations below average. Get on that!"

Special education can never be successful in terms of all or even most students with disabilities catching up with their nondisabled peers unless general education is really awful. In fact, if general education begins to provide truly effective instruction for all students, then we might expect that the population variance will increase and that the performance of students with disabilities will become more discrepant than ever from the mean. Perhaps our understanding of these problems at some level predisposes us to shy away from focusing on teaching and learning. After all, we tend to do things at which we are successful. If we are unable to achieve the goal of helping students with disabilities learn academic skills within a standard deviation or so of the normal population mean, then why not turn our efforts to things more easily accomplished: placing children in neighborhood schools and general education classes and telling their teachers to collaborate?

Unaware of Sociopolitical Drift

I think many of us tend to forget that education, including special education, is a social welfare program of government. All such programs are under attack today, especially if they are conceptualized as entitlement programs. In fact, special education is being attacked in the popular media and by some special educators as a wasteful and ineffective government entitlement program that should be drastically downsized or eliminated. Government assistance of all kinds—except, perhaps, that offered to business and industry—is increasingly difficult to obtain. The prevailing opinion of our citizens, as reflected by the people elected to public office, is that government benefits for children at risk and their families should be smaller and harder to get. Today, more of our children are being reared in poverty and under conditions that we would expect to produce elevated risk of disability. Yet today sentiment is building against the increasing number of students served by special education and the increasing cost of such services. We are being told—and some of us are buying the big lie—that government programs serving those with special needs, including special education, do not work and should be largely abandoned.

We are virtually certain, in my opinion, to be "downsized," possibly dramatically so in both the size of the population we now serve and the size of our budget. Perhaps a case can be made for turning back responsibility for some of the children we serve to general education. However, if we are to serve even the remaining students adequately, then surely we will need an increase, not a decrease, in the fiscal resources devoted to the task. Our expectations of our programs to normalize children have been unrealistically high, and our estimates of the cost of delivering high-quality services have been unrealistically low. Today, Americans want to ignore social welfare problems as much as possible, to abandon government commitments to all but the spectacularly needy, and to deal with what cannot be ignored by purchasing services from private vendors on the cheap. As a profession, we seem unaware that we are in grave danger of being torched by public sentiment and that some members of our profession are fueling the fire. Our vulnerability is being worsened by postmodern rejection of scientific evidence. Maybe we are attracted to any kind of claptrap if it seems to be capturing the popular imagination, as postmodern and deconstructionism are now doing.

Mesmerized by Postmodern/Deconstructivist Inanities

I recognize that mine may be an unpopular and risky position that in a few years will look silly or worse, but I now believe that some in our field today have taken a bad cognitive tumble into postmodernism and radical deconstructivist philosophy. I refer here specifically to essays on postmodern and deconstructivist descriptions of education, and more particularly of special education. In my view, their teachings undermine progress in serving the needs of students with disabilities. I am not able to identify any practical applications of these writers' work to special education or comprehend how applying their ideas might make a positive contribution to teaching students with disabilities or researching special education problems. This may reflect my own cognitive limitations, but if my assessment is widely shared among special education researchers, it may say something about the observation of an eminent scientist. "Consider this rule of thumb: to the extent that philosophical positions both confuse us and close doors to further inquiry, they are likely to be wrong." I do comprehend the value of context and understand the conditional nature of truth, but the recognition that scientific "truth" is tentative is not a uniquely postmodern insight, nor is the observation that science is affected by its social context a revelation of postmodernists.

The terms *posmodernism* and *deconstructivism*, though difficult to define precisely, are often linked (see Wilson, 1998). I refer to them together as "PD" to indicate the general notions that logical positivism (i.e., what we have come to know as science) is untrustworthy and that alternative ways of knowing or constructing truth have equal merit. The worldview presented by PD is singularly egocentric, as one's own experience (text or narrative) is the only one knowable. Much of the PD thinking put forward by educators is, in my view, based on nonsequiturs and serious misunderstandings of science. According to PD, disability is a social construction that we could eliminate (deconstruct, subvert, redefine), a view seriously at odds with the science of exceptionality. Elkind has suggested that postmodernism challenges the ideas of progress, universality, and regularity that are part of modern science. For example, Elkind noted:

> We acknowledge today that some phenomena, such as the weather, are inherently irregular. So too are phenomena such as the dispersion of cream in a coffee cup. Each time we place cream in a coffee cup, the dispersion pattern is different from what it was before. Some phenomena are, by nature, chaotic and have no underlying regularity.

First, it is important to understand that modern scientists do not claim to be able to predict all phenomena or all cases. In fact, it is precisely the irregularities in phenomena that give rise to shifts to new paradigms that can predict additional phenomena for which older ones could not account, bringing a new level of regularity and predictability to phenomena that previously were assumed to be chaotic. Second, the fact that some phenomena are or appear to be chaotic means neither that all are chaotic nor that the apparent unpredictability of a particular phenomenon will never be understood as a predictable sequence of events. Third, some chaotic phenomena are trivial for achieving a particular purpose in which they play a part. The fact that the dispersion of cream in coffee is chaotic in no way impairs our ability to predict with a high degree of accuracy, and with good effect, the color, taste, and caloric value of a given amount of coffee to which a given amount of cream is added. Likewise, the fact that an individual child's immediate response to a praise statement may be unpredictable in no way invalidates the use of social approval as a strategy for reinforcing desired behavior. Finally, the grand metanarrative of progress attributed to modern science by some proponents of PD is caricature, a clever and amusing set of exaggerations. But, if my understanding is correct, in the PD worldwide, caricature cannot be discriminated from reality.

The demise of the modern era and of logical positivism as the prevailing scientific paradigm are ballyhooed by those who speak—out of their academic element and inappropriately, I think—of a "paradigm shift." Many of those writers who urge a radical change in view invoke a book by Thomas Kuhn, who described the process by which science progresses from less defensible to more accurate and complete explanations of phenomena. But we are not experiencing a shift in scientific paradigm to postmodern or deconstructivist views in any sense compatible with the observations of Kuhn, who popularized the term *paradigm shift*. His treatise dealt only with how paradigms shift within science itself, in which replicable evidence in the positivist tradition is essential. "Any conception of nature compatible with the growth of science by proof is compatible with the evolutionary view of science developed here."

Those who say education paradigms are shifting have no reliable data—no proof—with which to create or legitimize a shift. In fact, PD rejects such proof as unnecessary. The changes of view proposed by PD are based on mere assertion. That is, the proponents of PD seem to suppose that a new paradigm can be created merely by saying or believing that science (that is, positivism) no longer provides valid explanations for our work. However, *scientific* paradigms are not shifted by chutzpah. A scientific paradigm shifts only if reliable, publicly verifiable data are obtainable in support of it; without the data, a new paradigm dies an ignominious death. Moreover, a new scientific paradigm does not necessarily discredit the old, as Kuhn has shown in the case of Newton's and Einstein's physics. Scientific paradigms offer solutions to problems; they are not merely interesting, novel ideas. Kuhn observed that "novelty for its own sake is not a desideratum in the sciences as it is in so many other creative fields." Nevertheless, in higher education, at least in the social sciences and humanities, data are often ignored for the glitter of novelty. ...

So far, I see no evidence that PD approaches to education offer superior solutions to puzzles (in fact, as I suggested earlier, I am unable to discern what the solutions suggested by PD might be). The absence of better solutions to educational problems offered by PD suggests to me an alternative view of shifting paradigms in education. Researchers during the past several decades have provided clear problem-solving theory. Education may be considered preparadigmatic in that no consensus has existed that teaching and learning can be studied scientifically or that educational policy decisions should be based on reliable data. The rise of applied behavior analysis and the formulation of an explicit and testable theory of instruction may represent the shift to a scientific paradigm of education against which PD assertions are now being directed. An initial scientific paradigm may emerge over a period of decades, and there are always countercurrents that seek to discredit science or, once established, the scientific paradigm that ultimately becomes dominant. To me, a plausible explanation of shifting paradigms in education is that PD represents a struggle to discredit the paradigm that ultimately will be adopted because it solves problems better than the nonpositivist alternatives.

In the end—in science, anyway—the paradigm that wins the wars is the one that offers the most practical and reliable tools for problem solving. As the history of science shows, though, paradigms can be squelched, at least in the short term, by political philosophy or religious beliefs or superstitions. Positivism has won the day in the natural sciences for several hundred years only because political and religious authorities have allowed it to emerge from the dark ages. But persons who do not believe the scientific data or do not like them can still squelch scientific evidence in favor of political correctness, religious faith, or greed, as has been demonstrated by despots, religious zealots, some industrial giants, and occasionally by scientists themselves.

We should not underestimate the popularity of nonscientific and aggressively *anti*scientific beliefs today. Nor should we dismiss the danger of such sentiments and frames of mind for education. *The New Yorker* magazine of April 14, 1997 devoted its entire "Talk of the Town" feature to commentary on the mass suicide of Marshall Applewhite and his Heaven's Gate cult. Applewhite and his followers rejected evidence in favor of belief in the supernatural. *The New Yorker* commentary concluded: "Though science is stronger today than when Galileo knelt before the Inquisition, it remains a minority habit of mind, and its future is very much in doubt. Blind belief rules the millennial universe, dark and rangy as space itself." As if to provide supporting evidence, *Life* magazine subsequently featured an article on the recent resurgence of belief in astrology, hyped on its cover under the banner "ASTROLOGY RISING: Why So Many of Us Now Believe the Stars Reflect the Soul." Belief in astrology has burgeoned in the past 20 years, in the absence of any scientific evidence whatever to support its claims and in the face of reliable scientific evidence that its perceived "success" is a function of people's suggestibility and desire for personal validation.

Postmodern/deconstructivist philosophy would have us embrace the subversion of the concepts of disability and special education, particularly their positivist research bases. It suggests that the scientific way of looking at things is a cognitive house of cards created solely by White males, mostly ones now dead. In fact, it would have us believe that all apparent realities are merely convenient constructions and power relations that need deconstructing. It is difficult, if not impossible, to construct a defensible philosophy of special education, or anything else, on the assumption that reality is always constructed to fit convenient power relations and fictions. Moreover, there is comic irony in the proposition that all realities are convenient fictions derived from power relations that enslave the powerless—except this one. It recalls the paradox embedded in any proposition made by someone who says, "I always lie." If we accept such notions we will be left with little or nothing but cognitive demolition debris. Guess who will be buried deepest in the rubble? Children with disabilities will be, of course.

The detonation of PD in our profession leaves us with profoundly weak defenses against the glossy assertions of charlatans that they have discovered something miraculous. We become easy marks for those peddling junk science and other frauds. Why wouldn't we believe a spaceship from comet Hale-Bopp might rescue us, if not our students, and transform our earthly vessels? Who is to say that it will not? I am reminded of the cartoon by Robert Mankoff in *The New Yorker* for April 14, 1997 (p. 6), with the caption, "What lemmings believe." Mankoff's drawing shows a stream of lemmings ascending into heaven rather than plunging off a cliff. As I have suggested elsewhere, our profession has a considerable history of enchantment by scam artists, and today's special education seems to me ripe for pied pipers.

An Easy Target for Scam Artists

In my view, PD philosophy helps make us sitting ducks for the quack—pun intended. The list of instructional and therapeutic procedures that have very little or no reliable data to support them is long. It would include such curious items as applied kinesiology and neurological organization technique (NOT) ocular training said to address learning disabilities, facilitated communication (FC), and a wide range of other new age nostrums. In some cases, these quack methods are popularized and sold shamelessly by special educators. ...

We have always had quacks, and we will have them in perpetuity. But PD notions of the invalidity of science and the arbitrary construction of truth have great potential for diverting us from progress and into perfidy. For example, in the 1990s, we have seen remarkable scientific progress in the positivist tradition in harnessing electronic technology to help individuals with highly specialized communicative needs to express themselves clearly, reliably, and independently. However, at the same time, we have seen the communication of some children with disabilities perverted by the inventive fantasies of "facilitators." What a cruel hoax—that some in our profession are now communicating *for* individuals with disabilities while pretending that these individuals are communicating for themselves. A predictable defense of such sham is that the phenomena of facilitated communication are beyond the reach of traditional scientific verification. This is the familiar dodge of accountability that is used by the magician, the charlatan, and cultist, or the astrologer.

My guess is that in 20 years or so many of those now believing in FC and other frauds will look back on today's quackery with considerable chagrin and wonder why they were so eager to play the fool. I think many of us will wonder why we thought we were about to be transformed, along with the rest of social science if not the world, by ideas that were disconnected from scientific method and not open to public verification. But even if we do not accept PD inanities and scams, we seem spellbound by the idea of systemic transformation, a notion that can distract us from the humbler task of ensuring the integrity and adequacy of *our* component of the array of services exceptional children need—special education.

... [T]he lure of postmodernism and radical deconstructivism is strong and growing. Anti-positivist sentiment is strong, and most citizens, including many teachers and teacher educators, have a very poor understanding of the methods and advantages of positivist science. We may well see even more virulent vilification and rejection of the scientific method by those who misunderstand the meanings and uses of evidence. Special education may lose much more of its focus on the scientific understanding of instruction and find itself lost in a cognitive dead end. We need to weigh very carefully the statements of those who would reform the foundational concepts of our field. We must think our way through the implicatons of propositions made with "little constraint from an external world of experiments and facts and numbers to limit the unleashed mind," especially propositions to subvert the idea of disability. We must remember that "disengagement from practice produces theoretical hallucinations." Minds unleashed from the constraints of external realities typically dodge responsibilities, leaving people with disabilities stuck in a social niche made more cruel by the avoidance of real-world issues.

A Note of Optimism

Our future looks bleak for many reasons, some of which I have addressed. We are a middle-aged profession that I believe is showing some signs of being "middle-age crazy," as the condition is called in the vernacular. As a professional group we seem to have lost our buoyancy, sense of purpose, and self-esteem. We appear to have forgotten much of our history, with two particular consequences. First, we tend to romanticize our profession's youth, when we were relatively free of regulation, definition, and responsibility, able to lead our professional lives ad hoc—without concern for the broader consequences of our actions. Second, we appear not to have learned much from our prior decades, as we seem ready to dismiss early mistakes as social aberrations and buy "new" ideas (or, if you prefer hype, "paradigms") with virtually no pragmatic analysis of their merits. This is not a pretty picture. If we are to get a grip on our situation and avoid decades of disastrous floundering, then we must do some serious stock-taking.

Our problem of conceptual foundations is not unique. Writers in many fields appear to be forcing a choice between common knowledge (universals) and idiosyncratic understandings of individuals or groups (constructivist knowledge). The differences in representation of truth are stark, and the consequences of rejecting common knowledge may be profound. But in the face of PD challenges, we can look with considerable confidence to the writing of numerous scholars in other fields who have studied the relationship of knowledge to culture and illuminated the value of common knowledge and truths that are independent of our idiosyncracies. The commentaries of several are particularly instructive and serve to give us hope that our profession will not abandon the science of human behavior for the alternatives:

> Some things in nature just are—even though we can parse and interpret such real items in wildly various ways. A lion is a lion is a lion—and lions are more closely tied by genealogy to tigers than to earthworms. (Of course, I recognize that some system of human thought might base its central principle upon a spiritual or metaphorical tie between lion and earthworm—but nature's genealogies would not be changed thereby, even though the evolutionary tree of life might be utterly ignored or actively denied.) (Gould, 1997, p. 17)

> No one can deny that science has often misunderstood the limits of its explanatory power, succumbing to a hubristic claim to the Truth. But hubris can be corrected without destroying the underlying confidence in the possibility of a common knowledge—or at least so one hopes. For without a common understanding, a common knowledge, prospects for coexistence among the world's many contending truths grow precariously faint. (Tolson, 1998, p. 12)

> How did they [liberal politicians since the 18th century] accomplish that [realize the goals of greater social justice]? Why, by identifying true (or nearly true) universals, such as the common origins, physiologies, aspirations, and feelings of all humankind, *and refuting the false ones,* such as the divine right of kings, natural slavery, and the general inferiority of women. Yes, by some scientists, and at various times, science has offered false universals, but those have been overthrown *only by better science.* And without reaching for true, or better-approaching-true commonalities, we would have only the idiosyncrasies of tribes, including those of whatever tribe you or I happen to belong to. (Gross, 1998, p. 48)

What these quotes have in common is the recognition that although individuals and groups may indeed see different truths from their idiosyncratic perspectives, there is also a body of information that is not only common or universal but able to free us from egocentrism and tribalism. Such universal knowledge—indeed, the admission of its existence and the recognition of its unique power to free people from separation into warring factions—is under serious attack as a modern failure. Nothing compels us to join the attack. The "modern" universal knowledge that has prevailed for several hundred years frees us as individuals and as a professional cadre to continue the pursuit of universally shared knowledge that brings the greatest liberation and habilitation to all people. The fact that contrary perspectives emerge should neither discourage us nor lead us to conclude that conceptual chaos is inevitable....

Looking only on the dark side is a serious mistake. Special education is a relatively young profession with a history that includes reliable empirical research on what works for students at the margins of the distribution of abilities and performance. We have considerable capacity for self-correction and finding order where others see disorder. We could turn our efforts unambiguously and forcefully to our historic mission of seeking reliable, common knowledge about how best to teach students with disabilities—researching and applying instruction that is intensive, urgent, relentless, goal directed according to individual need and delivered in the setting where it is most effective.

POSTSCRIPT

Is Special Education an Illegitimate Profession?

Danforth and Kauffman are both focused on the education and well-being of children in schools. Each is strongly convinced, however, that the viewpoint held by the other is not in the best interest of children.

Danforth asserts that normal learning differences have been magnified into labels that segregate and hobble children, causing adults to seek cures where none are needed. Like the perfectly thin model, the perfect learner may be an unattainable—in fact, an unnecessary—goal. According to Danforth, diversity in learning represents normal variation rather than a defect to be "remediated" by specially trained professionals.

In contrast, Kauffman worries that educators will be distracted by postmodern criticisms and lose direction. Significant learning differences exist, he says. Special education is still a new field. Educators are still seeking out the best way to meet the needs of children who have been on the outskirts of classrooms. However, noticing that individual attention helps some children learn, more teachers and parents seek that attention, whether or not their child has a disability. Kauffman concludes that perhaps the definitions of disability are not drawn tightly enough to ensure that the protection of the law is extended to those for whom it was intended.

The issues of postmodernism revolve around decisions of whose viewpoints are "in" and whose are "out." Those whose voices are "in" become important and shape policy and practice. Those who are "in" retain their influence by confining "others" to separate categories, which become less important. This view has been compared to the creation of maps (Smith, *Review of Educational Research*, 1999), in which boundaries are drawn to separate groups of people from each other. Smith maintains that the drawing of cultural or intellectual boundaries serves to create differences where none exist.

Rather than drawing boundaries to keep people out, modern science approaches to special education recognizes—and seeks to actualize—individual dignity and capability, according to Kleinert (*Mental Retardation*, 1997). Science, he says, uses descriptive terms and methods of systematic inquiry to demonstrate the potential within individuals who were previously "discarded as unteachable and of no value."

The polarity of this issue's points is expanded in discussions focusing directly on inclusion. Writing with William Rhodes (*Remedial and Special Education*, 1997), Danforth explores the idea that disability labels hinder inclusive education. If all children were viewed as individual learners rather than members of a category, they contend, teachers would easily accommodate individual needs instead of seeking assistance from specialists.

From another perspective, at least one proponent of modernist theories (Sasso, *The Journal of Special Education*, 2001) maintains that postmodernists have, in fact, found educating students with disabilities to be so difficult that their solution is to declare that differences have been artificially created. This declaration stifles systematic inquiry, abandoning the children to the very schools that once denied them access.

IDEA97 mandates that "services and placement needed by each child with a disability to receive [a free appropriate public education] must be based on the child's unique needs and not on the child's disability" (300.300(b)). Has the normal range of educational difference been forgotten in the race to seek scientific justification for special education? Or do the law's very words ensure that a child's needs are acknowledged and conveyed through the voices of his or her parents and teachers? Will the unique needs of all children be considered without the protection of law? Which will become invisible—the labels or the children?

ISSUE 2

Is Eliminating Overrepresentation Beyond the Scope of Public Schools?

YES: M. Suzanne Donovan and Christopher T. Cross, from *Minority Students in Special and Gifted Education* (National Academy Press, 2002)

NO: Daniel J. Losen and Gary Orfield, from *Racial Inequality in Special Education* (Harvard Education Press, 2002)

ISSUE SUMMARY

YES: M. Suzanne Donovan, a researcher in the areas of education and public policy, and Christopher T. Cross, who has been active in government and local board of education associations, represent the findings of a National Research Council (NRC) study on minority students in special and gifted education. They believe that overrepresentation issues are complex and not easily resolvable. While teachers can make a difference, environmental factors and poverty have a large impact and require interventions beyond schools.

NO: Daniel J. Losen and Gary Orfield, both policy experts, present the results of research commissioned by the Civil Rights Project of Harvard University. While agreeing with some of the NRC recommendations, these findings suggest that patterns will change with stricter enforcement of federal and state regulations.

As far back as 1968, Dunn (*Exceptional Children*, 1968) examined the developing field of special education and voiced concern that African American children were disproportionately placed in special education, resegregated into substantially separate classes for the mentally retarded.

Researchers and educators sometimes differ about how to calculate special education enrollment statistics. Some compare the percentage of each racial group in the overall school population with its proportion in special education. Others study the racial composition of individual disability categories.

Accurate analysis is complicated by the variable nature of racial designation and of disability definitions. Racial designations are reported by individuals and often governed by the categories provided on official forms. As society becomes more diverse, and more people have a multiracial heritage, choosing one racial "category" becomes complicated. Furthermore, eligibility qualifications for the disabilities differ across states. Some states use no discrete categories for students.

Whichever method of analysis is applied, and despite definitional complications, there is overall agreement that children of color are disproportionately represented in special education. This seems to be especially the case in the socially defined disabilities of mental retardation, emotional disturbance, and learning disabilities. IDEA97 attempted to address this imbalance by requiring states to collect and report special education enrollment information by race and ethnicity.

Coincidentally, in 2002, two major reports were issued. Because of their depth and the differences in their recommendations, these form the readings for this issue.

M. Suzanne Donovan and Christopher T. Cross edited a report representing the work of over a dozen researchers who are members of the National Research Council's (NRC's) Committee on Minority Representation in Special Education. Directed by NRC and Congress to update NRC's 1982 study of this same issue, their work was expanded to consider racial underrepresentation in gifted and talented programs. The Committee reviewed existent research studies to determine why disproportionality exists. Their conclusions and recommendations highlight environmental variables, suggesting that there may be reasons for overrepresentation that extend far beyond the school walls.

Daniel J. Losen and Gary Orfield share a professional commitment to studying the impact of law and public policy on the opportunities available for communities of color. Both have been heavily involved in designing and guiding policy formation, with a particular connection to the Civil Rights Project (CRP) at Harvard University. The impetus for their study was provided by the compelling voices of community leaders concerned about children wrongly placed in special education. To broaden the base of knowledge on the topic, CRP commissioned leading researchers to analyze conditions and contributing factors and to generate solutions. The collective findings led to recommendations that racial disproportionality should become a top school priority, facilitated (if necessary) through federal and state enforcement of school practices.

As you read the following selections, consider and debate the complex issues that are presented. When you compare and contrast the two summaries, what similarities and differences do you find in assumptions? methodology? conclusions and recommendations? Which findings correspond most closely to your own experiences, observations, and other reading? What is the real problem, and what is the right way to address it?

M. Suzanne Donovan and
Christopher T. Cross

 **YES**

Executive Summary

From the enactment of the 1975 federal law requiring states to provide a free and appropriate education to all students with disabilities, children in some racial/ethnic groups have been identified for services in disproportionately large numbers. Public concern is aroused by the pattern of disproportion. In the low-incidence categories (deaf, blind, orthopedic impairment, etc.) in which the problem is observable outside the school context and is typically diagnosed by medical professionals, no marked disproportion exists. The higher representation of minority students occurs in the high-incidence categories of mild mental retardation (MMR), emotional disturbance (ED), and to a lesser extent learning disabilities (LD), categories in which the problem is often identified first in the school context and the disability diagnosis is typically given without confirmation of an organic cause.

The concern is not new. In 1979 the National Research Council (NRC) was asked to conduct a study to determine the factors accounting for the disproportionate representation of minority students and males in special education programs for students with mental retardation, and to identify placement criteria or practices that do not affect minority students and males disproportionately. Twenty years later, disproportion in special education persists: while about 5 percent of Asian/Pacific Islander students are identified for special education, the rate for Hispanics is 11 percent, for whites 12 percent, for American Indians 13 percent, and for blacks over 14 percent. The NRC, at the request of Congress, has been asked to revisit the issue. In this case, however, the Office for Civil Rights in the U.S. Department of Education extended the committee's charge to include the representation of minority children in gifted and talented programs as well, where racial/ethnic disproportion patterns are, generally speaking, the reverse of those in special education.

Current Context

Since the 1982 NRC report, much has changed in general education as well as in special education. The proportion of minority students in the population of school-age children has risen dramatically—to 35 percent in 2000—increasing the diversity of students and of primary languages spoken in many schools. And state standards have raised the bar for the achievement expected of all students. More than 1 in 10 students is now identified for special education services: in the past decade alone, there has been a 35 percent increase in the number of children served under the Individuals with Disabilities Education Act (IDEA). And many more of these students are receiving special education and related services in general education classrooms.

The distribution of students across special education categories has changed as well. Identification rates for students with mental retardation today are about a quarter lower than in 1979. While the decline has applied across racial/ethnic groups, disproportionate representation of black students in that category has persisted. Just over 1 percent of white students but 2.6 percent of black students fall into that category.

Two decades ago, fewer than 3 percent of students were identified with learning disabilities (LD). That number approaches 6 percent of all students today. Only American Indian students are represented in disproportionately large numbers in that category. But for all racial/ethnic groups, the LD category accounts both for the largest number of special education students and for the largest growth rate in special education placements.

While these demographic and policy changes create a somewhat different context today from that confronting the earlier NRC committee, the problems are conceptually quite similar. At the outset, both committees confronted a paradox: if IDEA provides extra resources and the right to a more individualized education program, why would one consider disproportionate representation of minority children a problem? The answer, as every parent of a child receiving special education services knows, is that in order to be eligible for the additional resources a child must be labeled as having a disability, a label that signals substandard performance. And while that label is intended to bring additional supports, it may also bring lowered expectations on the part of teachers, other children, and the identified student. When a child cannot learn without the additional supports, and when the supports improve outcomes for the child, that trade-off may well be worth making. But because there is a trade-off, both the need and the benefit should be established before the label and the cost are imposed. This committee, like its predecessor, does not view the desirable end necessarily as one in which no minority group is represented in disproportionate numbers, but rather one in which the children who receive special education or gifted program services are those who truly require them and who benefit from them.

Who requires specialized education? Answering that question has always posed a challenge. The historic notion of a child with an emotional or learning disability or a talent conveys a "fixed-trait" model, in which the observed performance is the consequence of characteristics internal to the child. Assessment processes have been designed as an attempt to isolate those children with internal traits that constitute a "disability" or a "gift." And clearly there can be within-child characteristics that underlie placement in one of the high-incidence categories. Neurobiological investigations, for example, reveal different patterns of brain activity in dyslexic and nondyslexic children while reading.

However, in the past few decades a growing body of research has pointed to the critical role that context can play in achievement and behavior. The same child can perform very differently depending on the level of teacher support, and aggressive behavior can be reversed or exacerbated by effective or ineffective classroom management. In practice, it can be quite difficult to distinguish internal child traits that require the ongoing support of special education from inadequate opportunity or contextual support for learning and behavior.

Committee's Approach

The conceptual framework in which the committee considered the issue of minority disproportion in special education and gifted and talented programs, then, is one in which the achievement or behavior at issue is determined by the interaction of the child, the teacher, and the classroom environment. Internal child characteristics play a clear role: what the child brings to the interaction is a function both of biology and of experience in the family and the community. But the child's achievement and behavior outcomes will also reflect the effectiveness of instruction and the instructional environment.

The committee did not view the problem of disproportionate representation in special education as one of simply eliminating racial/ethnic differences in assignment. If special education services provide genuine individualized instruction and accountability for student learning, we consider it as serious a concern when students who need those supports are passed over (false negatives) as when they are inappropriately identified (false positives}. Likewise with respect to gifted and talented programs, we consider it a problem if qualified minority students are overlooked in the identification process, but consider it an undesirable solution if minority students are selected when they are not adequately prepared for the demands of gifted and talented programs. The committee's goal, then, was to understand why disproportion occurs. To address our charge, the committee asked four questions:

1. Is there reason to believe that there is currently a higher incidence of special needs or giftedness among some racial/ethnic groups? Specifically, are there biological and social or contextual contributors to early development that differ by race or ethnicity?

Our answer to that question is a definitive "yes." We know that minority children are disproportionately poor, and poverty is associated with higher rates of exposure to harmful toxins, including lead, alcohol, and tobacco, in early stages of development. Poor children are also more likely to be born with low birthweight, to have poorer nutrition, and to have home and child care environments that are less supportive of early cognitive and emotional development than their majority counterparts. When poverty is deep and persistent, the number of risk factors rises, seriously jeopardizing development.

Some risk factors have a disproportionate impact on particular groups that goes beyond the poverty effect. In all income groups, black children are more likely to be born with low birthweight and are more likely to be exposed to harmful levels of lead, while American Indian/Alaskan Native children are more likely to be exposed prenatally to high levels of alcohol and tobacco.

While the separate effect of each of these factors on school achievement and performance is difficult to determine, substantial differences by race/ethnicity on a variety of dimensions of school preparedness are documented at kindergarten entry.

> *2. Does schooling independently contribute to the incidence of special needs or giftedness among students in different racial/ethnic groups through the opportunities that it provides?*

Again, our answer is: "yes." Schools with higher concentrations of low income, minority children are less likely to have experienced, well-trained teachers. Per-pupil expenditures in those schools are somewhat lower, while the needs of low-income student populations and the difficulty of attracting teachers to inner-city, urban schools suggest that supporting comparable levels of education would require higher levels of per-pupil expenditures. These schools are less likely to offer advanced courses for their students, providing less support for high academic achievement.

When children come to school from disadvantaged backgrounds, as a disproportionate number of minority students do, high-quality instruction that carefully puts the prerequisites for learning in place, combined with effective classroom management that minimizes chaos, can put students on a path to academic success. While some reform efforts suggest that such an outcome is possible, there are currently no assurances that children will be exposed to effective instruction or classroom management before they are placed in special education programs or are screened for gifted programs.

> *3. Does the current referral and assessment process reliably identify students with special needs and gifts? In particular, is there reason to believe that the current process is biased in terms of race or ethnicity?*

The answer here is not as straightforward. The majority of children in special and gifted education are referred by teachers. If a teacher is biased in evaluating student performance and behavior, current procedures provide ample room for those biases to be reflected in referrals. Some experimental research suggests that teachers do hold such biases. But whether bias is maintained when teachers have direct contact with children in the classroom is not clear. For example, research that has compared groups of students who are referred by teachers find that minority students actually have greater academic and behavior problems than their majority counterparts.

Once students are referred for special education, they must be assessed as eligible or ineligible. Whether the assessment process is biased is as controversial as the referral process. However research shows that context, including familiarity with test taking and the norms and expectations of school, may depress the scores of students whose experiences prepare them less well for the demands of classrooms and standardized tests.

Whether the referral and assessment of students for special and gifted education is racially biased or not, are the right students being identified—students who need and can benefit from those programs? Here the committee's answer is "no." The subjectivity of the referral process allows for students with significant learning problems to be overlooked for referral, and the conceptual and procedural shortcomings of the assessment process for learning disabilities and emotional disturbance give little confidence that student need has been appropriately identified. Importantly, current procedures result in placements later in the educational process than is most effective or efficient.

4. Is placement in special education a benefit or a risk? Does the outcome differ by race or ethnic group?

The data that would allow us to answer these questions adequately do not exist. We do know that some specific special education and gifted and talented interventions have been demonstrated to have positive outcomes for students. But how widely those interventions are employed is not known. Nor do we know whether minority students are less likely to be exposed to those high-quality interventions than majority students. What evidence is available suggests that parent advocacy and teacher quality, both of which would be expected to correlate with higher-quality interventions, are less likely in higher-poverty school districts where minority children are concentrated.

At the core of our study is an observation that unites all four questions: *there is substantial evidence with regard to both behavior and achievement that early identification and intervention is more effective than later identification and intervention.* This is true for children of any race or ethnic group, and children with or without an identifiable "within-child" problem. Yet the current special education identification process relies on a "wait-to-fail" principle that both increases the likelihood that children will fail because they do not receive early supports and decreases the effectiveness of supports once they are received. Similarly, the practice of identifying gifted learners after several years of schooling is based on the "wait 'til they succeed" philosophy rather than a developmental orientation.

While this principle applies to all students, the impact is likely to be greatest on students from disadvantaged backgrounds because (a) their experience outside the school prepares them less well for the demands of schooling, placing them at greater risk for failure, and (b) the resources available to them in general education are more likely to be substandard. Early efforts to identify and intervene with children at risk for later failure will help all children who need additional supports. But we would expect a disproportionately large number of those students to be from disadvantaged backgrounds.

The vision we offer in the report is one in which general and special education services are more tightly integrated; one in which no child is judged by the school to have a learning or emotional disability or to lack exceptional talent until efforts to provide high-quality instructional and behavioral support in the general education context have been tried without success. The "earlier is better" principle applies even before the K-12 years. The more effective we are at curtailing early biological harms and injuries and providing children with the supports for normal cognitive and behavioral development in the earliest years of life, the fewer children will arrive at school at risk for failure.

Conclusions and Recommendations

... Here we give the conclusions we consider key, along with the recommendations. They are organized here in the following major categories: referral and eligibility determination in special education (SE) and gifted and talented education (GT); teacher quality (TQ); biological and early childhood risk factors (EC); data collection (DC); and expanding the research and development base (RD).

Special Education Eligibility

From our review of the current knowledge base, several important conclusions have led the committee to rethink the current approach to special education:

1. Among the most frequent reasons for referral to special education are reading difficulties and behavior problems.
2. In recent years, interventions appropriate for the general education classroom to improve reading instruction and classroom management have been demonstrated to reduce the number of children who fail at reading or are later identified with behavior disorders.
3. There are currently no mechanisms in place to guarantee that students will be exposed to state-of-the-art reading instruction or classroom management before they are identified as having a "within-child" problem.
4. Referral "for the high-incidence categories of special education currently requires student failure. However, screening mechanisms exist for early identification of children at risk for later reading and behavior problems. And the effectiveness of early intervention in both areas has been demonstrated to be considerably greater than the effectiveness of later, postfailure intervention.

These findings suggest that schools should be doing more and doing it earlier to ensure that students receive quality general education services to reduce the number of students with pronounced achievement and behavior problems. The committee's proposed alternative would require policy and regulatory changes at both the federal and state levels of government.

Federal-Level Recommendations

Recommendation SE.1: The committee recommends that federal guidelines for special education eligibility be changed in order to encourage better integrated general and special education services. We propose that eligibility ensue when a student exhibits large differences from typical levels of performance in one or more domain(s) and with evidence of insufficient response to high-quality interventions in the relevant domain(s) of functioning in school settings. These domains include achievement (e.g., reading, writing, mathematics), social behavior, and emotional regulation. As is currently the case, eligibility determination would also require a judgment by a multidisciplinary team, including parents, that special education is needed.

The proposed approach would not negate the eligibility of any student who arrives at school with a disability determination, or who has a severe disability, from being served as they are currently. But for children with milder high-incidence disabilities, the implications for referral and assessment are considerable. Assessment for special education eligibility would be focused on gathering information that documents educationally relevant differences from typical levels of performance, and that is relevant to the design, monitoring, and evaluation of treatments.

While eligibility for special education would by law continue to depend on establishment of a disability, in the committee view, noncategorical conceptions and classification criteria that focus on matching a student's specific needs to an intervention strategy would obviate the need for the traditional high-incidence disability labels such as LD and ED. If traditional disability definitions are used, they would need to be revised to focus on characteristics directly related to classroom and school learning and behavior (e.g., reading failure, math failure, persistent inattention and disorganization).

State-Level Recommendations

Regulatory changes would be required in most states for implementation of a reformed special education program that uses functional assessment measures to promote positive outcomes for students with disabilities. Some states have already instituted changes that move in this direction and can serve as examples. These states' rules require a systematic problem-solving process that is centered around quality indicators associated with successful interventions.

Recommendation 5E.2: The committee recommends that states adopt a universal screening and multitiered intervention strategy in general education to enable early identification and intervention with children at risk for reading problems. For students who continue to have difficulty even after intensive intervention, referral to special education and the development of an individualized education program (IEP) would follow. The data regarding student response to intervention would be used for eligibility determination.

Recommendation 5E.3: The committee recommends that states launch large-scale pilot programs in conjunction with universities or research centers to test the plausibility and productivity of universal behavior management interventions, early behavior screening, and techniques to work with children at risk for behavior problems. Research results suggest that these interventions can work. However, a large-scale pilot project would provide a firmer foundation of knowledge regarding scaling up the practices involved.

Federal Support of State Reform Efforts

Recommendation SE.4: While the United States has a strong tradition of state control of education, the committee recommends that the federal government support widespread adoption of early screening and intervention in the states.

Gifted and Talented Eligibility

The research base justifying alternative approaches for the screening, identification, and placement of gifted children is neither as extensive nor as informative as that for special education.

> *Recommendation GT.1: The committee recommends a research program oriented toward the development of a broader knowledge base on early identification and intervention with children who exhibit advanced performance in the verbal or quantitative realm, or who exhibit other advanced abilities.*

This research program should be designed to determine whether there are reliable and valid indicators of current exceptional performance in language, mathematical, or other domains, or indicators of later exceptional performance. Research on classroom practice designed to encourage the early and continued development of gifted behaviors in underrepresented populations should be undertaken so that screening can be followed by effective intervention.

School Context and Student Performance

School resources, class size, and indicators of teacher quality are associated with learning and behavior outcomes. However, their influence is exerted primarily through teacher-student interactions. Moreover, in the prevention and eligibility determination model the committee is recommending, general education assessments and interventions not now in widespread use are proposed as standard practice. Key to our proposals, then, are sustained efforts at capacity building, and sufficient resources, time, and coordination among stakeholders to build that capacity.

State-Level Recommendations
Teacher Quality: General education teachers need improved teacher preparation and professional development to prepare them to address the needs of students with significant underachievement or giftedness.

> *Recommendation TQ.1: State certification or licensure requirements for teachers should systematically require:*
> - *competency in understanding and implementing reasonable norms and expectations for students, and core competencies in instructional delivery of academic content;*
> - *coursework and practicum experience in understanding, creating, and modifying an educational environment to meet children's individual needs;*
> - *competency in behavior management in classroom and noninstructional school settings;*
> - *instruction in functional analysis and routine behavioral assessment of students;*

- *instruction in effective intervention strategies for students who fail to meet minimal standards for successful educational performance, or who substantially exceed minimal standards;*
- *coursework and practicum experience to prepare teachers to deliver culturally responsive instruction. More specifically, teachers should be familiar with the beliefs, values, cultural practices, discourse styles, and other features of students' lives that may have an impact on classroom participation and success and be prepared to use this information in designing instruction.*

While a foundational knowledge base can be laid in preservice education, often classroom experience is needed before teachers can make the most of instructional experiences.

- *States should require rigorous professional development for all practicing teachers, administrators, and educational support personnel to assist them in addressing the varied needs of students who differ substantially from the norm in achievement and/or behavior.*
- *The professional development of administrators and educational support personnel should include enhanced capabilities in the improvement and evaluation of teacher instruction with respect to meeting student's individual needs.*

Recommendation TQ.2: State or professional association approval for educator instructional programs should include requirements for faculty competence in the current literature and research on child and adolescent learning and development, and on successful assessment, instructional, and intervention strategies, particularly for atypical learners and students with gifts and disabilities.

Recommendation TQ.3: A credential as a school psychologist or special education teacher should require instruction in classroom observation/ assessment and in teacher support to work with a struggling student or with a gifted student. These skills should be considered as critical to their professional role as the administration and interpretation of tests are now considered.

Federal-Level Recommendations

This committee joins many others at the NRC and elsewhere in calling for improved teacher preparation. How to move from widespread agreement that change is needed to system reform is a challenge that will itself require careful study.

Recommendation TQ.4: The committee recommends that a national advisory panel be convened in an institutional environment that is protected from political influence to study the quality and currency of programs that now exist to train teachers for general, special, and gifted education. The panel should address:

- *the mechanisms for keeping instructional programs current and of high quality;*
- *the standards and requirements of those programs;*
- *the applicability of instructional programs to the demands of classroom practice;*
- *the long-term influence of the programs in successfully promoting educational achievement for pre-K, elementary, and secondary students.*

Direct comparison to other professional fields (e.g., medicine, nursing, law, engineering, accounting) may provide insight applicable to education.

Biological and Social Risk Factors in Early Childhood

Existing intervention- programs to address early biological harms and injuries have demonstrated the potential to substantially improve developmental outcomes. The committee concludes that the number of children, particularly minority children, who require special education can be reduced if resources are devoted to this end. In particular, the committee calls attention to the recommendation of the President's Task Force on Environmental Health Risks and Safety Risks to Children to eliminate lead from the housing stock by 2010.

Federal-Level Recommendations

The committee also looked at social and environmental influences on development with no clear biological basis that might differ by race or ethnicity. Because there is evidence that early intervention on multiple fronts, if *it is of high quality*, can improve the school prospects for children with multiple risk factors and reduce the likelihood that they will require special education, the committee recommends a substantial expansion and improvement of current early intervention efforts. Our recommendation is addressed to federal and state governments, both of whom currently play a major role in early childhood education.

> *Recommendation EC.l: The committee recommends that all high-risk children have access to high-quality early childhood interventions.*
>
> - *For the children at highest risk, these interventions should include family support, health services, and sustained, high-quality care and cognitive stimulation right from birth.*
> - *Preschool children (ages 4 and 5) who are eligible for Head Start should have access to a Head Start or another publicly funded preschool program. These programs should provide exposure to learning opportunities that will prepare them for success in school. Intervention should target services to the level of individual need, including high cognitive challenge for the child who exceeds normative performance.*
> - *The proposed expansion should better coordinate existing federal programs, such as Head Start and Early Head Start, and IDEA parts C and B, as well as state-initiated programs that meet equal or higher standards.*

While much is known about the types of experiences young children need for healthy development, improving the quality of early childhood programs will require refinement of the knowledge base in ways that are directly useful to practice, and bridging the chasm between what is known from research and best practice and is done in common practice. This will require a sustained vision and a rigorous research and development effort that transforms knowledge about what works and what does not work into field-tested program content, supporting materials, and professional development.

> *Recommendation EC2: The committee recommends that the federal government launch a large-scale, rigorous, sustained research and development program in an institutional environment that has the capacity to bring together excellent professionals in research, program development, professional development, and child care/preschool practice for students from all backgrounds and at all levels of exceptional performance.*

Improving Data Collection and Expanding the Research Base

The data documenting disproportionate representation are difficult to interpret in a variety of respects that make them a weak foundation on which to build public policy. Moreover, the data provide little if any insight into factors that contribute to placement or services that students receive.

Federal-Level Recommendations

> *Recommendation DC.1: The committee recommends that the Department of Education conduct a single, well-designed data collection effort to monitor both the number of children receiving services through the Individuals with Disabilities Education Act or through programs for the gifted and talented, and the characteristics of those children of concern to civil rights enforcement efforts.* A unified effort would eliminate the considerable redundancy, and the burden it places on schools, in the current data collection efforts of the Office for Civil Rights and the Office of Special Education Programs.

While a more careful data collection effort of the sort outlined here would improve the understanding of who is being assigned to special education and gifted and talented programs, it would do little to further understanding of the reasons for placement, the appropriateness of placement (or nonplacement), the services provided, or the consequences that ensue.

> *Recommendation DC.2: The committee recommends that a national advisory panel be convened to design the collection of nationally representative longitudinal data that would allow for more informed study of minority disproportion in special education and gifted and talented programs.* The panel should include scholars in special education research as well as researchers experienced in national longitudinal data collection and analysts in a variety of allied fields, including anthropology, psychology, and sociology.

In our study of the issues related to the representation of minority children in special education and gifted and talented programs, the existing knowledge base revealed the potential for substantial progress. We know much about the kinds of experiences that promote children's early health, cognitive, and behavioral development and set them on a more positive trajectory for school success. We know intervention strategies that have demonstrated success with some of the key problems that end in referral to special education. And we know some features of programs that are correlated with successful outcomes for students in special education. .

Between the articulation of what we know from research and best practice, and a change in everyday practice, lies a wide chasm. It is the distance between demonstrating that vocabulary development is key to later success in reading, and having every Head Start teacher trained and equipped with materials that will promote vocabulary development among Head Start children. It is the distance between knowing that classroom management affects a child's behavior, and the school psychologist knowing how to help a specific teacher work with a specific child in the classroom context. It is the distance between those who are most knowledgeable and experienced agreeing on what teachers need to know, and every school of education changing its curriculum. Bridging the chasm will require that we become better at accumulating knowledge, extending it in promising areas, incorporating the best of what is known in teacher training efforts and education curricula and materials, and rigorously testing effectiveness. It will require public policies that are aligned with the knowledge base and that provide the support for its widespread application.

Recommendation RD.1: We recommend that education research and development, including that related to special and gifted education, be substantially expanded to carry promising findings and validated practices through to classroom applicability. This includes research on scaling up promising practices from research sites to widespread use.

For medical problems like cancer, federal research programs create a vision, focus research efforts on areas with promise for improving treatments, conduct extensive field tests to determine what works, and facilitate the movement of research findings into practice. If the nation is serious about reducing the number of children who are on a trajectory that leads to school failure and disability identification as well as increasing the number of minority students who are achieving at high levels, we will need to devote the minds and resources to that effort commensurate with the size and the importance of the enterprise.

Daniel J. Losen and
Gary Orfield

Introduction:
Racial Inequity in Special Education

Before Congress passed the Education for All Handicapped Children Act—now known as the Individuals with Disabilities Education Act (IDEA)—nearly half of the nation's approximately four million children with disabilities were not receiving a public education. Of the children who were being educated in public schools, many were relegated to a ghetto-like existence in isolated, often run-down classrooms located in the least desirable places within the school building, or sent to entirely separate facilities. Since its passage in 1975, the IDEA has brought tremendous benefits: today, approximately six million children with disabilities enjoy their right to a free appropriate public education. IDEA's substantive rights and procedural protections have produced significant and measurable outcomes for students with disabilities: their graduation rates have increased dramatically, and the number of these students who go on to college has almost tripled since 1978 (though it is still quite low).

Despite these improvements, the benefits of special education have not been equitably distributed. Minority children with disabilities all too often experience inadequate services, low-quality curriculum and instruction, and unnecessary isolation from their nondisabled peers. Moreover, inappropriate practices in both general and special education classrooms have resulted in overrepresentation, misclassification, and hardship for minority students, particularly black children.

A flood of concerns expressed by community leaders about minority children being misplaced in special education prompted The Civil Rights Project at Harvard University to commission the research for [our] book. Since the early 1970s, national surveys by the Office for Civil Rights (OCR) of the U.S. Department of Education have revealed persistent overrepresentation of minority children in certain disability categories. The most pronounced disparities then were black children who, while only 16 percent of the total school enrollment, represented 38 percent of the students in classes for the educationally mentally retarded. After more than twenty years, black children constitute 17 percent of the total school enrollment and 33 percent of those labeled mentally retarded—only a marginal improvement. During this same period, however, disproportionality in the area of emotional disturbance (ED) and the rate of identification for both ED and specific learning disabilities (SLO) grew significantly for blacks.

To better understand this persistent overrepresentation trend, as well as growing reports of profound inequities in the quality of special education, The Civil Rights Project set out to find the best research available. In the original call for papers we asked leading scholars from around the country to document and clarify the issues for minority students with regard to special education. As researchers pursued this task and analyzed possible contributing factors, our fears about the persistence of these problems, the complexities of the contributing factors, and the lack of proven solutions were confirmed.

Our primary purpose in presenting this information is to identify and solve the problem, not to assign blame. This research is intended to inform the debate on special education and racial justice and to provide educators, researchers, advocates, and policymakers with a deeper understanding of the issues as they renew their efforts to find workable solutions. Using national-, state-, district-, and school-level data, these studies document the current trends for minority students regarding identification and restrictiveness of placement. They explore some of the most likely causes, dispel some myths and oversimplified explanations, and highlight the complex interplay of variables within the control of educators at all levels of government. Recognizing the critical role that advocacy has played in securing the rights of all children to educational opportunity, [our] book also provides analysis of the evolving role of the law in stopping inappropriate practices that harm children of color, and in guaranteeing equitable benefits from special education.

The findings [here] point to areas where much improvement is needed and offer an array of ideas for remedies and suggestions for continued research. It is important to recognize that concerns about special education are nested in concerns about inequities in education generally. Special education overrepresentation often mirrors overrepresentation in many undesirable categories—including dropping out, low-track placements, suspensions, and involvement with juvenile justice—and underrepresentation in desirable categories such as gifted and talented. Because special education inequities are often tied to general education issues, remedies should address shortcomings in both special and general education. The recommendations, which are aimed at improving policy and practice, were developed through extensive analysis of the efforts and experiences of educators, policymakers, attorneys, and civil rights enforcement agents. We hope the recommendations will help prevent harmful misidentification and inappropriate placements of minority students, and encourage effective and equitable leadership, enforcement, and distribution of resources to ensure that all children who need special education support receive appropriate and high-quality services.

Issues Explored and Findings

Much of the empirical research ... explores patterns of overrepresentation of minority children by disability category and whether, once identified, they experience relatively less access to the general education classroom than similarly situated white children. The evidence suggests that black overrepresentation is substantial in state after state. The studies reveal wide differences in disability identification between blacks and Hispanics and between black boys and black girls that cannot be explained in terms of social background or measured ability.

Both the statistical and qualitative analyses ... suggest that these racial, ethnic, and gender differences are due to many complex and interacting factors, including unconscious racial bias on the part of school authorities, large resource inequalities that run along lines of race and class, unjustifiable reliance on IQ and other evaluation tools, educators' inappropriate responses to the pressures of high-stakes testing, and power differentials between minority parents and school officials.

[We] ... examine whether the numerous causes of overrepresentation are likely race linked, which is a distinctly different inquiry from whether intentional racial discrimination is the primary cause. Absent a blatantly discriminatory (i.e., illegal as written) policy or practice, to establish that different treatment is purposeful and racist requires specific proof of intent, which is usually discovered through legal enforcement proceedings. The research [here] is obviously not specific enough to explore questions of intent.

Overidentification

On October 4, 2001, the U.S. House of Representatives Committee on Education and the Workforce convened hearings about the overidentification of minority students in special education. In his testimony, Representative Chaka Fattah concluded with the following story of Billy Hawkins:

> For the first fifteen years of his life Billy Hawkins was labeled by his teachers as "educable mentally retarded." Billy was backup quarterback for his high school football team. One night he was called off the bench and rallied his team from far behind. In doing so, he ran complicated plays and clearly demonstrated a gift for the game. The school principal, who was in the stands, recognized that the "retarded boy" could play, and soon after had Billy enrolled in regular classes and instructed his teachers to give him extra help. Billy Hawkins went on to complete a Ph.D. and is now Associate Dean at Michigan's Ferris State University.

Students like Billy Hawkins seldom get the "call off the bench" and an opportunity to shine in front of their principal. Instead, they are removed from the mainstream and never realize their talent. Unfortunately, some in Congress responded to findings we released in earlier reports and to stories like Dr. Hawkins' by opposing efforts to guarantee and fully fund special education at the level Congress originally intended, claiming a need to "fix" special education before providing more funds. [We address] discrete areas of deep racial inequity within a much larger system of special education. It would be wrong to restrict or withhold promised expenditures for all students with disabilities in every state of the nation based on the issues identified in this research.

Of the inequalities in education experienced by minority schoolchildren, those in special education are better documented than most. In 1998, approximately 1.5 million minority children were identified as having mental retardation, emotional disturbance, or a specific learning disability. More than 876,000 of these were black or Native American, and black students were nearly three times as likely as white students to be labeled mentally retarded. Mental retardation diagnoses are relatively rare for all children, and the last twenty years have witnessed a modest decrease in the percentages of students labeled mentally retarded for nearly all racial groups.

Despite this fact, U.S. Department of Education data from 2000–2001 show that in at least thirteen states more than 2.75 percent of all blacks enrolled were labeled mentally retarded. The prevalence of mental retardation for whites nationally was approximately 0.75 percent in 2001, and in no state did the incidence among whites ever rise above 2.32 percent. Moreover, nearly three-quarters of the states with unusually high incidence rates (2.75–5.41%) for blacks were in the South. This is arguably a continuation of the problem as a southern phenomenon that was first observed in the National Research Council's data from 1979, although both then and now many northern states also exhibit remarkably high rates. One positive sign is that southern states exhibited the largest decreases in sheer percentages since 1979.

The data in these studies are generally analyzed in one of three ways. In one, a given minority group's percentage enrollment in the general population is compared to that group's percentage identification in a given disability category. In the second, the actual risk level for a minority group is calculated by dividing the number of students from a given racial group with a given disability by the total enrollment of that racial group. And in the third way, these risk levels are calculated for each minority group and then compared. These comparisons are described as risk ratios and are usually reported in comparison to white children.

... Tom Parrish, a senior research analyst with the American Institutes for Research, calculates risk levels using U.S. Department of Education data based on the number of children eligible for special education reported by each state for children between the ages of six and twenty-one in 1998, and compares that with census estimates of children of the same age for each state for the same year. Parrish then calculates the risk ratios for each minority group by cognitive disability category for every state and for the nation.

He finds that black children are 2.88 times more likely than whites to be labeled mentally retarded and 1.92 times more likely to be labeled emotionally disturbed.

Blacks are the most overrepresented minority group in every category and in nearly every state. The gross racial disparities that exist between many minority groups and whites in terms of mental retardation also exist in other cognitive disability categories, but are less pronounced. Nationwide, blacks and Native Americans are less often overidentified for specific learning disabilities (i.e., black children are more than twice as likely as white children to be found to have a specific learning disability in only nine states).

Parrish also shows the extent of overidentification of other minorities in the ED and SLD categories. In the SLD category, for example, only in Hawaii are Asian Americans/Pacific Islanders identified at nearly twice the rate of whites. On the other hand, Native American children in six states are identified at more than twice the rate of whites.

Latinos and Asian Americans are generally underidentified compared to whites in most states and in most categories, raising the possibility of inadequate attention to their special needs; however, the state-level data may underreport the problem for some groups. According to a 1982 National Research Council (NRC) report, district-level data on Hispanics from 1979 suggested that a wide variety of both over- and underrepresentation tended to cancel each other out in aggregate state-level data. Neither the 2002 NRC report, "Minority Students in Special and Gifted Education," nor the studies [here] conducted a district-level analysis with national data comparable to that contained in the 1982 study of Hispanic identification rates. However, Alfredo Artiles, Robert Rueda, Jesus Jose Salazar, and Ignacio Higareda, in their analysis of large urban school districts in California, reveal that disproportionate representation in special education is far more likely for (predominantly Latino) English-language learners in secondary school than in elementary school. Thus, the problem may even be hidden when elementary and secondary school data are aggregated at the district level.

Edward Fierros and James Conroy's research ... , which does examine district-level data from throughout Connecticut and from selected U.S. cities, suggests that the state data may miss disturbing trends for minority overrepresentation in a given category or educational setting. Generally speaking, the most serious racial disparities (both under- and overrepresentation) become apparent when data on minority children are disaggregated by race/ethnicity subgroups, cognitive disability category, gender, and placement—at least down to the district level.

Educational Placement

Readers should not forget that students with disabilities are entitled to receive supports and services in a setting best suited to their individual needs, and not to be automatically assigned to a separate place, subjected to low expectations, or excluded from educational opportunities. While substantially separate educational environments are certainly best for some individuals, it is equally well established in research that students with disabilities benefit most when they are educated with their general education peers to the maximum extent appropriate, and this is reflected in the law.

Fierros and Conroy's work demonstrates that, once identified as eligible for special education services, both Latinos and blacks are far less likely than whites to be educated in a fully inclusive general education classroom and far more likely to be educated in a substantially separate setting. The data Fierros and Conroy explore show a consistent trend toward less inclusion for minority children at the national, state, and district levels. The relationship between race and greater exclusion, also not examined in the NRC's 2002 report, suggests that, among students with disabilities, black and Latino children with disabilities may be consistently receiving less desirable treatment than white children. Fierros and Conroy further disaggregate the racial data by disability type for the state of Connecticut and find a lower level of inclusion for blacks and Hispanics compared to whites among each of the three disability types examined (students with mental retardation, emotional disturbance, and specific learning disabilities).

The concern with the overrepresentation of minorities would be mitigated if the evidence suggested that minority children reaped benefits from more frequent identification and isolation. But as government officials acknowledge and as data demonstrate, this does not appear to be the case.

Low-Quality Evaluations, Supports, and Services

In their chapter, David Osher, Darren Woodruff, and Anthony Sims illustrate how the issue is often not as simple as the false identification of a nondisabled minority child. Many minority children do have disabilities but are at risk of receiving inappropriate and inadequate services and unwarranted isolation. Osher et al. point out that, for some children, receiving inappropriate services may be more harmful than receiving none at all. For others, not receiving help early enough may exacerbate learning and behavior problems. Both problems are reflected in disturbing statistics on outcomes for minority children with disabilities. As Donald Oswald, Martha Coutinho, and Al Best report in the opening lines of the book's first chapter, there are dramatic differences in what happens to minority students with disabilities after high school:

> In the 1998–1999 school year, over 2.2 million children of color in U.S. schools were served by special education (U.S. Department of Education, 2000). Post-high school outcomes for these minority students with disabilities are strikingly inferior. Among high school youth with disabilities, about 75 percent of African American students, as compared to 47 percent of white students, are not employed two years out of school. Slightly more than half (52%) of African Americans, compared to 39 percent of white young adults, are still not employed three to five years out of school. In this same time period, the arrest rate for African Americans with disabilities is 40 percent, as compared to 27 percent for whites (Wagner, D'Amico, Marder, Newman, & Blackorby, 1992).

In addition to these patterns, Osher, Woodruff, and Sims provide new data depicting substantially higher rates of disciplinary action and placement in correctional facilities for minority students with disabilities still in school. Based on their review of the data and other research, they suggest that investments in high-quality special education and early intervention are sorely needed and could reduce the likelihood that minority students with disabilities will develop serious discipline problems or eventually wind up in correctional facilities.

Racial Discrimination and Other Contributing Factors

In a society where race is so strongly related to individual, family, and community conditions, it is extremely difficult to know what part of the inequalities are caused by discrimination within the school. These studies, however, do uncover correlations with race that cannot be explained by factors such as poverty or exposure to environmental hazards alone. While the scope of this research does not attempt to depict a definitive causal link to racial discrimination, the research does suggest that unconscious racial bias, stereotypes, and other race-linked factors have a significant impact on the patterns of identification, placement, and quality of services for minority children, and particularly for African American children.

The researchers recognize that factors such as poverty and environmental influences outside of school contribute to a heightened incidence of disability in significant ways. All analysts who attempt to sort out the causes of inequality in U.S. institutions of course face the dilemma that some of the differences in subtracted control variables are themselves products of other forms of racial discrimination. For example, if a researcher determined that 40 percent of the association between race and shorter life expectancy could be explained by poverty, we have to understand that the poverty in question may be influenced by employment discrimination or be due in part to a second-generational effect of segregated schooling. Therefore, despite the importance of statistical controls, it is well established that many controls will lower the estimates of the effect of race when race is examined as an isolated variable. What happens in school is only a subset of the far more pervasive impact of racial discrimination that affects minority families and their children.

Even when researchers assume that poverty is independent of race and subtract race and other background variables, many of the trends highlighted by this research appear to contradict the theory that poverty is primarily to blame and that race is not a significant factor. Those trends include the following: (a) pronounced and persistent racial disparities in identification between white and black children in the categories of mental retardation and emotional disturbance, compared with far less disparity in the category of specific learning disabilities; (b) a minimal degree of racial disparity in medically diagnosed disabilities as compared with subjective cognitive disabilities; (c) dramatic differences in the incidence of disability from one state to the next; and (d) gross disparities between blacks and Hispanics, and between black boys and girls, in identification rates for the categories of mentally retarded and emotionally disturbed.

The data on disproportionate representation is compatible with the theory that systemic racial discrimination is a contributing factor where disparities are substantial. Moreover, the trends revealed in [our] book are consistent with the theory that different racial groups, facing different kinds of stereotypes and bias, would experience racial disparities differently. States with a history of racial apartheid under de jure segregation, for example, account for five of the seven states with the highest overrepresentation of African Americans labeled mentally retarded—Mississippi, South Carolina, North Carolina,

Florida, and Alabama. This trend suggests that the "soft bigotry of low expectations" may have replaced the undeniable intentional racial discrimination in education against blacks that once pervaded the South. In contrast, no southern state was among the top seven states where Hispanic children deemed mentally retarded were most heavily overrepresented.

The effects of poverty cannot satisfactorily explain racial disparities in identification for mental retardation or emotional disturbance. Regression analysis suggests that race, gender, and poverty are all significant factors. Oswald, Coutinho, and Best specifically asked whether, "taking into account the effects of social, demographic, and school-related variables, gender and ethnicity are significantly associated with the risk of being identified for special education." Their examination of each factor at the district level (based on all of the districts surveyed in OCR's database combined with the National Center for Education Statistics, Common Core of Data) finds that, although disability incidence often increases with poverty, when poverty- and wealth-linked factors are controlled for, ethnicity and gender remain significant predictors of cognitive disability identification by schools. Specifically, wealth-linked factors included per pupil expenditure, median housing value, median income for households with children, percentage of children in households below the poverty level, and percentage of adults in the community who have a twelfth-grade education or less and no diploma.

Most disturbing, was that in wealthier districts, contrary to the expected trend, black children, especially males, were *more likely to be labeled* mentally retarded. Moreover, the sharp gender differences in identification within racial groups, also described in the 2002 NRC report, are not explained by the poverty theory.

Large demographic differences among minority groups are also discussed by Parrish and by Fierros and Conroy, and each confirms that the influence of race and ethnicity is significant, and apparently distinct from that of poverty. For example, Parrish reviews the data for each racial group across all fifty states and finds that, in comparison to whites, each minority group is at greater risk of being labeled mentally retarded as their percentage of the total enrolled population increases.

That poverty does account for some of the observed racial disproportions in disability identification comes as no surprise. Certain minority groups are disproportionately poor. Logically, one would expect poverty to cause a higher incidence of "hard" disabilities (e.g., blindness and deafness) among members of low-wealth minority groups, due to the impact of poor nutrition and inadequate prenatal care. But the most recent research shows that blacks in any given state are substantially less likely to be overrepresented in these hard categories.

Finally, the theory that poverty and socioeconomic factors can explain all or most of the observed racial disparities fails to account for the extreme differences between black overrepresentation and Hispanic underrepresentation, differences that are even more significant in many states than disparities between blacks and whites. For example, blacks in Alabama and Arkansas are more than seven to nine times as likely as Hispanics to be labeled mentally retarded. Moreover, nationally and in many other states, the disparity in identification rates for mental retardation and emotional disturbance between blacks and Hispanics is greater than the disparity between blacks and whites. Yet Hispanics, like blacks, are at far greater risk than whites for poverty, exposure to environmental toxins in impoverished neighborhoods, and low-level academic achievement in reading and math. Thus, the high variation in identification rates among minority groups with similar levels of poverty and academic failure casts serious doubt on assertions by some researchers that it is primarily poverty and not bias that creates these deep racial disparities.

Multiple Contributing Factors

Most students with disabilities enter school undiagnosed and are referred by regular classroom teachers for evaluations that may lead to special education identification and placement. Therefore, the cause of the observed racial disparity is rooted not only in the system of special education itself, put also in the system of regular education as it encompasses special education. Most students referred for evaluation for special education are deemed in need of services. If differential referral is a key element, then the perceptions and decisions of classroom teachers, as well as school-level policies and practices that have an impact on students in regular classrooms, are, likewise, key elements.

Based on years of research, Beth Harry, Janette Klingner, Keith Sturges, and Robert Moore conclude in their chapter that "[t]he point at which differences [in measured performance and ability] result in one child being labeled disabled and another not are totally matters of social decisionmaking." Special education evaluations are often presented to parents as a set of discrete decisions based on scientific analysis and assessment, but even test-driven decisions are inescapably subjective in nature. The existence of some bias in test *content* is not the primary concern. Harry et al.'s research, for example, describes how subjective decisions creep into all elements of the evaluation *process*, including whom to test, what test to use, when to use alternative tests, how to interpret student responses, and what weight to give results from specific tests. All of these alter the outcomes. As Harry et al. point out, "a pen-stroke of the American Association on Mental Retardation (AAMR)" lowered the IQ score cutoff point for mental retardation from 85 to 70, "swiftly curing thousands of previously disabled children."

School politics, power relationships between school authorities and minority parents, the quality of regular education, and the classroom management skills of the referring teacher also introduce important elements of subjectivity that often go unrecognized. Other race-linked forces at work include poorly trained teachers who are disproportionately employed in minority schools (some of whom use special education as a disciplinary tool), other resource inequalities correlated to race, beliefs in African American and Latino inferiority and the low expectations that accompany these beliefs, cultural insensitivity, praise differentials, fear and misunderstanding of black males, and overcrowded schools and classrooms that are disproportionately located in school districts with high percentages of minority students. Add to these forces the general phenomenon of white parents' activism, efficaciousness, and high social capital exercised on behalf of their children compared to the relative lack of parent power among minority parents, and one can understand how the combination of regular education problems and the special education identification process has had a disparate impact on students of different races and ethnicities.

Sweeping reforms may also trigger harmful outcomes. For example, Artiles et al.'s preliminary examination of the "Unz Initiative," which eliminated bilingual education in California, suggests that English-language learners whose access to language supports is limited are more likely to be placed in restrictive special education settings. And as Jay Heubert describes in detail in his chapter, over the last ten years the use of high-stakes testing may have disproportionately punished poor and minority students, students with disabilities, and English-language learners: "There is evidence that states with high minority enrollments in special education are also likely to have high-stakes testing policies." Heubert goes on to cite evidence that "promotion testing is ... likely to increase, perhaps significantly, the numbers of students with disabilities and minority students who suffer the serious consequences of dropping out." He points out that the National Research Council has described simple retention in grade as "an ineffective intervention." The aspirational benefits of raising standards aside, Heubert concludes that minority students with disabilities are at "great risk ... especially in states that administer high-stakes promotion and graduation tests ... ."

The Status of the Law and Enforcement Policy

Beginning with *Brown v. Board of Education,* litigation and enforcement under civil rights law has been essential to improving racial equity in education. Title VI of the Civil Rights Act of 1964 provided an important lever for racial justice in education that was especially effective when the federal government made enforcement a high priority. Critically important was that, under the Title VI regulations, plaintiffs could use statistical evidence to prove that even a policy that was race neutral on its face had an adverse and unjustifiably disparate impact on children of color in violation of the law. As Daniel Losen and Kevin Welner describe in their chapter, the legal landscape shifted dramatically following the U.S. Supreme Court's 2001 ruling in *Alexander v. Sandoval* which declared that there is no implied private right of action to bring legal challenges under "disparate-impact" theory. Therefore, court challenges that would rely on serious statistical disparities to prove allegations of discrimination are nearly extinguished today. Although the government and individuals filing complaints with government agencies may still use the Title VI regulations to redress the racially disparate impact of neutral policies, enforcement of disparate impact regulations is more vulnerable to an administration's enforcement policy preferences than ever before.

Untouched by *Sandoval* is the potential to challenge policies or practices where the racial disparities in special education identification or placement arise in the context of hearings on school desegregation. For example, in Alabama in 2000, a court review of consent decrees in that state resulted in a settlement yielding comprehensive state- and district-level remedies for overidentification of minorities.

Losen and Welner point out that disability law is becoming a relatively stronger basis for leveraging remedies from states and school districts where overidentification, underservicing, or unnecessarily restrictive placements are an issue. They explain further how systemic legal actions are better suited for seeking effective comprehensive remedies that could address contributing factors in both regular and special education. In her chapter, Theresa Glennon closely examines and evaluates the Office for Civil Rights' enforcement efforts where disability law and Tide VI converge. Glennon's recommendations include better coordinated investigations and interagency information sharing, clearer guidance for schools, and more comprehensive compliance reviews by well-trained investigators.

Sharon Soltman and Donald Moore provide an extensive analysis of how to fashion a remedy through litigation in a case known as *Corey H.* Their thorough chapter combines many years of research on effective practices with models of school improvement. They set forth a roadmap for school district reform to ensure that children with disabilities in Illinois be educated in the least restrictive environment as required by law. The multitiered *Corey H.* remedy entails a ten-year process for change, in one set of schools each year. The plaintiffs also won a large infusion of state funding to make implementing the *Corey H.* requirements a fully funded mandate. Further research on the efficacy of the court-ordered remedy should prove extremely useful to policymakers and others seeking to guarantee that minority children with disabilities have appropriate educational opportunities.

The only study in this volume that explores restricting federal funds as a remedy does so in the context of analyzing the viability of the Department of Education's Office for Special Education Programs' (OSEP) enforcement mechanisms for redressing racial disproportionality. In that study, Thomas Hehir argues forcefully for more frequent exercise of partial withholding by enforcement agents that is narrowly targeted to leverage compliance by specific states or districts in certain areas. As Hehir points out, partial withholding would allow OSEP to ratchet up its enforcement efforts without wholesale withdrawal of federal funds, which would heighten the risk of political backlash and have a negative impact on students in properly run programs. Likewise, federal policymakers should improve IDEA implementation and civil rights enforcement without imposing wholesale limitations on federal special education funding, which would have a negative impact on children with disabilities nationwide. Of course, there may be extreme cases in noncompliant districts where the only way to end serious violations is to cut off general funds, which proved very effective in spurring the desegregation of southern schools.

Moreover, Tom Parrish's research suggests that some state funding formulas are contributing to problems of overidentification. Some of these formulas fail to follow the federal model, which relies on U.S. Census data to determine allocations. The most problematic state formulas instead channel funds by disability identification and/or program and are suspected of creating incentives for overidentification.

Recommendations

Theses studies and the NRC's 2002 report both suggest that special education issues faced by minority children often begin with shortcomings in the realm of general education well before teachers or parents seek an evaluation for special education eligibility. Therefore, policy solutions that fail to consider the connection with general education classrooms will unlikely bring about significant change.

A New Federal Initiative With Implications for State Accountability

Our nation's education policy is at a crossroads. Leaders demand an end to the "soft bigotry of low expectations" and our government has promised to improve the achievement of all children in 2002 through the new education reform act, known as the No Child Left Behind Act. Racial equity is rooted in the commitment to teach all children well, with particular attention to meeting the needs of minority children.

To tackle racial disparities in achievement and graduation rates, the president and Congress embraced three reform approaches: public reporting, accountability at all levels (school, district, and state), and mandatory enforcement. These three reform approaches could be used to address the gross racial disparities in special education identification, restrictiveness of placement, and quality of services

For policymakers, there is no need to pinpoint a specific cause or allege race discrimination in order to achieve racial equity. Scholars report that many schools today still operate under a deficit model, where school authorities regard students with disabilities as the embodiments of their particular disability and ask only *what the special educators are required to do in order to accommodate the student's problem.* A universal commitment to equity in special education would help erode this deficit model by shifting the focus to *what all public educators should do to improve educational opportunities and outcomes for all children.*

There is bipartisan acknowledgement that special education issues faced by minority children need a federal legislative response. This apparent consensus holds promise for effective federal reform. Reform attempts in the recent past can be improved upon. In 1997 the IDEA was amended to require states to collect and review data on racial disproportionality in both identification and placement and to intervene where disproportionality is significant. Before that, in 1995, the Office for Civil Rights made racial disproportionality in special education a top priority. The persistence of this problem suggests that states' legal obligations under IDEA and our civil rights enforcement priorities have not been met.

OCR was once a major force in the effort to desegregate our nation's schools, suggesting that the agency's efficacy is related to political will as much as it is to resources. It is apparent that there is a glaring need for stepped-up enforcement and oversight by both federal and state agencies. These actions must be geared toward encouraging the active participation of educators at all levels if there is to be any hope of meaningful and lasting improvement. Most important, aggressive efforts to remedy these issues are only the starting point. The efficacy of enforcement interventions and attempted reforms must be evaluated in terms of the outcomes for minority children.

Both general and special education teachers and administrators need better training to deliver effective instruction in the least restrictive, most inclusive environment appropriate. Meeting this need, along with the need for better data collection on racial and ethnic disparities and enhanced civil rights enforcement, would require an infusion of special education funds, which could be expected to result in net gains in education outcomes and savings in juvenile justice expenditures in the long term. By increasing federal oversight and by encouraging states to intervene where appropriate, the federal government could help improve the quality of instruction, supports, and services received by minority students in both regular and special education.

Although OCR still does not collect national data to determine racial disparities in the educational environment, the 1997 IDEA amendments obligate the states to collect sampled data. If the government required every state and school district to collect disaggregated data by race with disability category and educational setting (all three together), research on overrepresentation would benefit tremendously.

Moreover, much general education reform law is predicated on the concept that public pressure at the local level from parents and community stakeholders will stimulate meaningful improvements. To generate local reform pressure, the Bush education program requires public reporting of test achievement by a number of student subgroups, including disability status and major racial and ethnic subgroups. Policymakers could likewise stimulate meaningful improvements in special education by amending the IDEA to require public reporting of racial disparities in special education identification and placement.

IDEA should also require states to intervene under specified circumstances (they now have complete discretion) and to provide technical assistance to effect reforms. Such required intervention and assistance would likely foster greater self-reflection and improvement at the district level. While adopting mandatory interventions would be helpful, given the context of shrinking state education budgets, an emphasis on rewards and continued supports to foster successful efforts must be an integral part of any new enforcement efforts.

Finally, new mechanisms for minority children to exercise their rights under IDEA, including legal services support, would help considerably.

Toward Comprehensive Solutions to Systemic Problems at the District Level

The research and analysis presented in [the] volume are intended to serve educators, advocates, and policymakers alike. In addition to raising awareness of the issues, suggesting changes in legislation, and improving the enforcement of existing requirements, much can be accomplished with greater determination by school leadership.

For communities of color, disproportionate representation in special education is just one facet of the denial of access to educational opportunity. Denial begins in the regular education setting with school segregation, low tracking, test-based diploma denial and retention, overly harsh discipline, less access to programs for the gifted, and resource inequalities that have a distinctly racial dimension. Education leaders who suspect a problem at their school can accomplish a great deal by clearly stating that this problem is one that they and their staff can do something about, and that it has a racial dimension. By squarely shouldering responsibility and resolving to improve outcomes for all children as they tackle the racial disparities, school leaders can also reduce racial tensions among staff and in their school community and recover lives and talents that would otherwise be wasted. Tackling these issues should be a shared responsibility, not the duty of the principal or special education administrator alone. Furthermore, technical assistance can be sought from state and federal agencies, including OCR and OSEP, without triggering legal action. School leaders concerned with the issues raised above can also renew their efforts to involve parents and community in innovative ways. Some suggested methods include entering into partnerships with community organizations in order to boost minority parent involvement, and engaging school-based councils that would share decisionmaking power, working more closely with social service agencies to ensure that at-risk students receive high-quality services and that social workers and teachers are collaborating effectively, and increasing direct outreach to families.

Moreover, teachers need support to change their practice and improve classroom outcomes. In many cases regular classroom teachers have received little or no training in working with students from diverse backgrounds or with special education students, or have had little practicum experience in inclusive classrooms. Similarly, many special education teachers have not had the degree of training in the core curriculum or on how to work in a full-inclusion setting. Without both academic and multicultural training and time for special education and regular education teachers to collaborate, it is unrealistic to expect significant improvement.

Protecting the civil rights of all students benefits society at large. Obviously, it is much better if this problem is solved within the school than through external enforcement. Strong leadership at all levels could make an important difference. There is a great deal of work that can and should be done by schools, by districts, by states, and by federal lawmakers and enforcement agents that would improve educational opportunities for minority children in general, and make tremendous progress in solving the specific problems highlighted [here].

There are no quick fixes. The problems [we explore] have many roots, and creating better outcomes requires difficult changes at many levels. Far more research is needed on the practices that produce inequality and the reforms that can successfully correct them. We need to reach the point at which every child is treated as if he or she were our own child, with the same tirelessly defended and protected life possibilities. In schools where we can predict the racial makeup of a special education class before we open the door, we must have leadership, if possible, and enforcement, if necessary, to ensure that each child receives the quality academic support and special services he or she truly needs without diminishing any of the opportunities that are any child's right in American society. We hope [our] book will contribute to that dream.

POSTSCRIPT

Is Eliminating Overrepresentation Beyond the Scope of Public Schools?

Although these selections are longer than most in this book, they provide only a glimpse into the projects they represent. Reading both reports in their entirety delivers a much more textured appreciation of the extensiveness of each.

The studies share common ground in their concern about the issues surrounding overrepresentation. Their opening words, however, set the tone for their differences. Donovan and Cross endeavor not necessarily to end disproportionate representation, if it serves a purpose and delivers a benefit. Losen and Orfield would like to end disproportionality in special education, asserting that minority children with disabilities have not received much benefit.

In their literature review, Donovan and Cross find there may be some grounds for overrepresentation. Citing risks that come from poverty and environmental hazards, they conclude that children who have encountered these conditions come to school at greater risk. While experience is not unalterable, they say, there are actual differences in school readiness. Schools can address student performance, but environmental issues are matters of "political priority."

Losen and Orfield agree that environmental circumstances affect school readiness and performance, but they raise two compelling puzzles. First, if environmental issues are causal, why is there not overrepresentation in every disability category? Second, why is it that Hispanic children, who generally share economic status with African Americans, experience less overrepresentation?

Both studies agree that general education programs are critical. Indeed, while doctors identify the most visible disabilities, the majority of children in special education are referred by their classroom teachers. To what extent is overrepresentation affected by poor schools with inexperienced teachers and principals?

Racial bias is hard to evaluate, say the authors. The NRC study notes that the effects of prejudice are often subtle and intangible. Losen and Orfield comment that it is difficult to determine whether or not disproportionality results from intentional, biased behaviors but describe what happens in school as a "subset" of the racial impacts in society. Both sets of researchers agree educators must reexamine an evaluation process that can be subjective and influenced by cultural differences.

Many others have explored the issues surrounding disproportionality. Looking at environmental issues, Ness (*Rethinking Schools Online*, 2003), refers to the deleterious effects of lead toxins as "environmental racism," which results in lower school performance in children of poverty, many of whom are also children of color.

Artiles, Harry, Reschly, and Chinn (*Multicultural Perspectives*, 2002) explored a range of forces that impact disproportionality, including poverty, instructional and assessment factors, and cultural discontinuity. While concluding that many are "beyond the workscope" of schools, they believe that educators can draw attention to problems and strive to make positive changes.

Cultural and linguistic barriers that can affect the educational experience of African American children are discussed by Obi and Obiakor (*The Western Journal of Black Studies*, 2001). Since society is likely to become increasingly diverse, they emphasize the need for all educators to become more sensitive and responsive to linguistic and cultural differences.

Is disproportionality an issue for schools to solve or a broader societal challenge? If society committed the resources to address environmental problems and poverty, what differences would we see? Can communities and schools implement early intervention systems that would prevent referrals? Will the uniform expectations and accountability of No Child Left Behind ensure that everyone attends to the needs of all children rather than succumb to "the soft bigotry of lowered expectations"? Or is the answer to be found in stricter governmental oversight? These are not simple questions to ponder, much less answer. But they must be raised and addressed for the benefit of all children.

ISSUE 3

Do Funding Formulas Make Special Education Too Expensive?

YES: Teresa S. Jordan, Carolyn A. Weiner, and K. Forbis Jordan, from "The Interaction of Shifting Special Education Policies with State Funding Practices," *Journal of Educational Finance* (Summer 1997)

NO: Sheldon Berman, Perry Davis, Ann Koufman-Frederick, and David Urion, from "The Rising Costs of Special Education in Massachusetts: Causes and Effects," in C.E. Finn, Jr., A.J. Rotherham, and C.R. Hokanson, Jr., eds., *Rethinking Special Education for a New Century* (The Thomas B. Fordham Foundation & Progressive Policy Institute, 2001)

ISSUES SUMMARY

YES: Teresa Jordan, associate professor at University of Las Vegas–Nevada; Carolyn Weiner, president of Syndactics, Inc.; and K. Forbis Jordan, professor emeritus at Arizona State University, believe that the number of students identified as disabled is increasing at an excessive rate because of funding systems that encourage overidentification and that discourage flexible, creative, inclusive school programming.

NO: Sheldon Berman and Perry Davis (both school superintendents), along with Ann Koufman-Frederick, director of Technology Initiatives at the Massachusetts Association of School Committees, and David Urion, director of the Learning Disabilities/Behavioral Neurology Program at Children's Hospital (Boston) maintain that districts have been careful and conservative in identifying children with disabilities, but that enrollment and costs are increasing primarily because of the increased numbers of children with more significant disabilities.

Want to start a heated conversation? Walk into a room and ask if special education costs too much money. Sit at a school board meeting and listen to agonizing discussions of whether to spend sparse funds on new chemistry books or more special education staff. Can you already feel the heat?

Legislators knew that establishing and maintaining programs for students with disabilities would cost money. No one knew how much or came close to an accurate prediction. Passage of the first special education law came with Congress's promise to pay up to 40% of the cost of educating children with disabilities. Annually determined through Capitol Hill negotiations, the actual funding appropriated has never come close to this promise, ranging from seven percent to 15% of this cost.

Despite this continuing underfunding, districts eagerly reach for any financial assistance available. To qualify for federal funds, schools maintain detailed records documenting compliance with special education laws and regulations. Students are counted annually, along with the extent of their time in special education. These figures are reported to state and then to the U.S. Department of Education. Once budget wrangling ends, the total number of students with disabilities is divided into the funds available and checks are sent to each state.

After retaining some funds for the operation of overall special education activities, each state disperses the remaining federal funds among school districts. Sometimes the money that comes to a district amounts to less than $1000 per student.

At the district level, schools begin budget formation in September for the following educational year. Estimating the cost of new textbooks and salary increases is relatively simple, especially when the number of students can be predicted based on current enrollment and contracts are settled.

Predicting the number of students with disabilities and the extent of their need is an entirely different matter. Who can tell when a child will have a tragic accident? Or anticipate a child who has not yet moved to town or reached the age of eligibility for publicly supported education? Nevertheless, the budget built early in one school year must anticipate the children who will require education a full 18 months later.

No matter how rich the school district, there is never enough money to go around.

Teresa Jordan, Carolyn Weiner and K. Forbis Jordan explore the various ways that states fund special education concluding that most current systems encourage schools to identify more children as disabled to secure larger amounts of federal funds. The authors see this as counterproductive, limiting the flexibility of school districts and flying in the face of current efforts toward inclusion and site based management. Several alternative funding mechanisms are described, all with an eye toward halting the reward districts receive when they label children as disabled. Massachusetts is cited as a "trendsetter" state, altering regulations and funding formulas to reduce reliance on special education.

Sheldon Berman, Perry Davis, Ann Koufman-Frederick and David Urion analyze special education enrollment and funding patterns that followed these "trendsetting" policy changes in Massachusetts. Using data from districts throughout the state, and drawing parallels to national statistics, the authors find districts working assiduously to contain special education costs, struggling not to overidentify and creatively building responsive programs. Despite these efforts, special education expenditures continue to rise, driven by the increasing numbers of children with severe and complex needs and the shifting of costs to public schools.

As you read these articles, ask yourself whether federal funding helps defray the cost of expensive education or creates rigid expectations that limit the creativity of schools.

YES **Teresa S. Jordan, Carolyn A. Weiner, and K. Forbis Jordan**

The Interaction of Shifting Special Education Policies With State Funding Practices

Introduction

In the current atmosphere of education reform, school finance litigation, regulatory changes, deregulation, and shifts in economic and political philosophies, increasing attention is being given to state funding systems for special education programs. The interactive effects of limited funds, mounting costs of some special education placements, and the federal interest in deregulation are resulting in greater scrutiny being given to special education programs. As schools strive to respond to shifts in policy and pressures for education reform, they are confronted with state funding systems for special education that are based on a different set of assumptions. Most current state funding systems for special education assume identifiable students, quantifiable program standards, isolated and measurable services, and auditable expenditures. As school districts change delivery systems so that children with disabilities are integrated into classrooms that also include students without disabilities, changes in local district budgeting and cost accounting systems will be required to provide special education expenditure data. Thus, state funding approaches will need to accommodate these new instructional arrangements.

Even before the dramatic changes in political control in 1994 and emphasis on inclusion of children with disabilities in classrooms that also contain children without disabilities,... the future of special education was uncertain. Funding levels for all education programs are being questioned because of the competition among various social services for scarce funds.... .

For two decades, funding systems for special education in many states have allocated different levels of funding based on the child's disability classification. State funding allocations to provide programs and services for youth with disabilities typically have been based on instructional units, student weights, personnel reimbursement, reimbursement of the excess costs of educating these youth, or a flat grant.

Recently, in an effort to provide a disincentive for local districts to identify and serve more children with disabilities, Massachusetts, Montana, North

Dakota, Pennsylvania, and Vermont have enacted special education funding formulas that allocate funds on the basis of total school district enrollment and thus assume an equal proportion of students with disabilities in all school districts. Even though this approach may be attractive because of its simplicity and the elimination of the need to classify students to secure funds, a 1992 study reported that the statewide incidence of students in special education programs varied from just over 6 percent in Oregon to 17 percent in Massachusetts. State and district-level incidence data indicate that children with disabilities are not uniformly distributed among states or among districts within a state....

The adversarial competition for funds between students without disabilities and students with disabilities may not be evident in all states, but events in Massachusetts illustrate that the conflict can occur. Since the special education reform legislation was enacted two decades ago, dramatic improvements have been achieved in Massachusetts. This legislation was praised as a national model; at the time, programs for children with disabilities were fragmented, under-funded, and highly segregated. After 20 years, over 96 percent of the special education students were being served in the public schools and no mentally retarded students under the age of 21 were in state institutions. However, the number of students receiving services was increasing and the costs of special education services and programs were rising faster than overall funding. In addition, residential costs were becoming a problem with $53 million being expended annually for 830 children, almost $64,000 per student each year. As might be expected, a backlash against special education occurred after overall spending constraints occurred in 1991.

Recently, in response to concerns about the effects of this earlier legislation, Massachusetts has taken two steps that may be trendsetters in the education reforms of the late 1990s that affect special education. First, the concept of the special needs child was redefined.... Second, the state's education reform legislation addresses the underlying challenge to provide a high quality education for all students. The presumption is that arguments over pullouts, inclusion, and over-regulation will continue, but efforts to address the sufficiency of overall funding are expected to reduce the tension between general and special education. The state also changed its funding formula so that each district's funds for special education were based on total school population rather than the number of special education students being served....

The combination of programmatic reforms, fiscal constraints, and changing political philosophies suggest both the opportunity and the need to reexamine the ways that states fund special education programs and services....

Background

Even though most states had been funding special education for several years, the major impetus for full implementation of programs and services to serve youth with disabilities can be traced to the enactment of P. L. 94-142 in 1975. Enacted in a climate of social reform, this federal law resulted in the promulgation of federal and state regulations that each child be provided with a free and appropriate education. The Congress took this action in response to federal court cases affirming the right of an education for children with disabilities, research demonstrating that all children can learn, and intense lobbying by special education personnel and parent groups. As a result of this legislation, children with disabilities were guaranteed:

- a free appropriate education
- a comprehensive evaluation
- an individualized educational program (IEP)
- related services
- due-process procedures
- placement in the least restrictive environment

Amendments were made to the original legislation in 1986 and also in 1990 when the title was changed to the Individuals with Disabilities Education Act (IDEA).

In 1994–95, about 5.4 million students were being served in programs for youth with disabilities; this represents about 11 percent of the total school enrollment. Spending levels have been estimated to be over two times the expenditures for general education, with less than 10 percent from federal funds, about 54 percent from state sources, and about 36 percent from local sources.

Program Delivery

Programs and services for children with disabilities are provided through both public and private schools with the private placement often being supported by public funds. Referrals are most often initiated by a teacher or parent who notices a difficulty. Following a diagnostic process, the eligible child's educational and service needs are identified and formalized in an individualized education program (IEP). Historically, the child then has been assigned to the appropriate special education for specific periods of time.

... [T]he majority of students receiving special education are served in their home districts. Many public school officials contend that private placements are very costly options that benefit affluent parents who can afford legal counsel; these parents have the economic power to challenge the contention that their child can be served in the public school setting.

For several years, special education procedures have been subjected to a variety of criticisms. Much of the programmatic criticism has been related to the practice of removing the child from the classroom either to receive special services or to be placed in a self-contained classroom on a full-time basis....

Additional concerns have been that special education has become a "dumping ground" for students who are more difficult to teach and that there is a tendency for students once placed in special education programs to remain there.

Another area of criticism has been the use of labels to categorize children with disabilities.... The labeling or classification process has been criticized because it often lacks validity and reliability, results in isolation of students, and may consume as much as 20 percent of the total cost of educating the student. However, continued enforcement of the classification procedures and regulations has resulted in the persistence of these problems....

These criticisms suggest that labeling students by disability and funding on the basis of these labels is not compatible with the current interest in providing more flexible programs and services for students with disabilities....

An additional issue is that some current special education program and service delivery systems are not compatible with either the movement toward decentralization in local school districts or the efforts to implement inclusion for children with disabilities. Decentralization calls for each individual school to make decisions about the educational programs and services to be provided for the school's children. Current education reform recommendations call for all students to be provided with needed programs and services in classrooms that also contain students who have not been identified as disabled....

Districts do not receive funds for children with disabilities when they try to meet the needs of students without specific identification. Most current state funding systems encourage districts to identify as many students as possible so that state funding will be higher. Initially, these systems were developed to ensure that funds would be provided for every identified student receiving services and that the more expensive forms of service received more financial support; however, the result has been the segregation of students.

Effect of Funding Formulas

... When the values of weights are based on program types, the monetary value of a weight can encourage districts to classify students into a higher reimbursement category.... A uniform amount, or flat grant, for each child with an identified disability encourages districts to identify children with low-cost disabilities. Cost-reimbursement can encourage local school districts to become engaged in purposeful identification of students and fiscal accounting to maximize their state payment. A study of the effect of a change in Tennessee's funding formula for special education found that the number of children in a mid-level funding level category increased when the state used a weighted formula rather than a flat-rate system.

Commonly used state school finance formulas contain few incentives for serving children with disabilities in general classroom settings. State funding systems typically are based on traditional delivery systems that assume identifiable costs, services, and personnel assigned to special education. Cost accounting procedures require the assignment of staff time to a particular program, or in the case of special education to a sub-program. In an inclusion classroom, the time of the teacher would have to be assigned to the sub-program for each child with a disability as well as to general education. The record keeping and accounting burden would be significant. This is especially critical in those states that use a cost-reimbursement model in their state funding system. This funding approach tends to encourage schools to maintain status quo conditions. Higher funding levels for more intensive programs appear to result in the growth of these programs to serve children with disabilities in special classrooms.

Funding formulas influence the types of services and staff provided in a program. From a different perspective, when state funding systems are linked to location of service, the state funding system may not provide sufficient funds for local school districts that provide appropriate support services to students with disabilities. Thus, many state funding formulas may operate to the disadvantage of districts even if inclusion is judged to be the most preferable arrangement.

Current State Funding Practices

Traditionally, special education in many states has been funded as a separate categorical program.... Existing funding practices for programs and services for children with disabilities fall into four broad categories: pupil weights, instructional or classroom units, excess cost or percentage reimbursement, and flat grant. Pupil weighting and instructional unit systems typically are based on type of placement or disabling condition. Under the cost reimbursement method, state funds are based: (1) on allowable costs for programs and services or (2) on excess costs under which general program costs are deducted from the total expenditure levels for special education programs and services to determine the excess amount attributable to special education programs. Most states rely on a single funding method, but a few utilize some combination of funding methods.

Pupil weighting systems are used in 18 states; cost or percentage reimbursement methods are used in 11 states; flat grants are used in 10 states; and resource (i.e., instructional or classroom units) based funding is used in 11 states. In the 10 states that use the flat grant method, 5 states use the number of special education students to calculate the district's funds under the flat grant, and 5 states use population based funding (the district's total enrollment) to calculate the district's funds for special education....

Alternative Funding Responses

Various funding systems for special education are under discussion as efforts are being made to ensure that financing systems are compatible with the policy shift to inclusion of children with disabilities in the general classroom....

Delivery System Weights (DSW)

... The DSW option can accommodate a range of inclusion options. This formula does not include capital project funds that might be required for retrofitting classrooms or acquiring specialized equipment. *In contrast to funding programs for children without disabilities in which programs and services are reduced if funding is insufficient, school districts are required to provide programs and services (or a free and appropriate education) to children with disabilities consistent with the detail of the IEP. For that reason, the under-funding of special education programs does not reduce the services for these youth; however, if a financial shortfall occurs, the under-funding deficit is met by reducing programs for children without disabilities.* Thus, it is essential that sufficient base level funding be provided for children without disabilities.

The DSW funding methodology is different from traditional special education funding models.... It is still student-based, but is based on type of delivery system rather than type of disability.

The DSW funding model is currently used in several states and also was recommended in a recent study of schools serving American Indian students on Federal Indian reservation; these schools are funded by the Bureau of Indian Affairs (BIA).... These schools provided a unique opportunity for analyzing the effects of alternative funding models. Not only did they receive their funds in the form of a block grant, but also site-based management and decentralization were fully operational....

The DSW model was based on data from a cost study of BIA special education programs, an analysis of state practices, and information on preferred service delivery systems. The traditional service delivery approaches—consultation, resource, or self-contained—were reconfigured into a set of options that reflect current practices and recommendations: high service inclusion (HSI), moderate service inclusions (MSI), direct service (DS), and self-contained classroom (SC). The rationale for the new configuration was the need for a funding system designed to support recommended special education practices....

Based on the BIA cost study data, students in high service inclusion and self-contained classrooms were assigned a weight of 3.00, moderate service inclusion students a weight of 1.00, and students receiving related services a weight of 0.50.

This option is a form of per pupil allocation or child-based formula. Under this formula, the student's classification would be based on the provisions of the IEP. The amount of funds generated by this add-on weight would be based on the unweighted funding for students without disabilities.... Criteria for differentiating between *high service inclusion and moderate service inclusion* include the level (professional qualifications) and the quantity (time in person-hours) of service required. An example would be the proportion of an instructional aide's day required by a student and the number of students with whom a single aide could work at a given time.... This methodology is consistent with the theoretical assumptions about inclusion. Concerns would include the extent to which provision of related services within the general classroom would disrupt the general instructional program.

This latter approach for integrating the DSW funding methodology with the federal child count data is similar to the method used to fund special education under the Kentucky Education Reform Act. Special education directors in Kentucky supported the shift from the personnel unit methodology because it increased local flexibility and reduced the incentives for placing students into particular programs.

The DSW method recognizes differences in the educational needs of students among different school districts and requires that students be identified by the service being provided. Different amounts per student are based on the cost of the student's program. Local districts have flexibility in the use of funds, but, under this method, there is still no incentive to reduce services or change program or to determine that the child no longer needs the services or the special program....

Population Based Funding (PBF)

... In 1996, the Congress considered using the population-based approach with an adjustment for the percent of poverty students in making state allocations of federal funds for students with disabilities....

Massachusetts, Montana, North Dakota, Pennsylvania, and Vermont use the PBF method to allocate state funds for special education to local school districts. Vermont also uses the percentage reimbursement method. Motives for adoption varied from a concern about increasing costs to the desire to develop a funding system that would support inclusion.

The rationale for PBF is that a straight percentage of special needs funding should be allocated without recourse to testing or labeling. Districts then would not benefit from over-classification of students. A move to PBF at either the federal or state level would be a major shift in public policy. The economic incentives in many current state formulas to serve more children have been criticized, but this policy change would result in states and local school districts having a disincentive to either identify or serve children with disabilities. Since funding would no longer be based on programs being provided or the need for funds to serve children with disabilities, districts could use the released funds for other purposes. However,... currently available data document the contentions that children with disabilities are not equally distributed among either states or local school districts; therefore, the effect of a change to PBF would be that those states and districts with disproportionately larger numbers of children with disabilities would be penalized. This type of inequity was noted in the recent Ohio school finance litigation; the court noted the inequities that occur when the funding for students without disabilities is based on the residual that remains after funding has been provided for students with disabilities.

The primary rationales for PBF are that the number of students in special programs is increasing at an excessive rate because traditional state funding systems reward and encourage the over-identification of students with special educational needs. The assumption is that PBF would function as a block grant and that funding is based on a presumed percentage of children needing special education services; funds would not be attributable to a particular program or group of students.... The extent to which adequacy would be attained would be dependent upon the overall funding level. Local districts would have flexibility in the use of funds, and no penalty would be imposed for moving special needs students into general programs. The inherent assumption is that all districts have similar proportions of students with special educational needs.

PBF contains no incentive to identify students with special educational needs, and the district does not incur a gain or loss in state funds by identifying a student for a special program or moving a student from a special program to a general classroom. There is no incentive for over-classification; funding would not be dependent on labeling or classifying students. Funding would be predictable from one year to the next, but funding would not change if the districts had an increase in the number of students with special educational needs....

Educational Overburden Index (EOI)

... This funding index is a proxy for the magnitude of educational need. The process involves development of an index for each district based on a selected set of variables that reflect the differing educational and socioeconomic conditions among districts....

The first step in developing an EOI is to identify the educational and socioeconomic conditions that are to be considered in the index and then to select a set of common research-based variables or indicators for all school districts within a state. Data from the Decennial Census, state department of education, and local districts can be sources for the variables used in developing the index for use in the state funding formula. Potential variables include percent of students with IEPs, percent of unemployment, percent of children living below the poverty level, per capita income, percent of population with a high school education or higher, percent of youths 16 to 19 who were not in school and did not have a high school diploma (dropout), percent of persons with low English fluency, and percent of persons living elsewhere in a specific year (mobility). Data are converted into a common format to facilitate the statistical calculations that yield the EOI.

In the second step, districts within a state are clustered through the use of ... two forms of artificial neural networks....

Neural networks are information-processing systems that are able to deal with complex sets of multiple variables and group or cluster districts according to their relative needs without the traditional dependent variable. The first neural network assigns districts into groupings or clusters based on need. The second neural network refines the clusters by assigning each district an optimal weight reflective of its relative need in relationship to all districts in the state.

The results of this process yield a value that is converted into an index for each school district.... To determine the funding level for each district, the EOI [is] multiplied by the district's student membership to determine the number of funding units. This product [is] multiplied times the funding level per unit to calculate the district's state support level. In these calculations, the EOI is somewhat similar to population-based funding. However, unlike population based funding in which the index is a uniform percentage for all districts, the EOI is a *variable percentage* applied to the district's membership based on each district's differentiated need.

The educational overburden index is different from the other methodologies in that it can be used to recognize cost burdens on school districts associated with the full range of special needs youth, i.e., children with disabilities, at-risk youth, limited English proficient students, and disadvantaged youth. The strengths of the index are that the concept: (1) is consistent with the current emphasis on inclusion, (2) can accommodate differences in cost conditions among school districts, (3) provides a research-based proxy for the special educational needs of all youth without requiring that students be labeled or be served in separate programs, and (4) empowers schools to create innovative educational environments in which the unique needs of each student can be addressed.

The two rationales for the ... EOI are that the state's funding system should: (1) provide districts with sufficient flexibility to adopt creative reforms to improve instruction and learning and (2) recognize differences in the educational needs of students among different school districts without imposing additional paperwork. The ... EOI would function as a block grant; therefore, funding would be based on the predicted overall educational need of the districts and funds would not be attributable to a particular program or group of students.

The level of funding is based on an assumed incidence of special needs students derived from district educational and socioeconomic characteristics, but the district does not incur a gain or loss in state funds by identifying a student for a special program or moving a student from a special program to a general classroom.... Funding would be predictable from one year to the next because allocations would be based on projected differences in the special educational needs of the district's student population....

Conclusion

... Funding systems have been used to promote implementation of regulations and encourage traditional delivery systems. The policy shift to inclusion of students with disabilities in the general classroom, the broad interest in school reform, and the desire to implement new instructional arrangements for all students are potent forces that are contributing to changes in state funding systems for special education.

Inclusion assumes that programs and services for students with disabilities will be provided in an integrated educational environment that may not be compatible with the premises in many current school finance programs. *The delivery system weights, population-based funding,* and *educational overburden index* funding models have several advantages. First, these models empower districts to use diverse systems in providing appropriate services for children with disabilities in the least restrictive environment. Second, from an administrative perspective, they are supportive of and compatible with the concept of inclusion. Third, even though the federal legislation and regulations may still require districts to label students by type of disability, these systems are much less prescriptive.... [A]ll three funding systems could be designed in a manner that would reduce the paperwork burden. However, the authors have a concern about the *PBF* because of its assumption of uniform distribution of need among school districts in a state. This perhaps would not be critical in a time of sufficient resources, but it has the potential of resulting in the under-funding of general education programs.

Given the perceived negative reactions to the level of funding for special education programs, the challenge is to reduce the adversarial relationships among special education advocates, school finance theorists, special educators, local district administrators, and state policymakers. These diverse groups should join forces in efforts to conceptualize and implement more responsive funding systems for programs to serve students with disabilities.

NO

Sheldon Berman et al.

The Rising Costs of Special Education in Massachusetts

Introduction

Over the past decade states across the nation have seen rapid increases in the number of children requiring special education services. They have also experienced significant increases in the cost to school districts for these services. In states where additional funding has been provided to support education reform and school improvement, the rising costs of special education have consumed a disproportionate share of these funds, thereby compromising school-based and state-based efforts to support reform.

The causes of these increases, however, have been mis-diagnosed as the result of district policy and practice. In this case study of cost increases in Massachusetts, we determine that the increases schools have been experiencing have not been caused by school district policy and practice. In fact, just the opposite has been the case. School district policy and practice have been effective in containing and even reducing the percentage of children who require special education services in Massachusetts. Nonetheless, costs in Massachusetts have continued to increase....

[T]he root causes of these increases have been factors beyond the control of schools, such as advances in medical technology, the deinstitutionalization of children with special needs, privatization of services, and economic and social factors including increases in the number of children in poverty and the number of families experiencing social and economic stress. Although the focus of this paper will be on Massachusetts, national data on special education reveal that these factors are also influencing the increased number of special education children across the country....

A Case Study: Massachusetts

In the spring of 1996, the Massachusetts Association of School Superintendents (MASS) established a task force to study rapidly increasing special education costs across the state. These cost increases were significantly impacting school districts' ability to implement the state's education reform program....

This study has been updated with new data in 1999 and 2000, and again for this paper.

... [T]he task force found that the financial challenges facing districts as a result of rising special education costs were exacerbated by Massachusetts' new education reform funding formula. This formula was built on the inaccurate assumption that school district policy and practice were responsible for the cost increases and that the state could force school districts to change their practices by under-representing the costs of special education in the formula. Not only did the formula set unrealistically low percentages for students in special education, but also it allocated less than half of what would be required to pay for services for these students.

Finally, the task force found that increases in the numbers of children and severity of disabilities in early intervention programs serving 0- to 3-year-olds and special-needs preschool programs serving 3- to 5-year-olds indicated that costs would continue to increase in the future....

The Reality of Special Education Costs in Massachusetts

The special education components of the state's education reform funding formula, known as the foundation formula, were built on the assumptions that school districts did not effectively contain costs and that they identified more children than necessary as having special needs. Specific elements of the formula were designed as disincentives to these practices. For example, in all areas other than special education actual enrollment within a district is used to build the foundation budget. Additional allocations are provided for the number of students who are from low-income families or who are in bilingual or vocational programs. In contrast, allocations for special education are based on a preset percentage of children in special education set at a rate lower than the state average. In addition, the cost allocations for providing services to in-district preschool, in-district K-12 students, and out-of-district placements are set at levels well below the actual costs that districts incur for these students. These disincentives were designed to cause districts to be more rigorous in their use of the eligibility standards and to encourage more cost-effective placement of students.

Analysis of Massachusetts enrollment data shows that these assumptions are not accurate. In fact, schools have done a good job containing costs. They have rigorously applied eligibility standards and provided regular education and inclusive programming for children as alternatives to special education services.

Special education enrollments as a percent of total enrollment reached a high in FY92 of 17.4 percent. After that, new eligibility standards were implemented statewide. Beginning in FY93 and continuing through FY97 districts applied these new standards, and enrollment declined to a low of 16.6 percent. With the exception of a "spike" in FY99, special education enrollment has remained relatively steady at approximately 16.7 percent.

Massachusetts special education enrollment increases are also well below national trends. Between FY89 and FY98, special education enrollment in Massachusetts grew at less than half the rate of growth nationally (31.7 percent growth enrollment nationally compared to 13.3 percent growth in Massachusetts).

In its 1997 study, the Massachusetts Special Education Task Force observed sharp increases in special education preschool enrollments and predicted that these would impact enrollments and costs in future years. In fact, current special education increases are indeed being driven by significant increases in special education preschool enrollment. Between FY89 and FY00, special education preschool enrollment in Massachusetts rose by 83.8 percent, while other special education enrollments increased by only 13.1 percent and total enrollment by 17.8 percent. School districts continue to contain costs and effectively apply the eligibility standards but are seriously pressed by a greater number of children entering school districts at age 3 with a disability diagnosis. This sharp increase in preschool enrollment is also present nationally; overall enrollments of children ages 3 to 5 are growing at twice the rate of children ages 6 to 21.

Costs continued to increase over the past decade as districts enrolled a greater number of children with more serious needs. The task force found that between FY90 and FY99 per-pupil expenditures in special education increased ... from $6,675 to $10,249, while they increased by approximately one-third as much ... in regular education—from $4,103 to $5,487. During this period, special education expenditures grew ... at almost twice the rate of regular education expenditures.... The difference is even more significant when adjusted for inflation. In 1990 dollars, per-pupil regular education expenditures grew by only $186 or 4.5 percent, while per-pupil special education expenditures grew by $1,336 or 20 percent.

The Education Reform Act of 1993 resulted in the addition of $1.2 billion in state aid to local school districts. However, special education costs statewide increased by $476 million during those years, an equivalent of 38 percent of all the additional aid from 1993 to 1999....

The impact on education reform is clear when one compares the additional state aid provided to communities for education reform with the additional special education expenditures in those communities. The increases in special education exceeded the amount received in new state aid between FY93 and FY99 for 88 of the 300 school districts. For 36 more school districts, special education increases equaled between 75 percent and 99 percent of additional state aid. And for another 44 school districts, special education increases equaled between 50 percent and 74 percent of new state aid. This means that 56 percent of Massachusetts school districts spent the equivalent of 50 percent or more of new state aid on special education. There is no consistent pattern among these districts. They vary in size, wealth and region....

For most districts, the three primary causes of increased costs are students moving into the district with IEPs [individual education programs] requiring private placement, increases in the number of preschool children requiring special education services, and increases in the number of foster placements within the community requiring significant special-needs services. In fact, one factor in declining costs in some districts has been the movement of students with expensive private placements to another community. In all these districts, compromises have been made regarding implementation of education reform initiatives due to budget constraints presented by special education cost increases. Making headway on education reform is extremely difficult in the face of such increases.

Given the limited funds available to districts, even those districts with smaller increases in special education expenditures have had their education reform efforts compromised by a disproportionate share of new funds allocated to special education. In fact, the data the task force has provided may understate the problem. Most of the increases in regular education expenditures have simply covered the cost of inflation.

Significant increases in special education have the potential for starting a vicious cycle. Increases reduce the funds available for regular education classrooms, causing increases in class size and reduction in support services. These in turn make it more difficult for teachers to address the range of student needs in the regular classroom, producing more referrals to special education. This increases costs again, perpetuating the cycle. For many Massachusetts districts, education reform funds have prevented the perpetuation of this cycle by providing the infusion of new funds necessary to maintain regular education programs at a time of increasing special education costs. However, the price has been little improvement in regular education services for those districts—the original intent of the funding.

Associated Health Costs

Another cost trend impacting school districts is the increase in health and nursing expenditures. Over the past six years many school districts have experienced significant increases in the number of medically involved students who require nursing and other health-related care. These children are not necessarily classified as special education students, although they often receive extensive services.... [I]n analyzing the data on statewide health expenditures for school districts, we found that costs increased by 114 percent between FY90 and FY99....

At this point, we have not been able to secure data on how much has been expended for health education versus nursing services. However, we believe that the primary driver of costs in this area is the increasing number of students who need medical attention. This was not anticipated when the foundation formula was developed and remains an area of serious underfunding in the formula....

Ominous Trends

Based on increases in preschool and early intervention enrollments as well as trends in medicine and social services, we believe that special education costs will continue to increase well into the future. A significant factor in the increase in costs over the past decade has been the rapid rise in the number of children with moderate and serious disabilities who require special-needs preschool programs. Between FY89 and FY99, regular education enrollment rose by 17.8 percent. During this period, special education enrollment in all categories excluding preschool rose by 13.1 percent. However, special education preschool enrollment increased by 83.8 percent.

Preschool enrollment nationally has been growing at twice the rate of other special education enrollments. The increases in the Massachusetts preschool population parallel this trend.

Many districts reported to the MASS Special Education Task Force that not only were the number of children requiring special-needs preschool programs continuing to increase, but these children had more significant disabilities. These reports are confirmed by data provided by the Department of Public Health regarding children in early intervention programs. In FY92, 9,809 children were served by early intervention, with 59 percent of these children considered to have moderate or severe delays. By FY99, the number of children being served had increased by 105 percent.... However, the more ominous trend is that in FY99, the percent of children with moderate or severe delays had increased to 86 percent. Therefore the number of children with moderate to severe delays almost tripled during those years....

Major Causes of Rising Special Education Costs

Rather than school district policy and practice, the increases in special education costs are due largely to medical, economic, and social factors.

Changes in Medical Practice

Medical technology has advanced to such a degree that children who would not have otherwise survived due to prematurity or disability are now surviving. In addition, those whose disability would previously have placed them in hospital or institutional settings are now able to enter public school or private special education schools. The medical profession has also become increasingly aware of disabilities and is better able to diagnose them at an earlier age. Special education services are often recommended at infancy, and children are placed in early intervention programs. At age three, the responsibility for providing special education services is referred to the school district.

In particular, neonatology, the specialty of newborn medicine, has triumphed over the past decades. The last 20 years have seen increasingly premature infants survive at ever-lower mean birth weights.... Due to advances in medical technology, survival of children at a birth weight below 3.3 pounds has increased from 52 percent twenty years ago ... to 90 percent today. Although this development is laudable, it has left us with consequences. Multiple studies have shown a close correlation between prematurity/low birth weight and subsequent developmental outcome. Many premature infants are left with lifelong developmental and neurological problems.

Of infants born at birth weights less than 3.3 pounds, approximately 10 percent will develop classic cerebral palsy with seizures, severe spastic motor deficits, and mental retardation. All of these children, approximately 4,950 annually over the last five years, will have multiple medical issues that will necessitate the expansion of medical and nursing capabilities within the school responsible for them.

Fifty percent of children born weighing less than 3.3 pounds will have significant cognitive difficulties without spastic motor problems. Half of these ... will have measured intelligence in the borderline to mentally retarded range.

The other half will have significant to severe learning disabilities.

The actual number of children with disabilities resulting from prematurity, therefore, has increased markedly over the past 20 years. In fact, those numbers have almost tripled as medical technology has improved.

Prematurity and its consequences are not evenly distributed across society. The children of poor and marginalized populations are more likely to be born prematurely and suffer greater difficulties from this than children of middle- and upper-income families.... Thus, the social and economic burden of educating children with significant developmental problems resulting from their premature births is not evenly or equitably distributed across communities. Urban and rural communities bear a disproportionate share of poverty and a greater share of the disabilities resulting from prematurity.

Medical advances have enabled other populations of students to attend school who would not have been able to do so 20 years ago. For example, two of every 1,000 full-term infants are born asphyxiated because of various medical events in the delivery process. This number has been very stable over the last two decades. Two decades ago, however, there was a 35 percent risk of death in the newborn period after asphyxia. Now nearly all these infants survive, and all come to school with significant to severe motor and cognitive deficits.

Another example is children born with epilepsy. Increasingly effective anti-seizure medications have allowed larger numbers of children with epilepsy to attend school on a regular basis. Although only 60 percent of school-age children with epilepsy were able to attend school without significant interruptions 20 years ago, now more than 95 percent are in school full-time. One percent of the school-age population has epilepsy; 85 percent of these children have significant special education needs. Given the treatment regimens that allow for full-time schooling, essentially all will require nursing supervision of their anti-seizure medications in school.

Children with autism represent another population that is increasingly able to attend school. Autism spectrum disorders (frank infantile autism and pervasive developmental disorders) appear to be present in roughly 2 percent of the population. It is not clear whether the apparent increase over the last 20 years represents an absolute increase in numbers or increased recognition. However, increasingly effective medical treatments for elements of behavioral dyscontrol in children with autism, coupled with more effective behavioral treatment modes, have allowed a larger percentage of children with autism to be educated in public school or consortium environments. These children generally require extensive and costly services within the school environment.

Twenty years ago, roughly two percent of the school-age population had a medical diagnosis that impacted upon their ability to function in school, both from an academic/cognitive as well as physical standpoint. Currently, conservative estimates suggest that 7.5 percent of the school-age population have a medical diagnosis that has such impact that these children cannot expect to prosper in school without significant multimodal academic and medical assistance in the school setting. The burden is placed disproportionately upon communities that have less access to contemporary treatment and intervention strategies.

The research necessary to implement effective treatments that prevent disabilities associated with prematurity, birth asphyxia, epilepsy, and autism is only now in its very earliest stages. As a result, the number of students with these disorders attending schools and requiring extensive services is likely to continue to climb for at least the first two decades of this century.

Deinstitutionalization and Privatization

A second factor impacting costs have been the deinstitutionalization of special needs children and the privatization of special education services over the past decade. The best example is the Bureau of Institutional Schools (BIS). The Bureau of Institutional Schools was established within Massachusetts special education law to provide special education services for children residing in facilities under the control of the Departments of Mental Health, Retardation, Public Health, and Youth Services and the Country Houses of Corrections. However, in 1974, BIS primarily served two populations in state institutions. The first group was children with mental retardation; the second was children in hospital settings due to psychiatric or medical problems. BIS institutions and services for these populations were supported by state rather than local funds.

The number of children served by BIS, which has been reorganized as Educational Services in Institutional Settings (ESIS), has increased only slightly since 1974. However, the population is dramatically different from those served in 1974. Children with mental retardation are served directly through school district funds, either in programs within the district or in private or residential placements. This population, representing the majority of children served by BIS in 1974, is now the complete financial and educational responsibility of public schools. In addition, some children in hospital settings, who would have previously been served by BIS, especially those receiving psychiatric treatment, are also the responsibility of school districts. Currently, two-thirds of ESIS's caseload are incarcerated or detained youth served by the Department of Youth Services and the County Houses of Corrections, with the remainder coming from Departments of Public Health and Mental Health programs.

The shift away from state institutions toward a reliance on local school districts and collaborative or private placements is a positive one. It provides better services within a less restrictive environment. However, the financial resources to fund this shift have not come with the children.

Another example is a shift in policy at the Department of Social Services (DSS), especially in the new Commonworks Program. This program is designed to respond to the needs of hard-to-reach adolescents with multiple problems through out-of-home care. DSS typically has responsibility for out-of-home care but has sought to increase school districts' financial responsibility for children in the program. The Commonworks Program removes children from services they are receiving within a district and places them in private day or residential placements due to non-educational, family-related circumstances. School districts are then expected to share the cost of these placements. The request for proposals for lead agencies of the Commonworks Program contained specific references to the expansion of special education services, with DSS referring to school districts as a partner in paying for education services. DSS only set funding in place for educational services for 20 percent of the youth enrolled in Commonworks, however, creating an expectation that 80 percent of the youth enrolled in Commonworks would receive their educational services under cost-sharing agreements with school districts. The reality is that school districts lack the funding to support this new demand for services.

A third example is the increase in the number of children who are state wards placed in foster homes. These children receive services in public schools. However, the placement and movement of these children is controlled by DSS and the foster parent. The dilemma presented by the placement process is the large number of children placed in foster homes in some communities. In addition to the financial strain on these school districts, they are given late notification that a student with special needs will be placed in their community. A single foster home taking one special education foster child can require a school district to pay for an out-of-district tuition of over $30,000 plus daily transportation. The state does provide some additional funding for state wards, but no funding is available until the year after the costs are incurred. Plus, the funding is usually less than actual costs.

The children in both Commonworks and foster care deserve the services and education they receive. The problem is that both programs shift cost and responsibility from state level departments to local districts. Together with the deinstitutionalization of many children in ESIS, the financial and educational responsibilities now fall primarily on local communities without the funding to provide for these children.

Economic and Social Factors

A third cause of special education cost increases has been a higher percentage of children living in poverty. There is a correlation between poverty and special needs.... [B]etween 17 percent and 19 percent of Massachusetts children in primary grades lived in poverty for their early years.

The national data on children in poverty reveal that the percentage of children under six years of age living in poverty rose significantly during the 1980s and early 1990s to a high of 25.7 percent in 1993. The rate has steadily declined since 1993 and was approximately 18 percent in 1999. The high national level of children living in poverty since the 1980s may account for a portion of the increase in special education enrollments throughout the last two decades.

Adding to the impact of poverty is the increase in families experiencing social and economic stress. Many communities and school districts have seen increases in such indicators as child abuse and neglect, alcoholism and drug use, and dysfunctional family environments that lead to increases in children requiring special education services.

According to the Massachusetts Department of Social Services, reports of child maltreatment were more than two and half times higher in 1999 than in 1983, as was the number of cases of confirmed maltreatment through supported investigations. DSS's report *Child Maltreatment Statistics 1995* states that "families reported for child maltreatment displayed the following characteristics: substance abuse, poverty, economic stress (and the associated problems of poor housing and limited community resources), and a lack of specific parenting skills."...

If the Commonwealth of Massachusetts and other states wish to address the financial dilemma presented by special education, they need to recognize that the major causes of cost increases are not school district policy and practice. Instead, they are advances in medical technology, deinstitutionalization and privatization of services, and increases in children in poverty and families experiencing social and economic stress....

The Foundation Formula

Rather than helping school districts adequately address special education cost increases, Massachusetts' education reform foundation formula exacerbates the problem by underestimating the percentage of children in special education programs as well as the cost of these programs. For example, in FY99 16.7 percent of the total student enrollment statewide was being served in special education programs. However, the foundation formula locked in a figure of 14 percent of student enrollment being served 25 percent of the time in special education programs. The formula adds an additional 1 percent for out-of-district placements ... [which] is particularly problematic. Given the small size of many Massachusetts districts, enrollment can vary widely, especially high-cost out-of-district placements. Out-of-district placements, in fact, can vary between 1 percent and 3 percent with smaller districts—those that can least afford it—experiencing the greatest variation. The formula makes no accommodations for these variations between districts.

More significant, the formula underestimates the cost of services for these students....

As special education costs continue to rise, the low estimates built into the formula remain inflexible and unresponsive to these changes. Consequently, they produce unrealistic estimates for districts' foundation budgets and provide no additional state aid to address the problem. Massachusetts' failure to adequately fund the costs of educating students with severe disabilities is compromising school districts' ability to implement the kinds of instructional improvements intended in the state's Education Reform Act....

Recommendations

... [P]olicymakers should be realistic about the rising costs of special education. The increases in serious disabilities within the population in general and the increase in the number of young children with moderate and severe disabilities will require greater expenditures in special education. Even though districts in Massachusetts are making their best efforts to provide regular education programs and services as an alternative to substantially separate special-needs programs, these regular education programs and services require additional resources. Learning disabilities do not disappear just because a child is not classified as a special education student. These are realities that policymakers need to face.

The long-term solution requires that the state and federal government support school districts in meeting the responsibility for special education. Communities, especially smaller communities, cannot meet the needs of children who cost the district over $20,000 each without compromising other programs, but, under current law, communities pay the bill. This places an unfair burden on local communities when the responsibility for these children is best addressed through the collective efforts of all citizens within the state and throughout the nation.

One proposal for addressing the increasing costs is to have the local community pay the educational costs and the state or federal government pay for medical, psychiatric, physical therapy, and/or occupational therapy services. Although schools should not be required to address medical problems, it is so difficult to define which service is educational and which is medical that we believe that the only effective approach is to increase both the state's and federal government's financial responsibility for special education.

On a federal level, the landmark Education for All Handicapped Children Act of 1975 established a federal commitment to pay for 40 percent of the excess cost of its special education mandate. This mandate has never been met, and the federal government currently contributes approximately a modest 12 percent of the costs of special education. Additional resources provided at a federal level would help relieve the burden on states and local school districts.

Conclusion

We face a challenging dilemma. Children are entering our school system with significantly greater special needs, and these needs are often identified at a very early age. The increased cost of special education services is seriously compromising regular education programs and education reform in states throughout the country. We need a solution that addresses the financial crisis emerging in many districts while at the same time meeting the real and substantial needs of these children. In addition, we need a solution that does not blame the children or those working with them and does not pit regular education against special education.

The Massachusetts Education Reform Act set ambitious new standards and dedicated significant funds for the improvement of education. However, for the majority of districts the increase in special education spending has meant that little of the new funds have been available for the improvement of regular education. For all too many districts the situation is critical. The long-term interest of children with disabilities will not be served by pulling resources from regular education classrooms. Action on the part of the state of Massachusetts and the federal government is imperative so that the needs of both regular education and special education children can be well-served and the goals of education reform realized. It would be tragic if education reform, increased funding, and public education in general were declared failures when, in fact, the experiment was never really tried.

The long-term solution lies in addressing the underlying causes of the special-needs increases—the medical, social, and economic issues that cause increasing numbers of children to require special education. We need to invest in medical research directed toward the prevention of disabilities in premature infants. We also need to invest in reweaving the social and economic support systems for families. These are difficult problems to solve, but we encourage our state and federal legislators to work toward these long-term solutions.

POSTSCRIPT

Do Funding Formulas Make Special Education Too Expensive?

The Center for Special Education Finance (www.csef.org) estimates the cost of educating a child with disabilities at 1.90 times that of educating a typical child, down from a high of 2.28 times that amount. Expenditures vary widely based on need.

Currently studying the details of national spending, CSEF researchers place the costs of special education in the context of decreasing funds for schools in general. In sharp contrast to the 1970s, few taxpayers have children in school today. The first priority of the majority is not education. As schools struggle to fund the costs of education reform, the unpredictable, individual and unavoidable expenses of special education are cast into bold relief.

The solution, according to Jordan, Weiner and Jordan, is a funding system not tied to specific groups. Currently federal funds for at-risk students, bilingual children, those in poverty and those with disabilities must be used to address the needs of their target population of students. Combining these into one block grant resource would reduce bureaucracy and eliminate the tendency to label students in order to receive funds.

Although they believe schools are struggling to be reasonable about service delivery, Berman, Davis, Koufman-Frederick and Urion see darker times ahead, regardless of the funding system used. The beginnings of special education shifted educational responsibility from institutions and hospitals to schools. Managed care shifted financial responsibilities for medically related services from insurance companies to schools. The need for parents to work multiple jobs has shifted care responsibilities from families to schools. Tight fiscal conditions have shifted support responsibilities from social agencies to schools. Money has not accompanied this shift of responsibilities

Some suggest that the solution is for Congress to keep its promise of 40% funding of special education. Others wonder if this extra money would come with more strings, more bureaucracy and even less flexibility

In the midst of the baby-boom years, when special education legislation was created, few imagined a time when there would be any argument about paying for schools. Increasingly, funding mechanisms for education in general are hotly contested in the courts. The majority of school moneys come from local taxes. As academic expectations and standards (and the costs to meet them) rise, people are challenging the usual method of funding schools with property taxes as inequitable.

In parallel fashion, the various methods of special education funding are being found wonting. Alabama, Wyoming, Ohio and Michigan each support special education through different systems. Each mechanism was found to be illegal; resulting in the "encroachment" of special education into educational resources. The Ohio suit found the entire state financing system for education to be inadequate and inappropriate (Verstegen, *CSEF brief,* 1998).

Reviewing funding struggles in Michigan, where there is a fierce ongoing conflict about state funding of special education, Duff (2001) summarizes the entire issue by saying, there are "too many rules, too many lawyers, and not enough money."

There is agreement that special education is costly and that stressful financial times require difficult choices. Is this issue about the cost of special education or about scarce resources for all of education? Is this an argument about *how* to pay for the education of students with disabilities or *whether* to pay for the education of students with disabilities? What is the alternative—for all our children?

ISSUE 4

Does School Choice Open Doors for Students With Disabilities?

YES: Lewis M. Andrews, from "More Choices for Disabled Kids," *Policy Review* (no. 112, 2002)

NO: Barbara Miner, from "Vouchers: Special Ed Students Need Not Apply," *Rethinking Schools Online* (Winter 2003)

ISSUES SUMMARY

YES: Lewis M. Andrews, executive director for the Yankee Institute for Public Policy, reviews the experiences of a number of countries with considerable school choice experience. He maintains that children with disabilities will find unexpected opportunities in choice-sponsored schools.

NO: Barbara Miner, a freelance writer and former managing editor of *Rethinking Schools*, explores experiences with the pioneering Milwaukee voucher system and discusses exclusionary policies and practices that limit access for students with disabilities.

School choice, a major component of education reform, offers parents alternatives to their neighborhood school. Intradistrict options range from open-enrollment programs to magnet schools focusing on thematic education. Charter schools, which operate within the public school structure, are funded by direct transfers of funds from public schools. Dependent on state law, charter schools can be created from the ground up or converted from existent public schools. Finally, voucher programs grant families an amount of money that they can use across district lines to enroll in a suitable program, even in a private school. The goal of each of these options is to offer unique programs to children, stimulate creativity in public schools, and increase academic achievement.

Charter and private schools are exempt from many of the rules that structure (some say bind) public schools. Freedom from union contracts and many state rules and regulations—together with strict accountability for student performance—will, it is hoped, result in creative, innovative, nontraditional programs that offer more desirable alternatives for all children rather than bureaucracy-ridden, neighborhood public schools. In turn, the possibilities created by choice schools will hopefully stimulate public schools to move beyond their traditions and become creative in their own right.

The vast majority of states have some sort of school choice structure. No Child Left Behind (NCLB) expands the options further by mandating a range of interventions when a child's own school does not demonstrate sufficient progress toward meeting Adequate Yearly Progress. Many of the remedies open to parents include services outside the public school. Sometimes this can be enrollment in another school, which could be private. Sometimes the remedy can be supplemental services from a private provider.

While privately funded and charter schools are free from many regulations, including union contracts, they are required to abide by federal laws, including those governing the education of students with disabilities. Lively discussions have emerged about whether or not students with disabilities are welcome in the world of charter schools—and whether or not they are well served there.

Lewis M. Andrews acknowledges a frequently heard criticism, that school choice options will "skim" away the best students ("the cream") from public schools, leaving only those who have the most trouble learning. Lewis reviews the educational systems of the Netherlands, Sweden, and Denmark to demonstrate his contention that this is a baseless prediction.

Barbara Miner investigated voucher schools in Milwaukee and cites evidence that all is not rosy in the world of school choice—especially for students with disabilities. She talked with parents and researchers who found that many voucher schools find reasons not to be available to students with disabilities.

As you read the following selections, consider the alternatives open to all students. Are school choice options in the United States too new to have opened all the doors? Or are the doors to choice schools not open enough to the full range of children and their needs?

Lewis M. Andrews  **YES**

More Choices for Disabled Kids

If the opponents of school choice could have their way, the national debate over the use of public money to subsidize private schooling would turn on the subject of special education. With research demonstrating the overall success of school voucher programs in Milwaukee and Cleveland, and with the constitutional issue of public funding of religiously affiliated schools headed for resolution in a seemingly God-tolerant Supreme Court, defenders of the educational status quo have been reduced to fanning fears that government support of greater parental choice would transform public schools into dumping grounds for difficult-to-educate students.

Sandra Feldman, president of the American Federation of Teachers, repeatedly warns that, with private education more accessible to the poor and middle class, good students will "flee" to independent and parochial schools, leaving behind those kids who are physically and emotionally handicapped, are hyperactive, or have been involved with the juvenile justice system. "[P]rivate schools ... don't have to take [the learning-disabled]," agrees Tammy Johnson of the liberal activist group Wisconsin Citizen Action, so public schools would be left "to deal with those children." Even if private schools were required to take a certain percentage of disabled students, adds *Rethinking Schools*, an online publication of teachers opposed to school choice, they "tend not to provide needed services for children with special education needs or for children who speak English as a second language." NAACP president Kweisi Mfume predicts that the true cost of private education will always exceed what the government can afford to cover, so "those in the upper- and middle-income brackets will be helped the most ... as long as their kids don't have personal, behavioral, or educational challenges that cause the private school to pass them by."

Given the large number of parents who have come to rely on special education services provided through America's public schools, this strategy of conjuring a worst-case scenario for learning-disabled students would at first appear a promising one. According to the *Seventeenth Annual Report to Congress on the Implementation of the Individuals with Disabilities Education Act*, over 5.37 million children—97 percent of American students diagnosed with "special needs"—currently participate in public school special education programs; their parents, many of whom have become adept at using the legal system to access an estimated \$32 billion in annual services, are a potent political force. The vast majority of these parents have come to believe that their own son or daughter benefits most from being educated in the same classes as normal students—a remedial philosophy known as "inclusion"—and would vigorously oppose any policy that threatens to isolate special-needs children in separate schools for the learning-disabled.

The argument that school choice must inevitably create special education ghettos would appear to have been strengthened by the recent adoption of market-based education reforms in New Zealand. In the late 1980s, that country's Labour government undertook a sweeping reorganization of its highly centralized education system, replacing the Department of Education and its 4,000 employees with a new Ministry of Education staffed by only 400 people and putting each local school under the control of a community board of trustees. At the same time, the government abolished school zoning, allowing children to transfer freely between schools, even to private schools, at state expense.

A recent book on these New Zealand reforms by school choice opponents Edward Fiske and Helen Ladd, *When Schools Compete: A Cautionary Tale*, makes much of a flaw in the initial legislation, which permitted the more popular public schools to reject students who would be costly to educate or whose disabilities might drag down the test averages. The authors argue that this "skimming" or "creaming" of the better students—which did happen in some cases—is an inevitable consequence of any school choice program, a conclusion widely publicized in the United States by our teachers union.

Yet a closer look at how learning-disabled students are actually faring under a variety of school choice programs worldwide suggests that the special education card may not play out exactly as the opponents of market-based education reform are hoping. Take the case of New Zealand itself, which has largely remedied its original legislation with two amendments: a 1999 supplemental voucher program targeted at the country's indigenous population, the Maori, and a law requiring all schools accepting state funds to adopt a non-discriminatory admissions policy. Under the new Special Education 2000 policy, schools also receive supplemental funding for each learning-disabled child they take in; principals are free to spend the money on what they and the child's parents determine are the most appropriate services. And if the special-needs child leaves the school for any reason, the supplemental funding follows the child to his or her new placement. As a result of these modifications to the initial law, school choice now enjoys nearly universal public support, says Roger Moltzen, director of special education programs in the Department of Education at New Zealand's University of Waikato, and "is unlikely to be repealed."

The Dutch Experience

To see more clearly the impact of school choice on the treatment of learning disabilities, it is useful to compare the experience of three northern European countries: the Netherlands, Sweden, and Denmark. Each has adopted school choice as part of its national education policy, but with very different provisions in the area of special education. Consider first the Netherlands, where public funding of parental choice has been national policy since 1917 and where almost two-thirds of Dutch students attend private schools.

Until about 15 years ago, universal school choice for mainstream students coexisted with a separate, complex, and cumbersome arrangement for educating the learning-disabled. The Dutch had actually maintained 14 separate school systems, each geared to a particular learning disability—deafness, physical handicaps, mild mental retardation, severe mental retardation, multiple disabilities, and so on—and each mimicking as closely as possible the grade levels of conventional public and private schools.

This separate-but-parallel system did employ private providers; it also tested children regularly to determine whether any might be eligible for transfer to mainstream schools. But by the late 1980s the Dutch began to notice a disturbing increase in the percentage of pupils classified as learning-disabled. (The number of learning-disabled students actually remained constant, but this represented a sharp percentage increase, given the steady decline in the total number of school-age children.) There was widespread concern that the special education bureaucracy was expanding its services at the expense of children with mild-to-moderate learning problems, who were not being adequately integrated into mainstream society. The key to reform, many believed, was to create a financial structure that gave parents of special-needs children the same educational choices as other parents.

Under a "Going to School Together" policy adopted by the Netherlands in 1990, it became the stated intention of the Ministry of Education that parents of children with disabilities should ... be able to choose between [any] ordinary or a special school for their child." Children who required additional services for serious learning disabilities were awarded "a personal budget," which under Dutch law parents could spend at either a special or a mainstream school. To ensure equality of opportunity for all students, supplemental funding was provided to both public and private schools in economically depressed districts, where the percentage of learning-disabled students tends to be higher.

Today the Dutch educational structure enjoys strong support from all political quarters, but especially from advocates of greater inclusion for the learning-disabled. Already the number of separate special school systems has been reduced from 14 to only four.

The Swedes and the Danes

Compare the evolution of special education services in the Netherlands with Sweden, which in March 1992 adopted a "Freedom of Choice and Independent Schools" bill. It gave parents "the right and opportunity to choose a school and education for one's children" by granting all independent schools a municipal subsidy equal to 85 percent of the public school per-pupil cost multiplied by that private or parochial school's enrollment. Independent schools that received this funding were free to emphasize a particular teaching method, such as Montessori, an ethnic affiliation, or even a religious affiliation—but all had to be licensed by the national authority, Skolverket.

Like the Dutch, the Swedes had adopted a universal choice policy, but with one important limitation: The parents of special education students were not effectively granted the same freedom as parents of normal children. This omission was due in large part to Sweden's long history of pedagogic paternalism, which for decades had lowered testing standards, altered textbooks, and micromanaged both classroom and extracurricular activities—all in an effort to avoid making the learning-disabled feel in any way inferior. ("A handicap," according to official publications of the Swedish National Agency for Special Needs Education, "is not tied to an individual but is created by the demands, expectations, and attitudes of the environment.") When the Swedes finally adopted school choice for mainstream children, they were reluctant to risk letting learning-disabled students "flounder" in this new, more competitive educational marketplace.

The result today is that the majority of Sweden's deaf students are still educated in separate institutions. Other special-needs students, who supposedly have been integrated into the educational mainstream, continue to suffer under a centrally managed system in which support services are negotiated between school principals and municipal finance officers, with parents having little input. In theory, all conventional schools are supposed to have an action plan outlining a program of support for their special-needs students. According to a 1998 study by Sweden's National Agency for Education (NAE), however, only half of the country's schools maintain any such plans and fewer than 20 percent of affected parents feel they are able to participate.

One interesting consequence of this lingering paternalism is that the percentage of Swedish children classified as needing special education services is high relative to other industrialized countries and continues to grow at a disproportionate rate. Between the school years 1992–93 and 1996–97, according to the NAE, the number of students registered in schools for the mentally impaired rose by one-fifth. Furthermore, the severity of disabilities tends to be ranked higher within categories. For example, only 25 percent of Sweden's mentally retarded are considered mild cases, while 75 percent are labeled "moderate-to-severe." In the United States, by way of contrast, the proportions are exactly reversed. To what extent this reflects the failure of Sweden's centralized management of special education—or simply the tendency of a large bureaucracy to expand its client base—is unclear at present, but the failure of Sweden to make school choice truly universal has clearly undermined the government's stated goal of promoting greater inclusion.

Finally we come to Denmark, where political support for private education dates back to 1899 and where 11 percent of students attend more than 400 private schools with municipal governments covering 80–85 percent of the cost. Compared to Sweden and the Netherlands, the Danish education ministry has the longest history of, in its own words, letting "resources follow the [special-needs] child." Parents normally have the final say over what school their learning-disabled son or daughter attends, and if an independent school is chosen, the Ministry of Education pays a sum per pupil to the receiving school, with the student's hometown ultimately reimbursing the ministry. The Ministry of Education provides supplemental resources—such as class-room aids, extra courses, and after-hours tutoring—through special grants on a case-by-case basis.

The startling result is that only 0.7 percent of Denmark's 80,000 learning-disabled students are confined to specialized institutions—as compared to five times that percentage in the United States. The Paris-based Organization for Economic Cooperation and Development (OECD), which tracks special education statistics internationally, has praised the Danes for their exceptionally "strong commitment to inclusive education" and for years has held up Denmark's approach to schooling as a model to the rest of the world.

One obvious conclusion to be drawn from the three-way comparison of the Netherlands, Sweden, and Denmark—as well as from the experience of New Zealand—is that inclusion is not only possible under school choice, but with the right policy adjustments, may succeed to an extent not even imagined by American educators. The critical variable appears to be the willingness of legislators to extend freedom of choice to all parents, including the parents of the learning-disabled. In Australia, a school choice country where supplemental funding to support special education is provided to both private and public schools by the national government—but where individual territories have wide discretion in directing how the money is spent—those regions which provide the most flexibility to parents of the learning-disabled also have the best record of mainstreaming. From 1990 to 1995, the percentage of special-needs students successfully integrated into schools in New South Wales more than doubled, while the number of Schools for Special Purposes (the Australian euphemism for segregated special-needs schools) declined sharply. By contrast, West Australia retained most of its separate schools during that same period.

It is also worth noting that, regardless of the degree to which choice has been offered to parents of the learning-disabled, the subsidy of private education in foreign countries has not turned government schools into the "special education ghettos" American critics have predicted; rather it has led to a general increase in standards for all schools. According to studies by the European Agency for Development in Special Needs Education (EADSNE), the choice of an independent school in countries subsidizing private education is based far less on academic status than on a school's denominational affiliation, its political or social leanings, and, in some cases, the school's mix of instructional languages.

In a recently published review of education in Denmark, the Netherlands, and Sweden, EADSNE notes that private schools in these countries are "not generally considered elite" and that attending one confers "no added status or advantages." It is true in the case of the Netherlands that private schools have the legal right to impose admissions criteria, but in practice the vast majority follow an unrestrictive admissions policy. Sweden has seen a large increase in its number of private and religious schools since legalizing choice—an average annual growth of 15 percent—but this is from an extraordinarily low base created by a steeply progressive tax code that, prior to 1992, had made private education prohibitively expensive for all but the wealthiest families. Australia has a number of elite private boarding schools, which cater to parents of children from Hong Kong, Singapore, and Malaysia; but the domestic reality is that nearly half the enrollment in Australia's non-government schools is from families with a combined income of less than $27,000 (U.S.). In none of the 18 countries that in any way subsidize private or parochial education could the increase in the number of independent schools be described as a "massive flight" of the most capable students from public education.

Upon thoughtful consideration, the failure of school choice policies abroad to harm public education is not surprising. In the United States the concept of public funding of private education has become synonymous with the idea of a voucher system whereby parents receive a tuition coupon from the government for each of their children, which they are free to redeem at a school of their choosing. This equivalence between choice and vouchers in the American mind has allowed opponents of school choice to conjure up fearful scenarios in which wealthier families combine vouchers with their own resources to bid up and buy out limited slots at the most prestigious private schools.

Even if we put aside the appropriate counterargument—namely, that a free education marketplace would create as many good private schools as the public demanded—we have already seen that there are many ways other than vouchers to finance school choice, with as many protections for the poor and disabled as the state is willing to entertain. In Australia, where school choice was actually adopted as a populist reform in 1973 by a liberal-leaning Labor government, subsidies for private education are based on what is called a Social Economic Status (SES) model. Students attending private schools from wealthy towns receive assistance amounting to less than 25 percent of tuition, while students from poorer areas in the western part of the country can be reimbursed up to 97 percent. Technically speaking, school choice refers only to a method for making educators more accountable to parents—by empowering parents to choose their children's schools—not to any ideological bias involved in selecting among them any options for financing this method.

If there is a cautionary lesson to be learned from the experience of foreign countries, it comes from the United Kingdom, where in 1981 the parliament adopted the Assisted Places Scheme with the aim of providing private school tuition scholarships to 11-, 12-, and 13-year-old children from low-income families. By 1992 there were more than 26,000 voucher students attending almost 300 independent schools throughout England and Wales—and a separate parallel system had been established in Scotland.

Yet in spite of the program's apparent success, the annual enrollment cap of 5,000 was not raised, nor was there a serious effort to include children in their younger, more formative years. Instead, in 1988, Parliament enacted a more limited form of school choice, very similar to what Connecticut Sen. Joseph Lieberman and other Democrats are now advancing in the United States as a "moderate" alternative to a freer education marketplace. Under this "open enrollment" system all students were allowed to transfer between government-run schools on a space-available basis, but no funding could follow a student to private (what the English call "public") or religious schools, thus inhibiting the ability of education entrepreneurs to offer students real academic options.

The result of Britain's attempt to limit parental choice to government schools has been to create the very special education ghettos that opponents of school reform say they are against. "Popular schools in wealthy communities have devised many subtle ways to keep out expensive-to-educate students," observes Philip Garner, research professor in special education at Nottingham Trent University. Children with learning disabilities "are confined to failing schools in poorer districts, such as Liverpool, Tower Hamlets, and Hackney." In a telling indication of popular dissatisfaction with England's "moderate" approach to choice, the number of appeals brought before that country's special education tribunal reached 3 per week in the school year 1995–96. It was not until just before the last election, with polls showing a growing public anger over declining social services, that Parliament finally passed legislation allowing private companies and foundations to take over management of what the tabloids were calling "Britain's sink schools."

Inclusion and Achievement

So far we have seen that school choice is not only compatible with inclusion but may, under the right circumstances, be the most effective means of implementing it. Yet social inclusion is not a synonym for academic achievement. How, we must also ask, does a more competitive educational marketplace affect the intellectual development of learning-disabled students?

One clue comes from, of all places, the United States, where the same administrators who oppose choice for mainstream and moderately impaired children in their own schools tend overwhelmingly to favor private placements over public institutions for their towns' most difficult-to-educate students. According to Department of Education statistics, over 2 percent of the nation's learning-disabled population—100,700 students—are contracted out by local school boards to independent institutions, many operated by Catholics, Jews, Mennonites, Quakers, Lutherans, Baptists, Methodists, Presbyterians, and Episcopalians. Ironically, the states that rely most on private providers to teach the severely disabled have been among the staunchest opponents of market-based education reform: California, Connecticut, Illinois, Maryland, Massachusetts, New Jersey, New York, and Rhode Island.

American public school administrators are far less inclined to use private providers to teach students within their own walls; yet when they do, the results are instructive. In the school year 1999–2000, the school board of Hawthorne, California, hired Sylvan Learning Systems to offer remedial reading services to its learning-disabled students, while continuing to tutor normal children with regular teachers. According to the Hawthorne district's own standardized test, the special education students exceeded the gains of the non-special education students by five points for a total Normal Curve Equivalent (NCE) gain of nine. (NCEs are a common standard for measuring student progress in reading.) Special education students who completed a similar program in Compton, California, during the same school year made similar gains.

The overall academic success of special-needs students in school choice countries has led the European Agency for Development in Special Needs Education to conclude that the policy mechanisms for providing services to the learning-disabled may be just as important to their intellectual and social development as any teaching technique. In its recently published *Seventeen Country Study of the Relationship Between Financing of Special Needs Education and Inclusion*, EADSNE found that monopolistic public school systems characterized by "direct input funding"—that is, upping the budget for every increase in the number of learning-disabled students—produced the least desirable outcomes. Conversely, school systems characterized by multiple service providers, decentralization, accountability to parents, and an emphasis on teaching over such bureaucratic procedures as diagnosis and categorization "seem to be the most successful" at helping the learning-disabled to grow into happy, productive adults.

Again, it is useful to consider specific countries. In Sweden—where, as we have seen, choice is encouraged only for mainstream students—a telling split has developed in measures of parental satisfaction with the educational system. In 1993, a poll conducted by Sweden's National Agency of Education concluded that "85 percent of Swedes value their new school choice rights," a clear indication that parents of mainstream children were pleased with the academic results. On the other hand, studies by the same agency showed that the confidence of parents of learning-disabled children in Sweden's special education services was eroding at a rapid pace. It is "alarming," concluded the NAE in its 1998 report, *Students in Need of Special Support*, "that parents of more than 100,000 schoolchildren feel that the school system does not have the means to give their children the support they may need."

Halfway around the world in New Zealand, where exceptional efforts have been made in recent years to ensure that special-needs students benefit from school choice, experts such as Dr. David Mitchell of the School of Education at the University of Waikato record significant progress in the treatment of learning disabilities. Over the past three years, he notes, New Zealand's special education system has moved "from being relatively ad hoc, unpredictable, uncoordinated, and nationally inconsistent to being relatively coherent, predictable, integrated, and consistent across the country. It is moving away from ... seeing the reasons for failure at school as residing in some defect or inadequacy within the student to seeing it as reflecting a mismatch between individual abilities and environmental opportunities."

In Australia, a 1998 study funded by the national Department of Education, Training, and Youth Affairs found that many intellectually and physically disabled students who received an inclusive education under the nation's school choice program were "achieving in literacy and [math skills] at the same levels as their peers and, in some cases, much better than their classmates." Because the overwhelming percentage of non-government schools in that country are religiously affiliated, the internationally respected Schonell Special Education Research Centre at the University of Queensland has begun a previously unthinkable study to determine the extent to which faith improves academic achievement in the learning-impaired.

Current Dissatisfactions

All of which suggests that the more American parents of learning-disabled children become knowledgeable about the benefits of school choice around the world, the more the advocates of the status quo may regret ever trying to exploit the issue of special education in the first place. After all, notes Thomas B. Fordham Foundation president Chester E. Finn, it's not as if parents of learning-disabled children are anywhere near being satisfied with the services public schools now provide. "America's special education program has an urgent special need of its own," he writes. "It is, in many ways, broken." Jay Matthews, education reporter for *The Washington Post*, agrees, noting that journalists, himself included, "have done a terrible job telling this story. Special education systems are often too confusing, too bureaucratic and too bound by privacy rules to yield much useful information." What research is available, he adds, "suggests that the special education system has led to widespread, if well-intentioned, misuse of tax dollars and has failed to help kids."

To appreciate the unexpected way in which parental dissatisfaction with current services may shape domestic education policy, consider the surprising evolution of the "A+ Plan," the statewide voucher program adopted by the Florida legislature in 1999. Although initially regarded by some as a muted reform because children were not entitled to a private education unless their public school had failed to meet minimum academic standards in only two of four years, the law did authorize a sweeping pilot program for learning-disabled students in Sarasota County. Under this test project, the only requirement for a special-needs child to transfer to a private school was that his parents express dissatisfaction over his progress at meeting the goals of his individualized instructional plan.

So popular was the pilot program that just one year later, state senator John McKay was able to pass an amendment to the original A+ Plan, allowing the Sarasota County provision to apply to the entire state. According to the new law, known as the McKay Scholarship Program, private schools taking on a special-needs child could recover from the government from $6,000 to $20,000, depending on the severity of the child's disability. The only caveat was that any school wanting to participate in the program had to accept all learning-disabled applicants. In the school year 2000–01, 105 private schools in 36 of Florida's 67 districts signed up to enroll more than 900 special education students. Over the current academic year (2001–02), Florida state officials estimate the number of learning-disabled students receiving assistance will quadruple to 4,000, while the number of participating schools will triple to more than 300.

Although researchers have yet to identify the precise reasons the expansion of the McKay Scholarship Program had such easy political sailing, anecdotal evidence suggests strong backing from the largest group of eligible families: those with moderately disabled children who, while continuing to be promoted with their classmates, were nevertheless floundering academically. "My child needed a choice, an alternative. [She] was lost in middle school," says the mother of a scholarship recipient from the western part of the state. "She was held back early on, and the district did not want to keep holding her back, so even though she was not learning, she was moved along." Black clergy from Florida's cities, where the percentage of fourth-graders unable to read can soar as high as 60 percent, were also outspoken advocates of the McKay Scholarship Program.

Interestingly, a similar alliance of middle-class parents and minority clergy seems to have coalesced behind President Bush's recently enacted "No Child Left Behind" education bill. While stripped of its initial tuition voucher proposal for mainstream schools, the legislation nevertheless retained its "supplemental services" provision, which makes parents at over 3,000 poorly performing schools nationwide eligible for federal funding of remedial tutoring at an independent school or even a private company of their choice. Essentially a remedial education voucher program, it lets parents decide how and where the funds will be used.

While the prospect of advocates for the learning-disabled leading the charge for school choice here in the United States will doubtless come as a shock to the teachers unions and their political allies, it is hardly without precedent. Much of the shift toward the privatization of public education in Europe and elsewhere has come from political activism on behalf of special-needs students.

Indeed, it can be argued that opponents of school choice and parents of the learning-disabled were never very likely to stick together in the first place. Unlike mainstream students, most of whom can survive one bad year of mediocre instruction, a special-needs child can be permanently damaged by a single incompetent teacher, whose tenured position is protected by the current public school monopoly. In the end, the parents of learning-disabled students have the same goal as all market-oriented school reformers: to make every educator accountable to the highest possible standards.

NO

Barbara Miner

Vouchers:
Special Ed Students Need Not Apply

Susan Endress is into her second decade of demanding, cajoling, threatening, and doing whatever it takes to ensure that Milwaukee schools honor the rights of special education students.

On a recent afternoon, she shakes her head in weary frustration as she reads a summary of the special ed services provided (or, more likely, not provided) by Milwaukee voucher schools that receive public dollars yet operate as private schools.

"What do they mean, they can't serve children more than a year below grade level?" she says of one school's description. "That's terrible."

"Oh, here's a good one," she says as she continues reading. "'We cannot serve wheelchair-bound students.' And look at this one, it cannot serve 'students who are unable to climb stairs.'" She turns to a young man in a wheelchair working in the office with her at Wisconsin FACETS, a special education advocacy and support group for families. "Make sure you're bound to your wheelchair," she tells him good-naturedly. "And better learn to climb stairs."

Her moment of humor over, Endress turns serious again.

"You have to remember, it's only been a little over 25 years that special needs children have even had the right to attend a public school," she says. "And here we're moving backwards with the voucher schools, not forward. I'm personally scared to death of where this might lead."

Milwaukee's voucher program, the country's oldest, has long been seen as a prototype for what, in essence, is a conservative strategy to privatize education under the guise of "choice." With the U.S. Congress poised to start the first federally funded voucher program... in the Washington, D.C., schools, vouchers have once again jumped to the fore of educational debate.

Although Milwaukee's voucher schools receive tax dollars, they operate as private schools and thus can ignore almost all of the requirements and accountability measures that public schools must follow. They do not, for example, have to hire certified teachers, nor administer the same tests as public schools, nor report their students' academic achievement.

Nor do they have to provide the special education services required of public schools. While voucher supporters portray vouchers as a new Civil Rights Movement, disability activists see a different reality.

From *Rethinking Schools Online*, vol. 18, no. 2, Winter 2003. Copyright © 2003 by Rethinking Schools, Ltd. Reprinted by permission of the author.

Jim Ward, president of ADA Watch and the National Coalition for Disability Rights in Washington, D.C., warns that voucher programs threaten the rights of students with special needs. He cites a 1998 survey by the U.S. Department of Education that between 70 and 85 percent of private schools in large inner cities would "definitely or probably" not participate in a voucher program if required to accept "students with special needs such as learning disabilities, limited English proficiency, or low achievement." Among religious schools, the figure was 86 percent.

"The Supreme Court's 1954 *Brown vs. Board of Education* decision struck down 'separate but equal' schools, but voucher programs threaten to usher in a new form of segregation," Ward warns.

Milwaukee's voucher program shows that Ward's fears are well-founded. At a time when the percentage of special education students in the Milwaukee Public Schools (MPS) hovers around 16 percent and is projected to reach 19 percent by 2007, voucher schools are not legally obliged to provide special education services to their students.

The only official data on special ed and Milwaukee voucher schools is from a 2000 report by the Wisconsin Legislative Audit Bureau. It found that only 3 percent of the students in voucher schools in 1998-99 had previously been identified as needing special education services. It also noted that voucher schools likely served children with "lower-cost" needs such as speech, language, and learning disabilities.

Current data is sketchy, at best, because voucher schools do not have to collect or release information. The little information that's available paints a bleak picture.

A voluntary, unaudited survey by the Public Policy Forum in October 2002 found that almost half of the voucher schools provide no special ed services, even for students with mild learning disabilities. A significant number reported programs such as "Title I" or "smaller classes" that are generally not considered special education services. Some note that they work with MPS, which provides the special education services. One school said that special needs students are served through its "Jesus Cares Ministry."

A look at a website hosted by the University of Wisconsin-Milwaukee (www.uwm.edu/EPIC) is even more revealing. The site has information on most Milwaukee schools, private and public, and has a section where schools report on "categories of students which the school cannot serve." Some voucher schools do not report anything. Or, like Marquette University High School, they say the information is "n/a."

Many voucher schools succinctly note that they cannot serve "LD, ED, children with physical disabilities"—referring to learning disabled (LD) and emotionally disabled (ED). Some explanations are more elaborate. Blessed Sacrament, for example, says: "We believe that students who are 2-3 years below grade level cannot be realistically brought up to grade level because we do not have a tutorial/learning center to accommodate their needs. Students who have severe emotional or behavioral problems need specific programs to assist them—we do not have a counselor or social worker."

Some schools send mixed messages. St. Adelbert says: "We do not have specific services for ED students though we do have ED students. We do not have an elevator. However, we do have physically disabled students. We do have sight- and hearing-impaired students. We cannot service severe MR [mental retardation]."

A few voucher schools note they provide some special ed services, in particular for children with mild learning or physical disabilities. St. Gregory the Great, for instance, says, "We are able to accommodate most children with learning disabilities."

Services for special education students seem to be particularly limited at voucher high schools. Messmer, which had 398 voucher students last year, specifically notes on the EPIC website that it has "no special [ed] classes." Learning Enterprise, which had 175 voucher students, likewise said it cannot serve special education students. Pius XI, meanwhile, with 199 voucher students last year, is making an effort. While it says it cannot serve ED or EMR [educable mentally retarded] students, it provides services for LD students.

The Milwaukee voucher program is expected to cost about $76 million in taxpayer dollars this year, bringing the total to almost $350 million since its inception in 1990. This year it will serve almost 13,000 students, providing up to $5,882 for each child.

Funding Special Ed

Voucher proponents sometimes argue that voucher schools do not provide special education services because they do not get money to do so. But Endress of Wisconsin FACETS doesn't buy the money argument, whether it comes from public schools, charter schools, or voucher schools.

She understands why all schools may not be equipped to deal with students needing a full-time aide, such as medically fragile students or those with multiple physical, emotional, and medical needs. But such students are the exception, she says. Most special education students can be served without extraordinary accommodations.

"The main thing they have to do is have a teacher on staff that is licensed in special education that is cross categorical," she says. "There is no reason why these voucher schools can't have just one teacher. Think of all the support they could provide not just the students but also other teachers. To me, it just makes good educational sense."

The money argument assumes that public schools receive adequate funding for special education. But they don't. In MPS, for example, special ed spending is about $164 million this year, according to Michelle Nate, director of finance. Since the state and federal governments reimburse only 66 percent of that money, MPS must take $55 million from its overall budget to fund special education.

The Milwaukee Archdiocese, which oversees the largest bloc of voucher schools, does not have figures on special education. Nor does the Archdiocese provide special education teachers for its schools. Dave Prothero, superintendent for the Milwaukee Archdiocesan schools, says special education issues are dealt with at the school level. "Any parent that calls and says that their child has special needs, the response will be, 'Please come in to the school and talk about the specific needs of your child to see if we can meet those needs.'"

Special education experts, based on anecdotal evidence, say this often means that special ed children are "counseled out" of applying, or encouraged to leave if already enrolled, on the grounds that the school is not a good match.

"I think they are oftentimes discouraged from the very beginning," says Dennis Oulahan, an MPS teacher who provides special education assessments for bilingual children in both private and public schools. "The message might be, 'Don't apply.'"

Voucher schools are legally prohibited from discriminating in admissions against children with special needs and are only required to provide services that require "minor adjustments." Until the definition of "minor adjustments" is tested in the courts, it is doubtful that voucher schools will significantly change their practice.

As Oulahan notes, "Voucher schools don't have to deal with special ed. They are private schools. And as long as they don't have to deal with it, I don't think they are going to volunteer."

POSTSCRIPT

Does School Choice Open Doors for Students With Disabilities?

Project SEARCH, a three-year qualitative study of school choice policies and practices in 15 states (Rhim and McLaughlin, 2001), discovered that the inventiveness encouraged in charter schools can create an environment in which some students with some mild to moderate disabilities will flourish. However, sometimes this very focus can create "intentional and unintentional barriers."

Competing legislation complicates the situation. IDEA mandates that public schools adapt curriculum and instruction to ensure the meaningful participation of every child with a disability. School choice laws charge alternative programs to create break-the-mold structures and prove their success through solid test scores. One entity must be flexible to all students; the other must focus on results (Howe and Welner, 2002). Can both mandates be satisfied in any one school?

Lewis notes that parents of students with disabilities have long sought unique programs. He asserts that often, responsive options have been found in private special education schools—resulting in de facto segregation from typical schools. The choice between separation for special schooling and inclusion with typical peers is difficult. In fact, he predicts that these parents, who often find fault with their own district's education, will be major forces in extending the boundaries of both school choice and inclusion.

Miner also brings compelling experiences to light. She cites how one city's choice options do not extend to students who need specialized instruction or attention. And she sees dangerous echoes of the way schools were before special education law, when parents could be told that there was no place for their child in the educational system.

The Enrollment Options Project has been studying Minnesota's school choice experiences (Lange and Lehr, 2000). Parents of students with disabilities expressed pleasure with their child's charter school, citing the extensive series available. The only catch is that directors of these very same schools reported offering fewer services than the public schools. Is it possible that the environment counted as a "service," creating opportunities for success and support?

The challenge of understanding the "real story" is also evident in a 1998 publication from the U.S. Department of Education Office of Educational Research and Improvement. *Charter Schools and Students With Disabilities: Review of Existing Data* presents an extensive compilation of studies and reports, along with the caveat that the authors do not claim to evaluate or substantiate the validity of the referenced articles. Few compare practices across states. Many findings are contradictory. While one study maintains that students with disabilities are underenrolled in charter schools, another counters that they are simply undercounted or underreported. While some papers mention special education costs as prohibitive, the authors find no evidence that such expenses have ever threatened the financial existence of a school. They do, however, note that some charter school administrators are not skilled in seeking the federal funds to which they may be entitled. On still another front, some studies mention parental satisfaction with the responsiveness of charter schools, while others find that a single instructional approach may not respond to the needs of diverse learners.

The only clear answer is that there are many answers. And many questions. Will school choice creators and parents of children with disabilities discover creative ways to teach children? Will the corporate owners of private programs enforce admissions criteria so they can demonstrate increased test scores? Will students with unique and significant special education needs find themselves unable to access options that are open to their "typical" peers, or will their current access to a range of placement options be broad enough?

ISSUE 5

Does Society Have the Capacity to Prevent Emotional/Behavioral Disabilities?

YES: Hill M. Walker and Jeffrey R. Sprague, from "The Path to School Failure, Delinquency, and Violence: Causal Factors and Some Potential Solutions," *Intervention in School and Clinic* (November 1999)

NO: James M. Kauffman, from "How We Prevent the Prevention of Emotional and Behavioral Disorders," *Exceptional Children* (Summer 1999)

ISSUE SUMMARY

YES: Hill Walker and Jeffrey Sprague, educational researchers at the University of Oregon's Institute on Violence and Destructive Behavior, describe the path that leads from exposure to risk factors to destructive outcomes. They believe that society must recommit itself to raising children safely and advocate strong collaborative arrangements between schools, families, and communities.

NO: James Kauffman, professor of education at the University of Virginia, states that we know what needs to be done to prevent emotional and behavioral disorders, but that society as a whole has invented many reasons not to make prevention a reality.

Emotional Disturbance:

A condition exhibiting one or more of the following characteristics over a long periods of time and to a marked degree which adversely affects a child's educational performance:

- An inability to learn that cannot be explained by intellectual, sensory, or health factors;
- An inability to build or maintain relationships with peers and teachers;
- Inappropriate types of behavior or feelings under normal circumstances;
- A general pervasive mood of unhappiness or depression;
- A tendency to develop physical symptoms or fears associated with personal or school problems.

The term includes schizophrenia. It does not apply to students who are socially maladjusted, unless it is determined that they have an emotional disturbance. (IDEA-97)

The most well-mannered child needs to learn acceptable behavior, but may not always react appropriately, especially in times of stress, confusion or fatigue. The happiest siblings will struggle over the best seat in the car. Everyone has a bad day from time to time. When enough bad days occur in a short period of time, adults begin to wonder if a "real problem" exists and if those conditions are serious enough to fit the IDEA97 definition of emotional disturbance.

We spend a large amount of time talking about the increasingly troubled behavior of our children. We are particularly concerned with aggressive behavior that creates difficulties on the playground and endangers the safety and comfort of peers.

And then there are the silent children. The ones who never act out, but experience lives of internal pain and suffering, These are the children who do not call attention to themselves and, are noticeable only by their severely bitten fingernails, their unkempt hair, their worried faces, their failing grades. These children may not act out against others, but may cause harm to themselves.

As troubled children get younger and younger, attention turns to schools. Isn't it the job of schools to fix all the problems? Can't the schools do *something* to make the problems go away?

What should we do? Chalk the behavior up to an increasingly troubled society and try to adjust? Classify the children emotionally disturbed and ask schools to enroll them in special education programs, surrounded by other children with similar problems? Consider them ill and ask doctors to prescribe a medication? Blame poor parenting and urge families to provide stronger supports? Turn to the juvenile justice system?

Hill Walker has researched interventions for troubled and troubling behavior for over 40 years. In this article, Walker and his colleague, Jeffrey Sprague, trace the societal changes that continue to affect our children and their schools. They forecast the spiraling effects on society if we do not divert students from this path to societal violence and criminal behavior. They describe strategies we could put in place to ensure that risks are reduced, cautioning that we can never prevent all difficult behavior.

James Kauffman, a pioneer in the field of special education, agrees that interventions can be designed. He is concerned, however, that society always manages to find a way to avoid taking action. Kauffman lists the range of ways society prevents prevention and urges us to conquer these obstacles for the benefit of our children and society.

As you read these articles, consider the schools you know, the debates you have heard and the your own responses. Should schools be assuming all this responsibility? Can anyone help children in today's society?

**Hill M. Walker and
Jeffrey R. Sprague**

 **YES**

The Path to School Failure,
Delinquency, and Violence

Some years ago, we were developing a program for intervening with very aggressive children who teased and bullied others during school recess. Ritchie, a second grader, was referred as a likely candidate for the intervention. During a playground recess period, he was being observed to see if he qualified for this program. Suddenly, for no apparent reason, Ritchie attacked a kindergarten boy about two thirds his size. He knocked the smaller boy to the ground and proceeded to choke him. The playground supervisor quickly broke things up and called the principal and school counselor, who escorted Ritchie into the school to call his parents. We wanted to know what was in Ritchie's mind that prompted the attack. "Can you tell us why you were choking that little boy like that?" he was asked. Ritchie looked up in utter amazement and said, "Well, it was recess!"

Sarah was a fourth-grade girl who was commonly regarded as a terror by her teachers and peers. Sarah was aggressive, smart, a natural leader, able to manipulate others, charming—and a pain in the neck. Billie Webb was a school psychologist who served Sarah's school part time and visited her school several times weekly. Sarah was a regular customer of Billie's each time she came to the school, and they were on a first-name basis. One day, the principal and counselor were waiting for Billie at the school's front door to tell her the latest things Sarah had done on the playground. Billie called Sarah into a conference to hear her side of things. The following exchange ensued.

"Sarah, I understand you've been having problems on the playground again." Sarah just stared at Billie, saying nothing. Trying to engage Sarah in a problem-solving process, Billie asked another question. "What do you think people will say about that?" Sarah thought a minute, looked at Billie, and said: "Well, Billie, some people might say you're not doing your job!"

These true case examples illustrate how aggressive, antisocial children and youth tend to think about themselves and the world in which they live. They are often self-centered and very inconsiderate of others. The standards they have learned for governing their behavior are different from those of others. Children like Ritchie and Sarah are reluctant to assume responsibility for their actions. In very young children, these social characteristics are generally not destructive and can occasionally be amusing, even cute. However, in ado-lescents, they are highly destructive and anything but amusing.

Our society is producing thousands of children like Ritchie and Sarah who come from backgrounds in which they are exposed to a host of risk fac-tors that can be very damaging over time. There are strong and clearly estab-lished links between these risk factors, the behavioral manifestations and reactions that result from exposure to them, the short-term negative effects on the developing child that flow from this exposure, and finally, the destruc-tive, long-term outcomes that (a) too often complete this developmental pro-gression and (b) ultimately prove very costly to the individual; to caregivers, friends, and associates; and to the larger society....

As more and more young children experience a broad array of risk fac-tors from the moment of birth, we are seeing increasing numbers who are fol-lowing this unfortunate path, which too often ends in school failure and dropout, delinquency, adult crime, and sometimes violence.

Influence of Risk Factors

Risk factors operate at differing and sometimes overlapping levels. The con-texts in which these risk factors exist include the family, school and neighbor-hood, community, and, finally, the larger society. Across these contexts, key risk factors can include poverty, dysfunctional and chaotic families, drug and alcohol abuse by primary caregivers, incompetent parenting, neglect, emo-tional and physical abuse, negative attitudes toward schooling, the modeling of physical intimidation and aggression, sexual exploitation, media violence, the growing incivility of our society, and so on. These risk factors provide a fertile breeding ground for the development of antisocial attitudes and coer-cive behavioral styles among the children exposed to them.

The longer one is so exposed and the greater the number of risks involved, the more likely it is that a young child will develop an aggressive, self-centered, and dysfunctional behavioral style. Taunting and provoking others, mean-spirited teasing, bullying, hitting, yelling, tantrumming, defy-ing adults, and being cruel are examples of the early behavioral signs of long-term exposure to such risk factors. Too many children are coming to school with this behavior pattern already established; they are sometimes referred to as "early starters." That is, antisocial behavioral characteristics are manifested early in their lives primarily because of their early onset exposure to a host of such risk factors. These children tend to overwhelm teachers and peers with their destructive and highly aversive behavior. In adolescence, their behavioral characteristics often bring them into contact with the law from such activities as fire setting, cruelty to animals, burglary and robbery, assault, vandalism, drug and alcohol abuse, and so on.

Five specific risk factors have been identified through longitudinal research for both delinquency and youth violence. Adolescents who are involved in multiple risk conditions—(a) the mother and/or the father has been arrested, (b) the child has been a client of child protection, (c) one or more family transitions has occurred (death, divorce, trauma, family upheaval), (d) the youth has received special education services, and/or (e) the youth has a history of early and/or severe antisocial behavior—are at severe risk for adoption of a delinquent lifestyle. The Oregon Social Learning Center and the Lane County, Oregon, Department of Youth Services (DYS) jointly developed this profile of risk factors on the basis of careful research and analysis of severely at-risk adolescents referred to the corrections department of Lane County. Any combination of three of these five risk factors puts the youth at an elevated risk for chronic delinquency and a host of associated problems. DYS has reported that a number of youth they see have all five of these risk factors.

The American Psychological Association, in its 1993 seminal report on youth violence, identified four factors that seem to propel at-risk youth toward violent acts:

- Early involvement with drugs and alcohol;
- Easy access to weapons, especially handguns;
- Association with antisocial, deviant peer groups; and
- Pervasive exposure to violence in the media.

These conditions combine destructively far too often among youth who come from at-risk backgrounds. Furthermore, we find that larger and larger numbers of at-risk youth are in states of rage and carry high levels of agitation because of the myriad abuses they've experienced. Such youth are more likely to react aggressively to real or imagined slights and act upon them—often with tragic consequences. They are also more likely to misjudge the motives and social intentions of others toward them because of the hostility and agitation they carry. As a result, they are frequently engaged in hostile confrontations, and they sometimes issue threats of bodily harm to peers, teachers, and others.

Short-Term Effects of Exposure to Risk Factors

Several negative short-term outcomes are produced by antisocial behavior patterns resulting from exposure to the above risks. In the short term, they include lack of school readiness, antisocial attitudes, high levels of aggression and agitation, rejection by peers and teachers, affiliation with deviant peers, inability to regulate emotional behavior, severe tantrums, refusal to abide by school rules and adult expectations, and so on. Very often the academic engagement levels and academic achievement of severely at-risk students also lag well behind those of their classmates as well as grade-level expectations. These factors set the at-risk child up for school failure and eventual dropout. If school dropout does occur, the risks for delinquent acts skyrocket. It is estimated, for example, that 80% of daytime burglaries across the United States are committed by out-of-school youth.

Thus, the risks to which larger and larger numbers of our children and youth are exposed tend to put them on a path leading to very negative, destructive outcomes. Unless they are diverted from this path relatively early in their lives and school careers, severely at-risk children are very likely to adopt antisocial behavior as a lifestyle choice during their later development.

Long-Term Outcomes of an Antisocial Lifestyle

The long-term outcomes of investment in an antisocial behavior pattern are very destructive and extremely costly to our society. These longer term outcomes quite often include the following: delinquency, school failure and dropout, dishonorable discharges from the military, severe depression, alcohol and drug abuse, violence toward others, lifelong dependence on social service systems, appearance on community mental health registers, incarceration, and higher hospitalization and mortality rates.

We find that severely at-risk youth have a high frequency of discipline problems in school, with many referrals to the front office initiated by their teachers. By the later elementary grades, they tend to have chronic disciplinary problems. These same students often begin having contacts with law enforcement in the middle and high school years (or earlier). There is a moderately strong relationship between a very high level of conduct problems in school and arrestable offenses committed outside school. To the extent that this relationship is consistent, it may allow for the earlier identification of at-risk students who are likely to become offenders outside the school setting.

For example, we've found in our longitudinal studies of antisocial youth that it is possible to make relatively accurate long-term predictions about the arrest status of at-risk fifth graders by using three simple school measures:

1. The number of discipline contacts the student has during the school year,
2. The amount of negative behavior a student typically displays with classmates on the playground and that is reciprocated by peers, and
3. The teacher's impression of the student's social skills as reflected in teacher ratings....

We have the ability to find these at-risk children and youth early, but we generally prefer to wait—to not do anything—and hope that they grow out of their problems. In far too many cases, in the absence of intervention and appropriate supports for their emerging behavior problems, they grow into and adopt an antisocial behavior pattern during their school careers.

It should be noted that some students adopt an antisocial behavior pattern during adolescence but do not come from an at-risk background. These youth are referred to as "later starters." Although such students can become delinquent, they are much less at risk, as a general rule, than "early starters." Most will come out of this behavioral aberration within a few years. Occasionally, however, some of these youth will become severely delinquent and/or violent and retain their at-risk status into adulthood.

What Can Be Done?

What can be done to reduce and offset the effects of the risk factors to which more and more of our youth are being subjected? First and foremost, we need to reduce and eliminate as many of these risks as possible. As a society, we must recommit ourselves to raising our children safely and effectively. We seem to have lost our capacity to do so on a broad scale. Thousands of families are currently in crisis because of the stressors to which they are exposed (i.e., poverty, unemployment, domestic violence, drug and alcohol abuse, and so on). The resulting chaos negatively affects their children and provides a fertile breeding ground for the development of antisocial behavior.

Providing Parent Training and Supports

A very powerful knowledge base exists regarding parent–child relationships and the forms of parenting behavior that produce positive and negative outcomes in children. This knowledge base has provided the foundation for the development of a number of parent training modules, materials, and courses of instruction designed to teach positive and effective parenting practices. Providing supports, delivering respite care, and developing competent parenting skills are huge challenges that we as a society must confront in order to address this complex problem.

... [P]arenting practices that produce healthy, well-adjusted children ... involve consistent, fair discipline that is never harsh or severely punitive; careful monitoring and supervision of children's activities, peer associates, and whereabouts; positive family management techniques; involvement in the child's daily life; daily debriefings about the child's experiences; and the teaching of problem-solving techniques. We have to find ways to provide opportunities for families to become aware of these parenting skills and to learn how to master them. Insuring that family resource centers are attached to "X" number of schools across a school district to provide parental access to this information is an increasingly viable option for addressing family needs in this regard. We should also teach these parenting techniques to all our youth prior to their becoming parents.

School-Based Prevention Applications

We need to make the school's role in the prevention of disruptive, antisocial behavior patterns an effective reality. We, as educators, tend to give lip service to prevention strategies but are generally unwilling to invest in them at the necessary levels because of suspicions about their effectiveness and worries about their long-term costs.... Primary prevention strategies use universal interventions, such as schoolwide discipline and behavior management systems, grade-level teaching of violence prevention skills, and effective instruction, which are designed to keep problems from emerging. Secondary prevention strategies are more costly, intensive, and designed for addressing the problems and skill deficits of children and youth who are already showing clear signs of their at-risk status. Primary prevention strategies are not of sufficient intensity and strength to effectively remediate the problems of children and youth who require secondary prevention strategies. Finally, tertiary prevention strategies are designed for the most severely at-risk children and youth whom schools must attempt to accommodate. Generally, their problems demand resources, supports, interventions, and services that cannot be provided by schools alone (i.e., wraparound services and interagency partnerships are necessary to accommodate the needs of these students and their families).

... We currently have a pipeline literally filled with at-risk students who are experiencing traumatic behavioral events and outcomes as they progress through it. If we respond only reactively and rely exclusively upon secondary and tertiary strategies, applied after these destructive events and outcomes are manifested, we will continue to invest larger and larger amounts of our resources in return for weaker and weaker therapeutic effects and outcomes. There will always be students who come to school with such severe behavioral involvements that secondary and even tertiary supports and interventions will be necessary from day one of their school careers. That said, however, we can make much greater and more effective use of primary prevention strategies in the school setting than we traditionally have.

As noted, universal interventions are used for achieving primary prevention goals. It is estimated that 80% to 90% of a school's student population will respond positively, at some level, to these universal intervention strategies. Those who do not respond to primary prevention approaches (anywhere from 5% to 15% of the school's population) select themselves out as candidates needing secondary and/or tertiary prevention strategies and approaches. However, for those students who require more intensive, individualized interventions (approximately 1% to 7% of all students), the existence of a well-designed and carefully implemented primary prevention base in the school setting provides a powerful context for their effective application....

The Importance of Supporting Schools

As a society, we have to give greater support to our public school systems, which are struggling to educate an increasingly diverse and at-risk student population. Our schools are expected to compensate for the damaging effects of the background risks to which so many of our students are now exposed; those unfortunate effects spill over into the school setting. At the same time, we seem to be withdrawing fiscal resources from basic school operations and making it increasingly possible for nontraditional schools to access those resources and to pull the better students away from public education. Weakening the ability of our public schools to accommodate a diverse student population is a dangerous movement in our society.

Near the end of his life, in a speech delivered in upstate New York, Mark Twain spoke eloquently and perceptively about the issue of investing in public schools. He related a true story about a Missouri township that was considering closing several of its schools because they were too expensive and regarded as not needed. A farmer who had heard of this planned move attended a town meeting where the issue was being debated at length. After listening to the discussion, the farmer observed that he didn't see how the township would save any money because for every school that was closed, they'd just have to build a new jail. A century later, this prophecy is coming true as our society systematically underfunds public schools and builds jails at a rate unprecedented in our history.

Collaborative Interagency Prevention Approaches

In our view, a far better solution is to create full-service schools that (a) have an expanded capacity to address the complex needs of today's school population and (b) can address true prevention goals through effective collaborations forged between schools, families, and communities.

... We need to build effective partnerships between families, schools, social service systems, public safety departments, churches, and other agencies to create the socializing experiences that will give all our youth a chance to develop along positive lines....

Conclusion

We have a violent history as a country, and many experts argue that we are, by nature, a violent culture. As a society, we should hold up a mirror and examine ourselves in this regard in order to take a good look at what we have become, how we got here, and how we might change for the better.... The tragic spate of school shootings during the 1997–1998 school year offers grim testimony as to how the social toxins and violent images that increasingly pervade our daily lives are registering their negative effects upon our children and youth.

In spite of this grim picture, there are a few encouraging trends. According to recent annual reports of crime indices, adult crime seems to be on a downward spiral. It is imperative that we discover why this is the case and figure out how to make this trend continue. As we embark on a new century, we have the occasion to make a fresh start in this regard. We can ill afford not to.

NO

James M. Kauffman

How We Prevent the Prevention of Emotional and Behavioral Disorders

Prevention of emotional and behavioral disorders seems to be everyone's rhetorical darling, but I have come to the sad conclusion that most of our talk about prevention is of little substance. We often find ways to avoid taking primary or secondary preventive action, regardless of our acknowledgment that such prevention is a good idea. Other concerns take precedence, and as a result we are most successful in preventing prevention itself.

As a society, our actions often seem to thwart prevention of emotional or behavioral disorders at every level—especially primary and secondary prevention, but also prevention at the tertiary level. Primary prevention keeps disorders from occurring at all. It is focused on the universal application of safety and health maintenance interventions that reduce risk.... Once a disorder has emerged (become detectable), primary prevention is not possible; secondary prevention must be designed to keep the disorder from increasing in severity. The goal of secondary prevention is to arrest the growth of the disorder and, if possible, reverse or correct it....

Prevention of emotional and behavioral disorders sometimes occurs in our society and our schools, but it is not a predictable or pervasive phenomenon.... [T]hese programs reach only a very small fraction of those in need of them. Moreover, even if we had pervasive practice of what evidence to date suggests is best primary and secondary prevention, there is good reason to guess that emotional and behavioral disorders would still occur.... Nothing to date suggests that every such disorder can be prevented, although we have good reason to suspect that the pervasive use of our best primary and secondary prevention tools would reduce such disorders to a much lower level than we observe today. The problem I am discussing has much in common with other circumstances in which we fail to implement on a broad scale what we know are best practices, as in the case of teacher education.

If we show clear commitment as a society or as professional educators to prevention at any level, it is to tertiary prevention. We seldom hesitate to recommend intervention after a problem has become severe, protracted, and a clear threat to the community, even though our interventions are too late and only have a small chance of success even if they are not too little. Attempts at tertiary prevention are responses to crisis and often devolve into angry and punitive behavior on the part of adults. By the time tertiary prevention becomes the issue, many people are so angry that physical containment of the child and punishment of the behavior are viewed by the general public and by many educators as clearly defensible interventions, if not the best. Preventive practices at the tertiary level are often ignored in favor of more primitive interventions that are counterproductive but satisfy the desire for revenge.... Supportive interventions that earlier might have been effective are, at this point, perceived by the public as effete, as well they may be. It is too late to get good effects from best practices at the primary and secondary levels; we have allowed those opportunities to pass.

The reasons we do not implement prevention systematically may be related to public attitudes toward children and their schooling, but we professionals have developed and use regularly an extensive repertoire of behaviors that are highly effective in precluding prevention. Our professional attitudes and actions contribute to the public's unwillingness to make prevention a concern that reliably results in preventive acts....

I caution here that preventive *educational* intervention is only one facet of a comprehensive preventive strategy, which involves families, multiple service agencies, local communities, and state and federal governments. Children and youths may show the earliest signs of emotional or behavioral disorders in nonschool settings, and education alone cannot address the problem of prevention adequately.... However, the need for a systemic response to problems does not relieve us of the responsibility to make sure that each component of the system—in the present case, special education—functions properly. My particular concern in this article is the role of special education in prevention and how we avoid our responsibility....

Common Varieties of Prevention— Preventing Behavior

The gambits that stymie prevention are not mutually exclusive. In fact, they are often complementary. Like risk factors that are multiplicative rather than additive, they can become a witch's brew—individually not of great consequence, but combined a potent cocktail that easily wards off prevention.

Express Overriding Concern for Labels and Stigma

Perhaps the most frequent and fervid objection to preventive action is that the child will be labeled and stigmatized.... Either all students are treated the same or some are treated differently. Any student who is treated differently is inevitably labeled. We cannot speak of difference or needs without words (labels). Moreover, either our labels for emotional or behavioral difficulties signify concern (something unsettling, not positive) or they are worthless for describing what needs to be changed. The social reality of deviance cannot be hidden.... "Challenged," a euphemism of the 1990s, is already in our lexicon of derogations. We need to use the least offensive labels that clearly describe the problem, but we need not believe the fantasy that the label *is* the problem or that a new label will fool people for long....

Decades of investigation suggest that stigma typically precedes a formal label for disability, that such labels do not add appreciably to stigma, and that formal labels may, in fact, assist in the explanation of disability and the formation of a more positive identity than is possible to achieve with informally labeled deviance. Nevertheless, antilabeling sentiment remains a powerful anti-prevention force, particularly when it is wielded against the designation of children who are at highest risk of acquiring emotional or behavioral disorders. In fact, the sentiment against identifying any student as needing more or different treatment than another is so strong that I have heard colleagues argue against use of the term "at risk" applied to individuals; we should, they suggest, speak only of high-risk *environments*, thereby ascribing only *collective* characteristics. When we decline to use labels responsibly, the individuals whose problems they designate become rogues or unmentionables—those with unspeakable characteristics. Some may argue that "person first" language (i.e., "___*with*___" such as "child with behavioral disorder" or "person with mental retardation") is a partial solution, others that individuals do not actually *have* disabilities but are merely assigned them in some socially acceptable conspiratorial fashion or have merely developed a *reputation* for behaving in certain ways, or that we should label only programs or services, not the people who receive them. These are tortuous and self-serving philosophical games that delay and deny help to the suffering, whether they are the individuals who exhibit the problem behavior; those who must live, learn, play, or work with them; or those who simply care about them. When we are unwilling for whatever reason to say that a person has a problem, we are helpless to prevent it. In some instances, we call those who demonstrate such unwillingness to label a problem "enablers" because they support maladaptive behavior such as substance abuse or spouse abuse through their refusal to call it what it is. Labeling a problem clearly is the first step in dealing with it productively.

Most children with emotional or behavioral disorders are already labeled informally by their peers if not by adult authorities. They get the label du-jour among children for those who are misfits. Formal, adult labeling may, in fact, turn away some of the misunderstanding and rejection of their differences. Eventually, many of those with emotional or behavioral disorders are formally and informally labeled unequivocally, sometimes brutally. Their behavior often becomes so outrageous that its deviance cannot be denied. They become clients of a variety of.... social systems, including special education, mental health, and corrections. Their social spoilage is virtually assured by the fact that they did not have early and corrective treatment from these agencies....

Object to a Medical Model and to Failure-Driven Services

In the opinion of some, our labels should be abandoned because they reflect an inappropriate, medical conceptual model.... However, special education is much more aligned with the legal model than the medical model, and failuredrivenness is an inherent part of prevention. The mandatory and adversarial aspects of special education law... bespeak special education's gravitation toward a legal rather than a medical model.

... To complain that special education is flawed or badly structured because it is failure-driven is to use non sequitur to prevent prevention. Prevention is by necessity a structure designed to avoid or attenuate failure.

Prefer False Negatives to False Positives

No one has yet devised no-fault prevention in education or any other field of human services. That is, every known prevention strategy produces false positives and false negatives—in the context of this discussion, children mistakenly identified as having emotional or behavioral disorders when they do not, and children mistakenly assumed not to have disorders when they actually do.... Primary prevention is weighted toward false positives, as the intervention is assumed to be a no-risk, or very close to no-risk, strategy. Medical and dental primary prevention strategies include vaccinations, water fluoridation, and personal hygiene routines that pose near-zero risk of negative outcomes for individuals who would not acquire a health problem were the prevention strategy not practiced, and the benefit to those who would otherwise acquire the problem is obvious. Secondary and tertiary prevention in the medical-dental fields is somewhat more controversial and involves weighing personal and economic costs against benefits of specific procedures.

In medicine, false negatives (overlooking cases of pathology) are the primary concern; false positives (seeing pathology where none exists) are not taken lightly, but the primary concern of physicians tends to be making certain that pathological conditions are not missed. In law, however, the opposite is true—false conviction is the horror to be most carefully avoided, not false acquittal. Special education is much more like law than medicine in its preference for the errors we know as false negatives.

In education, primary prevention of school failure, including the socialization failure known as emotional or behavioral disorder, has never been practiced with anything approaching the universality of vaccination, fluoridation, or personal hygiene in spite of evidence that primary prevention of school failure could be practiced with extremely low risk of harm to anyone. Major obstacles to implementing such primary prevention include disagreement about what is to be prevented as well as disagreement about the legitimate processes of achieving particular outcomes.

However, additional barriers to prevention at all levels are either (a) making the exception the rule or (b) justifying the familiar as acceptable. In making the exception the rule, the comparatively unusual case is used as the rationale for rejecting prevention. In the health area, an example is using the vigorous health of an aged person who has smoked cigarettes for many decades to disprove the link between smoking and ill health; in education, examples are using the reading success of a young child who was never taught phonics to disprove the necessity of explicit instruction to teach phonemic awareness ... or the successful adulthood of an individual who engaged in serious antisocial behavior in school to disprove the need for intervention programs for antisocial children. In justifying the familiar as acceptable, the pervasiveness of a phenomenon is used as a rationale for disinterest in prevention. In education, the pervasiveness of uncivil or antisocial behavior is often used as a rationale for inaction: "Boys will be boys," "Lots of kids, probably most of them, threaten to kill somebody," "Every school has its bullies," "In our culture and our school, it's normal for kids to be loud and disruptive." Antisocial behavior is seen as an ordinary discipline problem, not as an incipient or emerging pathology. We shrink from the early recognition of social deviance that, full-blown, we find intolerable.

Recent shootings in schools have brought the issue of prevention to public attention and highlighted our tendency to prefer false negatives to false positives. To date, the shooters have been students not identified for special education services, although in most instances news accounts of these children's lives clearly suggest that they had long histories of antisocial behavior prior to their opening fire in school. Some or all of these killers may be found through psychiatric examination to be legally "sane" (i.e., to be competent to stand trial and unlikely to be found "not guilty by reason of insanity"). Our preference as a society and as educators, it seems, is for absolute certainty that an individual has become deviant before intervening—for after-the-fact recognition of problems, not anticipation of them. To anticipate, we fear, is to prejudge, to pigeonhole, to spoil or corrupt or limit by our expectation. School authorities may now suspend or expel students who possess weapons or drugs on school property or at school functions. However, this is anticipation only of horrendous possibilities, and it is intervention only after contraband is found. Furthermore, such action frequently results in terrible miscarriages of justice because the policy of zero tolerance is reaction with a single, severe sanction to behavior without consideration of its motivations or context.

High-profile cases of school violence may raise issues of prevention in the minds of the public and many professionals, but these cases are probably not the most important. Less riveting by far, but much more important to prevention, are the less highly visible and more common antisocial acts of students. These often do not result in public outrage, and often there is no intimation that they are a result of psychopathology. Coercion, bullying, disruption, social isolation, and threatening behavior are examples of the kind of conduct that *should* induce preventive action by educators. Nevertheless, such behaviors often are *not* sufficient to trigger identification of the student as having an emotional or behavioral disorder, full-blown or incipient. They may simply result in the student's exclusion from general education classrooms....

Propose a "Paradigm Shift"

Perhaps it is understandable that we look for alternative conceptualizations, or what have come to be known as "new paradigms," that avoid the problems of misidentification altogether. Those who propose a paradigm shift may assert that it will obviate the need for classification of students. In the new paradigm, all students will be taught well without the need for distinguishably different instruction or behavior management strategies; because everyone will be treated as an individual, no one need be distinguished as a special case.... Consequently, prevention will be a pervasive and imperceptible part of schooling. Prevention thus becomes at once a primary objective and impossible; we cannot prevent what we are unwilling to categorize as different from the typical or normative, nor can we practice anything other than primary prevention if we are unwilling to categorize interventions as special (not normative)....

A related "paradigm shift" argument is that we must not see the problem as in the child but in the environment. It is a truism that behavior always occurs in and is affected by a social context (a social ecology), but recognition of this fact can become an excuse not to intervene because the "real" trouble is assumed not to be the child. Apparently, we would rather assess diffuse and nonspecific "blame" for the trouble than confront the fact that the child is in trouble and needs help. This observation does not mean that ecological problems can be ignored or that addressing all of the various environmental contributors to the child's difficulty is unimportant.... In the face of ecological complexities, it is easy to become overwhelmed and conclude that what is alterable will make no significant difference. The danger in shifting our concern to the environment in general is that we will do nothing in particular to change what we can. Prevention requires lighting one candle at a time, even if all darkness is not dispelled thereby....

Call Special Education Ineffective

Sometimes the ineffectiveness of special education is merely intimated; sometimes the claim that special education has not "worked" or cannot work as currently structured is made directly and unequivocally....

Special education for students with emotional or behavioral disorders is in difficult straits for several reasons. First,... the meaning of "work" is unclear: What would we expect to happen if special education actually "worked"? Would we (could we) actually "work ourselves out of business"? What is a realistic measure of our "success"? Should our success be judged simply by students' staying in school, not dropping out? Should we expect that there be no significant difference between the performance of those receiving special education and those not receiving it? Second, students are typically identified for special education services only after their problems have become chronic and severe, making "works" by the standards of their successful return to general education, loss of identity as disabled, or high school graduation and gainful employment improbable with any known intervention. Much of our effort is spent on tertiary prevention—waiting until the primary issue is containment and prevention of complications, when it is too late to have realistic hope of correcting or eliminating the disorder. Evidence strongly suggests that if children who exhibit the pattern of aggression called conduct disorder are not identified before they are about 8 years of age, their disorder is much like any other developmental disability—very unlikely to be reversed or eliminated. Third, special education is often attempted by teachers who are poorly trained and poorly supported by infrastructure, and under such circumstances it is difficult to imagine that the students' education would be either special or effective....

Misconstrue Least Intrusive, Least Restrictive Intervention

Americans have a strong preference for leaving people alone as long as they are not clearly and immediately endangering others.... Our enthusiasm for minimally restrictive environments blinds us to the fact that the consequence of minimum restriction now may be greater restriction later. In the placement of individuals with disabilities, including the treatment of mental illness, we emphasize placement in the least restrictive environment, often misconstruing this placement as the same environment in which those without disabilities can thrive....

However, the interventions that are least restrictive and least intrusive are those that can be implemented earliest in a pattern of behavior leading to more serious misconduct. After misbehavior has accelerated, the *formerly* least intrusive, least restrictive intervention is very unlikely to be effective. An emphasis on minimizing the intrusion and restriction of consequences without careful attention to the nature of the behavior pattern results in a chain of increasingly intrusive and restrictive but decreasingly effective interventions. Implementing preventive, least intrusive, least restrictive practices *in the long term* thus requires something counter-intuitive and typically thought to be unacceptable in our legal model: stepping in earlier, more proactively, and with more positive assertiveness to avert maladaptive behavior patterns by anticipating them rather than waiting for misbehavior to occur.

If we give priority to the least intrusive and least restrictive *response* to misbehavior rather than to the most effective *preventive* interventions, then we will forever chase our tail—always and inevitably be ineffectual in preventing the escalation of misbehavior.... We wait for misbehavior to escalate until the *presumed* least restrictive or least intrusive response is very likely to fail and the *actual* least intrusion or restriction (prevention) is very unlikely or impossible. The correction of this failing requires something that is anathema to many: identifying and serving a larger portion of the child population.

Protest Percentage of Students Served by Special Education

A commonly heard opinion today is that special education has grown too large, not only in the percentage of time, effort, and money that schools spend on it but in the number of students and the percentage of the population identified for services. In the case of emotional or behavioral disorders, this view is extraordinarily problematic, for it is abundantly clear that far less than half of the population of youngsters with such disorders have been identified for special education and that students with these disorders are typically identified for special education only after several years of very serious difficulties.

Prevention in an underserved population demands that more individuals be identified, not fewer or the same number. If cases are to be caught earlier, and if many cases are missed (i.e., they are false negatives for considerable periods of time), then we must be ready to embrace a considerable increase in the number of students identified—unless, as seems to be the case, we are willing to forego prevention.

Complain That Special Education Already Costs Too Much

Prevention costs more money *up front* than nonprevention. True, it may save money in the long term, but that is not the immediate issue for politicians, school boards, and taxpayers.... The inescapable fact is simply this: If we were to initiate preventive action on a large scale, then we would be stuck with a large, immediate financial cost.... The necessary tasks cannot be accomplished without an infusion of revenues to provide proper training and support to a huge increase in the number and quality of school personnel.

... Legislators are typically reluctant to embrace programs that will not produce immediate results and cost savings for which they can take credit. In short, the near-term financial cost of widespread preventive programs is a powerful but usually not articulated argument against their implementation.

Maintain Developmental Optimism or Use Ineffective Early Education Practices

Those who work with young children tend to be overly optimistic about children's development, leading to the assumption that early signs of behavioral difficulty do not predict a stable or increasing pattern of maladaptive behavior. Their assumption seems to be that the child will "grow out" of the problem. Preventive action—deliberate correction of patterns of social difficulty—is thus delayed until the problem has become severe. Moreover, many individuals who work with young children have an apparent bias toward developmental approaches that do not involve explicit teaching and correction of the first signs of maladaptive behavior, which foils prevention.

Denounce Disproportionality, Defend Diversity, Deny or Dodge Deviance

The preceding arguments may persuade us not to take prevention action, but there remain other arguments predicated on our society's ambivalence about cultural and behavioral diversity. Guilt for our past ignorance, insensitivity, and brutality about racial, ethnic, and cultural differences and fear of returning to or being accused of such horrors may keep preventive action at bay. I discuss the tactics to which our guilt and fear give rise under a common heading because these tactics are frequently used together as well as in combination with other prevention-stopping arguments.

Denounce disproportionality.   There is no denying that students of color, those reared in poverty or in the lowest social classes, and males are served in special education for children and youth with emotional or behavioral disorders in proportions considerably higher than their proportions in the general school population (a phenomenon that may be defined as overrepresentation). The facts are clear, and concern about the causes and consequences of these facts is not misplaced. Nevertheless, these observations can be used counterproductively to thwart early intervention and prevention....

It is important to ask what causes the overrepresentation of any group in special education. Genetic differences are not acceptable as explanations of disproportional identification for special education services, but environmental circumstances are.... The environmental circumstances that lead to identification of disabilities fall into two major categories: (a) environmental circumstances known to heighten risk of disorders and (b) racial discrimination (i.e., racism in the social construction of disability or identification procedures).

Overrepresentation may be a result, at least in part, of racial discrimination In ... a variety of ... economic and social opportunities of parents that put children at risk for school failure. Racial discrimination creates conditions in which children and adults may strike out in anger and justifiable resistance to social control. These conditions must be addressed, but until they are corrected they may contribute significantly to the disproportional identification of students of color as having emotional or behavioral disorders....

Overrepresentation may, of course, be at least partly a result of racial discrimination in the identification process.... Given overwhelming evidence of the underidentification of emotional and behavioral disorders of children and youth, a plausible hypothesis is that many students—both minority and non-minority—who should be identified are not....

Overrepresentation of any group in special education or any other social service program is not a problem unless (a) the program is perceived as demeaning, there is an implication of hostile intent, or the program offers no benefit; or (b) the program is being provided to students who do not need it or is being denied to those who do. After all, it is the *under*representation of minorities in gifted education that is protested, precisely because gifted education is assumed to bring benefit to students and this benefit is being *denied* disproportionately to minority students.... Were identification of students for special education for those with emotional or behavioral disorders assumed to be beneficial, then the overrepresentation of minorities in such programs would likely not be the cause of protest (except, perhaps, by individuals unwilling to extend *benefits* disproportionately to minorities). But, as I discussed earlier, special education for students with disabilities is seen by some as thwarting opportunity, not as a helpful educational support. Perhaps, as I noted earlier, the problem is as much a self-defeating denial of the needs of students of all ethnic origins for special education as it is a racist or unintentional fabrication of deviance of children of color.

The rub for prevention is this: Disproportional identification of some groups for special education can be used as a rationale for nonidentification, nonintervention, waiting to take action out of fear that action will merely exacerbate the disproportion of the group to which the student belongs. The struggle against discrimination by race and class is not easy, and it includes resisting both the tendency to assume that disproportional identification can *only* be a consequence of unfair discrimination in identification for special services and the tendency to let an individual's color or social class inappropriately affect judgment of conduct.

Defend diversity.   In contemporary American educational jargon, differences are often lauded without thinking much about the differences among differences. Some differences are benign, but others are not.... In the desire to embrace diversity—difference—some may be tempted to extend acceptance to differences that are inimical to a just, multicultural, and benevolent society. In some instances, disrespectful or demeaning behavior towards others or rejection of academic learning may be defended as merely different from the ostensible white middle class standard or as an acceptable response to domination and oppression by the majority.

Prevention requires the recognition of diversity that is unacceptable. In today's social climate, however, there is reluctance to label difference unacceptable until it reaches the point of actual physical damage to another individual or to property. In the case of emotional and behavioral disorders, this means that there is pressure to allow behavior to escalate to extremely high levels before intervening, a response to difference that stops prevention in its tracks.

Deny deviance.   Differences of benign character should be accepted, if not celebrated. However, the harmful social conduct we call deviance must be discriminated from nonharmful difference. In contemporary American society there is a tendency to "define deviancy down" such that the consequences are deteriorating social justice and a lower level of benevolence. There is also a tendency to resist drawing lines that separate people into eligible and ineligible groups for any social service. Line-drawing has its costs of labeling and identity for the individual who is declared eligible, but refusing to draw a line has a more severe and an inevitable high cost—denial of service to that individual. We cannot have it both ways—special services and no eligibility lines....

There are a variety of ways to deny the deviance of children's behavior. Calling it mere cultural diversity is one such denial tactic. Another is saying that deviance and disability are social constructs and therefore somehow not "real." Deviance and disability are, indeed, social constructs, but so are childhood, adolescence, citizenship, success, social construct, democracy, justice, love, and nearly every other concept that we hold dear or that is necessary to a just and benevolent society. The point here is not that deviance is a social construct that can be changed arbitrarily but that it *is* changed—or people argue that it *should* be changed—in ways that prevent prevention. If we deny that an individual's current behavior is deviant, or that the behavior we wish to prevent is deviant, then it is highly unlikely that we will do anything to prevent it.

Sometimes we do not deny deviance but dodge responsibility for it. That is, we define behavior as deviant but claim that it is not a disability, concluding that it therefore does not fall within the purview of special education. The most common tactic is to conclude that a child is "socially maladjusted" or has a conduct disorder that is different from "emotional disturbance." Neither logical arguments nor reliable empirical studies support the distinction between social maladjustment and emotional disturbance. Furthermore, anti-social behavior, a form of social maladjustment that may be diagnosed as conduct disorder, is clearly among the most disabling emotional and behavioral disorders of children and youths. Unwillingness to include conduct disorder, antisocial behavior, or social maladjustment among the conditions for which special education interventions are appropriate is a dodge of responsibility for prevention that contributes to the unchecked acceleration of misconduct. If there is one emotional or behavioral condition for which every level of prevention (primary, secondary, and tertiary) is critical, it is conduct disorder. Dodging special education's responsibility for intervening early in conduct disorder virtually ensures that the child will become the responsibility of juvenile justice or another social agency specializing in tertiary prevention (containment)....

Suggestions for Attenuating the Problem

The arguments we can marshal against prevention must be taken seriously, as they raise important issues that we should not dismiss. Ignoring these legitimate concerns carries high costs, and I do not mean to demean them by pointing to the fact that they are often used to defeat prevention. My purpose is to bring into awareness the ways in which we may use them at the even higher cost of preventing prevention.

Myths—partial truths from which unwarranted generalizations or extrapolations are drawn—are pervasive in special education.... The arguments used to defeat prevention may be mythical if they occlude the larger truth that we would all be better off if we prevented serious misconduct. However, we must also recognize as myth any suggestion that we know in all cases precisely what behavior should be prevented and how to prevent it. Much of our knowledge of emotional and behavioral disorders is tentative. A great deal more research is required before we can, if ever, pinpoint for all children all the behaviors that should be prevented and prescribe the preventive action that is necessary and sufficient. Nevertheless, we now can identify many of the early signs of conduct that place children at very high risk for later negative life outcomes and describe preventive programs that can reduce these risks....

The attenuation of the problem will require assiduous attention to research and its application to instruction and behavior management. Prevention supportive sentiments must be balanced by knowledge of the costs, both fiscal and personal. If we are to achieve a balance of preventive behavior and the cautions that should accompany it, we might seek answers to the following questions in the individual case:

- Is the behavior in question, either the behavior being exhibited or the anticipated behavior, one that elevates risk of negative outcomes?
- If so, is the behavior preventable or can risk be lowered by any legitimate means?
- What are the possible negative side effects or risks associated with preventive action?

- If we estimate that the risks of nonintervention outweigh those of preventive action, can we offer social support for those who implement the preventive action—develop a professional community that reinforces prevention through social approval?
- When we encounter prevention-preventing behavior, can we provide counter arguments that effectively remove the blockade?

Individually and collectively we might work toward the following goals:

- Establishing common standards for judging evidence of the effectiveness of preventive interventions at all levels (primary, secondary, and tertiary).
- Abandoning and publicly condemning interventions for which evidence clearly is not supportive or negative or that make tertiary prevention inevitable because primary and secondary prevention are highly unlikely if not impossible.
- Increasing our immediate positive attention to and, when possible, prompt financial and social support of primary and secondary preventive action, thereby creating a professional culture more supportive of prevention.
- Understanding negative reinforcement as the primary process sustaining preventive behavior and legitimizing its function in primary and secondary prevention (i.e., teaching others that the avoidance of problems can be legitimately rewarding).

POSTSCRIPT

Does Society Have the Capacity to Prevent Emotional/Behavioral Disabilities?

The nuclear family with Mom at home baking cookies is not likely to re-appear, if it ever really existed. Video games, television and movies are not likely to become less violent. Guns are not likely to become less easy to get. Children will continue to reflect the turmoil of our society. There aren't enough hospital beds or jail cells to hold all the children who demonstrate troubling behavior. The institutions are gone.

Walker and Sprague agree with Kauffman about the difficulties our children face and the consequences for society if we fail to help children when the helping is easy. Examples of proactive, primary level interventions abound. Among the many are Reach Out to Schools (Stone Center, Wellesley College), the Responsive Schools, Success4 and yes, even DARE. Each is dedicated to helping students develop strong social skills which lead to conflict resolution and problem solving strategies for difficult times. After school programs to support latchkey children are more and more a common part of school systems.

Webber and Scheuermann (*Behavioral Disorders*, 1997) foreshadow the list of risk factors experienced by our children, augmenting them with recent public policy decisions that have further reduced community and family supports.

Noting that supportive counseling services have not been included in the current wave of education reform, Charles Lindahl (*Education Week*, October 18, 2000) cites recommendations by the American School Counselor Association for a student-counselor ratio of 250:1 and an actual national ratio of 561:1. The recommended levels of service could provide a safety net for students, teachers and families, all of whom are struggling to meet the pressures of higher expectations.

The journal *Behavior Disorders*, dedicated a thematic issue (*Vol. 24*, No. 4, 1999) to the topic of emotional and behavioral disabilities at the turn of the century. The wide ranging articles in this issue contain expansions by both Kauffman and Walker and Sprague, as well as others who are concerned with this field, especially as the number of students requiring intervention, rather than prevention, increases.

Observing that society often sees children as perpetrators rather than victims, Walker, Zeller, Close, Webber and Gresham (*Behavioral Disorders*, 1999) expand on the conditions facing children today. The consequence of this attitude is that children do not improve their behavior, but learn to avoid those who serve to judge it and who could possibly help them.

Landrum and Tankersley (*Behavior Disorders*, 1999) highlight the importance of early intervention as well as life-long services. They emphasize that general education teachers must learn and apply successful behavior management strategies (secondary intervention) and that special education services should acknowledge the value of specialized settings (tertiary intervention) to improve the functioning of children who have developed problem behaviors. They warn that even perfect application of each level of intervention will not eliminate all incidences of problem behavior.

Educators do employ a large number of strategies and interventions, argues Simpson (*Behavioral Disorders*, August 1999), but the methods themselves are rarely evaluated to determine if they are effective.

What will society choose to do? Will we use our collective power to implement early intervention strategies which will reduce risks for all our children—and their children? Will we adjust our expectations for an increasingly isolated group of children and families and an increasingly violent society? What is the ethical thing to do and what are the consequences of doing nothing?

ISSUE 6

Do Students With Disabilities Threaten Effective School Discipline?

YES: Kay S. Hymowitz, from "Who Killed School Discipline?" *The City Journal* (Spring 2000)

NO: James A. Taylor and Richard A. Baker, Jr., from "Discipline and the Special Education Student," *Educational Leadership* (January 2002)

ISSUE SUMMARY

YES: Kay S. Hymowitz, a regular contributing editor to *The City Journal*, cites inclusive education programming for students with disabilities and the legal limitations of IDEA97 as primary contributors to the destruction of effective discipline in today's schools.

NO: James A. Taylor and Richard A. Baker, Jr., president and vice president of Edleaders.com, respectively, believe that school administrators who design and implement an effective disciplinary code that applies to all students, including those with disabilities, can create a more orderly environment for everyone.

Barely a week goes by without reading about violence in schools. Politicians, school boards, teachers, and parents are all concerned. If there has not been a recent incident, then the media covers efforts that have been put in place to anticipate and prevent violence—more metal detectors, recent lockdown drills, and strengthened zero-tolerance policies.

When the local press covers an incident that has affected a community, it is not unusual to hear that the students involved experienced different consequences. Frequently, there is a comment that some of the youngsters involved are covered by special education and are remaining in school pending further evaluations, while their peers are given suspensions. Some suspensions have been revoked while parents seek evaluations to see if a disability could have caused the offending behavior. These situations elicit feelings of frustration, unfairness, and confusion.

IDEA97 significantly changed the procedures that administrators have to follow in disciplining students with disabilities. The changes attempted to address two goals. The first goal was to mesh special education laws with the Gun Free Schools Act, designed to protect against weapons in schools. The second goal was to ensure that, while doing so, those with documented disabilities are not ejected from school because of behavior beyond their control, thereby losing access to the free and appropriate public education to which they are entitled.

Despite the opinions of some, IDEA97 does not prohibit disciplining students with disabilities. It does require specific actions. If behavior problems are part of a student's disability, the Individualized Education Plan (IEP) must include services geared to improve this area. If a student's disability impacts her understanding of the behavior code (perhaps because the child has significant cognitive limitations and simply cannot comprehend some of the standards), alternate disciplinary expectations and interventions need to be stipulated.

If punishable behavior occurs repeatedly, educators must conduct a Functional Behavioral Assessment (FBA) to determine the cause of a behavior. Specific steps to address this behavior must be included in the IEP. Most importantly, if long-term suspensions are considered, the school must conduct a Manifestation Determination to learn if the behavior is a direct result of the disability and thus outside the student's control. If this is the case, appropriate changes in the educational program must be made.

Kay S. Hymowitz laments that such legalistic processes have turned principals into "psycho babbling bureaucrats," incapable of preventing harm or maintaining the most basic order in schools. James A. Taylor and Richard A. Baker, Jr. Assert that such beliefs are in error. They maintain that principals who understand the law and implement an effective disciplinary code will foster an improved climate for all students. With such standards in place, administrators actually have a broad array of actions at their disposal.

As you read the following selections, think about situations that have occurred in your own school or town. Do teachers and principals think that all students must follow the same behavior standards, or do they think that there must always be special treatment for students in special education? Seek out schools with reputations for differing climates. Talk to the teachers. Do you observe differences in the way behavioral expectations are communicated? Are all students treated fairly?

Kay S. Hymowitz  **YES**

Who Killed School Discipline?

Ask Americans what worries them most about the public schools, and the answer might surprise you: discipline. For several decades now, poll after poll shows it topping the list of parents' concerns. Recent news stories—from the Columbine massacre to Jesse Jackson's protests against the expulsion of six brawling Decatur, Illinois, high school students to the killing of one Flint, Michigan, six-year-old by another—guarantee that the issue won't lose its urgency any time soon.

Though fortunately only a small percentage of schools will ever experience real violence, the public's sense that something has gone drastically wrong with school discipline isn't mistaken. Over the past 30 years or so, the courts and the federal government have hacked away at the power of educators to maintain a safe and civil school environment. Rigid school bureaucracies and psychobabble-spouting "experts" have twisted such authority as remains into alien—and alienating—shapes, so that kids today are more likely than ever to go to disorderly schools, whose only answers to the disorder are ham-fisted rules and therapeutic techniques designed to manipulate students' behavior, rather than to initiate them into a genuine civil and moral order. What's been lost is educators' crucial role of passing on cultural values to the young and instructing them in how to behave through innumerable small daily lessons and examples. If the children become disruptive and disengaged, who can be surprised?

School discipline today would be a tougher problem than ever, even without all these changes, because of the nationwide increase of troubled families and disorderly kids. Some schools, especially those in inner cities, even have students who are literally violent felons. High school principal Nora Rosensweig of Green Acres, Florida, estimates that she has had 20 to 25 such felons in her school over the last three years, several of them sporting the electronic ankle bracelets that keep track of paroled criminals. "The impact that one of those students has on 100 kids is amazing," Rosensweig observes. Some students, she says, find them frightening. Others, intrigued, see them as rebel heroes.

But today principals lack the tools they used to have for dealing even with the unruliest kids. Formerly, they could expel such kids permanently or send them to special schools for the hard-to-discipline. The special schools have largely vanished, and state education laws usually don't allow for permanent expulsion. So at best a school might manage to transfer a student felon elsewhere in the same district. New York City principals sometimes engage in a black-humored game of exchanging these "Fulbright Scholars," as they jokingly call them: "I'll take two of yours, if you take one of mine, and you'll owe me."

Educators today also find their hands tied when dealing with another disruptive—and much larger—group of pupils, those covered by the 1975 Individuals with Disabilities Education Act (IDEA). This law, which mandates that schools provide a "free and appropriate education" for children regardless of disability—and provide it, moreover, within regular classrooms whenever humanly possible—effectively strips educators of the authority to transfer or to suspend for long periods any student classified as needing special education.

This wouldn't matter if special education included mainly the wheelchair-bound or deaf students whom we ordinarily think of as disabled. But it doesn't. Over the past several decades, the number of children classified under the vaguely defined disability categories of "learning disability" and "emotional disturbance" has exploded. Many of these kids are those once just called "unmanageable" or "antisocial": part of the legal definition of emotional disturbance is "an inability to build or maintain satisfactory interpersonal relationships with peers and teachers"—in other words, to be part of an orderly community. Prosecutors will tell you that disproportionate numbers of the juvenile criminals they now see are special-ed students.

With IDEA restrictions hampering them, school officials can't respond forcefully when these kids get into fights, curse teachers, or even put students and staff at serious risk, as too often happens. One example captures the law's absurdity. School officials in Connecticut caught one student passing a gun to another on school premises. One, a regular student, received a yearlong suspension, as federal law requires. The other, disabled (he stuttered), received just a 45-day suspension and special, individualized services, as IDEA requires. Most times, though, schools can't get even a 45-day respite from the chaos these kids can unleash. "They are free to do things in school that will land them in jail when they graduate," says Bruce Hunter, an official of the American Association of School Administrators. Laments Julie Lewis, staff attorney for the National School Boards Association: "We have examples of kids who have sexually assaulted their teacher and are then returned to the classroom."

✦❀✦

Discipline in the schools isn't primarily about expelling sex offenders and kids who pack guns, of course. Most of the time, what's involved is the "get your feet off the table" or "don't whisper in class" kind of discipline that allows teachers to assume that kids will follow the commonplace directions they give hundreds of times daily. Thanks to two Supreme Court decisions of the late 1960s and the 1970s, though, this everyday authority has come under attack, too.

The first decision, *Tinker v. Des Moines School District*, came about in 1969, after a principal suspended five high school students for wearing black armbands in protest against the Vietnam War. Tinker found that the school had violated students' free-speech rights. "It can hardly be argued," wrote Justice Abe Fortas for the majority, "that students or teachers shed their constitutional rights to free speech or expression at the schoolhouse gate." Schools cannot be "enclaves of totalitarianism" nor can officials have "absolute authority over their students," the court solemnly concluded.

Quite possibly the principal in *Tinker* made an error in judgment. But by making matters of school discipline a constitutional issue, the court has left educators fumbling their way through everyday disciplinary encounters with kids ever since. "At each elementary and middle school door, you have some guy making a constitutional decision every day," observes Jeff Krausman, legal counsel to several Iowa school districts. Suppose, says Krausman by way of example, that a student shows up at school wearing a T-shirt emblazoned WHITE POWER. The principal wants to send the kid home to change, but he's not sure it's within his authority to do so, so he calls the superintendent. The superintendent is also unsure, so he calls the district's lawyer. The lawyer's concern, though, isn't that the child has breached the boundaries of respect and tolerance, and needs an adult to tell him so, but whether disciplining the student would violate the First Amendment. Is this, in other words, literally a federal case?

And that's not easy to answer. "Where do you draw the line?" Krausman asks. "Some lawyers say you should have to prove that something is "significantly disruptive." But in Iowa you might have a hard time proving that a T-shirt saying WHITE POWER or ASIANS ARE GEEKS is significantly disruptive." Meanwhile, educators' power to instill civility and order in school dissolves into tendentious debates over the exact meaning of legal terms like "significantly disruptive."

In 1975, the Supreme Court hampered school officials' authority yet further in *Goss v. Lopez*, a decision that expanded the due-process rights of students. *Goss* concerned several students suspended for brawling in the school lunchroom. Though the principal who suspended them actually witnessed the fight himself, the court concluded that he had failed to give the students an adequate hearing before lowering the boom. Students, pronounced the court, are citizens with a property right to their education. To deny that right requires, at the least, an informal hearing with notice, witnesses, and the like; suspensions for longer than ten days might require even more formal procedures.

Following *Tinker's* lead, *Goss* brought lawyers and judges deeper inside the schoolhouse. You want to suspend a violent troublemaker? Because of Goss, you now had to ask: Would a judge find your procedures satisfactory? Would he agree that you have enough witnesses? The appropriate documentation? To suspend a student became a time-consuming and frustrating business.

⋅⟨⟨◉⟩⟩⋅

Students soon learned that, if a school official does something they don't like, they can sue him, or at least threaten to do so. New York City special-ed teacher Jeffrey Gerstel's story is sadly typical. Last year, Gerstel pulled a student out of his classroom as he was threatening to kill the assistant teacher. The boy collided with a bookcase and cut his back, though not badly enough to need medical attention. Even so, Gerstel found himself at a hearing, facing the student's indignant mother, who wanted to sue, and three "emotionally disturbed adolescents"—classmates of the boy—who witnessed the scuffle. The mother soon settled the dispute out of court and sent her son back to Gerstel's classroom. But by then, Gerstel had lost the confidence that he needed to handle a roomful of volatile teenagers, and the kids knew it. For the rest of the year, they taunted him: "I'm going to get my mother up here and bring you up on charges."

In another typical recent case, a Saint Charles, Missouri, high schooler running for student council handed out condoms as a way of drumming up votes. The school suspended him. He promptly sued on free-speech grounds; in previous student council elections, he whined, candidates had handed out candy. Though he lost his case, his ability to stymie adults in such a matter, even if only temporarily, could not but give him an enlarged sense of his power against the school authorities: his adolescent fantasy of rebellion had come true.

These days, school lawyers will tell you, this problem is clearing up: in recent years, they point out, the courts have usually sided with schools in discipline cases, as they did in Missouri. But the damage done by *Tinker, Goss,* and their ilk isn't so easily undone. Lawsuits are expensive and time-consuming, even if you win. More important, the mere potential for a lawsuit shrinks the adult in the child's eyes. It transforms the person who should be the teacher and the representative of society's moral and cultural values into a civil servant who may or may not please the young, rights-armed citizen. The natural relationship between adult and child begins to crumble.

The architects of IDEA, *Tinker,* and *Goss,* of course, thought of themselves as progressive reformers, designing fairer, more responsive schools. Introducing the rights of free speech and due process, they imagined, would ensure that school officials would make fewer "arbitrary and capricious" decisions. But lawmakers failed to see how they were radically destabilizing traditional relations between adults and children and thus eroding school discipline.

⋅⟨⟨◉⟩⟩⋅

School bureaucracies have struggled to restore the discipline that the courts and federal laws have taken away, but their efforts have only alienated students and undermined adult authority even more. Their first stratagem has been to bring in the lawyers to help them craft regulations, policies, and procedures. "If you have a law, you'd better have a policy," warns Julie Lewis, staff attorney for the American School Boards Association. These legalistic rules, designed more to avoid future lawsuits than to establish classroom order, are inevitably abstract and inflexible. Understandably, they inspire a certain contempt from students.

Putting them into practice often gives rise to the arbitrary and capricious decisions that lawmakers originally wanted to thwart. Take "zero tolerance" policies mandating automatic suspension of students for the worst offenses. These proliferated in the wake of Congress's 1994 Gun-Free Schools Act, which required school districts to boot out for a full year students caught with firearms. Many state and local boards, fearful that the federal law and the growing public clamor for safe schools could spawn a new generation of future lawsuits, fell into a kind of bureaucratic mania. Why not require suspension for *any* weapon—a nail file, a plastic Nerf gun? Common sense went out the window, and suspensions multiplied.

Other districts wrote up new anti-weapon codes as precise and defensive as any corporate merger agreement. These efforts, however, ended up making educators look more obtuse. When a New York City high school student came to school with a metal-spiked ball whose sole purpose could only be to maim classmates, he wasn't suspended: metal-spiked balls weren't on the superintendent's detailed list of proscribed weapons. Suspend him, and he might sue you for being arbitrary and capricious.

Worse, the influence of lawyers over school discipline means that educators speak to children in an unrecognizable language, far removed from the straight talk about right and wrong that most children crave. A sample policy listed in "Keep Schools Safe," a pamphlet co-published by the National Attorneys General and the National School Boards Association (a partnership that itself says much about the character of American school discipline today), offers characteristically legalistic language: "I acknowledge and understand that 1. Student lockers are the property of the school system. 2. Student lockers remain at all times under the control of the school system. 3. I am expected to assume full responsibility for my school locker." Students correctly sense that what lies behind such desiccated language is not a moral worldview and a concern for their well-being and character but fear of lawsuits.

⋘◉⋙

When educators aren't talking like lawyers, they're sounding like therapists, for they've called in the psychobabblers and psychologists from the nation's ed schools and academic departments of psychology to reinforce the attorneys in helping them reestablish school discipline. School bureaucrats have been falling over one another in their rush to implement trendy-sounding "research-based programs"—emotional literacy training, anti-bullying workshops, violence prevention curriculums, and the like—as "preventive measures" and "early interventions" for various school discipline problems. Of dubious efficacy, these grimly utilitarian nostrums seek to control behavior in the crudest, most mechanical way. Nowhere is there any indication that adults are instilling in the young qualities they believe in and consider integral to a good life and a decent community. Kids find little that their innate sociality and longing for meaning can respond to.

Typical is "Second Step," a widely used safety program from a Seattle-based nonprofit. According to its architects, the goals of "Second Step" are "to reduce impulsive and aggressive behavior in children, teach social and emotional skills, and build self-esteem." Like many such therapeutic programs, it recommends role-playing games, breathing exercises, and learning to "identify feelings," "manage anger," and "solve problems." The universal moral values of self-control, self-respect, and respect for others shrink to mere "skills," as scripted and mechanical as a computer program.

In this leaden spirit, the National Association of School Psychologists newsletter, *Communiqué*, proposes a "Caring Habit of the Month Adventure," a program now in use in Aliquippa Middle School near Pittsburgh. Each month, school officials adorn school hallways with posters and stickers that promote a different caring habit or "skill." The skittish avoidance of moral language is a giveaway: this is a program more in love with behavioral technique than inducting children into moral consciousness. It's not surprising to find that *Communiqué* recommends dedicating a month to each "skill," because "[r]esearchers say a month is about the length of time it takes to make a habit out of consistently repeated action."

The legal, bureaucratic, and therapeutic efforts make up what Senator McCain would call an "iron triangle," each side reinforcing the others. Consider the fallout from last year's Supreme Court decision *Davis v. Monroe County School District,* which held that school districts could be liable for damages resulting from student-on-student sexual harassment. Now every school district in the country is preparing an arsenal to protect itself against future lawsuits: talking to lawyers, developing bureaucratic policies, and calling in therapeutic consultants or even full-time "gender specialists" to show a "proactive" effort to stamp out harassment. Experts at universities across the U.S. are contentedly churning out the predictable curriculums, with such names as "Flirting and Hurting" and "Safe Date," as cloying and suspect to any normal adolescent as to a grownup.

The full consequence of these dramatic changes has been to prevent principals and teachers from creating the kind of moral community that is the most powerful and dependable guarantor of good discipline ever devised. When things work as they should—in the traditional manner familiar all over the world and across the ages—principals forge a cohesive society with very clear shared values, whose observance confers a sense of worth on all those who subscribe to them. People behave morally primarily because they assent to the standards of the group, not because they fear punishment. A community of shared values cannot be legalistic or bureaucratic or based on moronic behavior exercises; it must be personal, enforced by the sense that the authority figure is protective, benevolent, and worthy of respect.

That's why good principals have to be a constant, palpable presence, out in the hallways, in the classrooms, in the cafeteria, enforcing and modeling for students and staff the moral ethos of the school. They're there, long before the school day begins and long after it ends; they know students' names, joke with them, and encourage them; and they don't let little things go—a nasty put-down between students, a profanity uttered in irritation, even a belt missing from a school uniform. They know which infraction takes only a gentle reminder and which a more forceful response—because they have a clear scale of values and they know their students. They work with their entire staff, from teachers to bus drivers, to enlist them in their efforts.

For such principals, safety is of course a key concern. Frank Mickens, a wonderful principal of a big high school in a tough Brooklyn neighborhood, posts 17 staff members in the blocks near the school during dismissal time, while he sits in his car by the subway station, in order to keep students from fighting and bullies from picking on smaller or less aggressive children. Such measures go beyond reducing injuries. When students believe that the adults around them are not only fair but genuinely concerned with protecting them, the school can become a community that, like a good family, inspires affection, trust—and the longing to please.

◦⟨◉⟩◦

But how can you create such a school if you have to make students sit next to felons or a kid transferred to your school because he likes to carry a box cutter in his pocket? June Arnette, Associate Director of the National School Safety Center, reports that, after Columbine, her office received numerous e-mails from students who said they wouldn't bother reporting kids who had made threats or carried weapons because they didn't think teachers or principals would do anything about them. A number of studies show that school officials rarely do anything about bullies.

How can you convince kids that you are interested in their well-being when from day one of the school year you feel bureaucratic pressure to speak to them in legalistic or quasi-therapeutic gobbledygook rather than a simple, moral language that they can understand? How can you inspire students' trust when you're not sure whether you can prevent a kid from wearing a WHITE POWER T-shirt or stop him from cursing at the teacher? It becomes virtually impossible, requiring heroic effort. Even when good principals come along and try to create a vibrant school culture, they are likely to leave for a new job before they have been able to effect any change.

Since heroes are few, most principals tend to become what John Chubb and Terry Moe in *Politics, Markets and American Schools* call "lower level managers," administering decisions made from above. Teachers often grumble that principals, perhaps enervated by their loss of authority, retreat into their offices, where they hold meetings and shuffle papers. It's not that they don't make a show of setting up "clear rules and expectations," as educators commonly call it, but they are understandably in a defensive mood. "Don't touch anyone. Mind your own business," was the way one New York City elementary school principal summed up her profound thinking on the subject.

In tough middle and high schools presided over by such functionaries, this defensive attitude is pervasive among teachers. "Protect yourself," one New York City high school teacher describes the reigning spirit. "If kids are fighting, stand back. Call a supervisor or a security guard. Don't get involved." That teachers are asked to rely for the safety of their students on security guards—figures unknown to schools 30 years ago—says much about the wreckage of both adult-child relations and of the school as a civil community. It also serves as a grim reminder that when adults withdraw from the thousand daily encouragements, reminders, and scoldings required to socialize children, authoritarian measures are all that's left.

The effect of the collapse of adult authority on kids is practically to guarantee their mistrust and alienation. Schools in this country, particularly high schools, tend to become what sociologist James Coleman called an "adolescent society," dominated by concern with dating, sex, and consumerism. The loss of adult guidance makes it certain that adolescent society—more powerful than ever, if we're to believe TV shows like *Freaks and Geeks* and *Popular*—will continue in its sovereignty. Quaking before the threat of lawsuits and without support from their superiors, educators hesitate to assert the most basic civic and moral values that might pose a challenge to the crude and status-crazed peer culture. When they do talk, it is in a language that doesn't make any sense to kids and cannot possibly compel their respect.

⚜

Though under the current system it's easy to lose sight of this truth, there's nothing particularly complex about defining moral expectations for children. At one successful inner-city middle school I visited, a sign on the walls said, WORK HARD, BE KIND; BE KIND, WORK HARD: and if the school can instill just those two values, it will have accomplished about all we could ask. Educators who talk like this grasp that a coherent and meaningful moral environment is what socializes children best. Paul Vallas, CEO of the Chicago public schools, has introduced character education, community service requirements, and a daily recitation of the Pledge of Allegiance. "It's the Greek in me," explains Vallas. "I take Aristotle's approach to education. We are teaching kids to be citizens." Two and a half millennia later, Aristotle's approach remains a surer recipe for disciplined schools than all the belawyered conduct codes and all the trendy life-skills programs that the courts and the bureaucrats have given us.

**James A. Taylor and
Richard A. Baker, Jr.**

Discipline and the Special Education Student

John is a special education student who attends only one resource class each day. Otherwise, he participates in regular education classes. During English class, the teacher corrects him for disruptive behavior, but he continues to make inappropriate comments. The teacher asks him to step into the hallway so that she can address his behavior privately. As she begins speaking to him, he walks away, then turns to her and says, "Shut up, you bitch." The teacher submits a referral to the assistant principal, who consults the district handbook and recommends that John spend three days in the supervised suspension center.

Because of John's status as a special education student, however, personnel at the district level—without conducting a hearing or a meeting with John's individualized education program (IEP) team—allow John to spend the three days at home. The district's concern is with John's protections under the Individuals with Disabilities Education Act. But is the district's action in compliance with federal law?

The general belief among teachers and administrators is that the Individuals with Disabilities Education Act insulates special education students from experiencing consequences for their disciplinary infractions and sets them apart from the school's regular disciplinary procedures. Horror stories abound about students whose behavior, like John's, threatens the safety of staff and students, disrupting learning for themselves and other students.

The misperception that educators are supposed to tolerate such behavior is largely the result of the unclear administrative procedures outlined under the Education for All Handicapped Children Act of 1975 (Public Law 94-142) and the Supreme Court decision in *Honig v. Doe* (1988). Aware of these unclear procedures and educators' common misunderstanding of the law, the U.S. Congress took care, when reauthorizing the Education for All Handicapped Children Act as the Individuals with Disabilities Education Act in 1990 (Public Law 101-476) and 1997 (Public Law 105-17), to address the issue of appropriate disciplinary procedures for special education students. Educators need to know the provisions of the current law as they develop schoolwide discipline

From *Educational Leadership*, December 2001/January 2002, pp. 28-30. Reprinted with permission of the Association for Supervision and Curriculum Development (ASCD). © 2001 by ASCD. All rights reserved.

plans and the individualized education programs required for special education students.

The 1997 Individuals with Disabilities Education Act amendments clarify that the only disciplinary procedure that applies exclusively to special education students is the determination of a long-term change of placement—that is, a long-term suspension or removal to an alternative school setting. If the disciplinary measure for behavior infractions lasts for 10 or fewer days, and 45 or fewer days for weapon or drug infractions, the special education student receives the same treatment that students without disabilities receive. If, however, the special education student's suspensions are recurrent and add up to more than 10 days in a school year or more than 45 days for a serious infraction, the local education agency must conduct an assessment of the student's behavior and implement an intervention plan to address the student's behavior problems.

After conducting classroom observations and closely examining the evaluation of the student's disability and the implementation of the student's individualized education program, a committee designated by the local education agency must decide whether or not the student's behavior is a manifestation of the student's disability. If the committee determines that it is, the student's IEP team must immediately rewrite the student's program to correct the behavior. If the committee determines that the behavior is not a manifestation of the disability, the child must be disciplined "in the same manner... applied to children without disabilities" (Individuals with Disabilities Education Act, 20 U.S.C. § 1415 [k][5]).

In the case of John, the district should have applied the same disciplinary measures that it applies to students without disabilities. If the district plans to treat John differently, or if the behavior is recurrent and disciplinary measures have exceeded 10 days, the district must hold a meeting with the IEP team to determine whether this behavior is a manifestation of John's disability. If the team decides that it is not a result of the disability, the district must assign the same disciplinary consequences to John that it assigns to students without disabilities.

A Discipline Policy for All Students

To meet the federal standard, schools need a humane and just administration of discipline that respects and protects all students' rights to a free and public education. Comprehensive discipline guidelines must cover the treatment of students with and without disabilities. Moreover, the discipline plan must do more than take corrective action for offenses; it must also prevent discipline problems and support positive behavior (Charles, 1999).

As administrators and IEP teams develop behavioral intervention plans for students with disabilities, they should keep in mind the overall goal of implementing a schoolwide discipline system that is more than merely corrective. Special education students must understand that they are subject to the same disciplinary measures as other students. Such practices as before-school and after-school detentions, weekend detentions, additional written work, or required community service, commonly found in school discipline plans, do not create a change in special education placement and may serve as corrective measures for disciplinary infractions that are not directly related to the safety of fellow students or disturbance of the learning environment. Integrating these alternatives into behavioral intervention plans for special education students reminds them of the consequences of their choices. The discipline plan for all students should also incorporate preventive and supportive discipline measures.

Preventive Discipline

Preventive discipline promotes behaviors that are beneficial to the learning environment. By affirming and practicing them and reflecting on their meaning, everyone can practice showing concern, modeling courtesy, and supporting one another. Translating classroom rules and procedures into affirmative "we" statements to which the students and teachers commit themselves helps to identify good behaviors and strengthens the sense of belonging that both learners and adults need.

For example, Mr. Boudreaux has taught 7th graders for several years and knows that they will enter the classroom in an energetic, boisterous manner. Without a preventive discipline plan, the students will take a long time to settle down and focus on the lesson. Mr. Boudreaux, however, meets the students at the door and requires them to enter according to a specific procedure. First, he says, we enter in silence, then go to the materials shelf, read the assignments on the board, and assemble our materials. Instruction begins within three minutes of classroom entry, with all students having materials in place. In this way, Mr. Boudreaux meets all students' need for structure, limits, and routine.

Learning experiences that are worthwhile and enjoyable provide the foundation of a quality preventive discipline plan. Three elements—fun, focus, and energy—are essential components of a preventive discipline plan (Taylor & Baker, 2001), particularly for students with disabilities, whose classes and activities are often unchallenging and devoid of opportunities for creative expression.

Supportive Discipline

Supportive discipline helps students channel their own behaviors productively. As a weight lifter needs a spotter to provide support during a challenging lift, students need positive intervention. The teacher and students need a set of common signals so that either can ask for or offer assistance without judgment or confrontation. Such agreed-upon techniques as "eye drive" (a deliberate look that signals affirmation or correction), physical proximity, silent signals, and head movement can communicate the need for a refocus to productive behavior.

The teacher's goal is not to control the students but rather to support students as they learn to control themselves. A supportive disciplinary action is an offer to help, not a judgment or imposition of will. To minimize the need for corrective discipline, educators need to explain the supportive elements of this approach to students with disabilities and to their parents.

Several supportive techniques have been developed by Mr. Boulanger, an 8th grade teacher. His signals remind students that they are responsible for controlling themselves. When he stands in front of the room and looks intently from student to student, they understand and respond to his signal by focusing on the task at hand. Through routine and consistent reinforcement, each student learns that the purpose of these signals is to help them achieve the level of excellence they desire.

Corrective Discipline

Even the best preventive and supportive approaches sometimes fail, at which point corrective action becomes necessary. Educators must administer corrective discipline expeditiously, invoking well-known guidelines about consequences for certain kinds of behavior. The purpose of corrective discipline is not to intimidate or punish but to provide natural consequences for disciplinary infractions that disrupt the learning environment.

The person in authority must never ignore disruptive behavior. One helpful technique for remaining calm is to administer corrective action in a matter-of-fact manner, adopting the demeanor of a state trooper. "May I see your driver's license, insurance card, and automobile registration? You were traveling 50 miles per hour in a 35 miles per hour zone."

Invoke the insubordination rule when necessary. Use a predetermined plan to command assistance if it is necessary to correct the situation. The behavior intervention plan that the Individuals with Disabilities Education Act regulations now require must include clear corrective procedures.

For example, Mrs. Thibodaux has developed a set of consequences for the most common infractions. Each student knows that being late to class will mean a period of after-school detention for a certain number of school days. Each knows that repeated failure to complete assignments will result in a telephone conference with a parent during work hours. Educators must work out these corrective measures ahead of time. Although the measures are not harsh or excessively punitive, they should be consistently inconvenient for the students and parents.

The U.S. Congress has now made it clear that schools should not allow children with disabilities to disrupt learning environments. All students need guidance to become respectful, responsible citizens who enjoy and effectively exercise their rights. If educators make excuses for special education students' behaviors, they deny them the benefits contained in the laws. All students deserve well-disciplined learning environments that are fun, focused, and full of creative energy. Developing discipline systems that combine preventive, supportive, and corrective measures for all students will move our schools toward that ideal.

POSTSCRIPT

Do Students With Disabilities Threaten Effective School Discipline?

Many people agree with Hymowitz that too much of the behavior seen in schools hurts the overall learning climate. Conflicting laws dealing with freedom of speech as well as disabilities can dominate the thinking of administrators and teachers who should be focusing on teaching and learning.

Responses from a survey of middle and high school parents and teachers (Teaching Interrupted; Public Agenda 2004) revealed that behavior is a major concern to both groups. Teachers and parents agree that a few persistent troublemakers create the most problems. Teachers report that documentation requirements are overwhelming. Surprisingly, the majority of teachers and parents believe that the primary problem is that parents do not teach discipline to their children. They believe that this, in combination with a "culture of disrespect" and overcrowded classrooms, results in behavior problems. Teachers also report that lack of parental support and fear of lawsuits impact th kind of behavior they tolerate.

IDEA97 seems to recognize that the issues are more complex. Its provisions clearly encourage schools to develop and communicate clear behavioral expectations for all students, to ensure that faculty respond consistently and fairly to misbehavior, and to treat students fairly. Taylor and Baker descibe a system where these practices create an orderly climate in which students meet the expectations that are set for them. Individualized responses can be crafted for students who need specialized instruction to learn how to abide by these expectations.

The ramifications of IDEA97 are wide ranging. Schools must walk a fine line between managing effective disciplinary practices and upholding legal rights based on disabilities (Yell, Katsiyannis, Bradley, and Rozalksi, *Journal of Special Education Leadership*, 2000). While the requirements of the law may be clear, the practices of implementation are sometimes cloudy.

Discipline for students with disabilities is a major focus of the IDEA reauthorization debates. House and Senate members are deliberating whether or not to relax some of the requirements on schools, most notably those requiring a Functional Behavioral Assessment and a Manifestation Determination when long-term suspensions are considered.

In this time of research-based practice demands, both of these practices have been questioned by credible researchers. Sasso, Conroy, Stichter, and Fox (*Behavioral Disorders*, 2001) acknowledge that although functional assessments are a fine tool to use with individuals with retardation, it may not yet be possible to determine the function of a behavior demonstrated by students with emotional and behvioral problems.

Similarly, Katsiyannis and Maag (*Exceptional Children*, 2001) believe that there are no valid current tools to help a school decide if a particular behavior is a manifestation of a disability. They suggest that the key questions to answer include whether or not the student has the skills to engage in appropriate behavior, to analyze situations and craft acceptable responses, and to interpret a situation accurately.

There is no doubt that some children with disabilities exhibit significant behavior problems. There is also no doubt that some typical children do as well. Are students with disabilities being targeted as the cause of school disciplinary problems when the real issue is much broader? Would there be more positive results if schools and parents worked together to establish and support solid behavioral expectations for all students? Do the requirements of IDEA97 support students with disabilities or overwhelm educators and provide excuses for some students? Will the reauthorization of IDEA resolve some of these issues or make them more complicated?

ISSUE 7

Will More Federal Oversight Result in Better Special Education?

YES: National Council on Disability, from *Back to School on Civil Rights: Advancing the Federal Commitment to Leave No Child Behind* (January 25, 2000)

NO: Frederick M. Hess and Frederick J. Brigham, from "How Federal Special Education Policy Affects Schooling in Virginia," in Chester E. Finn, Jr., Andrew J. Rotherham, and Charles R. Hokanson, Jr., eds., *Rethinking Special Education for a New Century* (Thomas B. Fordham Foundation & Progressive Policy Institute, 2001)

ISSUE SUMMARY

YES: The National Council on Disability (NCD), an independent federal agency dedicated to promoting policies, programs, practices, and procedures that guarantee equal opportunity and empowerment for all individuals with disabilities, found that all 50 U.S. states are out of compliance with special education law, a condition that the council argues must be remedied by increased federal attention.

NO: Frederick M. Hess, an assistant professor of education and government, and Frederick J. Brigham, an assistant professor of education, both at the University of Virginia, maintain that increased federal monitoring will only deepen the separation between general and special education, drawing resources away from true educational excellence for all.

Federal and state laws regarding special education were written to compel school districts to design and deliver education to students with disabilities. The rules and regulations for IDEA97, the federal special education law, can be found in full at http://www.ideapractices.org/finalregs.htm. Hard copies of the regulations fill over 100 pages of the Federal Register, in tiny type. These regulations translate IDEA97 into operational elements, ranging from definitions of terms to the contents of an individual education program (IEP), to the substance, form, and timelines of communications with families, to reporting responsibilities to federal agencies. In short, the regulations guide the daily practices of schools.

Comparable regulations exist for Section 504 of the Rehabilitation Act of 1973. These regulations are designed to eliminate discrimination on the basis of disability in any program or activity that receives federal funds. Beyond these, each state has its own specific statutes and accompanying regulations governing the education of nondisabled children and those with disabilities. Although there is much similarity between state and federal requirements, states are free to exceed federal requirements and to add unique local expectations.

Interpreting and implementing these layers of laws and regulations is not a one-time task. Changes in any of these laws mean changes in school practice. Parents who do not believe that the rights of their children are being preserved may seek resolution through administrative hearings or action before a state or federal court. As legal cases clarify the meaning of any of these laws, schools adjust to these interpretations.

As with most situations in which the weight of law is used to force action, the process of ensuring compliance is complicated and detailed. Each state is audited by the federal government periodically. In turn, states evaluate the performance of each school district. Some oversight takes place in regular reports of practices and finances. Periodically, more extensive study occurs during on-site visits to districts, which include record reviews and interviews with educators and parents. States and districts that refuse to correct identified faults run the risk of losing federal special education funds.

In an extensive study of federal monitoring and enforcement of elements of IDEA, the National Council on Disability (NCD) found that, despite more than 20 years of effort, there is not one U.S. state that fully and accurately complies with IDEA's requirements. In the following selection, the NCD delineates how the promises of IDEA—and the educational rights of children with disabilities—remain unmet by weak oversight procedures, poor follow-through, and lack of consequences for repeated failings. The NCD recommends implementing changes to ensure the civil rights of children with disabilities and a strong special education system.

In the second selection, Frederick M. Hess and Frederick J. Brigham, reflecting on the impact of federal regulations in Virginia, assert that the current emphasis on compliance forces districts to focus more on procedures than on children. Filling out forms according to regulation takes precedence over ensuring good programs for children. Also, money spent on compliance details reduces money spent on services for children. Hess and Brigham hold that strict adherence to rigid procedures creates an adversarial system that engenders distrust between families and educators and unnecessary divisions in school districts.

As you read these selections, ask yourself whether or not meeting the letter of the law prevents meeting the spirit of the law. Does holding states and districts to exacting standards help or hinder the implementation of an effective educational program?

 **YES**

Back to School on Civil Rights

Executive Summary

Twenty-five years ago, Congress enacted and President Gerald Ford signed the Education for All Handicapped Children Act, one of the most important civil rights laws ever written. The basic premise of this federal law, now known as the Individuals with Disabilities Education Act (IDEA), is that all children with disabilities have a federally protected civil right to have available to them a free appropriate public education that meets their education and related services needs in the least restrictive environment. The statutory right articulated in IDEA is grounded in the Constitution's guarantee of equal protection under law and the constitutional power of Congress to authorize and place conditions on participation in federal spending programs. It is complemented by the federal civil rights protections contained in section 504 of the Rehabilitation Act of 1973, as amended, and Title II of the Americans with Disabilities Act.

This report, the second in a series of independent analyses by the National Council on Disability (NCD) of federal enforcement of civil rights laws, looks at more than two decades of federal monitoring and enforcement of compliance with Part B of IDEA. Overall, NCD finds that federal efforts to enforce the law over several Administrations have been inconsistent, ineffective, and lacking any real teeth. The report includes recommendations to the President and the Congress that would build on the 1997 reauthorization of IDEA. The intent is to advance a more aggressive, credible, and meaningful federal approach to enforcing this critical civil rights law, so that the nation's 25-year-old commitment to effective education for all children will be more fully realized.

Background

In 1970, before enactment of the federal protections in IDEA, schools in America educated only one in five students with disabilities. More than 1 million students were excluded from public schools, and another 3.5 million did not receive appropriate services. Many states had laws excluding certain students, including those who were blind, deaf, or labeled "emotionally disturbed" or "mentally retarded." Almost 200,000 school-age children with mental retardation or emotional disabilities were institutionalized. The likelihood of exclu-

From National Council on Disability, *Back to School on Civil Rights: Advancing the Federal Commitment to Leave No Child Behind,* (January 25, 2000). Washington, D.C.: U.S. Government Printing Office, 2000. Notes omitted.

sion was greater for children with disabilities living in low-income, ethnic and racial minority, or rural communities.

In the more than two decades since its enactment, IDEA implementation has produced important improvements in the quality and effectiveness of the public education received by millions of American children with disabilities. Today almost 6 million children and young people with disabilities ages 3 through 21 qualify for educational interventions under Part B of IDEA. Some of these students with disabilities are being educated in their neighborhood schools in regular classrooms. These children have a right to have support services and devices such as assistive listening systems, braille text books, paraprofessional supports, curricular modifications, talking computers, and speech synthesizers made available to them as needed to facilitate their learning side-by-side with their nondisabled peers. Post-secondary and employment opportunities are opening up for increasing numbers of young adults with disabilities as they leave high school. Post-school employment rates for youth served under Part B are twice that of older adults with disabilities who did not benefit from IDEA in school, and self-reports indicate that the percentage of college freshmen with a disability has almost tripled since 1978.

Findings

As significant as the gains over time are, they tell only part of the story. In the past 25 years states have not met their general supervisory obligations to ensure compliance with the core civil rights requirements of IDEA at the local level. Children with disabilities and their families are required far too often to file complaints to ensure that the law is followed. The Federal Government has frequently failed to take effective action to enforce the civil rights protections of IDEA when federal officials determine that states have failed to ensure compliance with the law. Although Department of Education [DoED] Secretary Richard W. Riley has been more aggressive in his efforts to monitor compliance and take formal enforcement action involving sanctions than all his predecessors combined, formal enforcement of IDEA has been very limited. Based on its review of the Department of Education's monitoring reports of states between 1994 and 1998, NCD found:

- Every state was out of compliance with IDEA requirements to some degree; in the sampling of states studied, noncompliance persisted over many years.
- Notwithstanding federal monitoring reports documenting widespread noncompliance, enforcement of the law is the burden of parents who too often must invoke formal complaint procedures and due process hearings, including expensive and time-consuming litigation, to obtain the appropriate services and supports to which their children are entitled under the law. Many parents with limited resources are unable to challenge violations successfully when they occur. Even parents with significant resources are hard-pressed to prevail over state education agencies (SEAs) and local education agencies (LEAs) when they or their publicly financed attorneys choose to be recalcitrant.

- The Department of Education has made very limited use of its authority to impose enforcement sanctions such as withholding of funds or making referrals to the Department of Justice, despite persistent failures to ensure compliance in many states.
- DoED has not made known to the states and the public any objective criteria for using enforcement sanctions, so that the relationship between findings of noncompliance by federal monitors and a decision to apply sanctions is not clear.

DoED Monitoring Model

The oversight model adopted by the Department of Education is multitiered and multipurpose. The Office of Special Education Programs (OSEP) distributes federal IDEA funding to the states and monitors the SEAs. The SEAs in turn monitor the LEAs to make sure they are in compliance with IDEA. In this tiered oversight model, the same Department of Education office (OSEP) distributes federal funds, monitors compliance, and enforces the law where violations are identified. The politics and conflicts inherent in administering these three disparate functions have challenged the Department's ability to integrate and balance the objectives of all three.

Data Sources and Summary of Analyses

As mentioned above, NCD found that the most recent federal monitoring reports demonstrated that every state failed to ensure compliance with the requirements of IDEA to some extent during the period covered by this review. More than half of the states failed to ensure compliance in five of the seven main compliance areas. For example, in OSEP's most recent monitoring reports, 90 percent of the states (n = 45) had failed to ensure compliance in the category of general supervision (the state mechanism for ensuring that LEAs are carrying out their responsibilities to ensure compliance with the law); 88 percent of the states (n = 44) had failed to ensure compliance with the law's secondary transition services provisions, which require schools to promote the appropriate transition of students with disabilities to work or postsecondary education; 80 percent of the states (n = 40) failed to ensure compliance with the law's free appropriate public education requirements; 78 percent of the states (n = 39) failed to ensure compliance with the procedural safeguards provisions of the law; and 72 percent of the states (n = 36) failed to ensure compliance with the placement in the least restrictive environment requirements of IDEA. In the two remaining major compliance areas, IEPs [individual education programs] and protection in evaluation, 44 percent of the states (n = 22) failed to ensure compliance with the former and 38 percent of the states (n = 19) failed to ensure compliance with the latter.

Enforcement Authority

Currently, the U.S. Department of Education has neither the authority nor the resources to investigate and resolve individual complaints alleging noncompliance. The Department does consult with and share some of its enforcement authority with the U.S. Department of Justice (DOJ), which has no independent litigation authority. Yet between the date it was given explicit referral authority in 1997 and the date this report went to the printer, DoED had not sent a single case to DOJ for "substantial noncompliance," and had articulated no objective criteria for defining that important term. The Department of Justice, whose role has been largely limited to participation as an amicus in IDEA litigation, does not appear to have a process for determining what cases to litigate.

Overall Enforcement Action

Despite the high rate of failure to ensure compliance with Part B requirements indicated in the monitoring reports for all states, only one enforcement action involving a sanction (withholding) and five others involving imposition of "high risk" status and corrective action as a prerequisite to receiving further funds have been taken. The only withholding action occurred once for a temporary period and was overruled by a federal court. Overall, the DoED tends to emphasize collaboration with the states through technical assistance and developing corrective action plans or compliance agreements for addressing compliance problems. There appear to be no clearcut, objective criteria for determining which enforcement options ought to be applied and when to enforce in situations of substantial and persistent noncompliance.

Recommendations for Strengthening Federal Enforcement

NCD makes the following recommendations to strengthen the capacity of both the Department of Education and the Department of Justice to more effectively enforce IDEA:

- Congress should amend IDEA to create a complaint-handling process at the federal level to address systemic violations occurring in a SEA or LEA. Congress should designate the Department of Justice to administer the process and allocate adequate funding to enable the Department to take on this new role. This new federal complaint process should be designed to complement, not supplant, complaint procedures and the due process hearing at the state level. The federal process should be simple to use and easy to understand by parents and students.
- Congress should amend IDEA to provide the Department of Justice with independent authority to investigate and litigate cases brought under IDEA. The Department of Justice should be authorized to develop and disseminate explicit criteria for the types of alleged systemic violation complaints it will prioritize given its limited resources.
- Congress should include in the amendment that the Department of Education and the Department of Justice shall consult with students with disabilities, their parents, and other stakeholders to develop objective criteria for defining "substantial noncompliance," the point at which a state that fails to ensure compliance with IDEA's requirements will be referred to the Department of Justice for legal action.
- Congress should ask the General Accounting Office (GAO) to conduct a study of the extent to which SEAs and LEAs are ensuring that the

requirements of IDEA in the areas of general supervision, secondary transition services, free appropriate public education, procedural safeguards, and placement in the least restrictive environment are being met. In addition, the DoED Office of Inspector General (OIG) should conduct regular independent special education audits (fiscal and program). The purpose of the audits would be to examine whether federal funds granted under IDEA Parts B and D (State Program Improvement Grants) have been and are being spent in compliance with IDEA requirements. These audits should supplement OSEP's annual compliance-monitoring visits, and the audit results should be in DoED's annual report to Congress. To the extent that the DoED OIG lacks the subject-matter expertise to conduct program audits under IDEA, the OIG should contract with independent entities having such expertise when a program audit is necessary.

- The Department of Education should establish and use national compliance standards and objective measures for assessing state progress toward better performance outcomes for children with disabilities and for achieving full compliance with Part B.
- The Department of Education should consult with students with disabilities, their parents and other stakeholders in developing and implementing a range of enforcement sanctions that will be triggered by specific indicators and measures indicating a state's failure to ensure compliance with Part B.
- When Congress and the President approve an increase in the funding to be distributed to local schools under Part B, Congress and the President should appropriate at the same time an amount equal to 10 percent of the total increase in Part B funding to be used to build the Department of Justice's and the Department of Education's enforcement, complaint-handling, and technical assistance infrastructure to effectively enable the federal agencies to drive improvements in state compliance and ensure better outcomes for children.

Personnel Training Needs

Regular and special education teachers in many states are frustrated by the mixed messages regarding compliance from school administrators, local special education directors, state oversight agents, school district attorneys, and federal oversight agents. Teachers ultimately bear the responsibility to implement interventions and accommodations for students with disabilities, often without adequate training, planning time, or assistance. They must function within an educational system that often lacks adequate commitment, expertise, or funding to deliver appropriate services to every child who needs them. School administrators, special education directors, school principals, and agents of federal, state, and local governments must stop working at cross purposes and commit to working together to resolve, not conceal or ignore, these very real problems. If the Federal Government continues to refrain from taking enforcement action in the face of widespread failures to ensure Part B compliance, this atmosphere of questionable commitment to the civil rights of students with disabilities will continue.

Advocacy Service Needs

Pervasive and persistent noncompliance with IDEA is a complex problem with often dramatic implications on a daily basis for the lives of children with disabilities and their families. Too many parents continue to expend endless resources in confronting obstacles to their child's most basic right to an appropriate education, often at the expense of their personal lives, their financial livelihoods, and their careers. Students are frustrated—their skills undeveloped and their sense of belonging tenuous. When informal efforts have failed to end unnecessary segregation or inappropriate programming for individual children, many have used the rights and protections afforded by IDEA to successfully challenge these injustices. Advocacy and litigation have been essential to ending destructive patterns of recurring noncompliance. Litigation has resulted in important victories for the children involved and better outcomes for other students with disabilities by exposing and remedying systemic noncompliance with IDEA. Yet legal services are often far beyond the financial reach of many families of students with disabilities.

Children with disabilities and their families are often the least prepared to advocate for their rights in the juvenile justice, immigration and naturalization, and child welfare systems when egregious violations occur. Children with disabilities and their families who are non-English speaking, or who live in low income, ethnic or racial minority, and rural communities, are frequently not represented as players in the process. These individuals must be included and given the information and resources they need to contribute and advocate for themselves.

Recommendations for Training and Advocacy

Accordingly, NCD makes the following recommendations:

- When Congress and the President approve an increase in the funding to be distributed to local schools under Part B of IDEA, Congress and the President should appropriate at the same time an amount equal to 10 percent of the total Part B increase to fund free or low-cost legal advocacy services to students with disabilities and their parents through public and private legal service providers, putting competent legal assistance within their financial reach and beginning to level the playing field between them and their local school districts.
- The Department of Education should give priority support to the formation of a comprehensive and coordinated advocacy and technical assistance system in each state. The Department should develop a separate OSEP-administered funding stream to aid public and private advocacy entities in each state in collaborating to expand and coordinate self-advocacy training programs, resources, and services for students with disabilities and their parents throughout the state. Elements of the coordinated advocacy and technical assistance systems should include:

—The availability of a lawyer at every state Parent Training and Information (PTI) Center, a protection and advocacy agency, legal services, and independent living center to provide legal advice and representation to students with disabilities and their parents in advocating for their legal rights under IDEA.

—Self-advocacy training programs for students with disabilities and their parents focused on civil rights awareness, education and secondary transition services planning, and independent living in the community.

—The establishment of a national backup center with legal materials, training, and other supports available for attorneys working on IDEA cases and issues at the state level.

—Expansion of involvement by the private bar and legal services organizations in providing legal advice to students with disabilities and their parents in advocating for their legal rights under IDEA.

—Training in culturally sensitive dispute resolution to meet the needs of growing populations of citizens from racial and ethnic backgrounds having diverse traditions and customs. Multiple language needs and communication styles must be accommodated in all training.

Full compliance with IDEA will ultimately be the product of collaborative partnership and long-term alliances among all parties having an interest in how IDEA is implemented. For such partnerships to be effective, all interested parties must be well prepared to articulate their needs and advocate for their objectives. To that end, coordinated statewide strategies of self-advocacy training for students with disabilities and their parents are vital. To make this happen, NCD recommends the following:

• The Department of Education should fund additional technical assistance, training, and dissemination of materials to meet continuing needs in the following areas:

—Culturally appropriate technical assistance, which should be available to ensure that American Indian children with disabilities, their families, tribal leaders, and advocates in every interested tribe can participate as full partners in implementing IDEA in their communities. Culturally appropriate training and technical assistance should be developed and delivered through the satellite offices of newly created disability technical assistance centers (DBTACs) managed and staffed primarily by Native Americans that serve American Indian communities around the country.

—Training to enhance evaluation skills for parents to assess the effectiveness of their states' IDEA compliance-monitoring systems.

—Training of the appropriate agents (officials, advocates, and other stakeholders) in the immigration and naturalization and child welfare systems in IDEA's civil rights requirements.

—Training of the appropriate agents (officials, advocates, and other stakeholders) in the juvenile justice system in IDEA's civil rights requirements, how they apply within the juvenile justice system, and ways the law can be used to help minimize detention of children with disabilities in the juvenile justice system.

A Six-State In-Depth Sample

NCD looked in depth at a sampling of six states, using the last three monitoring reports to assess the compliance picture in those states over time. The first two of the monitoring reports for these six states (covering a period from 1983–1998) included failure to ensure compliance with a total of 66 Part B requirements. Only 27 percent (n = 18) of the 66 violations had been corrected by the time of the third report. Based on the reported data, in 73 percent (n = 48) of the 66 violations, either the six states still failed to ensure compliance or no compliance finding was reported at all in the last monitoring report.

To date federal compliance-monitoring and enforcement efforts have not fully dealt with the root causes of widespread noncompliance, and children with disabilities and their parents have suffered the consequences. This report details NCD's findings and recommendations for improving the effectiveness of federal efforts to ensure state compliance with IDEA and related legislation. NCD calls on Congress and the President to work together to address the inadequacies identified by this report so that children and families will have an effective and responsive partner in the Federal Government when they seek to ensure that IDEA's goals of enhanced school system accountability and improved performance outcomes for students with disabilities move from the language of the law to the reality of each American classroom.

IDEA mandates that school systems respond to the needs of individual children with disabilities, making education accessible to them, regardless of the severity of their disabilities. Teachers today know that education tailored to individual needs and learning styles can make all the difference in the quality of a child's learning, whether or not she has a disability. Very few public schools consistently and effectively deliver this individualized approach for all children. Accordingly, many children fall through the cracks, as performance on achievement tests across the nation demonstrates. Alternatives to traditional public education such as charter and private schools, as well as political calls for vouchers, indicate growing public dissatisfaction with schools that do not educate all children effectively. IDEA calls for a responsive public education system that meets the individual learning needs of students with disabilities. It also contains a blueprint for the future of public education—where no child is left behind, and all children have an equal opportunity to gain the knowledge and skills they need to fulfill their dreams.

Ultimately, the enforcement of the civil rights protections of IDEA will make a difference to every child, not only children with disabilities. At the national summit on disability policy hosted by NCD in 1996, more than 350 disability advocates called for a unified system of education that incorporates all students into the vision of IDEA. NCD's 1996 report, *Achieving Indepen-*

dence, presents the outline of a system in which every child, with or without a disability, has an individualized educational program and access to the educational services she or he needs to learn effectively. IDEA leads the way in reshaping today's educational system from one that struggles to accommodate the educational needs of children with disabilities to one that readily responds to the individual educational needs of all children.

NO

Frederick M. Hess and
Frederick J. Brigham

How Federal Special Education Policy Affects Schooling in Virginia

Federal special education legislation has an honorable heritage and a laudable purpose. Unfortunately, the manner in which Congress and the executive branch have pursued that purpose now impedes the ability of state school systems to serve children in both general and special education.

The current system of oversight and resource allocation focuses less on educational attainment and more on procedural civil rights. Problems result from the federal government's use of this legalistic approach. In most areas of education, Washington offers supplementary funding as a carrot to encourage desired state behaviors. The challenge of compelling states to abide by federal dictates in special education, however, has produced a reliance on procedural oversight with deleterious effects for the federal-state partnership in education.

Under the present system, educators are restricted in their ability to make decisions regarding how best to assist children with disabilities. Instead, in response to federal dictates, states press school districts toward a defensive posture in which educators may spend more time attending to procedural requirements than to students' instructional and behavioral needs. Most discussions of reforming special education at the federal level ask what policy changes would alleviate this problem of excessive proceduralism. We suggest that such an approach is too narrow, that over-reliance upon procedural regulation actually arises from Washington's attempt to compel behaviors with insufficient incentives or guidance.

While seeking to get states to do its bidding with respect to children and youths with disabilities, Congress has provided neither inducements for them to cooperate nor flexibility in how they comply with federal direction. Lacking the capacity to implement special education policy on its own—considering that it does not operate public schools or employ their teachers—Washington has instead relied upon micro-managing state procedures and using the threat of legal action as a primary enforcement tool.

Lacking explicit federal direction or support, state officials cope by crafting their own muddled guidelines. This permits the state, like the federal government, to forestall messy conflict over details regarding program eligibility and services by pushing such questions down to districts and schools. Principals and teachers complain that the nested levels of governance deepen the confusion as the rules grow more convoluted and cumbersome at each stage....

The Federal Role in Special Education ...

The IDEA [Individuals With Disabilities Education Act]

In making special education law, Congress and the executive branch have relied heavily upon judicial precedents rooted in the Equal Protection and Due Process Clauses of the 14th Amendment. Whereas most federal legislation is framed as a compromise between competing interests and claims, this more absolutist orientation means that special education policies turn on endowing claimants with an inviolable set of rights. That mindset is illustrated by the "inclusion" proponent who prominently argued, "It really doesn't matter whether or not [full inclusion] works ... even if it didn't work it would still be the thing to do."

Under the IDEA, a satisfactory program is defined as one that adheres to due process, regardless of its results. Critics suggested that this orientation fed lower expectations for students with disabilities. In response, the 1997 IDEA reauthorization sought to emphasize academic performance by insisting upon "meaningful access to the general education curriculum to the maximum extent possible" for students with special needs....

Section 504

In theory, states are free to disregard the IDEA. The only federal sanction is the ability of the Office of Special Education Programs (OSEP) to withdraw IDEA grants. These grants amount to less than ten percent of state special education spending. This apparent freedom is illusory, however, because any state that fails to comply with the IDEA's requirements would still be liable under Section 504 of the Rehabilitation Act of 1973. Section 504 is designed ... "to eliminate discrimination on the basis of handicap in any program or activity receiving Federal financial assistance." Although it supplies no funding, Section 504 applies to any entity receiving any federal funding, meaning that all states must abide by its directives....

Although the IDEA offers guidelines regarding various disability conditions, the provisions of Section 504 are so nebulous that it becomes extremely difficult to distinguish students entitled to special education services from those not entitled. As one administrator said, "In my opinion, IDEA is much more precise, much more specific.... 504 is the same as saying, 'you have a problem here.' [Anybody can identify some problem] 'substantially limits' [a life activity].... What's the line there? So you're wide open."

Special Education in Virginia

Special education comprises a substantial share of Virginia's K–12 educational expenditures. Between 1995 and 1998, special education students made up 13 percent to 14 percent of the state's student population, while the special education budget consumed 23 percent to 25 percent of the state's education budget....

In Virginia, federal special education directives are interpreted and implemented by a designated group of professionals in the state Department of Education (DOE). Within the larger DOE, headed by the state Superintendent of Education, is a directorate for special education headed by a Director of Special Education and Student Services (SESS). Historically, the directorate for Special Education did nothing else. In 2000, DOE merged "Special Education" with "Student Services," the unit responsible for activities such as school health and safety. Despite this reorganization, Special Education remains relatively isolated from the other areas of the DOE. In January 2001, SESS included 23 positions devoted to oversight of special education. These individuals include specialists in learning disabilities, emotional disturbance, mental retardation, early childhood, and severe disabilities. Not one member is explicitly charged with coordinating policy with the other parts of the DOE.

Virginia's DOE essentially runs parallel school systems, one staffed by special educators for students with disabilities, the second staffed by general educators for everyone else. Each side exhibits distrust and frustration with the other. A local special education administrator observed, "People in general education don't listen to us or even ask us about the kids in our caseloads." A state-level administrator said, "We have consistent problems with some of our districts," explaining that the state deals with such challenges by using legal and administrative sanctions to coerce general educators into "playing ball." General educators voice reciprocal concerns. One administrator spoke for many, saying, "I have all I can handle right now without attending to students with wildly varying educational and behavioral needs."...

The current structure ensures that special education policy decisions are mostly made by people removed from actual school practice and from the general decisionmaking process for K–12 curriculum and instruction. This makes it less likely that services for students with special needs will be integrated or coordinated with the larger educational program.... The structure of the DOE helps to divide general and special education personnel, while encouraging professionals to think differently about different categories of children, despite Congress' insistence that its goal is to eliminate distinctions among students.

Special Education Litigation

Despite the visibility of special education cases that reach the courts, such actions are relatively rare in Virginia. The most common legal or quasi-legal actions are complaints and due process hearings. The Commonwealth devotes considerable time and energy to these. Due process hearings are a quasijudicial, adversarial procedure overseen by part-time hearing officers trained by the DOE.

Between 1992–93 and 1999–2000, 799 due process requests were filed with the DOE.... All such requests require formal notification to the Department that the plaintiff is exercising his right to a due process hearing. Ninety-three percent of these requests were filed by parents. The remaining 7 percent were filed by school districts, usually when the district was concerned that parents were refusing to allow it to provide the services it deemed appropriate. These figures indicate that formal legal proceedings may be less of an issue than critics sometimes fear.

Of these 799 cases filed, 586 were resolved in the same year. Of the 586, 176 (30 percent) led to decisions by a hearing officer while the rest ended through withdrawal of the complaint or settlement prior to a hearing. Of the 176 decisions rendered, three-quarters were resolved wholly in favor of the school district. The other 25 percent either favored the parent or split the difference between parent and district.

There are at least two ways to interpret these outcomes. One is that a substantial percentage of the requests filed lack merit. A second is that some schools respond to parental concerns only when faced with the threat of legal sanctions. A significant number of hearing requests are withdrawn after districts make concessions....

The larger problem is not the number of formal complaints or their resolution, but the incentives that this legalistic mechanism creates for local educators. Presently, the desire to avoid legal sanctions and officer-ordered costs and services is the clearest incentive for schools to make extraordinary efforts to serve students with disabilities. Such efforts may cause the district to divert resources from other worthy purposes. Educators have cause to focus on what services and accommodations will forestall complaints, rather than on which are cost-effective and educationally appropriate. The result is that districts are caught between a desire to "cut corners" on special education expenditures and the impulse to provide services in order to avoid the threat of legal action. By encouraging schools and parents to adopt adversarial roles, the legalistic emphasis makes cooperative solutions more difficult and shifts the focus of decision-making from educational performance to the avoidance of potential liability.

The Institutional Shape of Special Education

Here we examine three key program dimensions used by the federal government to define special education and to ensure that it is delivered in an acceptable manner....

FAPE and LRE

The key IDEA mandates affecting instruction and student placement are FAPE (free appropriate public education) and LRE (least restrictive environment). FAPE addresses the elements of a student's education program, although LRE addresses the integration of disabled students into the general education system. Often, the two mandates embody contradictory impulses. Legal scholar Anne Dupre has observed, "The friction between 'appropriate' education and 'appropriate' integration has baffled the court and led to a confusing array of opinions on inclusion." While educators must attend to both considerations, in Virginia it appears that the balance is tipped in favor of inclusion, even at the cast of effective education. An attorney who often represents parents of children with disabilities said, "[t]he intensity of the programs offered for students with mild disabilities fell after the push for more inclusion. Now we more often have to pursue formal action to get these students the services they need."

The most difficult aspect of FAPE involves the meaning of "appropriate," which is clearer for some disabilities than others. Few question the need for Braille tests for students who are blind or ramps for those with limited mobility. For students with less obvious disabilities, however, program appropriateness ought to take into account curricular demands on the student as well as the larger educational context of the school....

Although the challenge of validating the appropriateness of a given student's educational program is daunting, it is overshadowed by the problems surrounding the LRE requirement. Few areas of special education are as controversial. Much effort is invested in determining the LRE for individual students, closely watched by a group of educators and advocates who call for "full inclusion" of disabled youngsters in regular education classes....

In Virginia, as a result of the push for "inclusion," many of the services formerly available to students with mild disabilities ... have been cut back or eliminated. Such programs frequently have been replaced by "collaborative" or "consultative" models, in which students with special needs are enrolled full-time in general education classrooms. One result has been that a continuum of placement options has been replaced with a starker choice between intensive (for example, self-contained) classes and limited services (for example, enrollment in general education programs). This shift has left both general and special education teachers with fewer ways to respond to the needs of students, which reduces their ability to make effective professional judgments about what works for children in their schools....

The current approach to FAPE and LRE fails to resolve the tension between maximizing achievement and maximizing integration, leaving these competing desiderata to be worked out by administrators, teachers, and parents without clear guidelines. Yet educators are blocked from using their professional judgment in weighing these two imperatives and are subjected to administrative or judicial review and sanction if deemed to have proceeded in an inappropriate manner. In other words, district officials are granted an ambiguous autonomy and expected to make appropriate decisions but are prevented from relying upon their professional determinations of efficiency and efficacy in reaching those decisions. The system is faintly redolent of a star chamber in which one is not sure the criteria to which one is being held.

Funding

One of most significant impacts of FAPE is on state education funding. Because Congress has imbued disabled children with particular rights, the state is legally required to give budgetary priority to their needs. States are legally vulnerable to charges that they have failed to provide adequately for students with special needs, while parents of general education students cannot make similar claims. The consequence is that states have a difficult time making the case against the provision of even very expensive special education services and tend to fund these by dipping into the pool that would otherwise fund general education....

Monitoring Special Education

In theory, federally inspired monitoring ensures that special education programs provide an appropriate education to all eligible students. In reality, the monitoring focuses more on procedural compliance than on either the appropriateness or effectiveness of the education being delivered. Given the lack of evidence that procedural compliance equates to more effective services, it is not clear that federal monitoring is effectively promoting quality special education. Moreover, such an emphasis undermines teacher professionalism by forcing educators to invest significant time in managing procedures and documenting processes, rather than on instruction.

OSEP's policy, adopted after the 1997 IDEA amendments, monitors states predominantly by requiring them to conduct self-studies. A key problem in this process is that the reporting requirements are both complex and vague. For example, the phrase "free appropriate public education" sounds straightforward and easily implemented, but a closer look proves otherwise.

Assuming that "free" means no cost to the parents, interpreting this part is straightforward. But, what does "appropriate" mean? In order to define this term, one must first determine the goals of the education program and ask the question, "Appropriate for what?" The IDEA is silent on that point, meaning that this question must be revisited in the case of each student. OSEP plainly is unable to monitor the "appropriateness" of a given decision in the case of a particular child. Therefore, it winds up monitoring processes and procedures—for example, the way that the decision was made. In practice, the guidelines are daunting, elaborate, and time-consuming even for many special education professionals—let alone the parents and students they are intended to protect. As one state official commented, "Monitoring used to be a part of my job, now it's all I do. Running the monitoring program has become my whole job."

Virginia's SSEAC [State Special Education Advisory Committee], which is supposed to identify critical issues and advise DOE on carrying out special education programs, scrapped its entire agenda for 2000–2001 in order to concentrate on the issue of program monitoring. The state DOE has had to add additional staff to handle these responsibilities.

In early January 2001, the SSEAC met to discuss the self-study that comprises the initial stage of Virginia's federal monitoring. At the beginning of the meeting, a facilitator asked each committee member why he or she had given up the time to attend this particular meeting. The most common response was to attain closure on the process. The facilitator pointed out that the federal monitoring process, being continuous, could never result in closure.

Reports were presented regarding programs for both school-aged and pre-school children. Each report was several hundred pages long. After the meeting, several parent representatives remarked that they saw little connection between the activities conducted through the federal monitoring and discernible improvements in the educational services offered to their children. The best that can be said of the self-study is that it allows parents and special educators to voice their concerns. However, there is little reason to suspect that this unfocused airing of grievances is likely to produce substantive improvements in special education. More likely, because the state officials who led the self-study procedure were diverted from their responsibilities to monitor and support local education agencies (LEAs), the federal monitoring program is likely to result in decreased attention to the problems faced by children and youths with disabilities, their families, and the schools that serve them.

The Practice of Special Education...

IEPs

As originally conceived, IEPs were to be a flexible tool for creating specialized programs responsive to student needs as well as parental and school concerns. However, Virginia practice emphasizes *pro forma* compliance with IEPs in order to protect educators from administrative and legal actions. A typical IEP form offers 45 boxes for committees to check off before they even begin to describe the student's own education program. Rather than a flexible pedagogical tool, the IEP is often a ritualized document. As one special education administrator said, "Of course, all of our special ed students have IEPs. But how relevant are [the IEPs] to what our teachers are doing on a day-to-day basis? Not very."

Parents are not alone in their dissatisfaction. Teachers often complain that IEPs do little but absorb time and repeat platitudes....

IEPs have historically reflected a given student's particular instructional regimen, rather than provided a road map for helping that child accomplish the general education goals promulgated by the school or state. A result is that they are often written with little input from general education teachers and scant regard for the standards of general education programs....

The 1997 amendments required that general education teachers be included in IEP meetings and that IEPs yield "meaningful access to the general education curriculum." Unfortunately, both changes appear to hold only limited promise. So long as special education policy is driven by rights and legalisms, inserting general education teachers into IEP planning sessions is unlikely to produce significant changes in practice. As for "meaningful access to the general education curriculum," the phrase is so nebulous as to serve no real purpose, while creating yet one more interpretive minefield for school personnel.

The trouble with most efforts to improve IEPs is that they fail to address the contradiction at the heart of the process. On the one hand, professional educators are charged with designing flexible programs that respond to the needs of each student with disabilities. On the other hand, these plans are devised and implemented in a context shaped by compliance-based rules and marked by legal peril. The result is that IEPs cease to be useful pedagogical tools.

Discipline Policy

The IDEA requires the development of distinct disciplinary policies for students with disabilities. Some of these distinctions make sense. It is unreasonable to discipline a wheelchair-bound student for failing to stand during the national anthem. The IDEA prevents schools from punishing students in such situations (although we see no evidence that Virginia schools, left to their own judgment, would engage in such practices). The IDEA requires a "zero reject" model that extends special education services to *all* students with disabilities. Under this logic, schools may not interrupt or withhold services for any such students save for infractions involving guns or possession of drugs. Such interruption of services has been deemed to violate the IDEA's procedural safeguards....

IDEA regulation of discipline may serve a legitimate purpose. It is well established that students with disabilities are frequently "over-punished" for behavior infractions. Many parents of children with disabilities report that their children feel singled out by school officials for behavior that rarely leads to sanctions for other students....

Unfortunately, the IDEA also has a number of undesirable disciplinary consequences. School officials must determine the extent to which an act of misbehavior results from a disability. Judgments regarding the motivation of a specific act have eluded philosophers and psychologists through the ages, yet are required by the IDEA. Such deliberations are bound to yield variable results, even as they consume substantial time. Effective disciplinary procedures require that acts and consequences be closely linked in time and consistent over time if they are to have the desired effect. The IDEA's procedural mandates make such practices doubly difficult when the child has any sort of disability.

Despite the frequent voicing of such concerns, the IDEA constraints do not actually result in many disciplinary measures being challenged or overturned in Virginia.... Still, the fear of such a challenge reportedly causes many teachers and administrators to shy away from punishing students with disabilities for infractions for which others would be disciplined.... The perception in Virginia that the IDEA creates a class of students licensed to "terrorize schools and teachers" undermines public trust in school safety and support for special education.

State Education Standards

... Much special education practice draws heavily on the philosophy of progressive education, emphasizing notions of personal relevance more heavily than traditional academic skills and knowledge.... The IDEA's ethos of individualized instruction is at odds with systems of standards-based accountability that seek to improve education by requiring all students to perform at a measurably high level on a specified set of objectives.

In the past, this conflict was often accommodated by exempting special education students from standardized assessments. In the 1990s, however, special educators began to assert that such policies caused disabled students to be denied effective and equitable instruction. Consequently, the 1997 IDEA amendments mandated that students with disabilities be included in testing programs to the maximum feasible extent. As a result, students with special needs now participate in Virginia's SOL [Standards of Learning] testing regime.

This change places schools and districts in an awkward position, as the state simultaneously asks them to raise test results and to include students who have shown historically poor performances on standardized assessments. The IDEA requires educators to take greater responsibility for the achievement of students with disabilities. However, the law can also encourage educators to look for loopholes to relax the standards for students who are unlikely to fare well on high-stakes assessments. An example of this tendency was the SSEAC recommendation in early 2000 that the state extend the category of "developmental disabilities" up to the federal maximum age of nine so that more students would be afforded special accommodations on the SOL tests. The nature of this request suggests the fundamental tension between special education provisions and the push toward high uniform standards....

Perhaps the central dilemma for states pursuing high-stakes accountability is how best to serve those students with mild disabilities who find attaining acceptable levels of performance a daunting challenge. On the one hand, it is sensible to hold these students and their teachers to the same high level of expectations to which we hold others. On the other hand, these students may find assessments frustrating or insurmountable and may drop out of school altogether. This bifurcation is partly a function of the Virginia SOL's virtually exclusive focus on academic preparation. Although this emphasis is understandable, it leads to de-emphasis of programs such as vocational education and the arts that can provide other forms of useful instruction and skill-based learning for students with mild or moderate disabilities.

Conclusion

Surveying the six dimensions of policy and practice in which special education poses significant challenges, we can see that the key problems have much in common. FAPE and LRE demand that educators abide by open-ended and ill-defined directives, even as the court-enforced right of a select group of children to "free and appropriate education" prohibits measured decisions regarding the allocation of resources. The monitoring of special education relies upon documentation and paper trails, requiring much time and effort and forcing educators to base program decisions upon procedures rather than determinations of efficiency or effectiveness. IEPs intended as flexible instruments of learning have evolved into written records of compliance with formal requirements. In the area of school discipline, protections afforded to special education students have caused educators to look askance upon these children and have made it more difficult to enforce clear and uniform standards in schools. And in jurisdictions such as Virginia, which have moved to a standards-based curriculum and a results-based accountability system, the question arises of how to track the progress of disabled students and whether they will be treated as part of the reformed education system or (reminiscent of pre-IDEA discrimination) as a separate educational world.

Reformers have sought to tackle one or another of these issues in isolation, acting in the belief that incremental policy shifts could remedy the particular problem. For example, the 1997 IDEA reforms sought to emphasize outcomes by requiring schools to test all students and enhancing schools' ability to discipline disabled students who misbehave. Such efforts have not worked very well, however, because they fail to recognize that the enumerated problems are symptomatic of a deeper tension at the heart of the federal-state relationship.

In sum, special education policy today is unwieldy, exasperating, and ripe for rethinking. Congress has demanded that states and schools provide certain services, but it has refused to pay their costs. States are obliged to deliver special education, yet lack substantive control over its objectives and policy design and the nature and shape of its services. But Washington does not actually run the program, either. Instead it tells states, albeit in ambiguous terms, what they must do, no matter whether these requirements are in the best interests of children, schools, or the larger education enterprise. Whatever the cost of compliance, states and districts are obliged to pay it, regardless of the effect on other children, programs, and priorities. The result is a hybrid reminiscent of the "push-me, pull-you" that accompanied Dr. Doolittle in Hugh Lofting's legendary children's tales. Like that mythical two-headed creature, the special education system is constantly tugged in opposite directions. To compel state cooperation with its directives, Washington relies upon a rights-based regimen of mandated procedures and voluminous records, enforced by the specter of judicial power. Yet because states and districts end up paying most of the bill for special education, Congress is hesitant to order the provision of particular services or to demand specific results. The consequence is that educators must interpret vague federal directives while operating under the shadow of legal threat.

Arguably, this produces the worst of two very different policy regimes. If special education were an outright federal program, like the National Park Service, the Weather Bureau, or Social Security, Washington would run it directly, in uniform fashion, with all bills being paid via Congressional appropriation. If it were a state program, Congress might contribute to its costs but states would determine how best to run it. Today, however, it is neither, and the result is not working very well.

These are two obvious solutions. The first is for Congress to pay for the special education services that it wishes to provide disabled children. The second is for Washington explicitly to decentralize special education, granting substantive authority to states, districts, and schools.

Either remedy, of course, would bring its own new problems. Full federal funding, for example, may encourage local overspending. Similarly, decentralization raises the likelihood that substantial variation will occur between states.

Yet these problems are likely to be less vexing than those we now face and apt to be more amenable to solution. The intergovernmental confusion would diminish. Those setting policy would be directly in charge of those delivering services. And a shift away from today's emphasis on rights and procedures will increase flexibility and foster innovations responsive to the distinctive needs of individual students, the judgments of expert educators, the preferences of parents, and the priorities of communities. This, we believe, would be good for children. And that, we believe, is the main point.

POSTSCRIPT

Will More Federal Oversight Result in Better Special Education?

A frequently heard comment is that IDEA is the "full employment for attorneys" act. Sometimes it feels that way. There is a long distance between the dream of helping all children learn and the reality of legal time deadlines, shifting interpretations, and confusing terminology.

In writing *Back to School on Civil Rights*, from which the NCD's selection was excerpted, the authors interviewed 14 parents from nine states, each of whom trusted that their children would receive an appropriate education in the least restrictive environment. Each shared the disillusionment and distrust that resulted from finding their rights sidestepped or ignored. The NCD found substantiation in their review of monitoring activities. Without increased federal attention to legal detail and requirements, the authors worry that schools will continue to avoid meeting the requirements of the laws. In the full report, the NCD expresses dismay that education reform efforts and budgetary cutbacks have siphoned away state funds that could have been used for compliance monitoring. They urge restoration of this money so that no more ground (or time) is lost.

In sharp contrast, Hess and Brigham assert that much ground has been too easily surrendered because districts fear costly litigation that might find them out of bureaucratic compliance with special education laws. The impact of individual challenges to school performance provides the protection that a global state audit could not—perhaps preventing educators from selecting effective practices that could benefit the whole school. Unfortunately, according to the authors, the confusing tangle of regulations often prevents schools from focusing on the more appropriate target of accountability for the progress of all children.

IDEA97 made a shift from compliance to accountability, requiring that all students have access to the general curriculum and can participate in the large scale testing that is part of education reform. Regretting a lost opportunity, Wolf and Hassel (Finn, Rotheram, & Hokanson, 2001) argue that this change has succeeded only in adding another layer of bureaucratic responsibilities while reducing none.

Providing the perspective of attorneys who have represented both parents and schools, Lanigan et al. (Fordham, 2001) see the situation this way:

> Special education staff members in the public schools devote their professional lives to educating children with disabilities, are truly dedicated to the endeavor, and genuinely want to provide appropriate special education and related services to the students they are charged with educating. Yet

school resources are not unlimited, budget pressures are real, and the IDEA allows districts to take program costs into account only so long as they still are meeting the FAPE requirement. This is the fundamental source of school district conflict with parents.

Parents (and other guardians) who devote their lives to raising children with disabilities genuinely want to make sure that their children receive at least appropriate special education and related services. In truth, however, what these parents really want—indeed what all parents want—is an education that will allow their children to maximize their potential. The IDEA does not require this. This is the fundamental source of parents' conflict with school officials.

Does monitoring of complex federal regulations waste time and resources that could be devoted to the education of children? Do these very regulations protect the rights of children with disabilities to an equitable education? Can two well-meaning people interpret the law in two different ways yet both care deeply about the children they share? If so, how can they resolve their differences? How do your local educators view the controversy? What do they do now because of oversight? What would they do better if there were closer scrutiny? What would they do if no one checked to see if they were complying—would students with disabilities benefit from creative new programs, or would options be foreclosed because no one was watching?

ISSUE 8

Should One-on-One Nursing Care Be Part of Special Education?

YES: John Paul Stevens, from Majority Opinion, *Cedar Rapids Community School District v. Garret F.,* U.S. Supreme Court (March 3, 1999)

NO: Clarence Thomas, from Dissenting Opinion, *Cedar Rapids Community School District v. Garret F.,* U.S. Supreme Court (March 3, 1999)

ISSUE SUMMARY

YES: U.S. Supreme Court justice John Paul Stevens, writing for the majority of the Court, affirms the "bright line test," establishing that school districts are required by IDEA to provide one-on-one nursing services and any other health-related services that can be delivered by individuals other than a licensed physician.

NO: U.S. Supreme Court justice Clarence Thomas, representing the dissenting minority opinion, asserts that continuous one-on-one nursing services for disabled children are indeed medical and, as such, beyond the scope of congressional intent in IDEA. He concludes that such services are not the responsibility of special education programs within school districts.

Recognizing that some children need more than traditional educational services, IDEA directs schools to provide "related services" necessary to enable a child with a disability to access the special education program designed by the school team (IDEA, Section 300.24). Like the program, these must be provided at no cost. Related services include speech, occupational and physical therapy, and transportation. School health services and "medical services for diagnostic or evaluation purposes" are also mentioned in IDEA, though not medical procedures or treatment.

Court cases about related services began almost as soon as IDEA was passed. The first to reach the Supreme Court questioned whether a sign language interpreter was a required related service for a child with a hearing impairment (*Board of Education v. Rowley,* 1982). The Court determined that this service was not required because it felt that the child was making effective school progress with the operative special education program.

Concurrent with *Rowley*, the first medically related cases were moving through the courts. The landmark case was *Irving Independent School District v. Tatro* (1984), in which the Supreme Court required school personnel to perform clean intermittent catheterization, a procedure used to empty a child's bladder, so that she could remain in school and benefit from special education services. Although the school district felt that this procedure crossed the line into medical services, the Supreme Court established its own "bright line": If a procedure could be performed by a trained, supervised individual, it fell within the realm of the school's responsibilities. The Court acknowledged, however, that there are likely some medically related services that are too financially burdensome or complicated to be included.

Following *Tatro*, court decisions split into two lines of reasoning. Initially, lower courts adopted the "burden" and "complexity" elements of the decision, finding some medical services (tracheostomy care and cardiopulmonary resuscitation, for example) to be beyond the professional and financial responsibility of schools. About 10 years later, courts emphasized the "bright line" standard, finding that cost and complexity should not pose a barrier to access to education.

The issue crystallized with Garret Frey, a high school student who had been paralyzed since childhood. Academically successful in school, Garret required continuous medical support in order to attend. Having exhausted available personal funds, and believing that the services were well within the capacity of trained staff, Garret's parents turned to the school district. However, the district believed that the bright line standard should be overridden in this case by overall consideration of cost, complexity, time, and amount of services required, as well as liability for improper services.

In *Cedar Rapids Community School District v. Garret F.*, the Supreme Court voted 7-2 in favor of the bright line standard. The majority and dissenting opinions are reprinted in the following selections. Writing for the majority, Justice John Paul Stevens finds the continuous nursing services required by Garret to be well within the confines of school health services, noting that current federal law does not permit districts to consider the total cost or complexity of medically related assistance.

Justice Clarence Thomas, writing for the dissenting minority, holds that the services required by Garret—indeed, those discussed in *Tatro*—are medical and clearly outside the boundaries of school responsibility as written in IDEA. The minority opinion identifies financial and professional limits to the extent of a school's responsibility as well.

As you read these Supreme Court opinions, ask yourself these questions: What is the difference between medicine and education? Should there be a limit to a school's responsibilities to provide access? Where do you draw the line?

John Paul Stevens

 **YES**

Majority Opinion

Cedar Rapids Community School District *v.* Garret F.

Justice Stevens delivered the opinion of the Court.

The Individuals with Disabilities Education Act (IDEA), 84 Stat. 175, as amended, was enacted, in part, "to assure that all children with disabilities have available to them ... a free appropriate public education which emphasizes special education and related services designed to meet their unique needs." 20 U.S.C. § 1400(c). Consistent with this purpose, the IDEA authorizes federal financial assistance to States that agree to provide disabled children with special education and "related services." See §§1401(a)(18), 1412(1). The question presented in this case is whether the definition of "related services" in §1401(a)(17)[1] requires a public school district in a participating State to provide a ventilator-dependent student with certain nursing services during school hours.

I

Respondent Garret F. is a friendly, creative, and intelligent young man. When Garret was four years old, his spinal column was severed in a motorcycle accident. Though paralyzed from the neck down, his mental capacities were unaffected. He is able to speak, to control his motorized wheelchair through use of a puff and suck straw, and to operate a computer with a device that responds to head movements. Garret is currently a student in the Cedar Rapids Community School District (District), he attends regular classes in a typical school program, and his academic performance has been a success. Garret is, however, ventilator dependent,[2] and therefore requires a responsible individual nearby to attend to certain physical needs while he is in school.[3]

During Garret's early years at school his family provided for his physical care during the school day. When he was in kindergarten, his 18-year-old aunt attended him; in the next four years, his family used settlement proceeds they received after the accident, their insurance, and other resources to employ a licensed practical nurse. In 1993, Garret's mother requested the District to accept financial responsibility for the health care services that Garret requires during the school day. The District denied the request, believing that it was not legally obligated to provide continuous one-on-one nursing services.

From *Cedar Rapids Community School District v. Garret F.*, 119 S. Ct. 992 (1999).

Relying on both the IDEA and Iowa law, Garret's mother requested a hearing before the Iowa Department of Education. An Administrative Law Judge (ALJ) received extensive evidence concerning Garret's special needs, the District's treatment of other disabled students, and the assistance provided to other ventilator-dependent children in other parts of the country. In his 47-page report, the ALJ found that the District has about 17,500 students, of whom approximately 2,200 need some form of special education or special services. Although Garret is the only ventilator-dependent student in the District, most of the health care services that he needs are already provided for some other students.[4] "The primary difference between Garret's situation and that of other students is his dependency on his ventilator for life support." App. to Pet. For Cert. 28a. The ALJ noted that the parties disagreed over the training or licensure required for the care and supervision of such students, and that those providing such care in other parts of the country ranged from nonlicensed personnel to registered nurses. However, the District did not contend that only a licensed physician could provide the services in question.

The ALJ explained that federal law requires that children with a variety of health impairments be provided with "special education and related services" when their disabilities adversely affect their academic performance, and that such children should be educated to the maximum extent appropriate with children who are not disabled. In addition, the ALJ explained that applicable federal regulations distinguish between "school health services," which are provided by a "qualified school nurse or other qualified person," and "medical services," which are provided by a licensed physician. See 34 CFR §§300.16(a), (b)(4), (b)(11) (1998). The District must provide the former, but need not provide the latter (except, of course, those "medical services" that are for diagnostic or evaluation purposes, §1401(a)(17)). According to the ALJ, the distinction in the regulations does not just depend on "the title of the person providing the service"; instead, the "medical services" exclusion is limited to services that are "in the special training, knowledge, and judgment of a physician to carry out." App. to Pet. for Cert. 51a. The ALJ thus concluded that the IDEA required the District to bear financial responsibility for all of the services in dispute, including continuous nursing services.[5]

The District challenged the ALJ's decision in Federal District Court, but that Court approved the ALJ's IDEA ruling and granted summary judgment against the District. Id., at 9a, 15a. The Court of Appeals affirmed. 106 F.3d 822 (CA8 1997). It noted that, as a recipient of federal funds under the IDEA, Iowa has a statutory duty to provide all disabled children a "free appropriate public education," which includes "related services." See id., at 824. The Court of Appeals read our opinion in Irving Independent School Dist. v. Tatro, 468 U.S. 883 (1984), to provide a two-step analysis of the "related services" definition in §1401(a)(17)—asking first, whether the requested services are included within the phrase "supportive services"; and second, whether the services are excluded as "medical services." 106 F.3d, at 824–825. The Court of Appeals succinctly answered both questions in Garret's favor. The Court found the first step plainly satisfied, since Garret cannot attend school unless the requested services are available during the school day. Id., at 825. As to the second step, the Court reasoned that *Tatro* "established a bright-line test: the services of a physician (other than for diagnostic and evaluation purposes) are subject to the medical services exclusion, but services that can be provided in the school setting by a nurse or qualified layperson are not." *Ibid.*

In its petition for certiorari, the District challenged only the second step of the Court of Appeals' analysis. The District pointed out that some federal courts have not asked whether the requested health services must be delivered by a physician, but instead have applied a multi-factor test that considers, generally speaking, the nature and extent of the services at issue. See, *e.g., Neely* v. *Rutherford County School,* 68 F.3d 965, 972–973 (CA6 1995), cert. denied, 517 U.S. 1134 (1996); *Detsel* v. *Board of Ed. of Auburn Enlarged City School Dist.,* 820 F.2d 587, 588 (CA2) (*per curiam*), cert. denied, 484 U.S. 981 (1987). We granted the District's petition to resolve this conflict. 523 U.S. (1998).

II

The District contends that §1401(a)(17) does not require it to provide Garret with "continuous one-on-one nursing services" during the school day, even though Garret cannot remain in school without such care. Brief for Petitioner 10. However, the IDEA's definition of "related services," our decision in *Irving Independent School Dist.* v. *Tatro,* 468 U.S. 883 (1984), and the overall statutory scheme all support the decision of the Court of Appeals.

The text of the "related services" definition, see n. 1, *supra,* broadly encompasses those supportive services that "may be required to assist a child with a disability to benefit from special education." As we have already noted, the District does not challenge the Court of Appeals' conclusion that the in-school services at issue are within the covered category of "supportive services." As a general matter, services that enable a disabled child to remain in school during the day provide the student with "the meaningful access to education that Congress envisioned." *Tatro,* 468 U.S., at 891 ("'Congress sought primarily to make public education available to handicapped children' and 'to make such access meaningful'" (quoting *Board of Ed. of Hendrick Hudson Central School Dist., Westchester Cty.* v. *Rowley,* 458 U.S. 176, 192 (1982)).

This general definition of "related services" is illuminated by a parenthetical phrase listing examples of particular services that are included within the statute's coverage. §1401(a)(17). "Medical services" are enumerated in this list, but such services are limited to those that are "for diagnostic and evaluation purposes." *Ibid.* The statute does not contain a more specific definition of the "medical services" that are excepted from the coverage of §1401(a)(17).

The scope of the "medical services" exclusion is not a matter of first impression in this Court. In *Tatro* we concluded that the Secretary of Education had reasonably determined that the term "medical services" referred only to services that must be performed by a physician, and not to school health services. 468 U.S., at 892–894. Accordingly, we held that a specific form of health care (clean intermittent catheterization) that is often, though not always, performed by a nurse is not an excluded medical service. We referenced the likely cost of the services and the competence of school staff as justifications for drawing a line between physician and other services, *ibid.*, but our endorsement of that line was unmistakable.[6] It is thus settled that the phrase "medical services" in §1401(a)(17) does not embrace all forms of care that might loosely be described as "medical" in other contexts, such as a claim for an income tax deduction. See 26 U.S.C. § 213(d)(1) (1994 ed. and Supp. II) (defining "medical care").

The District does not ask us to define the term so broadly. Indeed, the District does not argue that any of the items of care that Garret needs, considered individually, could be excluded from the scope of §1401(a)(17).[7] It could not make such an argument, considering that one of the services Garret needs (catheterization) was at issue in *Tatro*, and the others may be provided competently by a school nurse or other trained personnel. See App. to Pet. for Cert. 15a, 52a. As the ALJ concluded, most of the requested services are already provided by the District to other students, and the in-school care necessitated by Garret's ventilator dependency does not demand the training, knowledge, and judgment of a licensed physician. *Id.*, at 51a–52a. While more extensive, the in-school services Garret needs are no more "medical" than was the care sought in *Tatro*.

Instead, the District points to the combined and continuous character of the required care, and proposes a test under which the outcome in any particular case would "depend upon a series of factors, such as [1] whether the care is continuous or intermittent, [2] whether existing school health personnel can provide the service, [3] the cost of the service, and [4] the potential consequences if the service is not properly performed." Brief for Petitioner 11; see also *id.*, at 34–35.

The District's multi-factor test is not supported by any recognized source of legal authority. The proposed factors can be found in neither the text of the statute nor the regulations that we upheld in *Tatro*. Moreover, the District offers no explanation why these characteristics make one service any more "medical" than another. The continuous character of certain services associated with Garret's ventilator dependency has no apparent relationship to "medical" services, much less a relationship of equivalence. Continuous services may be more costly and may require additional school personnel, but they are not thereby more "medical." Whatever its imperfections, a rule that limits the medical services exemption to physician services is unquestionably a reasonable and generally workable interpretation of the statute. Absent an elaboration of the statutory terms plainly more convincing than that which we reviewed in *Tatro*, there is no good reason to depart from settled law.[8]

Finally, the District raises broader concerns about the financial burden that it must bear to provide the services that Garret needs to stay in school. The problem for the District in providing these services is not that its staff cannot be trained to deliver them; the problem, the District contends, is that the existing school health staff cannot meet all of their responsibilities and provide for Garret at the same time.[9] Through its multi-factor test, the District seeks to establish a kind of undue-burden exemption primarily based on the cost of the requested services. The first two factors can be seen as examples of cost-based distinctions: intermittent care is often less expensive than continuous care, and the use of existing personnel is cheaper than hiring additional employees. The third factor—the cost of the service—would then encompass the first two. The relevance of the fourth factor is likewise related to cost because extra care may be necessary if potential consequences are especially serious.

The District may have legitimate financial concerns, but our role in this dispute is to interpret existing law. Defining "related services" in a manner that *accommodates* the cost concerns Congress may have had, cf. *Tatro*, 468 U.S., at 892, is altogether different from using cost *itself* as the definition. Given that §1401(a)(17) does not employ cost in its definition of "related services" or excluded "medical services," accepting the District's cost-based standard as the sole test for determining the scope of the provision would require us to engage in judicial lawmaking without any guidance from Congress. It would also create some tension with the purposes of the IDEA. The statute may not require public schools to maximize the potential of disabled students commensurate with the opportunities provided to other children, see *Rowley*, 458 U.S., at 200; and the potential financial burdens imposed on participating States may be relevant to arriving at a sensible construction of the IDEA, see *Tatro*, 468 U.S., at 892. But Congress intended "to open the door of public education" to all qualified children and "require[d] participating States to educate handicapped children with nonhandicapped children whenever possible." *Rowley*, 458 U.S., at 192, 202; see *id.*, at 179–181; see also *Honig* v. *Doe*, 484 U.S. 305, 310–311, 324 (1988); §§1412(1), (2)(C), (5)(B).[10]

This case is about whether meaningful access to the public schools will be assured, not the level of education that a school must finance once access is attained. It is undisputed that the services at issue must be provided if Garret is to remain in school. Under the statute, our precedent, and the purposes of the IDEA, the District must fund such "related services" in order to help guarantee that students like Garret are integrated into the public schools.

The judgment of the Court of Appeals is accordingly

Affirmed.

Notes

4. "The term 'related services' means transportation, and such developmental, corrective, and other supportive services (including speech pathology and audiology, psychological services, physical and occupational therapy, recreation, including therapeutic recreation, social work services, counseling services, including rehabilitation counseling, and medical services, except that such medical services shall be for diagnostic and evaluation purposes only) as may be required to assist a child with a disability to benefit from special education, and includes the early identification and assessment of disabling conditions in children." 20 U.S.C. §1401(a)(17). Originally, the statute was enacted without a definition of "related services." See Education of the Handicapped Act, 84 Stat. 175. In 1975, Congress added the

definition at issue in this case. Education for All Handicapped Children Act of 1975, §4(a)(4), 89 Stat. 775. Aside from nonsubstantive changes and added examples of included services, see, e.g., Individuals with Disabilities Education Act Amendments of 1997, §101, 111 Stat. 45; Individuals with Disabilities Education Act Amendments of 1991, §25(a)(1)(B), 105 Stat. 605; Education of the Handicapped Act Amendments of 1990, §101(c), 104 Stat. 1103, the relevant language in §1401(a)(17) has not been amended since 1975. All references to the IDEA herein are to the 1994 version as codified in Title 20 of the United States Code—the version of the statute in effect when this dispute arose.

5. In his report in this case, the Administrative Law Judge explained that "[b]eing ventilator dependent means that [Garret] breathes only with external aids, usually an electric ventilator, and occasionally by someone else's manual pumping of an air bag attached to his tracheotomy tube when the ventilator is being maintained. This later procedure is called ambu bagging." App. to Pet. for Cert. 19a.

6. "He needs assistance with urinary bladder catheterization once a day, the suctioning of his tracheotomy tube as needed, but at least once every six hours, with food and drink at lunchtime, in getting into a reclining position for five minutes of each hour, and ambu bagging occasionally as needed when the ventilator is checked for proper functioning. He also needs assistance from someone familiar with his ventilator in the event there is a malfunction or electrical problem, and someone who can perform emergency procedures in the event he experiences autonomic hyperreflexia. Autonomic hyperreflexia is an uncontrolled visceral reaction to anxiety or a full bladder. Blood pressure increases, heart rate increases, and flushing and sweating may occur. Garret has not experienced autonomic hyperreflexia frequently in recent years, and it has usually been alleviated by catheterization. He has not ever experienced autonomic hyperreflexia at school. Garret is capable of communicating his needs orally or in another fashion so long as he has not been rendered unable to do so by an extended lack of oxygen." Id., at 20a.

7. "Included are such services as care for students who need urinary catheterization, food and drink, oxygen supplement positioning, and suctioning." Id., at 28a; see also id., at 53a.

8. In addition, the ALJ's opinion contains a thorough discussion of "other tests and criteria" pressed by the District, id., at 52a, including the burden on the District and the cost of providing assistance to Garret. Although the ALJ found no legal authority for establishing a cost-based test for determining what related services are required by the statute, he went on to reject the District's arguments on the merits. See id., at 42a-53a. We do not reach the issue here, but the ALJ also found that Garret's in-school needs must be met by the District under an Iowa statute as well as the IDEA. Id., at 54a-55a.

9. "The regulations define 'related services' for handicapped children to include 'school health services,' 34 CFR § 300.13(a) (1983), which are defined in turn as 'services provided by a qualified school nurse or other qualified person,' §300.13(b)(10). 'Medical services' are defined as 'services provided by a licensed physician,'

§300.13(b)(4). Thus, the Secretary has [reasonably] determined that the services of a school nurse otherwise qualifying as a 'related service' are not subject to exclusion as a 'medical service,' but that the services of a physician are excludable as such.

... *"By limiting the 'medical services' exclusion to the services of a physician or hospital,* both far more expensive, the Secretary has given a permissible construction to the provision." 468 U.S., at 892–893 (emphasis added) (footnote omitted); see also *id.,* at 894 ("[T]he regulations state that school nursing services must be provided only if they can be performed by a nurse or other qualified person, not if they must be performed by a physician").

Based on certain policy letters issued by the Department of Education, it seems that the Secretary's post-*Tatro* view of the statute has not been entirely clear. *E.g.,* App. to Pet. for Cert. 64a. We may assume that the Secretary has authority under the IDEA to adopt regulations that define the "medical services" exclusion by more explicitly taking into account the nature and extent of the requested services; and the Secretary surely has the authority to enumerate the services that are, and are not, fairly included within the scope of §1407(a)(17). But the Secretary has done neither; and, in this Court, she advocates affirming the judgment of the Court of Appeals. Brief for United States as *Amicus Curiae;* see also *Auer v. Robbins,* 519 U.S. 452, 462 (1997) (an agency's views as *amicus curiae* may be entitled to deference). We obviously have no authority to rewrite the regulations, and we see no sufficient reason to revise *Tatro,* either.

10. See Tr. of Oral Arg. 4–5, 12.
11. At oral argument, the District suggested that we first consider the nature of the requested service (either "medical" or not); then, if the service is "medical," apply the multi-factor test to determine whether the service is an excluded physician service or an included school nursing service under the Secretary of Education's regulations. See Tr. of Oral Arg. 7, 13–14. Not only does this approach provide no additional guidance for identifying "medical" services, it is also disconnected from both the statutory text and the regulations we upheld in *Irving Independent School Dist. v. Tatro* 468 U.S. 883 (1984). "Medical" services are generally *excluded* from the statute, and the regulations elaborate on that statutory term. No authority cited by the District requires an additional inquiry if the requested service is both "related" and non-"medical." Even if §1401(a)(17) demanded an additional step, the factors proposed by the District are hardly more useful in identifying "nursing" services than they are in identifying "medical" services; and the District cannot limit educational access simply by pointing to the limitations of existing staff. As we noted in *Tatro,* the IDEA requires schools to hire specially trained personnel to meet disabled student needs. *Id.,* at 893.
12. See Tr. of Oral Arg. 4–5, 13; Brief for Petitioner 6–7, 9. The District, however, will not necessarily need to hire an additional employee to meet Garret's needs. The District already employs a one-on-one teacher associate (TA) who assists Garret during the school day. See App. to Pet. for Cert. 26a–27a. At one time, Garret's TA was a licensed practical nurse (LPN). In light of the state Board of Nursing's recent

ruling that the District's registered nurses may decide to delegate Garret's care to an LPN, see Brief for United States as *Amicus Curiae* 9–10 (filed Apr. 22, 1998), the dissent's future-cost estimate is speculative. See App. to Pet. for Cert. 28a, 58a–60a (if the District could assign Garret's care to a TA who is also an LPN, there would be "a minimum of additional expense").

13. The dissent's approach, which seems to be even broader than the District's, is unconvincing. The dissent's rejection of our unanimous decision in *Tatro* comes 15 years too late, see *Patterson* v. *McLean Credit Union*, 491 U.S. 164, 172–173 (1989) (*stare decisis* has "special force" in statutory interpretation), and it offers nothing constructive in its place. Aside from rejecting a "provider-specific approach," the dissent cites unrelated statutes and offers a circular definition of "medical services." *Post,* at 3–4 ("'services' that are 'medical' in 'nature'"). Moreover, the dissent's approach apparently would exclude most ordinary school nursing services of the kind routinely provided to nondisabled children; that anomalous result is not easily attributable to congressional intent. See *Tatro,* 468 U.S., at 893. In a later discussion the dissent does offer a specific proposal: that we now interpret (or rewrite) the Secretary's regulations so that school districts need only provide disabled children with "health-related services that school nurses can perform as part of their normal duties." *Post,* at 7. The District does not dispute that its nurses "can perform" the requested services, so the dissent's objection is that District nurses would not be performing their "normal duties" if they met Garret's needs. That is, the District would need an "additional employee." *Post,* at 8. This proposal is functionally similar to a proposed regulation—ultimately withdrawn—that would have replaced the "school health services" provision. See 47 Fed. Reg. 33838, 33854 (1982) (the statute and regulations may not be read to affect legal obligations to make available to handicapped children services, including school health services, made available to nonhandicapped children). The dissent's suggestion is unacceptable for several reasons. Most important, such revisions of the regulations are better left to the Secretary, and an additional staffing need is generally not a sufficient objection to the requirements of §1401(a)(17). See n. 8, *supra.*

Dissenting Opinion of Clarence Thomas

Justice Thomas, with whom Justice Kennedy joins, dissenting.

The majority, relying heavily on our decision in *Irving Independent School Dist.* v. *Tatro*, 468 U.S. 883 (1984), concludes that the Individuals with Disabilities Education Act (IDEA), 20 U.S.C. § 1400 *et seq.*, requires a public school district to fund continuous, one-on-one nursing care for disabled children. Because *Tatro* cannot be squared with the text of IDEA, the Court should not adhere to it in this case. Even assuming that *Tatro* was correct in the first instance, the majority's extension of it is unwarranted and ignores the constitutionally mandated rules of construction applicable to legislation enacted pursuant to Congress' spending power.

I

As the majority recounts, *ante*, at 1, IDEA authorizes the provision of federal financial assistance to States that agree to provide, *inter alia*, "special education and related services" for disabled children. §1401(a)(18). In *Tatro, supra,* we held that this provision of IDEA required a school district to provide clean intermittent catheterization to a disabled child several times a day. In so holding, we relied on Department of Education regulations, which we concluded had reasonably interpreted IDEA's definition of "related services"[1] to require school districts in participating States to provide "school nursing services" (of which we assumed catheterization was a subcategory) but not "services of a physician." *Id.*, at 892–893. This holding is contrary to the plain text of IDEA and its reliance on the Department of Education's regulations was misplaced.

A

Before we consider whether deference to an agency regulation is appropriate, "we first ask whether Congress has 'directly spoken to the precise question at issue. If the intent of Congress is clear, that is the end of the matter; for the court, as well as the agency, must give effect to the unambiguously expressed intent of Congress.' " *National Credit Union Admin.* v. *First Nat. Bank & Trust Co.*, 522 U.S. 479, 499–500 (1998) (quoting *Chevron U.S.A. Inc.* v. *Natural Resources Defense Council, Inc.*, 467 U.S. 837, 842–843 (1984)).

From *Cedar Rapids Community School District v. Garret F.*, 119 S. Ct. 992 (1999).

Unfortunately, the Court in *Tatro* failed to consider this necessary antecedent question before turning to the Department of Education's regulations implementing IDEA's related services provision. The Court instead began "with the regulations of the Department of Education, which," it said, "are entitled to deference." *Tatro, supra*, at 891–892. The Court need not have looked beyond the text of IDEA, which expressly indicates that school districts are not required to provide medical services, except for diagnostic and evaluation purposes. 20 U.S.C. § 1401(a)(17). The majority asserts that *Tatro* precludes reading the term "medical services" to include "all forms of care that might loosely be described as 'medical.'" *Ante*, at 8. The majority does not explain, however, why "services" that are "medical" in nature are not "medical services." Not only is the definition that the majority rejects consistent with other uses of the term in federal law,[2] it also avoids the anomalous result of holding that the services at issue in *Tatro* (as well as in this case), while not "medical services," would nonetheless qualify as medical care for federal income tax purposes. *Ante*, at 8.

The primary problem with *Tatro*, and the majority's reliance on it today, is that the Court focused on the provider of the services rather than the services themselves. We do not typically think that automotive services are limited to those provided by a mechanic, for example. Rather, anything done to repair or service a car, no matter who does the work, is thought to fall into that category. Similarly, the term "food service" is not generally thought to be limited to work performed by a chef. The term "medical" similarly does not support *Tatro's* provider-specific approach, but encompasses services that are "of, *relating to, or concerned with* physicians *or* the practice of medicine." See Webster's Third New International Dictionary 1402 (1986) (emphasis added); see also *id.*, at 1551 (defining "nurse" as "a person skilled in caring for and waiting on the infirm, the injured, or the sick; *specif:* one esp. trained to carry out such duties under the supervision of a physician").

IDEA's structure and purpose reinforce this textual interpretation. Congress enacted IDEA to increase the *educational* opportunities available to disabled children, not to provide medical care for them. See 20 U.S.C. § 1400(c) ("It is the purpose of this chapter to assure that all children with disabilities have ... a free appropriate public education"); see also §1412 ("In order to qualify for assistance ... a State shall demonstrate ... [that it] has in effect a policy that assures all children with disabilities the right to a free appropriate public education"); *Board of Ed. of Hendrick Hudson Central School Dist., Westchester Cty.* v. *Rowley*, 458 U.S. 176, 179 (1982) ("The Act represents an ambitious federal effort to promote the education of handicapped children"). As such, where Congress decided to require a supportive service—including speech pathology, occupational therapy, and audiology—that appears "medical" in nature, it took care to do so explicitly. See §1401(a)(17). Congress specified these services precisely because it recognized that they would otherwise fall under the broad "medical services" exclusion. Indeed, when it crafted the definition of related services, Congress could have, but chose not to, include "nursing services" in this list.

B

Tatro was wrongly decided even if the phrase "medical services" was subject to multiple constructions, and therefore, deference to any reasonable Department of Education regulation was appropriate. The Department of Education has never promulgated regulations defining the scope of IDEA's "medical services" exclusion. One year before *Tatro* was decided, the Secretary of Education issued proposed regulations that defined excluded medical services as "services relating to the practice of medicine." 47 Fed. Reg. 33838 (1982). These regulations, which represent the Department's only attempt to define the disputed term, were never adopted. Instead, "[t]he regulations actually define only those 'medical services' that are owed to handicapped children," *Tatro*, 468 U.S., at 892, n. 10) (emphasis in original), not those that *are not*. Now, as when *Tatro* was decided, the regulations require districts to provide services performed " 'by a licensed physician to determine a child's medically related handicapping condition which results in the child's need for special education and related services.'" *Ibid.* (quoting 34 CFR § 300.13(b)(4) (1983), recodified and amended as 34 CFR § 300.16(b)(4) (1998).

Extrapolating from this regulation, the *Tatro* Court presumed that this meant "that 'medical services' not owed under the statute are those 'services by a licensed physician' that serve other purposes." *Tatro, supra,* at 892, n. 10 (emphasis deleted). The Court, therefore, did not defer to the regulation itself, but rather relied on an inference drawn from it to speculate about how a regulation might read if the Department of Education promulgated one. Deference in those circumstances is impermissible. We cannot defer to a regulation that does not exist.[3]

II

Assuming that *Tatro* was correctly decided in the first instance, it does not control the outcome of this case. Because IDEA was enacted pursuant to Congress' spending power, *Rowley, supra,* at 190, n. 11, our analysis of the statute in this case is governed by special rules of construction. We have repeatedly emphasized that, when Congress places conditions on the receipt of federal funds, "it must do so unambiguously." *Pennhurst State School and Hospital* v. *Halderman,* 451 U.S. 1, 17 (1981). See also *Rowley, supra,* at 190, n. 11; *South Dakota* v. *Dole,* 483 U.S. 203, 207 (1987); *New York* v. *United States,* 505 U.S. 144, 158 (1992). This is because a law that "condition[s] an offer of federal funding on a promise by the recipient ... amounts essentially to a contract between the Government and the recipient of funds." *Gebser* v. *Lago Vista Independent School Dist.,* 524 U.S. 274, 276 (1998). As such, "[t]he legitimacy of Congress' power to legislate under the spending power... rests on whether the State voluntarily and knowingly accepts the terms of the 'contract.' There can, of course, be no knowing acceptance if a State is unaware of the conditions or is unable to ascertain what is expected of it." *Pennhurst, supra,* at 17 (citations omitted). It follows that we must interpret Spending Clause legislation narrowly, in order to avoid saddling the States with obligations that they did not anticipate.

The majority's approach in this case turns this Spending Clause presumption on its head. We have held that, in enacting IDEA, Congress wished to require "States to educate handicapped children with nonhandicapped children whenever possible," *Rowley*, 458 U.S., at 202. Congress, however, also took steps to limit the fiscal burdens that States must bear in attempting to achieve this laudable goal. These steps include requiring States to provide an education that is only "appropriate" rather that requiring them to maximize the potential of disabled students, see 20 U.S.C. § 1400(c); *Rowley, supra,* at 200, recognizing that integration into the public school environment is not always possible, see §1412(5), and clarifying that, with a few exceptions, public schools need not provide "medical services" for disabled students, §§1401(a)(17) and (18).

For this reason, we have previously recognized that Congress did not intend to "impos[e] upon the States a burden of unspecified proportions and weight" in enacting IDEA. *Rowley, supra,* at 176, n. 11. These federalism concerns require us to interpret IDEA's related services provision, consistent with *Tatro,* as follows: Department of Education regulations require districts to provide disabled children with health-related services that school nurses can perform as part of their normal duties. This reading of *Tatro,* although less broad than the majority's, is equally plausible and certainly more consistent with our obligation to interpret Spending Clause legislation narrowly. Before concluding that the district was required to provide clean intermittent catheterization for Amber Tatro, we observed that school nurses in the district were authorized to perform services that were "difficult to distinguish from the provision of [clean intermittent catheterization] to the handicapped." *Tatro,* 468 U.S., at 893. We concluded that "[i]t would be strange indeed if Congress, in attempting to extend special services to handicapped children, were unwilling to guarantee them services of a kind that are routinely provided to the nonhandicapped." *Id.,* at 893–894.

Unlike clean intermittent catheterization, however, a school nurse cannot provide the services that respondent requires, see *ante,* at 3, n. 3, and continue to perform her normal duties. To the contrary, because respondent requires continuous, one-on-one care throughout the entire school day, all agree that the district must hire an additional employee to attend solely to respondent. This will cost a minimum of $18,000 per year. Although the majority recognizes this fact, it nonetheless concludes that the "more extensive" nature of the services that respondent needs is irrelevant to the question whether those services fall under the medical services exclusion. *Ante,* at 9. This approach disregards the constitutionally mandated principles of construction applicable to Spending Clause legislation and blindsides unwary States with fiscal obligations that they could not have anticipated.

⋅⦿⋅

For the foregoing reasons, I respectfully dissent.

Notes

14. The Act currently defines "related services" as "transportation and such developmental, corrective, and other supportive services (including speech pathology and audiology, psychological services, physical and occupational therapy, recreation, including therapeutic recreation, social work services, counseling services, including rehabilitation counseling, and medical services, *except that such medical services shall be for diagnostic and evaluation purposes only*) as may be required to assist a child with a disability to benefit from special education...." 20 U.S.C. § 1401(a)(17) (emphasis added).

15. See, *e.g.*, 38 U.S.C. § 1701(6) ("The term 'medical services' includes, in addition to medical examination, treatment and rehabilitative services ... surgical services, dental services, ... optometric and podiatric services, ... preventive health services, ... [and] such consultation, professional counseling, training, and mental health services as are necessary in connection with the treatment"); §101(28) ("The term 'nursing home care' means the accommodation of convalescents ... who require nursing care and related medical services"); 26 U.S.C. § 213(d)(1) ("The term 'medical care' means amounts paid—... for the diagnosis, cure, mitigation, treatment, or prevention of disease").

16. Nor do I think that it is appropriate to defer to the Department of Education's litigating position in this case. The agency has had ample opportunity to address this problem but has failed to do so in a formal regulation. Instead, it has maintained conflicting positions about whether the services at issue in this case are required by IDEA. See *ante*, at 7–8, n. 6. Under these circumstances, we should not assume that the litigating position reflects the "agency's fair and considered judgment." *Auer* v. *Robbins*, 519 U.S. 452, 462 (1997).

POSTSCRIPT

Should One-on-One Nursing Care Be Part of Special Education?

As with most complex legislation, the implementation of IDEA has been defined through court decisions. Garret's case—and others like it—highlight the complexity involved in designing education that includes all learners. All members of the Supreme Court agreed that Garret's services were costly and complicated. The majority found that these factors do not matter, almost requesting a renovation of IDEA to be more specific about limits in this area. In short, while it did not seem very happy about the decision, the majority felt that it was the only choice under the current law. The bright line may not be the best line, but it is clear and easy to apply. Now it is clear that schools have no choice.

The minority contends that *Garret* and *Tatro* have crossed a boundary that was very clear in IDEA. Schools cannot fulfill their educational mission when their energies are focused on medical care. If Congress had meant to include daily medical attention, it would have said so. IDEA limits medical services to diagnosis and evaluation, argues the minority. Continuous care does not fall within that limit.

Despite the clear connections to health-related conditions, parental medical insurance is not a resource for schools. Because families of children with significant disabilities can easily exceed lifetime limits on coverage or be placed in financial risk categories with costly premiums, courts have upheld exclusionary clauses that prohibit insurance coverage for services or equipment that the insured is entitled to under IDEA (Katsiyannis and Yell, *Exceptional Children*, 2000).

As more children come to school in a fragile condition—and as the procedures to support them become more complex—district personnel must be prepared to deliver emergency care, sometimes in life-threatening situations. The consequences of not reacting fast enough or with sufficient wisdom and skill raise fears of liability among educators. To date, this issue has not been tried in the courts, which have determined that concerns about consequences should not prohibit implementation of accommodations and services by individuals who have been adequately trained.

As medical science continues to advance, will schools soon be required to provide even more extensive and expensive medical services? Is this what IDEA meant? Should the federal law be rewritten to refocus human and financial resources on education and to delegate medical responsibilities to other agencies? Can the line be drawn more clearly in a different location, or will any change simply spawn more debate? Should there be any line at all?

Center for Law and Education

This Web site is operated by the Center for Law and Education, which is based in Washington, D.C., and Boston, Massachusetts. It is a source for information about legal access issues for students with disabilities, with a special focus on those who have the added challenge of low income. This site has numerous links to current legal issues, upcoming changes in regulation, and hot issues such as curriculum access, discipline, and testing.

http://www.cleweb.org

Institute on Disability/UAP

This site details the actions of the Institute on Disability/University Affiliated Program, located at the University of New Hampshire in Durham, New Hampshire. The institute has a wide scope of activities designed to promote active and effective inclusion of individuals with disabilities in school and work settings.

http://www.iod.unh.edu

National Association of the Deaf

The National Association of the Deaf (NAD) is a nonprofit organization dedicated to advocacy for Individuals who are deaf or hard of hearing. This site provides extensive information and links regarding the array of issues pertinent to those who are Deaf and those who are deaf/hard of hearing.

http://nad.org

Circle of Inclusion

This Web site, funded by the U.S. Office of Special Education Programs, is targeted to providing information and resources about the effective practices of inclusive educational programs for children from birth through age eight. Links to additional resources and videoclips can be found on the home page.

http://www.circleofinclusion.org

National Resource Center for Paraprofessionals in Education and Related Services

The National Resource Center for Paraprofessionals addresses questions of policy and practice regarding the work done by paraprofessionals. Bibliography entries on paraprofessionals, articles, and research updates enhance knowledge about this growing group of educators.

http://www.nrcpara.org

PART 2

Inclusion

*A*fter talking with educators, parents and aspiring teachers for years, I am convinced that the definition of inclusion is infinitely variable. It is a term so widely used that some may think it synonymous with special education. The practice of balancing a Free Appropriate Education (FAPE) and the Least Restrictive Environment (LRE) is delicate. Inclusive programming is not easily accomplished, and inclusionary programs are not strategies for saving money. Like all good education, inclusion requires careful attention to individuals. Awareness of the dimensions of the debate keeps everyone's eyes on the best interest of each child.

- Does Inclusion Work?
- Does Full Inclusion Deliver a Good Education?
- Are Residential Schools the Least Restrictive Environment for Deaf Children?
- Should Students with Disabilities Be Exempt from Standards-Based Curriculum?
- Are the Least-Trained Teaching Our Most Needy Children?

ISSUE 9

Does Inclusion Work?

YES: Dorothy Kerzner Lipsky and Alan Gartner, from "Taking Inclusion Into the Future," *Educational Leadership* (October 1998)

NO: Daniel P. Hallahan, from "We Need More Intensive Instruction," *LD Online,* http://www.ldonline.org/first_person/hallahan.html (June 30, 2001)

ISSUE SUMMARY

YES: Dorothy Kerzner Lipsky, director of the National Center on Educational Restructuring and Inclusion at the City University of New York, and professor of educational psychology Alan Gartner emphasize that IDEA97 supports inclusion as the best way to educate students with disabilities and discuss the ingredients that contribute to successful inclusionary practices.

NO: Daniel P. Hallahan, a professor of education at the University of Virginia in Charlottesville, fears that students with disabilities will lose access to necessary, specially designed instruction in the inclusionary rush to return them to the very classrooms in which they experienced failure.

In 1986 Madeline Will, then-assistant secretary of education, launched the Regular Education Initiative (*Exceptional Children,* 1986). While acknowledging that the first 10 years of mandated special education had provided opportunities for many children, Will decried the separate nature of special education. She challenged general education administrators to take responsibility for the education of students with mild to moderate disabilities and to accept "the general applicability of special education techniques beyond the confines of the special education class." In words that could have been spoken last week, Will predicted that less-segregated programming would "prepare all children to identify, analyze and resolve problems as they arise; to increase their ability to cope in a flexible manner with change ... and to enter the community as informed and educated citizens who are capable of living and working as independent and productive adults."

Information from the *Annual Reports to Congress* indicates that the percentage of children with disabilities increased consistently and substantially from 1988 to 1995, especially students identified as having learning disabilities, health or orthopedic impairments, or communications disorders. In general, these students are considered to have mild disabilities, and the services and supports that they need are not viewed as intense.

The impact of these disabilities is deceptive, however. Although children with mild disabilities might look, think, and behave more like their nondisabled peers than students with severe disabilities, they encounter significant challenges mastering the basic building blocks of reading, writing, and math. Educators and researchers labor mightily to identify specialized teaching methods to overcome the hurdles posed by nimble minds that are stymied by tasks that others learn easily.

As special education developed, many children with mild disabilities received their specially designed instruction in small self-contained rooms, with little connection to their age-mates. Alternatively, some children would be enrolled in typical classes but "pulled out" of class to receive help from a specialist. School days focused on intensive instruction and remediation. The goal was to help students conquer the basic skills so that they could return to their "regular" classes. While this remediation occurred, students often missed the curriculum and activities of the general classroom. Two separate educational systems existed; Will proposed that they merge, sharing responsibility for the education of all children.

In the following selection, Dorothy Kerzner Lipsky and Alan Gartner support that merger and review the elements of IDEA97 that will propel schools to make the structural changes necessary to create inclusive environments. The authors assert that combining the classroom teacher's curriculum knowledge with the special educator's ability to individualize instruction increases options for all children. Such collaboration will eliminate the need to make a choice between remediation and curriculum.

In the second selection, Daniel P. Hallahan contends that inclusion represents a step backward in time—one that ignores research findings about the effectiveness of specially designed instruction. Instead of combining expertise to create a whole larger than the sum of the parts, Hallahan fears that inclusionary collaboration dilutes the effectiveness of both educational environments, helping no one and widening the educational gap between children with mild disabilities and their grade-level peers.

As you read these selections, ask yourself whether inclusionary programs for students with mild disabilities are doorways to expanded learning or barriers preventing access to critical remediation.

**Dorothy Kerzner Lipsky
and Alan Gartner**

 **YES**

Taking Inclusion Into the Future

To improve education for children with disabilities, we cannot address special education by itself. Rather, we must look toward educational restructuring—changing the nature and practice of education in general, not just education called "special." The reauthorized Individuals with Disabilities Education Act (IDEA) reflects these needs and propels them further.

Until 1975, with the passage of the Education of All Handicapped Children Act, children with disabilities were not ensured what was a right of their nondisabled siblings and peers, the right to attend public schools. The 1975 law granted a "free appropriate public education" to all children, regardless of the nature or severity of their handicap. In the two decades since then, the U.S. public education system has provided students with that access, an achievement unparalleled anywhere in the world. As such, it both marks what schools can do and provides a basis for what still needs to be done—educational outcomes of high quality for all students.

Special Education, Both Separate and Unequal

Too often in the past, providing access meant that students with disabilities were served in separate special education classes and programs—despite the 1975 law's "least restrictive environment" (LRE) mandate. This mandate required that students with disabilities be educated to the maximum extent with children who were not disabled, and that students with disabilities be removed from regular classes only when they could not be educated in a regular setting with supplementary aids and support services. After more than two decades, the most recent data from the U.S. Department of Education reports that 55 percent of children with disabilities, ages 6 through 21, are not fully included in regular classes. This, despite the fact that more than 71 percent of the five million students with disabilities, ages 6 through 21, served through IDEA in the 1995–96 school year had the least severe impairments—learning disabilities (51 percent) and speech or language impairments (20 percent) (*U.S. Department of Education*, 1997, Tables II-6).

Throughout the 1980s and into the current decade, the experience of students with disabilities, their parents, and their teachers is that a dual system of education fails all students, primarily those with disabilities, in terms

From *Educational Leadership*, October 1998, pp. 78-81. Copyright © 1998 by Association for Supervision and Curriculum Development. Reprinted by permission. The Association for Supervision & Curriculum Development is an international education association for educators at all levels and of all subject matter, dedicated to the success of all learners. To learn more, visit ACCD at www.ascd.org

of student learning, drop-out rates, graduation rates, participation in postsecondary education and training, and community living (see Lipsky & Gartner, 1997). The most recent federal study reports that the graduation rate for students with disabilities was 57 percent, as compared with 76 percent for students without disabilities. (*U.S. Department of Education*, 1997, p. IV-11).

Longitudinal studies and research findings confirmed the experience of students, parents, and teachers that the separate system was flawed and unequal; this led to many championing a new inclusive design. This model holds to several principles: students are more alike than different; with effective educational practices, schools can educate well and together a wide range of students with better outcomes for all; and separation is costly, a civil rights violation, and a cause for limited outcomes for students with disabilities.

IDEA 1997

Similar beliefs motivated the administration and Congress to reauthorize the federal law. Culminating a two-year process, the reauthorized IDEA emphasizes two major principles: The education of students with disabilities should produce outcomes akin to those expected for students in general, and students with disabilities should be educated with their nondisabled peers. These features are expressed in the law's "findings" section, its implementation provisions, and the funding provisions as they concern inclusive education. Although the reauthorization does not mention "inclusive education" (nor had previous laws), one might think of IDEA 1997 as the Inclusion Development and Expansion Act.

Findings: Congress asserted that the education of students with disabilities would be more effective by "having high expectations for students and ensuring their success in the general curriculum...."; "[ensuring] that special education can become a service for such children rather than a place where they are sent."; and "providing incentives for the whole-school approaches...." The House and Senate Committee reports that accompany the law highlight the primary purpose of the new Act: to go beyond access to the schools and to secure for every child an education that actually yields successful educational results.

Implementation: Two sets of requirements will have direct consequences for students: student evaluation requirements and instruction and assessment requirements. In determining a student's classification and special needs, schools must consider whether factors other than disability will affect the student's performance. Specifically, the law states that a student may not be identified as disabled if the determining factor is inadequacy of instruction in reading or math. In other words, if the failure lies in the school's services, then the remedy is not labeling the student but fixing the school's program.

IDEA consistently reinforces the expectation that a student with a disability will be educated in the general education environment. For example, if a student is or may be participating in the general education program, the individual education program (IEP) team must include a general education teacher. If the child is currently in a general education classroom, the classroom teacher is to be a member of the IEP team. This brings to the IEP process someone familiar with the general education curriculum, which will be the basis of the student's program. And since the IEP meeting is supposed to be a decision-making event in which parents also participate, a school might be vulnerable to a legal challenge if it fails to include a general education teacher.

Further, should the school system propose that a child with a disability not participate with nondisabled students in academic, extracurricular, or nonacademic activities, it must justify such nonparticipation. In other words, supplemental aids and support services in the general education environment and in the curriculum should be considered the norm; schools must justify and explain exclusion in any of these areas. Only then may they consider other placements.

Schools must develop performance goals drawn from general classroom students for all students with disabilities. They then must develop performance indicators to assess achievement of these goals, with necessary adaptations and modifications. The school's and district's public reports must incorporate the results of performance. This is a requirement for all schools and covers all students.

Funding: States must change their funding formulas for supporting local school districts by removing incentives for placing students in more (rather than less) restrictive environments. This will require changes in all but a handful of states. Additionally, the previous provision that IDEA funds may not be used to benefit nondisabled students has been rescinded. Further, given that general education teachers will have a major role in providing services to students with disabilities, IDEA personnel-preparation funds may be used to train them. Indeed, in language accompanying the appropriations bills, Congress has emphasized that the substantial new funds must be used for such activities.

Implementing Inclusive Education Programs

In the implementation of the new federal mandate, a growing body of experience can guide practice. Over a two-year period, the National Center on Educational Restructuring and Inclusion (NCERI) surveyed school districts identified by each chief state school officer as implementing inclusive education programs (*NCERI*, 1994, 1995). The reports from nearly 1,000 school districts provide a basis for understanding the factors necessary for successful implementation. These are congruent with the findings of a Working Forum on Inclusive Schools, convened by 10 national organizations (*Council for Exceptional Children*, 1995) and reported in an Association for Supervision and Curriculum Development publication (Thousand & Villa, 1995).

The NCERI study identified seven factors for the successful implementation of inclusive education:

1. *Visionary leadership.* This leadership can come from many sources, including school superintendents, building administrators, teachers,

parents, school board members, disability advocates, and universities. Whatever the initial impetus for inclusive education programs, all stakeholders must ultimately take responsibility for the outcome.

2. *Collaboration.* The process of inclusive education involves three types of collaboration: between general and special educators, between classroom practitioners and providers of related services, and between those involved in student evaluation and program development (that is, the IEP team) and classroom practitioners. Each group needs time for collaboration.

3. *Refocused use of assessment.* Schools must replace the traditional screening for separate special education programs with more authentic assessment that addresses student strengths as well as needs and that provides useful guidance for classroom practitioners. Schools must develop and use adapted methods to assess student knowledge. They must question the use of traditional measures of potential (such as IQ tests) and opt for curriculum-based assessment.

4. *Support for staff and students.* School staff must have time to work together and have effective professional development programs. Staff development should be sensitive to the needs of adult learners and involve more than one-shot experiences. Support for students should include the full panoply of supplemental aids and services that the law mandates, such as curriculum modifications; alternative instructional strategies; adapted assessment measures; and procedures, technology, and roles for paraprofessionals and other support personnel.

5. *Appropriate funding levels and formulas.* Data from school districts about special education funding are limited and difficult to compare. School districts reporting in the *National Study* (NCERI, 1994, 1995) indicate that although there are initial start-up costs for planning and professional development activities, a unitary system over time is not more expensive than separate special education. Funds that follow the student with special needs into the general education environment can provide preventive services for some students and enhanced learning opportunities for others, thereby making inclusive education no more costly over time. However, districts that continue to operate under a dual system will be more costly.

6. *Parental involvement.* Because parental involvement is essential, schools report creative approaches to make parents an integral part of the school community. This goes well beyond the procedural due process requirements of the law. For example, in New York City's Community School District 22, pairs of general and special education parents have been instructed about the basis of inclusive education and its benefits for all students.

7. *Effective program models, curriculum adaptations, and instructional practices.* There is no single model of inclusion. Most common is the pairing of a general and a special education teacher to work together in an inclusive classroom with general and special education students. At one middle school, a special education teacher and his or her class become part of the team. In other settings, a special education teacher serves as a consultant to several general education teachers, in whose classes students with disabilities are included.

Increasingly, districts are seeking teachers who are dual licensed and, thus, can themselves teach inclusive classrooms.

Special education teachers often report their lack of knowledge about the general education curriculum, whereas general education teachers often report their lack of knowledge about individualizing instruction. However, after a year of collaboration, both report greater knowledge and comfort in these areas. They use many of the same instructional strategies in the inclusive education classroom that are effective for students in general classrooms. These include cooperative learning, hands-on learning, peer and cross-age tutoring and support models, instruction based on students' multiple intelligences, classroom technology, and paraprofessionals and classroom assistants (not "Velcroed" to the individual child but serving the whole class).

As Congress pointed out in the reauthorized IDEA, special education should be understood as a service, not a place. Thus, a student (labeled either special or general education) may receive services in a variety of settings or groups. Though not a legal term, inclusion is best expressed in the student who is on the regular register, attends homeroom with her or his peers, participates equally in all school activities, receives instruction suited to her or his needs, is held to the school's common standards, and receives the same report card as other students. As a New York City Public Schools superintendent stated, "Inclusion is about 'ownership.' They are all our students."

The Future of Inclusive Education

As Edmonds (1979) declared two decades ago concerning the education of minority students, we know how to provide effective education at the school level, but we have yet to do so on a districtwide basis. So, too, with inclusive education. We have numerous pilot programs and, increasingly, whole-school approaches for inclusion. However, inclusion as yet remains largely a separate initiative, parallel to, rather than integrated within, broad school reforms. Some of the national reforms, especially Slavin's Success for All, Levin's Accelerated Schools, Sizer's Coalition of Essential Schools, Comer's School Development, and Wang's Community for Learning, incorporate inclusive models (Wang, Haertel, & Walberg, 1998).

Beyond these efforts, other factors are conducive to the expansion of inclusive education. They include the success of inclusive education programs; the now firm legal mandate to educate students with disabilities with their nondisabled peers, especially the requirement that their performance be included in school and district performance reports; public concern for the costs of separate programs that do not serve students with disabilities well; and the growing insistence from parents not only that their children with disabilities be served in the public schools, but also that their children's education be of high quality, preparing them to participate as full and contributing members of an inclusive society. These changes need to occur in more than just school. Commensurate changes must occur in the universities, in the workplace, and in the community.

Inclusion goes beyond returning students who have been in separate placements to the general education classroom. It incorporates an end to labeling students and shunting them out of the regular classroom to obtain needed services. It responds to Slavin's call for "neverstreaming" by establishing a refashioned mainstream, a restructured and unified school system that serves all students together.

NO    Daniel P. Hallahan

We Need More Intensive Instruction

I would like to sketch out a few of my major concerns related to the field of special education, generally, and to learning disabilities, in particular. Although I don't view myself as a whiner by nature, I was surprised at just how many concerns flashed through my mind as I set about preparing for this article. I really do think that special education, and especially learning disabilities, is in trouble. And I guess, if I had to pinpoint the one thing that pervades most of my concerns, it would be that the field has lost its instructional momentum. Or as my respected colleague, Doug Fuchs, remarked at a recent meeting, the field has lost its instructional intensity.

What do I mean by instructional momentum or instructional intensity? Back in the early 1980s the field had a focus on instructional issues and methodology. Researchers were focused on testing interventions for students. And special education teachers were actually teaching students with learning disabilities—in small groups, in large groups, or individually.

In the past 10 years or so, however, researchers and practitioners, alike, have been pulled away from this concentration on instruction. Any focus on instruction has been lost to a seeming obsession with where instruction takes place. Starting with Madeline Will's call in 1986 (Will, 1986) for a regular education initiative, to the call for the total annihilation of special education by the full inclusionists, up to the present-day love affair with collaborative teaching and the general education curriculum, we have lost our resolve to teach students with learning disabilities to read better, do math better, attend-to-task better, and/or interact with their peers better.

Researchers have been diverted from pursuing topics related to instruction in order to try to put out brush fires set by those who would gut the continuum of placements in favor of full inclusion. Teachers have been forced into hastily conceived models of inclusion and collaborative teaching. And those of us in teacher education have all too often caved in to pressures from the marketplace to prepare teachers certified to teach students from two or three different categories of disability as well as general education students. On top of this, we're expected to prepare novice preservice teachers to be ready to teach collaboratively with general education colleagues, some of whom have several years of teaching experience.

Please don't get me wrong. Collaborative teaching can work. I'm sure many [such teachers] have engaged in some very successful collaborative teaching arrangements. But I'm also sure [they] recognize that, when it does work, it's because of a very special relationship [they] forged with [their] general education colleague—a relationship that research shows is not easily established and maintained. Collaborative teaching can be a very effective model under the right circumstances for some students—maybe even many students—but not for all students. In a collaborative model, what happens to those students who require intensive instruction? Who provides it? My fear is that the current emphasis on collaboration leads teachers away from actual teaching. They are spending their time consulting with general education teachers rather than teaching. Or, at best, they are teaching, but the effects of their instruction are diminished because it's spread over large numbers of students, some of whom are not learning disabled.

A recent study by Budah, Schumaker, and Deshler (1997) is important here. This is one of the few well controlled studies of collaborative teaching. In a secondary setting, they found that both teachers (the general education and special education teacher) spent over half their time engaged in noninstructional behaviors. Furthermore, they spent less than 10% of their time presenting content. Not surprisingly, they also found that the outcome measures for the students with learning disabilities were very disappointing.

Also, don't get me wrong on another point—it is important that students with learning disabilities have access to the general education curriculum. A very legitimate criticism of the resource room model of the 1980s is that far too often the special education teacher and his or her students had no idea what was transpiring in the general education classroom. I fear, however, that folks are going to translate the 1997 IDEA [Individuals with Disabilities Education Act] emphasis on the general education classroom to mean exclusive placement in general education classrooms. Why can't students with learning disabilities learn the general education curriculum with the help of special educators in special education settings? Furthermore, let's not forget that failure in the general education curriculum is what got many of these students into special education in the first place. Just maybe there's something wrong with the general education curriculum. Access to the general education curriculum is great, but how about access to instruction?

I have to wonder if there isn't a connection between the current zeitgeist and the tremendous teacher attrition problem in special education. The irony is that learning disabilities teachers are working harder than ever, but they're spending less and less time actually teaching. Special education teachers have lost their identity as teachers. Instead, they find themselves in a limbo-like state somewhere between special and general education. In fact, their strongest identity with special education is probably linked to the IEP [individual education program]. And with the new IDEA Amendments, the paperwork associated with that document is only going to increase. In short, special education teachers often find themselves being glorified aides and paper-pushers.

Perhaps one of the major reasons we're in the mess we're in is because people don't take learning disabilities seriously enough. It's almost as if they view it as a minor inconvenience rather than the life-long serious condition [we] know it can be, and often is. This carefree attitude toward learning disabilities, coupled with the mantra of reformers, "all children can learn," ends up short-changing students with learning disabilities. Sure, all children can learn, but they have to be instructed first. Sure, all children can learn, but not to the same degree and not with the same facility. At the core of special education are the ideas that some children are able to learn better than others and that some children will find learning some things virtually impossible. That's why we have special education. It's the erosion of these core beliefs that many reformers would like to see happen—reformers who assert that students with learning disabilities can be served in general education classrooms, with, at most, a little consultation from special educators.

I'd like to end by referring to Martha Minow's (1985) idea of the "dilemma of difference." She wrote a chapter on bilingual education, in which she talked about the dilemma one faces by either ignoring or recognizing differences in children. To recognize that some children are different, carries the risk of labeling and stigmatizing them. However, to ignore differences runs the risk of neglecting student's instructional needs. It's unfortunate that so many are opting to ignore the differences. It seems to me that ignoring differences is a totally unsatisfactory solution to the dilemma. A better course is to admit that the dilemma of difference doesn't have a completely satisfactory solution. In lieu of a perfect solution, we need to recognize, not ignore, the differences students with learning disabilities exhibit. We need to find ways to diminish these differences. And the way to do this, I think, is through intensive instruction. If we ignore differences, the children won't learn plus they'll be stigmatized anyway because of their learning problems. But if we recognize differences and actually do something about them through intensive instruction, the children will at least learn.

POSTSCRIPT

Does Inclusion Work?

Debates about inclusion often take place in hearing rooms and courts, with schools and parents supporting their preferred programs. The direction of preference is not at all predictable. Schools sometimes advocate for services delivered in the regular education classroom rather than intensive specialized programs. At other times, the same schools may favor a more restrictive, separate program. Some parents feel that the regular education classroom holds the key to generalized learning and growth. Others feel that a private school focuses on direct and intensive programming that will ensure success for their children. It is likely that the position held is governed by direct experience with school programs. One's position is also affected by the individual child.

As might be expected, legal decisions regarding inclusive programming have also varied in outcome, although there is a guiding decision point. In light of the language of "least restrictive environment," the courts place the burden on the party seeking a more restrictive program to prove that it is most beneficial to the child (McCarthy, Educational Horizons, 1998). To prevail, this party must make a solid argument demonstrating that genuine efforts to support education in the mainstream have not resulted in school progress.

The efforts to support inclusion are significant. Lipsky and Gartner discuss factors that are critical to successful programs, ranging from leadership to financial and professional support. Students, teachers, and parents, they say, will not be helped by programs that are mandated by administration directives to unprepared faculty or by programs that are understaffed. Also, school and district administrators who support and value inclusion must help teachers and parents solve the most difficult problems.

Energies for successful inclusion are so substantial that Hallahan wonders if they will overburden special education faculty, who he feels are already buried beneath required paperwork. When more time is devoted to meetings and collaboration, less is available for direct contact with students who are crying out for professional expertise.

Hallahan's concerns about the effectiveness of inclusion programs are echoed by Baker and Zigmond (*Journal of Special Education*, 1995), whose extensive study of five schools found numerous examples of admirably adapted assignments for whole classes but few situations in which the education was specially designed and delivered to meet the specific educational needs of students with disabilities within those classes.

How do the schools that you know address inclusion? What factors do they consider when making decisions to balance classroom participation and intensive remediation? How are inclusion efforts supported? What do teachers, parents, and students say about the compromises that have been struck?

ISSUE 10

Does Full Inclusion Deliver a Good Education?

YES: Susan Shapiro-Barnard et al., from *Petroglyphs: The Writing on the Wall* (Institute on Disability/UAP, 1996)

NO: Gary M. Chesley and Paul D. Calaluce, Jr., from "The Deception of Inclusion," *Mental Retardation* (December 1997)

ISSUE SUMMARY

YES: Susan Shapiro-Barnard and her colleagues in the Institute on Disability at the University of New Hampshire affirm the positive outcomes of full inclusion at the high school level for students with significant cognitive disabilities.

NO: Public school administrators Gary M. Chesley and Paul D. Calaluce, Jr., express their concern that full inclusion of students with significant cognitive disabilities does not provide appropriate preparation for successful life following school.

Ask a group of people about the definition of *inclusion* and they will usually come up with a statement like, "All children being educated in the same school." Ask again, "Do you mean *all* children?" The reply is likely to be a bit less certain: "Well, maybe not *all*." Probe a bit further and someone is likely to admit (with a bit of trepidation) that inclusion should mean "all students except ..." The words that follow might vary, but usually there are exceptions for students with severe cognitive challenges—those who have mental retardation or those who have disabilities in multiple areas and require complex and broad levels of support in order to communicate, move, and learn. So inclusion, for many people, does not really include *all* children.

Proponents of full inclusion would have a very different answer. They would say—and mean—all children being educated in the same school. Full inclusion advocates insist that all children, regardless of level of need, have a moral and legal right to attend their home school, be enrolled in a general education class, and receive all necessary supports within that class. In a full inclusion environment, students do not need to fit into the school; the school needs to adapt to all students. This means that services are brought to the child; children are not sent out (or away) because what they need is not available.

Those who oppose full inclusion cite the difficulties of adapting instruction, meeting student needs, and acquiring needed supports. Accustomed to a traditional academic curriculum for some students and a vocational, life skills–based curriculum for others, they ask how the needs of both can be met.

The challenge of full inclusion is perhaps greatest for high schools, which focus on distinct academic disciplines and college hopes. Communication among high school teachers is complicated by the increased number of people who interact with each student and the large numbers of students taught by each educator. The specialization and concentration of high schools has become even more intense with the advent of high-stakes testing, causing some to wonder if the needs of every child can be met within a typical classroom.

Susan Shapiro-Barnard, Carol Tashie, Jill Martin, Joanne Malloy, Mary Schuh, Jim Piet, Stephen Lichtenstein, and Jan Nisbet have worked with numerous high schools across New Hampshire, overcoming long-held assumptions about possibilities and individual potential. In the following selection, the authors look beyond what they "used to think" and reflect on the accomplishments of students with disabilities and fully inclusive high school programs.

In the second selection, Gary M. Chesley and Paul D. Calaluce, Jr., advise caution, noting that the solutions and suggestions of full inclusion proponents are complex, time consuming, and challenging. They express concern that full inclusion of students with significant disabilities—especially at the high school level—might appeal to everyone's sense of fairness and goodness but result in precious little time spent on the skills and knowledge that are essential for adult success.

As you read these selections, ask yourself, Is it educationally reasonable to expect the general education classroom to meet the needs of every student? And can a student be truly included in the adult world if that process does not begin in school?

Susan Shapiro-Barnard et al.  **YES**

Petroglyphs: The Writing on the Wall

Although inclusive education has taken a strong hold in schools throughout the country, high school students with disabilities still face the real and frightening possibility of segregation. We used to accept this. We used to think that high schools could not embody both excellence and equity. But we now know better. By challenging existing beliefs and practices, [we] advocate ... change. Change that disturbs the universe of special education. Change that goes beyond a revelation to become part of a revolution. Change that is more than a nodding of the head.

Frederick Douglas once wrote, "People who advocate freedom, yet deprecate agitation, are people who want crops without plowing the ground." It's time to turn the soil. Douglas continued, "Without struggle, there is no progress." [We] honor ... the struggle in all of us. The struggle to embrace our old thinking for a moment, learn from it, and then push it aside. With confidence. For the writing is on the wall.

We used to think students with disabilities couldn't learn academics in regular high school classes. That functional-daily-living-skills were more important than reading and writing and math. That cooking skills were more important than knowledge. So we taught students to read safety words while their peers were reading books. We took students to the bowling alley while their classmates studied physics. We equated not being able to read Shakespeare, with not being able to appreciate it. Not being able to raise your hand in class, with having nothing to say.

We now know seven of the most dangerous words in our vocabulary are "she won't get anything out of it." We now know students with disabilities can learn academic skills. And that it's advantageous to do so. We now know literacy is probably the most functional skill in our society. And there is great value in knowledge. We now know about the "least dangerous assumption." So when we aren't sure whether or not a student understands, we must assume that she does. We now know the high price of assuming she does not.

We used to think if a student wasn't able to open a biology book and answer the questions on page seventy-two, that the student would be better off in a special education classroom. But then we learned about the importance of inclusion. And so, when the teacher said turn to page seventy-two, we no longer asked that student to leave. Instead, we handed her something else

From Susan Shapiro-Barnard, Carol Tashie, Jill Martin, Joanne Malloy, Mary Schuh, Jim Piet, Stephen Lichtenstein, and Jan Nisbet, *Petroglyphs: The Writing on the Wall* (Institute on Disability/UAP, 1996). Copyright © 1996 by The Institute on Disability/UAP, University of New Hampshire. Reprinted by permission.

to do—something "on her level." And we called on a special education teacher to create it. And we called on a paraprofessional to implement it. But the student never got called on, because the biology teacher didn't know what the student was doing.

We now know we can do better. That it is possible for students with disabilities to learn from the regular education curriculum. That the barrier to this happening isn't the student's ability, but often it is our own. We know "no man is an island," but without modifications and supports, sometimes students with disabilities in regular classrooms can be. We now know the difference between alternative and modified. That "being in" isn't the same thing as "being with." And that ultimately we need to stop talking about curriculum modification and start talking about inclusive curriculum design.

We used to think students with disabilities didn't need guidance counselors. Or lockers, or notebooks, or an excuse for being late to class. We used to think students with disabilities couldn't be sent to the principal's office. Didn't need transcripts. Couldn't make the team. When students needed to practice communication skills we sent them to the speech room—we forgot about the cafeteria. When students got sick, the special education teacher called home—we forgot about the school nurse. And when classmates were getting homework assignments, we forgot to give students with disabilities anything at all.

We now know about natural supports. And that "only as special as necessary" are words to live by. We now know about the people, places, and things that support all high school students. So instead of "checking in" each morning to the special education room, students check into homeroom. Instead of aides being assigned to students, instructional assistants are assigned to classrooms. And instead of IEP [individual education program] progress notes, all students get report cards. We now know that including students without natural supports just moves the self-contained classroom into regular education. It only changes the place where supports are provided. Not the way. Not the who. Not the how.

We used to think making a bed, change for a dollar, and a grilled cheese sandwich were important skills for students with disabilities to learn during high school. That achieving these skills would lead to a full—and fulfilling—life. Of course, we had heard about inclusion. Of course, we had heard stories of students learning academics, gaining friendships, and trying out for the school play. It sounded great. It sounded wonderful. But it sounded like something was missing. When did these students learn functional skills?

We now know when—and how—students with disabilities can learn functional skills during a typical high school day. We now know money skills can be taught in math class, the cafeteria, and the school store. That cooking can be learned in culinary arts. And let's face it, just how important is "bed-making" anyway? At the same time, we realize these things are not enough. That learning to work in a group, solve a problem, and ask for help are essential skills for all people in the real world. At home. Around town. On the job. And these things are taught in regular education classes. Everyday. To all students.

We used to think it was a good idea for students with disabilities to spend a portion of their day out in the community separated from their peers. We used to think they needed "the exposure." We used to think when students left school in the middle of the day, they didn't really miss anything. And if it's true actions speak louder than words, then it can be said we thought going to the mall was more important than going to class. It's as if we thought once a student had the skills to eat in a restaurant, buy a bus ticket, and cross the street, something magical would happen. We used to think only students with disabilities needed to learn in the community. But then students without disabilities began leaving school during the day. And we wondered what they were doing.

We now know community-based instruction is not the same as community service. Job shadowing isn't an internship. And walking the mall is walking the mall. We now know that community-based-instruction is rooted in the notion that—in the name of skill acquisition—it's okay to separate students with disabilities from their peers. (Didn't we used to call that segregation?) We still recognize that some skills need to be learned outside of the school building. But we now know this can happen at times when all students are out of school. For there are still too many students who can eat in a restaurant but have no one to eat with. Too many students who are buying vowels instead of bus tickets.

We used to think being included from seven-thirty until two was enough. That a full day of classes equaled a full life. We thought if students were well supported during the school day, we had done our job. Yes, there were stories of students sitting in front of the television everyday after school. Yes, parents asked for ideas, names, and activities. And yes, we were concerned. But what could we do? After-school was not our responsibility. Surely there was an agency that could help.

We now know life does not end after the last bell. That all students need to be supported to have full after-school lives. That clubs, sports, teams, and just "hanging out" matter as much as classes. And sure, we still struggle to get students the right after-school supports. In the right places. At the right times. And it's not always easy to find that ride home. And we still worry about the limits of our responsibility. But we're talking about people's lives, so can we really just say, "It's not my job"?

We used to think friendships for students with disabilities couldn't happen. That it was too hard. That the only way to get people involved was to pay them. We used to think peer support was friendship. And that it was okay if the aide was the student's "best friend." We used to think having people say "hello" in the hallways was enough. And that we were working on friendship if socialization goals were written on the IEP. As if maintaining eye contact could fill a Saturday night.

We now know we were right about friendships being hard work, but wrong to think they couldn't happen. We now acknowledge what we should have known all along—students absolutely must share time and space. There is no other way. We have learned this from students who tell us they are lonely. We have learned this from parents who would trade all of their child's therapy units for a single phone call. And, as hard as it is to hear, we have learned this from classmates who tell us that adults often stand in the way—literally—of real friendships happening. Their advice: take a step back, don't force it, trust us.

We used to think high school students with disabilities needed to learn prevocational skills. That sorting forks from spoons, nuts from bolts, and red from yellow would lead to gainful employment. But how many jobs are there sorting nuts and bolts? We used to tell students they had plenty of jobs to choose from. (As if working with food, cleaning supplies, and plants was choice enough.) And that they needed job coaches by their sides. Because employers didn't have the training. Or the time. We used to think going to work was more important than going to class. That a student couldn't learn job skills in school. And that filling a soda machine was more important than geography.

We now know the best kind of job training for any student is a well rounded education. That students with disabilities shouldn't have to choose between classes and work. That real jobs happen after and beyond school. And involve a paycheck at the end of the week. We now know the best person to teach the job is a person who knows the job—a co-worker. Because the job coach has never worked in a bank, or a record store, or a law office. We now know that being on time, working with others, and organizing materials are skills for work as well as school. That they can be learned in regular classes. And that prevocational training only gets a student ready to get ready to get ready to get ready ...

We used to think students with disabilities didn't need to graduate. We used to think that getting a diploma didn't matter. Caps, gowns, photographs, and graduation parties—well, those things just weren't very important. And not only did we believe that students shouldn't graduate, we thought students should come back to school after their senior year. And the year after that. And sometimes even longer. It was an entitlement, so we did it. And afterwards, students went through the graduation ceremony with a class they didn't know. We used to think that made sense.

We now know graduation is one of the only remaining "rites of passage" for most young people in our country. And that it does matter. We learned this when a high school "graduate" had to get his GED [general equivalency diploma] in order to go to college. We learned this when a student confessed it was embarrassing to be a third year senior. We learned this when the bus stopped coming the day after a student's 21st birthday. We now know that students with disabilities should graduate. That some students may need continued school district support. And that we have both the power and the responsibility to figure out a way for one not to cancel out the other. Students cannot be held hostage to policy that lags behind practice.

We used to think we needed to make schools better. We still think that, and we probably always will. But we used to think schools could get better without being better for all students. That when we improved education for students without disabilities, we had improved education. We used to think ninety percent of the student population was the whole school. Or close enough. And though we never dared to say it aloud, we secretly questioned whether it was even possible to design a school that met the needs of all students. Therefore, it wasn't even our goal.

We now know equity and excellence are both possible. That they are partners when educational reform is meaningful, sustainable, and real. In fact, without equity there can be no true excellence. We now know we need to include everyone in school reform. Parents. Students. With and without disabilities. But we also know we can't wait for schools to be perfect before students with disabilities are included. (Can a school be perfect if not everyone belongs?) We now understand inclusion is not a guarantee for a flawless education—it's an assurance of a typical one. Isn't that only fair?

We used to think getting a student "into" a job was supporting her to plan for her future. That aptitude tests and vocational assessments would tell us everything we needed to know. And if the student wasn't successful, well, we did our best. But we forgot to ask students what they wanted to study. We forgot to ask students where they wanted to work. And sometimes we even forgot to ask students to attend and direct the meetings where all of these decisions were being made.

We now know that nobody has the right to plan somebody else's future. So we've stopped telling students what they should be. We've stopped telling students what they can't be. And we have started listening to what students want to be. We now know work is just one of many options for a new high school graduate. That college is a possibility for everyone. That passions and interests are just as important as skills and abilities. And "being realistic" often results in shattered dreams.

We used to think disabilities were bigger than people. That students' days were best filled with what someone said they couldn't-wouldn't-shouldn't do. So we pulled students out of English class to do physical therapy. Out of math to work on speech. Out of lunch to learn social skills in a restaurant. And although it's difficult to admit, we often believed that a student with disabilities was in need of repair. So if we could remediate the disability, we could help the student learn more. Live more. Become a better person.

We now know students with disabilities are not broken. That unlike automobiles, people don't need to be fixed. We now see past a student's label and learn the student's name. Past the IQ score to find the student's talent. We now know people are people. (Scary to think that this is something new.) And so we talk with students, not about them. We work with students, not on them. We plan with students, not for them. We follow, not lead. Ask, not tell. Respect, not change.

We used to think inclusion was a good idea for little kids, but it couldn't work in high school.

That professionals wouldn't make it work.

That high school students would be too cruel.

We now know high school inclusion can happen.

Is happening.

And continues to get better.

(The end, or maybe just the beginning.)

**Gary M. Chesley and
Paul D. Calaluce, Jr.**

The Deception of Inclusion

Our national obsession with the inclusion of special education students into the mainstream is analogous to the description of a liberal as an individual who frantically throws 200 feet of rope to a drowning swimmer struggling only 100 feet from the shore. This liberal throws the rope in the conviction that he is saving another. Then he scampers frantically down the beach, seeking other souls to save, before he pulls the original dying victim to safety. His good intentions are misguided and provide us with a lesson about how schools treat individuals with disabilities.

Today, far too many special needs children are drowning. They are being short-changed in the name of socialization. We are truly reliving the myth of the "Emperor's New Clothes." Everyone is afraid to state the obvious. Full inclusion for all is a myth that exists in the hearts of its supporters—those who have lost sight of practical reality. Harsh words perhaps, but they express a sentiment that needs to be addressed so that we may best prepare students with disabilities to become successful participants in our society. Once again the educational pendulum has taken a good idea to the extreme.

Inclusionists argue that children with disabilities make the greater gains when they are completely educated, *included*, in general education classes. Although there is a good deal of evidence that supports the argument that social gains can be made by students with disabilities in full inclusionary programs, the professional literature is devoid of documentation in support of the argument that full inclusionary programs improve the cognitive development of students with disabilities.

Inclusionists also contend that through cooperative planning, students with disabilities receive lessons that are modified to meet their specific needs while remaining fully involved in general education classes. On the surface this contention seems instructionally plausible and the politically correct philosophical stance for a school system to take. For those of us who walk through the halls of our nation's schools, it is clear that this strategy is flawed for several fundamental reasons.

The instructional coordination required in many of these cases sets up situations where the left hand cannot know what the right hand is doing. It is extremely difficult for a principal to provide all of the staff generally involved in supporting a fully mainstreamed child with the time necessary to adjust and to enhance curricular experiences for one child. As a result, too much planning is done "on the fly" and without a timely effort to assess the value of the modifications. In reality, many students with disabilities go through their educational career with a paraprofessional assisting them in class after class. Recently, a parent complained that her son, who had severe handicaps, had received less than an A in his English class. She contended that the boy's B+ was a result of the paraprofessional not following completely the classroom teacher's direction. What is the student actually learning in such a case, and does anyone really care?

Equally problematic is the general education curriculum's lack of focus on functional and vocational skills. Curricular demands as early as first grade do not match the educational needs of many students with disabilities. Even with an infinite amount of planning, the educational interests of some students with disabilities cannot be met through modifications to the general education curriculum. Meanwhile, the performance of special education students on state-mandated performance instruments, such Connecticut's CAPT (Connecticut Academic Performance Test), are a siren call for many to criticize the overall performance of our schools. These results, in reality, indicate the need for more aggressive and intensive remediation for our lowest achievers. Sufficient remediation is not likely to occur when a special needs student is fully included with peers who are zooming ahead academically.

Many students who have handicaps graduate from high school without the skills required to be successful in the adult world. These skills cannot, and should not, be the main focus of the general education curriculum. Classroom modifications are becoming so intrusive that many special needs students are, in the end, responsible for just a small sampling of the curriculum requirements that their peers take for granted; and this is precisely where the educational establishment is blinded at the sight of the emperor's new clothes. Too often, we feel warm and fuzzy at the mere presence of a child with disabilities mainstreamed in a regular classroom. Mom and Dad are pacified and "a program is in place"; but warm and fuzzy does not necessarily translate into academic results. When headlines scream out that high school graduates do not demonstrate basic academic skills, it is too often the special education students who are not making the grade. These young people have not acquired the cognitive skills needed to be competitive in our society nor the functional and vocational skills required for independent living. Parents tend to accept this reality only when their child is approaching graduation and the safety net of public education is about to be removed. Recently, the parents of a child who has been totally included for his entire school career petitioned a school district for an out-of-state residential placement for the student's senior year. When asked why they were requesting a program diametrically opposed to that for which they had advocated throughout the previous 10 years, their stunning response was that the child (in the end) was not prepared for the adult world.

Another fundamental requirement of a full inclusionary program is the commitment of a regular education teacher with the expertise and the perseverance to modify instruction appropriately for one, two, three or more students in a single classroom setting. In theory, all teachers provide differentiated instruction that recognizes learning styles and modalities appropriate to all students. Teaching that recognizes the needs of learners who have disabilities is sound instruction for all children. That is the theory we all know. In reality, even our best trained and most willing teachers have difficulty meeting the diverse needs of their heterogeneously grouped classes, let alone the special requirements of students with moderate to severe disabilities. *"I have twenty-five children in my second-grade class, and you can't expect me to take on more students with special needs,"* has become the oft-heard plea in school after school. This sentiment carries some grain of truth to even the most hard-core supporters of inclusion and clearly illustrates one of the legitimate road blocks to a full inclusionary program. It is inconceivable to imagine a third-grade teacher being asked to focus an entire curriculum on life skills and functional academics. Yet, it is precisely this type of program that is required by many students with severe disabilities. Yasutake and Lerner (1996) reported that 41.9% of regular educators feel that inclusion is not workable, regardless of the level of support provided, with only 4.6% responding very positively about the academic results of inclusion.

It is very disconcerting to attend a Planning and Placement Team meeting where loving parents insist that all services recommended for their child be implemented within the regular classroom. Services, such as speech and occupational therapy, are tightly focused and require a special approach and setting to maximize their effectiveness. These services, and others like them, are not delivered productively in the general education classroom. It is also common practice for independent evaluators, experts from the world outside the public schools, to recommend individual one-to-one instruction to remediate learning and language difficulties; however, these services too belong as a supplement to regular instruction.

In addition, parental demands for inclusion are often unrealistic, and at times absurd. Recently, the parent of a student with almost total intellectual and language impairment insisted that her son be included in a high school French class. Other parents of a child with multiple disabilities, including mental retardation and chronic health problems, demanded that she attend a week-long outdoor nature excursion while hooked to a life support device rather than the alternative educational experience planned for general education students not participating. The parent was making this demand on purely philosophical grounds, dismissing the fact that the field trip would be dangerous and educationally incomprehensible to the student.

Today's public schools are a microcosm of the communities that they serve. We have the opportunity to use a public school experience to teach children with disabilities the many cognitive and social skills needed for assimilation into the community. The socialization gains are important but need to be placed within a valid educational context. Proponents of inclusion assume that through mainstreaming skills will be assimilated as they are taught in the regular classroom. A better solution is to work intensively on skill development and remediation first in a more intensive setting, with the goal being to mainstream children incrementally when they can best benefit from being included. Students with disabilities should be educated to the maximum extent possible with peers who do not have disabilities, but they should not be asked to sacrifice cognitive and vocational preparation for social interaction.

The original guiding philosophy of P. L. 94-142 acknowledged that students with disabilities require individually designed educational plans that offer the child a blend of specialized instruction in different settings. A continuum of service options and integrated social experiences in mainstream classes was the vision in this legislation. We should return to that philosophy. Local schools should develop a practical litmus test that guides the placement of children with disabilities. Issues such as planning time, the preparation and commitment of teachers, the acceptance of the child's peer group, how and where services are best delivered, and a clear identification of targeted skills should guide the placement process. Quite simply, we need to ask whether the classroom teacher can achieve the best academic results for the identified child.

Teachers and parents of special education students must look carefully and forthrightly at the real needs of our children and recommend the programs and learning environments that will best prepare them for academic as well as social success as adults. We must remove the emperor's cloak of inclusion and substitute it with a warm woolen coat, one that will provide the practical academic foundation to serve children well for years to come.

POSTSCRIPT

Does Full Inclusion Deliver a Good Education?

In some schools, "fully included" children sit isolated in the back of general education classrooms, their education addressed by a stream of specialists with whom they work individually or in small groups. Interaction with the rest of the class is limited. This arrangement offers the worst of both options—the student with disabilities receives a separate education in a way that prominently advertises his difference. He is a class of one.

Increasing numbers of schools—particularly at the elementary level—are discovering creative ways of addressing the academic needs of a wider range of students in general education classrooms. Supportive adults become functional classroom members rather than appendages. Extensive summer workshops foster faculty communication about universally designed educational practices. And differentiated instruction—so much the rage in general education—embraces all children, especially in these days of high content standards.

Shapiro-Barnard and her colleagues invite educators to make the "least dangerous assumption" and expect academic ability rather than assume limitations based on a disability. They see an opportunity to develop a world of social justice for all within a fully inclusive school environment that makes few assumptions about students except that each can excel in all areas. The theme of social justice is echoed by Gerrard (*Equity and Excellence*, 1994), who maintains that the entire inclusion debate is moot because students with disabilities have already "won" the right to be included through IDEA.

Chesley and Calaluce believe in individual potential but are doubtful that the potential of each child can be reached in today's general education classroom. They argue that the ability to provide numerous services, supports, and modifications within a finite school day stretches the capability of a system. Such a stretch limits educational opportunities for students who need to develop specialized skills.

Macmillan, Gresham, and Forness (*Behavioral Disorders*, 1996) argue that full inclusion creates an ideological debate in which the "where" of education takes precedence over the "what" of education. Rather than saying that one location or approach applies equally to every student, the authors advise readers to be open to multiple options to meet divergent needs at different life stages. As fully included students move to highly academic secondary schools, will instructional practices change? Does full inclusion tear down barriers constructed by a needlessly protective educational system? Or does full inclusion focus on a dream of belonging at the cost of the acquisition of needed life skills with trained educators?

ISSUE 11

Are Residential Schools the Least Restrictive Environment for Deaf Children?

YES: Harlan Lane, Robert Hoffmeister, and Ben Bahan, from *A Journey Into the Deaf-World* (DawnSignPress, 1996)

NO: Tom Bertling, from *A Child Sacrificed to the Deaf Culture* (Kodiak Media Group, 1994)

ISSUE SUMMARY

YES: Harlan Lane, a faculty member at Northeastern University; Robert Hoffmeister, director of the Deaf Studies Program at Boston University; and Ben Bahan, a deaf scholar in American Sign Language linguistics, value residential schools as rich cultural resources that enable Deaf children to participate fully in the educational experience.

NO: Tom Bertling, who acquired a severe hearing loss at age 5 and attended a residential school for the deaf after third grade, favors the use of sign language in social situations but views residential schools as segregated enclaves designed to preserve the Deaf culture rather than to develop adults who can contribute fully to society.

Hearing Impairment—Impairment in hearing, whether permanent or fluctuating, that adversely affects a child's educational performance but that is not included under deafness in this section

Deafness—A hearing impairment so severe that the child is impaired in processing linguistic information through hearing, with or without amplification, that adversely affects a child's educational performance.

— IDEA 97

The term *hard of hearing* includes individuals whose hearing acuity is not equal to that identified as "normal." Most individuals covered by this definition can perceive some conversation with a hearing aid, although it might not be sufficient for school learning. The term *deafness* is reserved for a more restricted range of hearing. Although an aid might increase sensitivity to some sounds, clear access to conversation is not possible.

Apart from medical descriptions of deafness lives the powerful cultural discussion of Deafness (capital letter intended). In deference to the authors of the following selection, the term will be capitalized here as it is in their writing. The Deaf believe that they are linguistically different, not disabled. Members of the Deaf culture maintain that they have not "lost" anything but, instead, belong to a unique group with its own language, traditions, and social life. Some people who are deaf do not join the Deaf culture. Others who are very much a part of the Deaf culture may hear.

Several visual languages, codes, and signing systems have been part of the education of deaf individuals. These include idiosyncratic signs, developed at home; oralism (emphasizing the development and use of speech without signing); and finger spelling of English words and total communication (combining pantomime, drawing, finger spelling, and oral language). Several formal systems of signed language also exist, which differentially represent the word order and practices of spoken English. Each of these methods has its supporters. The language of the Deaf culture is American Sign Language (ASL).

With its own grammar and syntax, ASL is not a translation of spoken English but its own language, fully developed and complex (as detailed in the works of Stokoe, Bellugi, and Klima). Emphasis on ASL as the natural language of the Deaf has increased in the last 30 years.

Residential schools for the deaf have been an established element of life for Deaf children. While lessons are presented either in ASL or spoken English, the Deaf child is surrounded by others who "speak the same language." Dorm life is a pivotal component, a rich environment within which to convey culture and develop lifetime friendships. However, IDEA and the inclusion movement challenge the existence of residential schools, asking if they truly offer the least restrictive environment to deaf children.

In the following selection, Harlan Lane, Robert Hoffmeister, and Ben Bahan argue that residential schools for the Deaf, while appearing to be very restrictive for deaf children, actually provide a freer educational environment, with role models who use the natural language of the children to create strong cultural bonds and to enhance self-esteem. In contrast, they see public school programs as isolating in terms of language, social interaction, and exposure to role models.

Although his mother is involved in the Deaf culture and he is fluent in ASL, Tom Bertling considers the Deaf culture a social invention, which he does not embrace. In the second selection, Bertling shares the feelings of isolation he experienced after moving to a residential school for the deaf. He decries the limited expectations of the residential school, maintaining that he lost more than he gained by his attendance.

Harlan Lane, Robert Hoffmeister, and Ben Bahan

Educational Placement and the Deaf Child

What if you were a child and you had to go to a school where you didn't understand the teacher in your classroom? At the very least, your access to the subject matter would be limited, dependent on what you could learn from texts. But what if you couldn't read very well either? What if you were thirteen before you were able to understand print, and even then your comprehension was extremely limited? What if, on entering junior high school, you were reading at the third-grade level, which is the situation for the typical Deaf child? ...

Suppose you were unable to understand even your peers, so that your only meaningful interactions at school took place between you and one other adult, your interpreter or teacher, who "filtered" all information from the environment for you. What would you learn then? How would your psychological and social development proceed? How could your teacher evaluate your progress?

... [Y]oung Deaf children often face educational environments like this. We will examine some of the forces that place these obstacles in the way of their education: the hearing parents' natural desire to have their children schooled close to home; the small numbers of Deaf children; the higher academic quality of many local schools compared to specialized programs; and especially, the dominant educational philosophy, which views Deaf children as children with a disability and has a single solution for virtually all categories of children with disabilities—inclusion in mainstream schools and programs....

Deaf Education and the Law

...Under IDEA [Individuals with Disabilities Education Act], the Federal government became responsible for defining "appropriate education" for children with disabilities, and it proceeded to issue guidelines specifying a range of acceptable placement options. At the time the law was passed, many children with disabilities, in particular those with mental retardation, lived in separate residential facilities, where they frequently received poor educational and social training. IDEA was intended in part to ensure that such separate facilities, often referred to as "institutions," would be the last place a state or a public school district would choose to send a child with a disability. To this end, the act specified that every such child was entitled to an education in the "least restrictive environment" (LRE) possible; thus, the range of acceptable placements for the child became a hierarchy in which residential facilities ranked at the bottom. In fact, according to the strictest interpretation of the principle of the LRE by the Office of Special Education and Rehabilitation Services of the federal Department of Education (OSERS), the preferred locale of educational services for the child with a disability is the neighborhood school, and the child should be placed in as close proximity as possible to his or her peers without disabilities, which in the case of the Deaf would be hearing children in a regular classroom.

The problem for the Deaf was, and still is, twofold. First, under the LRE principle as interpreted by OSERS, the residential schools for the Deaf, which are a core element in the very identity of many members of the DEAF–WORLD, and where the Deaf children of hearing parents may encounter peers and adults fluent in ASL [American Sign Language] for the first time, are referred to as "institutions" and hence positioned at the bottom of the placement hierarchy. Second, most Deaf children require the use of a unique, visual language, which is the language neither of instruction nor of conversation in the preferred setting for the education of most children with disabilities, that is, regular public schools. Thus, the laws that were created to protect those with disabilities carry with them conflicts for the Deaf child and, often, for the Deaf adult who wishes to obtain a quality education. These conflicts are grounded in the issues of language and culture that mark the interface between the DEAF–WORLD and the hearing world....

Placement Options

... Determining the educational placements where Deaf students will be most successful is becoming a very complex business. Increasingly, special-education professionals desire inclusion of the Deaf child with an interpreter in a regular classroom in the midst of hearing pupils. Many hearing parents may be reluctant to accept a school where signing is used. Professionals in audiology and related medical fields continue to push for an emphasis on speech; if the child has had cochlear implant surgery, the hospital team and the parents may insist on special classes for Deaf children where primarily spoken language is used. In some settings, the content of the curriculum may be simplified to make it accessible, and teaching staff may be isolated from the latest developments in pedagogical practice. In others, a Deaf child may have no peers with whom he or she can communicate.

For 150 years, separate facilities, either residential schools or, in large cities, day schools, were the main setting for the education of the Deaf. Since the 1960s, various forms of what is called generically *mainstreaming* have been encouraged, ranging from the self-contained day class within a regular public school (with interaction, if any, with hearing students limited to activities outside the academic program), to *full inclusion* of the Deaf in hearing classrooms. More recently, ... there has been a strong push for inclusion, with (or without) the provision of signed language interpreters and other support services like resource rooms and itinerant teachers.

In the following pages we will look at these options largely in terms of three factors parents should consider in determining where and how to obtain the highest quality education for their Deaf child. These factors are the language of instruction; the academic quality of the program, including the subjects offered and the level of instruction; and the degree of social interaction.

... [R]esidential schools for the Deaf—large, centrally located schools providing education from preschool through high school (and, in some cases, adult education)—were at one time the center of the DEAF–WORLD. However, ... starting in the 1860s, ... oralists took control of the residential schools in the U.S. and abroad, virtually eradicating the influence of the DEAF–WORLD. From then on, the teaching staff and administrators were hearing, instruction in almost all schools was oral throughout the elementary years, and the Deaf staff were relegated to nonacademic posts with less influence on academic achievement, posts such as dormitory supervisor, coach, shop instructor, and custodian.

As a result of these changes, the students acquired much of their information and, unless they had been born into the DEAF–WORLD, all of their language, from other Deaf students or the after-school staff. The elementary and middle school academic personnel especially did not know ASL and therefore could not communicate effectively with their students. Since the students' success was measured by what they knew in English, but most had great difficulty learning English (or much else) through oral instruction, the level of accomplishment was low, both as measured, and in fact. The result was drastically lowered expectations and, in consequence, the drastic lowering of curriculum content. The advent of the special education laws and the change from strictly oral instruction to the combined use of signs from ASL and speech in the 1960s improved matters somewhat, but one of the major drawbacks of the residential schools remains to this day. That is the low expectations they have for many of their students, and the low quality and limited variety of their academic offerings.

Residential schools typically are divided into a lower school, a middle school, and an upper school—designations that may signal the low expectations of the staff. The upper school will include students of high-school age but may well not offer high-school-level instruction. At each grade level, the curriculum that many residential schools offer is much less demanding than that offered to hearing students at the same grade level in most regular public schools, and materials are created or adapted to match the low reading levels of the students. Isolated and insular, the schools find it difficult to incorporate new educational strategies into the curriculum, and they even tend to lose sight of what hearing students of a given age are expected to know.

These are admittedly generalizations; happily, there are residential schools that have changed and that challenge many students appropriately. However, a consequence of the situation generally is that residential school graduates tend not to enroll in college, nor are they prepared to do so. Most students are encouraged to pursue vocational training in high school, with courses in printing, computer data entry, or auto body repair, rather than precollege courses.... Sometimes ... the residential schools collaborate with local vocational centers and high schools for hearing students to permit the Deaf students to attend classes.

If, however, most residential schools are below par academically, they do have a great advantage for the average Deaf student: as they always have, they do an excellent job of socialization. There are several reasons for this. For one, since all the children in the school are Deaf, participation in extracurricular functions, such as school government, sports, or dramatic performances, is not dependent on the level of speech one may have, or on the use of an interpreter, as it is in non-residential programs. Moreover, because all their students are Deaf, some hearing teachers in residential schools become proficient in some form of signed communication (though usually not ASL) and are therefore able to converse with students and with Deaf staff to a much greater extent than their counterparts in general education. Children in residential schools can thus participate in every aspect of their schooling beginning very early in their academic careers.

The most important advantage of the residential schools in this regard is the large number of Deaf staff who traditionally work in them (residential schools are the largest single employer of educated Deaf adults). Although some Deaf staff are teachers, most, as we have noted, are employed in noneducational activities as dorm counselors, groundskeepers and cooks—all the many functions besides teaching that make a boarding school work. These people are able to communicate fluently and efficiently with the Deaf students. In addition, like Deaf parents, they tend to have high expectations for Deaf children....

In fact, nowhere other than the residential school, is the Deaf child likely to come into contact with so many Deaf role models, including not only Deaf staff, but older Deaf students and alumni as well. The latter, with whom the residential schools maintain strong ties, support their schools as centers where the Deaf may meet, hold workshops and become involved with students. It is through these contacts that Deaf children, especially Deaf children of hearing parents, may begin to understand that there is a Deaf society, a Deaf culture— a DEAF-WORLD—where they may feel at home. They also have the opportunity to learn a great deal from a Deaf perspective about how to function as a Deaf person in the hearing world.

As a result of all this, most students graduate from the residential schools with healthy self-esteem. Integrated into the DEAF-WORLD by virtue of their attendance at the school, especially if they were residents, they have many friends and are able to take advantage of the DEAF-WORLD's sophisticated networks as they begin their adult lives....

Before the 1960s almost eighty percent of the Deaf children in the U.S. attended residential schools. Today only about thirty percent do. This sharp reversal is mostly a result of the push of the mainstreaming and inclusion movements, coupled with the expansion of interpreter training programs, which have changed the way residential facilities operate. When Deaf students get older, some tend to move to mainstream settings to take advantage of the wider course offerings available in regular high schools. And as enrollments decline, funding becomes a more and more serious problem. Not only does the hearing world consider the mainstream to be the most inclusive and positive educational setting (the Least Restrictive Environment) for all students with disabilities, among whom the Deaf are included, but also the desire of state legislatures to minimize state expenditures on residential schools reinforces the bias in favor of the mainstream placement.

By contrast, the DEAF-WORLD considers the residential school, one of its core institutions, to be the most inclusive and the best placement (the Least Restrictive Environment) for Deaf students....

[M]any students, typically fifty to seventy percent of the school population, commute daily even to the residential schools, which effectively also makes them function as day schools.

Since the commuting time for students is limited to an hour each way by law, separate day schools are located in urban areas and tend to serve inner-city populations. Many have large minority populations and their students may also come from immigrant families, where English is a second language. As a result, the day schools must be concerned not only with the problems of the education of Deaf children per se, but with the functioning of the Deaf child within a multicultural framework.

Day schools have the disadvantages of many of the residential schools, without their advantages. That is, generally the teaching staff is hearing, and because of difficulties in communication and low expectations, the curriculum is severely degraded. There is no large number of Deaf non-teaching staff with whom the students may associate after school. If there are Deaf staff members, they tend to be aides in classrooms. Because they leave for home after classes, younger pupils at day schools also seldom come into contact with the older students.... The lack of Deaf role models means that the child attending such schools often does not discover the DEAF-WORLD until much later in life.... [I]dentity crises can be severe. As in the residential schools, pressure is now being exerted by individuals in the local DEAF-WORLD where the day school is situated, and by local and state associations of the Deaf, to see that more Deaf teachers are hired....

Least Restrictive Environment and Inclusion

By definition, *least restrictive environment* means the most appropriate educational placement for the child, the setting in which the child's capacities may be developed to the greatest possible extent. We have noted ... that the hearing world in general, and special educators who are not familiar with the DEAF-WORLD in particular, tend to see the full integration of the Deaf child into the hearing classroom as providing the least restrictive environment for the education of that child. The DEAF-WORLD clearly sees things differently....

The Paradox of Inclusion

... Advocates of full inclusion for children with disabilities seek to make the educational system keep the promise that mainstreaming in special self-contained classes failed to keep, namely real integration in school—education of children with disabilities alongside children who have none. And for many children with disabilities, special classes are indeed not necessary, though for others, such as some children with multiple severe handicaps, they are. But from the perspective of the DEAF–WORLD, full inclusion is a disaster....

So, what is the Least Restrictive Environment for [Deaf] children ... ? For one thing, it seems to change between elementary and high school. Many Deaf students who have been in putatively integrated and even in self-contained settings for their elementary years, and who may have the academic skills to go to a hearing high school, may opt to attend a residential school so that they can have some social interaction with their peers. On the other hand, those Deaf students who have been in attendance in a residential school may well feel competent and secure enough to enter into a regular hearing high school because they have the social development and peer network to make the experience meaningful, as well as the language skills (English and ASL) to function well in the regular classroom, where the academic level is generally higher than in residential or day programs for the Deaf.

The education of the Deaf student in any setting is a problem. The overall dropout rate of Deaf high schoolers has been estimated at twenty-nine percent. One in every five Deaf students who "graduate" does not meet the academic requirements for a diploma and leaves with a certificate instead. Thus only half the Deaf students who enter high school graduate with a diploma. The lowest dropout rates are found in the residential schools, seventeen to twenty-three percent. For Deaf students who are placed in integrated settings in regular high schools, the dropout rate is thirty-seven percent. If a Deaf student is placed in a self-contained program and is not integrated into the school's regular classes, the dropout rate almost doubles to fifty-four percent (recall that many of these programs will not have any Deaf teachers or contact with the DEAF–WORLD). Different kinds of Deaf students go into different kinds of programs, so the dropout rate reflects both the kinds of students and the type of programming. In all types of programs, if a Deaf student has disabilities, such as a putative learning or behavior disorder or blindness, the dropout rate is fifty-seven percent, and if the Deaf student is Hispanic, the rate is thirty-six percent. Thirty-three percent of Deaf females drop out of high school.

In general, the Least Restrictive Environment for Deaf students is probably the one that allows the freest and fullest communication with teacher and peers, which is a prerequisite to academic progress and psychological and social development. For the vast majority of Deaf students, enjoying the communication conditions that their hearing counterparts take for granted requires teachers and peers fluent in a visual/manual language—ASL in most of North America. That requirement, combined with the small numbers of children who are Deaf, favors specialized educational programs with significant numbers of Deaf children. If we further seek not to restrict the Deaf student in participation in extra-curricular activities and in exposure to pertinent role models, the LRE is the residential school.

In concluding in favor of the residential schools, we must acknowledge the pain that hearing parents (but, significantly, not Deaf parents) feel at the prospect of sending their young child to a boarding school. We Americans like to keep our children close to home. The hearing parents must wonder, too, whether an institution can give their children the attention and care they need. It should be reassuring that Deaf parents who have attended such schools and know what they have to offer are grateful to *their* parents for having sent them there, and they do likewise with their own children if Deaf, even though they are in some ways in a better position than hearing parents to provide at home what the Deaf child requires. The sense of shared language and culture at these schools and the presence of healthy, happy and smart Deaf children is a counterpoise to the regimentation and anonymity that can arise in boarding schools. We have repeatedly cited drawbacks in the residential schools, but many of those drawbacks can be corrected and are being corrected in the most progressive schools today. Teachers have better training and higher expectations, and curricula are being enhanced. Meanwhile the residential schools' traditional strengths, such as better communication, more Deaf role models, and opportunities for personal growth, are being reinforced....

Deaf children should receive what we desire for hearing children as well: an education delivered in their best language. Anything less is not equal educational opportunity. Since their best language is different from that of their hearing peers, their education needs to be conducted separately, at least in part.

A Childhood's End

The first year at the deaf school, I was ten years old in the fourth grade. My first class of the day was leather shop. The classroom was at the far end of the institution grounds facing one of the main streets through town. I spent much time in the storage room looking out the window at the activity across the street. There were businesses plus a public elementary school much like the one I had gone to before being sent here.

The street became a symbol of the stark reality of where I was and the "outside world" to which I had once belonged. I would watch the grade school kids walk to school in the playful and happy manner I had done myself once upon a time. I have never felt as sad as I did watching the world go on without me.

As the months went by, I found it easier to fight back the tears as I looked out the storeroom window, but forever etched in my mind are those dark dreary November mornings that my childhood came to an end.

A few months earlier, on the first morning of the new school year at the state deaf school, all the children gathered in the auditorium for assignment to teachers and classes. The names of the students were called in sign language; then assigned to a teacher and reported to class.

Not having any knowledge of sign language, I sat through the whole process, not knowing if my name was called, not to mention the bewilderment of not being sure of what was going on and what might eventually happen to me. On top of all that, I was dealing with a sense of abandonment for being sent here. I felt I was being punished for not hearing better when I was in the public school.

After nearly everybody had finally dispersed did somebody show concern for me. I was made to wait in a foyer for quite a while until there was enough finger pointing done at me and a flurry of conversations in sign language giving me the impression of their being mystified about what to do with me.

Then somebody led me from the intermediate school building and started to walk me to a different building where the first through third grades were taught. I would have entered fifth grade had I remained in public school and now here I was being led to the primary school.

I remember vividly wondering what I might have done wrong to be headed toward this fate. Was it because I did not see my name being fingerspelled out? Did I look at somebody wrong? I did not know the proper way for a deaf person to behave and remember thinking that I must have done something wrong.

The walk to the school building seemed to take years. With an unexplained ominous future looming ahead, I was reliving what was a happy childhood prior to being sent here. All the scenes were replaying as I walked. It seemed slowly what was my life was now becoming someone else's. Although I did not know it at the time, for the rest of my time at this deaf school things felt somewhat as one would describe being transcendental. I would from then on be present but mentally distanced as a way to cope.

I was told to sit in a chair in the hall outside the administration office apparently used for disciplinary purposes. Drawing stares and mockery by ignorant students unaware of my plight, I became embarrassed and angry for not knowing what was happening to me.

I dared not ask anybody for fear of making another mistake. I felt hurt over the loss of my old life and was disturbed by not knowing what I had done, resulting in being placed in this deaf school.

It was after lunch before the primary school principal led me to my new classroom and told me it was the second grade as I entered the room. As I took my seat after the hearing teacher pointed to a chair, I noticed that the other children were about my age as the teacher resumed writing on the blackboard. After getting over the initial shock of a new setting, I came to realize what my new teacher was teaching that day.

The teacher had written on the blackboard a list of colors such as gold, gray and silver and a few others. Another list had names of common animals. The lesson for the day was "difficult colors." We were to look at pictures she showed us and write down the appropriate color and name of animal.

Disbelief and confusion reigned in my head. I would have been in the fifth grade had I not been sent here. I knew the names of all the astronauts who have flown in space and today, here I was, being taught new colors I learned years ago.

The transformation was nearly complete. What did I do that was so bad to end up being sent here? I remember thinking I should have tried harder to hear when I was in public school and maybe I would not be here. I was heartbroken as I looked out the second floor window glancing at the tall chain-link fencing that ran far as I could see. The thought of running away slipped away when I remembered I lived 200 miles away and felt as if I had done something so bad that my Mom and Dad did not want me anymore. The realization set in, my world had come to an end, and I had nowhere to go.

I was to remain in that 2nd grade class for a few weeks before I was moved up into the fourth grade. By then the damage had been done. Apparently, the deaf school had the practice of placing a new student in a class with his age group. Perhaps making an adjustment later in the school year instead of evaluation by testing and utilizing placement exams. Nobody bothered to tell me what was going on and I did not feel that it was safe to ask. I already felt enough harm had been dealt me without asking for more.

Perhaps I was a bit spoiled. At the public school my teachers were always asking me if I understood what was going on. I had special speech classes and teachers concerned with my education. I never felt left out or mystified at what was happening to me. But here at this deaf school, I was just another deaf kid. No speech classes anymore. Nobody cared.

My first week on the campus ended up being a lesson in restrictions. Seems like since I first walked, I always rode some sort of a bicycle. It was part of my life and all my friends from the public school went everywhere with them. But, here at this school of 350 students, bikes were banned. The only bikes to be seen were the ones ridden across the street by kids not penalized for being deaf.

Reality continued to set in. I wasn't going anywhere anymore. My whole world was being shrunk into a closely controlled and monitored situation where decisions I once used to make were now being made for me.

Personal radios and television sets were not allowed in the dormitory. There was one small set in the "sitting room" that was usually on something the dorm staff wanted to watch and the volume low not to "disturb" the hearing staff. In the "sitting room" were enough chairs for all the boys on the floor. If the boys were not in their bedrooms, they were expected to be in the "sitting room." Except for school, mealtimes and supervised extracurricular activities, my life was now confined to this area. The only alternative to watching television, (this being before widespread closed-captioning) was a stack of decades-old obsolete magazines donated to the school. Nothing which a ten-year-old boy would find of interest. By the end of the year I had read them all several times anyway.

Personal items or toys that could not be shared with everybody were rounded up and locked away. I could see that the dorm staff were going to select all my activities outside of school hours, and individualism, which was my nature, was not going to be allowed. Outside world contact barely existed. "Warehousing kids" accurately describes the conditions.

My whole life prior to coming to this place, I had never once considered myself "deaf." I always knew that I had a hearing loss and needed to wear a hearing aid, but I took it in stride much the same way other people need to wear glasses. I considered myself the same as everybody else and the term "deaf" never applied to me.

I remember staring at deaf children who were using sign language before being sent to this institution and thinking it was good that I wasn't "deaf."

But now here I was, dumped together with "them," confined to the school grounds, segregated from the mainstream world, forced to learn sign language and live in a dormitory with strangers, separated from my Mom, Dad, brothers and childhood friends, placed in demeaning classes never being able to do what normal people do. No more bike rides, no more building forts, no more watching space launches. And now I was also "deaf."

I was born with normal hearing. I was about three years old when my hearing started to deteriorate. By age 5, I had an 85 to 95 db hearing loss in both ears. Fortunately, I had already developed language and speech skills before my hearing loss arrested further development.

Before entering pre-school I was fitted with a hearing aid. Although I clearly remember hating it, I eventually ended up wearing it nearly all the time. Being deprived of a sense was not to my liking, so the bulky electronic device was tolerated.

Although my Mom had hearing loss similar to mine, and knew sign language, (along with her parents and numerous other relatives) our family communicated by voice only and I never learned sign language until the first day at the deaf school. My Dad had normal hearing and had one brother who was also hard-of-hearing and two others with normal hearing.

At the public school I attended, I had an hour a day with a speech therapist. Along with extra concern for me by my first and second grade teachers in the public school, the use of amplification at an early age, and the exclusive use of voice communication at home contributed to my having a normal language development in spite of a very severe hearing loss.

My childhood prior to coming to the deaf school was filled with happiness and fun. The days were full of adventures and challenges. I had future plans and dreams. My hearing disability barely existed. There was not anything I could not do, it seemed. Life was good to me.

My first grade teacher and especially my second grade teacher in the public school had genuine concern for their students. If any of their students were to fail later in life, it certainly was not anything that happened in their early school years. The biggest impact was the introduction of music into my life. The teacher, for the first hour of class every morning would play the piano and sing childhood songs and contemporary hits of the day, placing an importance on class participation.

By the time I was in the third and fourth grade at the public school, extracurricular activities started to have an impact in the way of social skills and a diversified education. There was Cubs Scouts, roller skating and swimming lessons. At school, band instrument music lessons, papier mache projects, and even though I hated it, square dancing came into play. Once, a select few of us with a strong interest in music were chosen to learn Christmas songs in order to go caroling at senior citizen centers during the Christmas season. I remember a visitor came to school once for the purpose of teaching us to sing a certain Christmas song in German.

The rest of my times were spent with my neighborhood friends. One of my friends and classmate at school and I always had numerous construction projects going on. By the time I was in the fourth grade at the public school, we had built a fort in my friend's backyard, one behind the back fence at my house, another up in a tree that our parents did not know too much about and a fourth we started to build with scraps from a subdivision under development. My Dad tore that one down after it started to get taller than all the new houses going up around it.

Other times, we would be on our bikes riding to areas farther and farther away from our houses. For eight-year-olds, the sense of discovery and curiosity overwhelmed the danger we might face from our parents for exceeding the boundary of the "immediate neighborhood."

One of our discoveries was Trouble Lake. In deep woods near our neighborhood, only a few kids and supposedly, no parents knew of its existence. Tales of snakes and other water creatures kept most kids away. The trail to the lake resembled the Amazon rain forest to an eight-year-old. Things crawled and slithered along the trail.

We built a raft and went on imaginary expeditions, and when the lake froze over during the winter, we pretended to conquer Alaska. Our creature fearing friends were left behind.

Once, during a heavy snowstorm, we were checking out the lake and my little brother ended up in water up to his waist. I do not remember the excuse I gave my parents, but it must have been good because I did not have to mention Trouble Lake, named after the trouble you would be in if your parents found out you were there.

On occasion, we would go with my Mom to visit her culturally-deaf friends. In one instance, we visited a deaf couple who had a deaf son attending a "special" school for the deaf in another part of the state. Their son came home once every few weeks for the weekend and it would be my first time meeting him.

He did not have any speech ability and I did not know sign language. The hearing aid that was helping me overcome a hearing loss was of no use in this circumstance. I thought how glad I was to not be like him and never once thought I was "deaf" like him.

It was in instances like this that parents of deaf children had seeds sown by members of the deaf culture encouraging them to send their child to a state residential school for the deaf and convincing them of its being the best possible option for their deaf child.

This culturally-deaf couple were eager to bring another deaf child whom they did not even know into their culture regardless of the consequences, which if in error, would be difficult to reverse. This is typical of leaders and members of the deaf culture trying to preserve their culture. I had no idea they were conspiring to send me to this deaf school.

During the summer before entering the deaf school in the fall, I was still unaware of the changes that lay in store for me. Part of the summer was spent at my grandparents' house across the country. Days were spent building yet more forts, swimming, watching lightning from the evening thunder storms and catching fireflies.

Late at night I'd go down into the basement and listen to the transistor radio my grandpa gave me. I would hold it to my ear and would be fascinated how clear I could hear things and the variety of the medium.

Little did I know a cruel trick was being played on me. In a few weeks that radio would be the only thing I would have left from my childhood and my only connection to the world I would be taken from.

POSTSCRIPT

Are Residential Schools the Least Restrictive Environment for Deaf Children?

Deaf linguists Padden and Humphries (*Deaf in America: Voices From a Culture*, 1988) describe the richness of the Deaf culture: the dramatic range of storytelling and the National Theatre of the Deaf; the active community life of Deaf clubs; and the prevalence of Deaf sports, including the Deaf World Games, which have been held since 1924 and which now feature more than 4,500 athletes from 75 countries in the summer and about 400 athletes from 20 countries in the winter. Could these exist without the links that are forged in residential schools? Should the culture that supports their existence be underwritten by special education?

In the remaining chapters of the book from which his selection was taken, and in his other writings, Bertling expands his position that separate education is not in the best interests of the deaf, who he feels really should be part of the national culture. While acknowledging that sign language is sensible for social interaction, he maintains that deaf individuals must master English in order to maximize learning and to participate fully in society. Focusing on the narrow range of deaf experiences, says Bertling, severely limits a child's horizons and wastes time that could be spent becoming more proficient in written English and academic learning.

Lane, Hoffmeister, and Bahan, in the balance of the book from which their selection was taken (and in their other writings), emphasize the profound isolation that a Deaf person experiences in the hearing world. The authors cite higher dropout rates of Deaf children enrolled in hearing schools to bolster the benefits of early exposure to ASL and the residential school as truly effective education, opening the door for a Deaf child to develop complex language, thought, and social relationships that lead to productive adulthood.

Despite their opposing positions on the value of residential schools, both sides agree that academic expectations for deaf children are too low, regardless of the setting. Not surprisingly, their solutions differ. Bertling would increase exposure to written and spoken English. Lane, Hoffmeister, and Bahan would hire more speakers of ASL to respond to increasing academic standards.

Citing research evidence that use of ASL from birth provides language access resulting in "normal and successful language acquisition," which serves as the foundation for literacy and learning, Dragow (*Exceptional Children*, 1998) supports increased use of ASL, despite the fact that there is no parallel written form of the language. The challenge for the field, according to Drasgow, is to identify the most successful ways in which written language can be acquired.

A third position, which supports Deafness as a linguistic entity, is Deaf-Bilingual Bicultural (DBiBi), in which ASL is introduced as early as possible, matching the critical period of language learning. Early education focuses on teaching ASL and Deaf culture. Written English is later taught as a second language. Spoken English can be taught, but it is not emphasized. This model more closely resembles that of bilingual education, which uses a child's first language and culture to support the development of a second language. This option has the highest level of applicability for children whose parents are fluent speakers of ASL—but will it work for children whose parents use spoken English as their first language?

What is the balance between least restrictive environment (LRE) and free appropriate public education (FAPE) for students who are deaf? Does a residential, ASL-based education enable a deaf child to take advantage of the critical period of language acquisition, or does it waste time that could be spent learning English and gaining access to the printed word? What will be the future for Deaf individuals in a world that focuses on high-stakes testing? Will residential schools for the Deaf increase academic expectations and outcomes? Can the high academic standards of the public school somehow be blended with the cultural connections of Deaf culture to create the best possible outcome? What is the most inclusive?

ISSUE 12

Should Students with Disabilities Be Exempt from Standards-Based Curriculum?

YES: **Rex Knowles and Trudy Knowles**, from "Accountability for What?" *Phi Delta Kappan* (January 2001)

NO: **Jerry Jesness**, from "You Have Your Teacher's Permission to Be Ignorant," *Education Week* (November 8, 2000)

ISSUE SUMMARY

YES: Rex Knowles, a retired college professor, and his daughter Trudy Knowles, an education faculty member at Westfield (MA) State College, feel that federal mandates for all students to master the same curriculum fail to consider individual differences and needs.

NO: Jerry Jesness, a special education teacher, stresses that students who complete school without learning the basics will be ill-equipped to succeed as adults and that any program that avoids teaching these essentials fails to address the long-term needs of students.

In 49 of the 50 states, standards based education is the watch-word. Curriculum expectations are changing. The range and dimension of these expectations differ widely across the country. Some states are designing high level academic programs to meet world class standards. Others have embraced literacy standards that measure the basic skills students will need to be successful in the world of work. Some states have designed their standards to apply to all students. Others have formulated separate sets of standards for students with severe disabilities. Still others do not expect their standards to apply to all students with disabilities.

IEP expectations are changing as well. While eligibility for special education has always hinged on the disability's adverse impact on classroom academic performance, once a student has entered special education, the IEP has frequently become the curriculum, seldom referencing classroom content.

IDEA97 alters this pattern with its stipulation that students with disabilities must have access to the general curriculum and that IEPs must focus on ways in which this access can be facilitated.

As might be expected, this shift in special education has required some major alterations. Historically, special education programs have focused on goals that include academics, but sometimes go beyond them to the types of skills students will need to succeed independently in the workplace. For some students, with significant disabilities, this has meant a heavy focus on communication and community-based application of a more limited range of academic skills. IDEA97 mandates a closer connection with the learning that happens in more typically academic programs.

Rex and Trudy Knowles, both college professors, believe that individual differences warrant differences in instruction and, sometimes, different curricula. They feel society bestows too much reverence on the mastery of reading, which is a supreme struggle for some children with disabilities and not terribly relevant to many rewarding jobs. Forcing the same curriculum on everyone means that some children learn to hate school, feel like failures, and do not gain the competence that they could bring to adult life.

Jerry Jesness, who teaches bilingual children with disabilities, feels holding all students to high level curriculum may help children overcome some struggles to reach greater heights. Warning that lowered expectations can lead students into a false sense of competence, Jesness cautions that we should not confuse difficulty learning with an inability to learn or to need the same skills for lifelong success.

As you read these articles consider these questions. How much struggling is detrimental to a child's self-confidence and when does hard work lead to success and personal accomplishment? How would you decide whether to stop driving for mastery of the skill of reading (or math or any other academic subject) and shift to teaching skills more related to the expected workplace? When would you make this decision? What would the student say about this change now? In twenty years? What options would this open? Close?

Have your state standards included students with disabilities or are there separate, less academic standards for students covered by special education? How was your state's decision made and how does it impact the education of all students? How does your own state's curriculum affect your reaction to this issue?

Accountability for What?

America instituted public education and compulsory attendance partly to save its children from exploitation. We wanted all children to be freed from the demands of sweatshops and farm labor that filled the days of 10-year-olds.

What started as a noble attempt to save children from forced labor has ended up as a daily sentence to a six- to seven-hour prison from which they have no escape. We refuse to let them leave if they feel bad; we regiment their hearing, speaking, seeing, walking, eating, arrival, departure, and bowel movements. We even tell them when they have to wear a coat.

Child abuse is a very strong term, and it rightly makes us angry. That much is clear. But our schools practice child abuse every day. That is also clear.

Every day we ask children to do what they can't do, at least at the moment we ask them. And then we grade them, as if they were eggs. "You're grade A." "You're grade B." "You're rotten." We shame them, and we embarrass them.

We could tell many stories. One lovely, considerate, and gentle 11-year-old girl studied for four hours for a spelling test. The next day she took the test and failed. According to the girl, when her teacher handed back the papers, she said to her, within earshot of the rest of the class, "You're lazy. If you'd put in any time at all on your work, you would get an A. You're just lazy! We're not going to let you hold this class back."

That young girl spells quite well orally. She is helpful and responsible around the home. She is well liked by her peers and adored by her younger brother and sister. She is bright beyond her years. And she is absolutely terrorized by school. She has a perceptual-motor problem. Writing is just not her thing. The internal details regarding the figures she draws and the words she writes get mixed up. While these facts were carefully explained to the teacher, she continued—either from ignorance or cruelty—to insult the girl. That's child abuse. And it's not an isolated incident.

A bright young man with attention deficit disorder and a severe organizational deficit consistently posted failing grades on major assignments because he couldn't seem to keep all the materials together that he needed to hand in. When it was suggested that the teacher help the student set up a system for keeping track of materials, the response was, "He's going to have to figure out how to get by in the real world sometime. Might as well do it now."

The young man continued to fail until his severe depression resulted in his being taken out of school and put in a homebound tutoring program.

We think it's time to start yelling. We have been treating our children badly for a long time now. With the new emphasis on "accountability," the abuse will only multiply. "The word in education is accountability," according to one state commissioner of education—a view no doubt shared by many of his peers. That is a worrisome sentiment. The easy acceptance of the statement by parents and teachers is even more worrisome.

If the word meant that teachers are to be accountable for the respect they show to children, we would rejoice. If it meant that teachers are to be accountable for helping students to find joy in learning and to become lifelong contributors to their society, we would rejoice. If it meant that teachers are to be accountable for ensuring that all children are successful and that those teachers will be required to find the means to guide students and to assess students in multiple ways, we would rejoice.

But "accountability" in today's discussions of education means that teachers will be held accountable for how well their students read and for what they score on achievement tests. Everyone in the class will be performing above average—or else. Teachers' salaries and promotions will depend on their ability to bring children up to grade-level norms.

Even the most naive statistician knows that half of all people who take a norm-referenced test will be below average. That's what average means. Statistical accountability automatically makes some children "leftovers." It is not true that any good teacher can teach any child to read at grade level, any more than any good physical education teacher can teach any child to be an above-average baseball player.

Reading and throwing a baseball are skills. If you're not a Greg Maddux or a Pedro Martinez, reading is probably a more important skill, but a skill it remains. Why do we make this particular skill the sine qua non of education?

Through training, almost anyone can improve his or her skills, but individual differences will remain. Some children will always be terrible baseball players (often to their shame), and some children will always be terrible readers (always to their shame). To base the notion of the "good teacher" on such "objective measurements" as test scores is to create teachers who teach not for creativity, fun, imagination, freedom, exuberance, and the love of learning, but rather for test results. And teaching merely to get test results not only deprives students of the opportunity to think, question, reason, or disagree, it also informs 50% of the group that they are below average and tells 10% that they are just no good at all!

If teachers are to be held accountable, will those students who are below average in reading be pushed, mauled, and remediated? Shouldn't we instead tinker with the regular education regimen and get on with the process of educating the child? But that's not what we do. Instead, we say, "If a child doesn't learn to read, we can't teach him anything." So we make him spend extra time working on this particular skill. If another child can't get the assigned reading in one hour, should we make her spend two? We take children with eyes that won't focus, fingers that won't cooperate, sensory pathways that won't coordinate, association areas that won't associate, neurons that don't fire appropriately, connections that aren't connected, brains that won't attend, and we say, "Sorry, but you must read anyway. And if you don't read, you're educationally and vocationally shot. (And I don't get my raise.)" The combination of school and homework is for some students far more arduous than the 19th-century sweatshops.

Parents sometimes get angry at brutish physical education teachers who shame children who can't throw a ball because they aren't physically coordinated to do so. In enlightened schools, we even excuse some children from physical education. But we do nothing about teachers who shame children who can't read because they aren't physically coordinated to do so. And we never excuse them from reading. Instead, we pile on more. It's about accountability, after all.

Our emphasis on accountability fails to take into consideration the single clear fact of life: *children are different.* It is the only psychological truth accepted by all psychologists. Children are different. Certainly educators know this to be true. Howard Gardner has been espousing the idea of multiple intelligences for years. Teacher educators have been teaching it for years. Why, then, do federal and state mandates for accountability result in what teachers know will never work: a foolish emphasis on sameness—same classes, same books, same chronological age in the classroom, same program, same assignments, same tests, same curriculum, same instruction?

The tremendous variation in children is not abnormal, but squeezing them into a common learning mold is. In our emphasis on accountability, we operate as though individual differences *don't* exist. That's just plain stupid. But we also operate as though differences *shouldn't* exist, and that's just plain cruel.

The child with low reading ability is not diseased. That child is different in a very normal way, and if you shove a book into his or her hand, you are limiting that child's education.

There has been no essential change in schooling in more than a hundred years—except in the number of inmates being schooled. We still think students can learn only through the sacred tool of reading. We still act as if a child learns more under conditions of stress and seem to believe that the more stress, the more learning. We still think that children ought to be punished if they aren't the same as the rest and that differences—in responses, attitudes, movements—are deviant, disabling, and disturbing. We still teach children that, unless they are successful in school, they are losers. And we still hold teachers accountable for the failure of children to read.

Many school systems are guilty of child abuse, dehumanizing children, and teaching them that they are an educational waste. When children are having trouble with reading, they learn that they are not okay and that school is not where they belong.

Check the dropouts. Many of them were diagnosed with learning disabilities. A great many have attention deficits. They became problem children—hyperactive, demanding attention, disruptive, aggressive, truant. They didn't really drop out by choice. They were forced out of school. In fact, they are not learning disabled; the schools are teaching disabled.

Why is it that we insist on calling a child "learning disabled" if he has difficulty reading, but we don't label a child "disabled" if she can't compose a song? Educators have set up altars to reading. They worship at its shrine and intone the doctrine "Outside of reading, there is no salvation." And if the child can't read, there are the stocks, the pillories, solitary confinement—all the torture devices.

A graduate student who teaches in a high school for students with language learning disabilities recently asked for help with some strategies for teaching *Huckleberry Finn*. She said she was having a hard time getting students to appreciate or understand the story. While thinking about strategies she could use, it suddenly became clear that perhaps there was really no point in trying to get these students to appreciate classic literature. They are a group of students who will rarely, if ever, pick up a novel to read for pleasure.

A student who recently graduated from college with a 3.7 grade-point average told us that she had to read 32 novels in high school. For her it was a painful, tearful, agonizing experience. She has never picked up a book to read for pleasure, because for her there is no pleasure in reading.

Let's be honest. Is the skill of reading classic literature that important? For students to become successful citizens, it is certainly helpful to have a command of the written word. But do we need to expose all students to courses in fiction and literature as ninth-graders, in poetry and drama as 10th-graders, in American literature and folklore as 11th-graders, and in British literature as 12th-graders? Can you pick out the slow readers and the nonreaders as you walk down the street? Does a person who hears well, remembers adequately, and works in a nonwriting or nonreading vocation (which includes most) suffer greatly from a reading disability? Only until commencement day, if there is one. The disability disappears as soon as such a student leaves school. Why should school be such an agony? Who declared that reading was so important?

Art can be viewed and created without reading. Concerts can be heard and instruments played. History can come in the form of videos, movies, photographs, and plays. Social studies and current events flow from the television sets. Films, videos, cassette tapes, records, pictures, demonstrations, and the spoken word are all available as ways of learning. And yet where do we force education to abide? In the textbook. In the written word. Imagine a book designed to show students how to assemble an engine. Then imagine a written test to see if the students have learned how to assemble an engine. Then imagine having your car fixed by a student who had passed the test but had never worked on an engine.

We "do" physical education. Why can't we "do" art and music and history and science and math? If there are good readers around, let them review the literature as their contribution. Why must everyone do so? The library is not necessarily the center of the educational process. And if learning by reading is torturous, arduous, even impossible, let's forget the reading. Give every child every opportunity to learn to read, but let's not make failure to acquire this skill mean failure in virtually all school learning. If the skill of reading makes each day a torment, makes the child feel devalued, and interferes with the acquisition of knowledge, then away with it! Let's put reading in its rightful place and get on with the learning process.

The "three R's" of reading, 'riting, and 'rithmetic are the marks of an educational elite, excellent hallmarks for what schools were meant to do a hundred years ago. We are appealing for a new way of looking at schooling, for more recognition of individual differences, for more concern for true democracy, and for fewer objective tests.

Accountability? Sure. But accountability for what? Let's make teachers accountable only for their humane treatment of children. Let's make them accountable not for how well their children test in the three R's, but for how well they function in the three "L's": living without fear or shame, loving themselves and others, and learning about this wonderful world at their own speed and in their own way.

NO

Jerry Jesness

You Have Your Teacher's Permission to Be Ignorant

I once read a cheery story about a caring teacher who helped her failing students by shortening their assignments. "Don't worry," the teacher assured a crying child as she handed him a shortened list of spelling words, "I will give you an assignment at which you can succeed." The implication was that the teacher, by crossing some words off of a list, "gave" the student success. We teachers are familiar with this line of thought. It is almost a rite of passage for first-year teachers to be called into their principals' offices to be chastised after releasing their first round of grades. "If you want to fail these children," the principal begins, as if the teacher is issuing failing grades for her own pleasure. "We want these children to succeed," the teacher is told. "We don't want them to experience failure."

We teachers remember with pain, laughter, or both, the in-service sessions in which we learned to empathize with our students, to feel their pain. At one such session, a presenter gave several commands in rapid succession. "Fold your paper in nine equal parts," he commanded, and rapidly added: "Draw a tetrahedron in the upper left corner. Write the name of the capital of Outer Mongolia in the square directly above the lower left-hand corner. Write the square root of 386 rounded to the nearest whole number in the square closest to the center. Put down your pencils! Why aren't you finished?" he shouted in feigned anger.

At another workshop, participants were asked to write while viewing their hands and writing in a mirror. At another, participants were asked to assemble jigsaw puzzles which, in reality, contained mismatched pieces. The moral of these sessions was always that it hurts to fail; therefore, give the kids tasks that they can perform with relative ease. Success is good and failure is bad, so let us give our students the former.

It is truly absurd to suggest that teachers are so powerful that we can somehow grant and withhold success with mere strokes of our pens. Sixty-nine percent represents failure, 70 percent represents success, and 90 percent represents honor. So, according to this way of thinking, a teacher can bring students success or honor by simply simplifying the assignments or by devising an excuse to tack on a few extra points.

From Jerry Jesness, "You Have Your Teacher's Permission to Be Ignorant," *Education Week*, vol. 20, no. 10 (November 8, 2000). Copyright © 2000 by Editorial Projects in Education. Reprinted by permission of *Education Week* and the author.

It is a linguistic fluke that the word "fail" means both to lack success and to score below a set standard. Real success is based on what the student knows, not on what a teacher ordains. If a 1st grade student learns to read, he has succeeded. A classmate who did not learn to read has failed, even if the teacher declares him a success by giving him a passing grade. A well-read, knowledgeable recent high school graduate has the tools for success. In fact, so does a well-read, knowledgeable dropout. A barely literate graduate armed only with an undeserved diploma and a transcript filled with inflated grades is, however, going to have problems. Only knowledge is power.

Some of the greatest frustrations that we teachers feel result from conflicting expectations placed on us. On the one hand, we are expected to honestly evaluate our students' knowledge, skills, and progress. On the other, we are expected to assure that all, or at least most, "succeed," even if we have to fabricate that success by watering down the material or inflating the grades. Teachers are expected to both follow a curriculum and to manipulate that curriculum so that all students at least enjoy the illusion of success.

Low standards, particularly for students who have known little else, can actually make a teacher look good. Feel-good activities and mind-numbing busywork can be very effective classroom-management techniques. While challenging assignments may motivate students who have come to expect them, students who have never been pushed are likely to react to such assignments by misbehaving. Veteran teachers will tell you that some of their best teaching may have appeared to be their worst. The student who refuses to open his literature textbook in August, yet somehow develops a love for reading by the following May, or one who quivers with anger or frustration while attempting new algorithms, yet becomes enthusiastic about math after mastering them, should warm our hearts.

Many competent readers had to be dragged, screaming and kicking, through their first novels, and many top math students once had to have the multiplication tables drilled into them. Helen Keller first reacted to Anne Sullivan's finger-spelling lessons by screaming, kicking, and biting. Unpleasant confrontations, however, may result in poor evaluations from administrators or complaints from parents. Smiling faces and busy fingers make for the best public relations.

[Recently] a journalist for a Houston newspaper visited an inner-city high school and observed some classes. He wrote disparagingly of an English teacher whose 11th grade students were performing dismally on a test covering a Shakespeare play, but praised an algebra teacher who captured his students' attention by using games of chance to teach them about probability. What's wrong with this picture? Probability is not a part of algebra. While I do not know the teachers in question and therefore cannot judge their abilities, it is clear that the English teacher was, however unsuccessfully, covering high-school-level literature, while the algebra teacher had abandoned his assigned subject and replaced it with basic math.

I recently had a conversation with a probationary teacher who had just been told that her contract would not be renewed. I was quite impressed by both her general knowledge and her knowledge of the subject she taught. She explained to me that, despite the fact that most of her 11th graders came to her reading at only a 4th or 5th grade level, she had managed to lead them through Rudolfo Anaya's *Bless Me Ultima*, a novel appropriate for students who can at least read at a high school level. She had also managed to coax research papers from most of them. Earlier this year, she had been called into her principal's office and asked to "adjust" some of her student's grades. She was also asked to apologize to the parents of some discontented students. She refused to do either, and she is now looking for another job. She refused to give her students permission to be ignorant, so now she will pay the price.

While most teachers who give their students permission to know less than their peers do so by turning a blind eye to their failures, we special education teachers put that permission in writing. Each year, we meet with an administrator, a student's parents, and others responsible for the student's education to discuss his or her individual educational program, or IEP. At these meetings, we set the student's educational goals for the year.

I never cease to be awed by this responsibility. It is not that it is wrong to hold those of lesser skills and abilities to a lower standard. We certainly should not, for example, demand that Down's syndrome children perform differential calculus. Nor should we require illiterate children to analyze great works of literature. Still, the responsibility of determining the standard to which a child should be held is an awesome one.

⟐

It is easy to succumb to the temptation to teach special-needs children at their comfort levels. The system allows and often encourages us to do so. This, however, is rarely in the child's best interest.

My school once had a 4th grade child come from a neighboring district unable to subtract or to write in cursive handwriting. Although her IEP included only the most rudimentary literacy and math skills, the girl seemed to be fairly bright, so we wrote her new IEP near her grade level. After some pushing and prodding, she mastered her basics and is now comfortably working with regular 4th grade material. Another 4th grader was reduced to tears several times in the process of learning long division, a procedure he eventually mastered. It is fortunate that I was not observed during some of those students' more difficult moments in my class.

There is nothing more heart-wrenching than a special-needs child in tears, but there is nothing more heartwarming than the smile of a child for whom schoolwork has ceased to be a mystery.

We teachers should imagine ourselves as swimming instructors whose charges will someday be thrown out of a boat half a mile from shore. If we certify that a nonswimming student is a competent swimmer, he will still sink like a stone when thrown from the boat.

In like manner, a graduate who lacks real academic skills, who has only the trappings of scholarly success, will have a difficult time swimming in the real world. Failure is failure, with or without our permission.

POSTSCRIPT

Should Students with Disabilities Be Exempt from Standards-Based Curriculum?

More exacting standards—for teachers, students and schools—are here. There is no changing this reality. And yet—how should the reality impact students with disabilities?

Vohs, Landau and Romano, authors of PEER (2000), an extensive parent information document on standards-based curriculum and assessment, acknowledge that while state standards range from broad to specific, all share the common goal of raising expectations—from which all students can benefit. The report concedes it is certainly easier to include all students in broad, literacy based frameworks, but that all students can participate at some level of the new standards, with appropriate support. Addressing the specific needs of some students with more significant disabilities, the authors advocate for individualized performance standards within the common content, even for vocational goals.

Although Knowles and Knowles might be more at ease with standards stressing basic literacy, they are still concerned that some students will be unnecessarily hurt by the rigor of today's new expectations—finding that the short term misery and struggle of learning specific skills deprives a child of the ability to feel empowered to develop life skills in which they really are competent.

In a study of legal and practical considerations for graduation of students with disabilities, Lanford and Carey (*Remedial and Special Education*, 2000) maintain that, since most students with disabilities spend most of their time in general education classes, they should work within the same curriculum. However, they also indicate that a total academic curriculum may not be appropriate for all students with disabilities, whose programs should be clearly stated in their IEPs.

Jerry Jesness would counsel teachers and parents not to stray from the standard curriculum too easily, lest opportunities for success be lost. And yet, Jesness acknowledges that high expectations do not mean the same expectations for everyone. The challenge is in knowing how to balance the curriculum and individual needs.

In *Educating One and All*, exploring the involvement of students with disabilities in standards based reform, McDonnell and McLouglin (National Research Council, 1997) wrestle with the complex balance between individualized programs and statewide standards. Referencing research concluding that post-school employment possibilities are broadened with supported community-based training best begun while students are in school, they wonder how these activities will mesh with a standard curriculum that does not include vocational or career goals.

Related to all these puzzles is the recent backlash against standards-based programs that focus on academics. In his Seventh Annual State of American Education Address (2000), then Secretary of Education Richard Riley called for a "midcourse review" of the standards movement. Urging educators to continue increasing expectations, Riley counseled that standards need to be stimulating for all, but reachable by more than just a very few.

Since educational standards are decided on a state-by-state basis, the involvement of students with disabilities will likely be determined that way as well, guided by the mandates of IDEA97. And yet, that very strategy brings a number of questions to mind. Does what you learn depend on where you live? And if that's the case, will parents of children with disabilities move to locations where the specific needs of their children are best met? Does everyone need to learn the same curriculum or are different life paths best served by different programs? Is there a core curriculum that everyone needs to learn? If so, who decides what that is to be? For students with complex needs, does a vocationally-related course of study limit horizons, provide time on task for relevant skills or offer opportunities for creative connection with academic frameworks? And who makes these decisions?

ISSUE 13

Are the Least-Trained Teaching Our Most Needy Children?

YES: Michael F. Giangreco et al., from "Helping or Hovering? Effects of Instructional Assistant Proximity on Students With Disabilities," *Exceptional Children* (Fall 1997)

NO: Susan Unok Marks, Carl Schrader, and Mark Levine, from "Paraeducator Experiences in Inclusive Settings: Helping, Hovering, or Holding Their Own?" *Exceptional Children* (Spring 1999)

ISSUE SUMMARY

YES: Michael F. Giangreco, a research associate professor specializing in inclusive education, and his colleagues assert that untrained teacher assistants spend too much time closely attached to individual students, often hindering the involvement of certified teachers and nondisabled peers.

NO: Susan Unok Marks, Carl Schrader, and Mark Levine, of the Behavioral Counseling and Research Center in San Rafael, California, find that professionally trained classroom teachers are often less prepared than some assistants to work with children in inclusive settings and that, unprepared to supervise assistants, they use this lack of knowledge to avoid teaching children with disabilities.

Teacher assistant, paraprofessional, teacher's aide, inclusion aide, special education paraeducator; whatever the title, every district has many dedicated, hard-working people who support children in inclusive classroom settings. What do we know about what they do? And what do *they* know about what *they* do?

Teacher assistants first appeared in U.S. schools in the 1950s to address the teacher shortage that arose as baby boom children came of age. Their first roles were clerical, helping the classroom teacher with routines such as copying, maintaining bulletin boards, and taking attendance. By 1965 there were about 10,000 teacher assistants in U.S. schools. Tasks and responsibilities remained clear: the aide helped; the teacher taught.

In the full flower of the inclusion movement, as well as the special education teacher shortage, there are now over 500,000 teacher assistants in schools across America. More than half of them work with children who have disabilities, frequently spending all day with a single child who is enrolled in a general education classroom.

While paralegals and paramedics have clearly delineated job responsibilities separating their roles from those of the professionals whom they assist, such is not the case with paraeducators (French and Pickett, *Teacher Education and Special Education,* 1997). Few states require specific qualifications for paraprofessionals. Many districts have a single job description (if that) covering individuals who help with the cafeteria and the lunchroom as well as those who assist with medical procedures, support children with severe behavior problems, assist in separate classrooms, or work as inclusion supports.

Michael F. Giangreco, Susan W. Edelman, Tracy Evans Luiselli, and Stephanie Z. C. MacFarland devote much of their time to designing and supporting inclusive educational programs to maximize student participation. In the following selection, they supplement the comments of teachers, therapists, parents, and paraprofessionals with their own observations of the assistants' activities. Parents and teachers want paraprofessionals in the general classrooms so that students with significant disabilities can be adequately supported. Unfortunately, say Giangreco et al., by their close physical presence assistants often prevent active inclusion, frequently hovering over their charges rather than encouraging involvement and natural supports. Training for the assistants rarely occurs—most frequently they learn from each other. The result, according to the authors and the people they interviewed, is that the paraprofessional assumes full responsibility for teaching the child—and is the least trained to do so.

Susan Unok Marks, Carl Schrader, and Mark Levine collaborate closely with school staff to design positive behavioral support plans for students with challenging behaviors. Their interviews with a number of paraprofessionals, which they discuss in the second selection, echoed many of the same themes found by Giangreco et al. Assistants say that they willingly assume significant responsibilities, including the role of "expert." The difference is that Marks et al. found the assistants, in fact, to be the experts. Most of the classroom teachers did not attend training or know the inclusion students well enough to feel comfortable taking charge of instruction. In fact, according to Marks et al., the teachers are the least trained, and they are not teaching the children.

As you read these selections, you will hear the voices of the people who are most closely connected to children whose needs require extra assistance. These voices convey commitment as well as concern. Who is teaching the neediest students? Are they prepared to do so? Are teachers delegating responsibilities to support personnel fairly, or have teachers abdicated their own responsibility to teach a wide range of children?

Michael F. Giangreco et al.

 **YES**

Helping or Hovering?

As students with disabilities increasingly are placed in general education schools and classes, the use of instructional assistants has greatly expanded. Recent national figures estimate that over 500,000 instructional assistants are employed in public schools, and increases are anticipated in the coming years. Although their changing roles and responsibilities have gained recent attention, the proliferation of instructional assistants in public schools often has outpaced conceptualization of team roles and responsibilities, as well as training and supervision needs of instructional assistants. Nowhere is this more evident than in schools where students with severe or multiple disabilities are included in general education classrooms.

In our work in public schools, we have noticed intructional assistants playing increasingly prominent roles in the education of students with disabilities. With pressure from parents, who want to ensure that their children are adequately supported, and general educators, who want to make sure they and their students are adequately supported, the use of special education instructional assistants has become a primary mechanism to implement more inclusive schooling practices. Although we have been encouraged by situations where students with disabilities have been provided with previously unavailable educational opportunities, we are concerned that some current approaches to providing instructional assistant support might be counterproductive....

The purpose of this study was to ... [highlight] some of the key issues we observed in general education classrooms where students with disabilities were supported by instructional assistants. The nature of these findings holds important implications for evaluating how we use, train, and supervise instructional assistants so that their work can be supportive of valued educational outcomes for students with disabilities and their peers without disabilities in general education classrooms....

One of the most prominent findings that emerged from [our observations] was that instructional assistants were in close proximity to the students with disabilities on an ongoing basis. This was evidenced by (a) the instructional assistant maintaining physical contact with the student (e.g., shoulder, back, arms, hands) or the student's wheelchair; (b) the instructional assistant sitting in a chair immediately next to the child; (c) the student sitting in the instructional assistant's lap when classmates were seated on the floor; and (d) the instructional assistant accompanying the student with disabilities to virtually every place the student went within the classroom, school building, and grounds.

Although study participants indicated that some level of close proximity between students with disabilities and instructional assistants was desirable and sometimes essential (e.g., tactile signing, instructional interactions, health management), they also recognized that unnecessary and excessive adult proximity was not always necessary and could be detrimental to students. As one mother who had observed her son's classroom stated:

> At calendar time in the morning she (instructional assistant) doesn't have to be right by his side. She could kind of walk away. She doesn't have to be part of his wheelchair. That's what it feels like. I just think that he could break away a little bit (from the instructional assistant) if he were included more into all the activities with the regular classroom teacher.

A speech/language pathologist from the same team independently stated, "I think there is some unnecessary mothering or hovering going on."

... [Eight] subthemes pertaining to proximity between instructional assistants and students with disabilities ... are presented in the following sections.

Interference With Ownership and Responsibility by General Educators

Most of the classroom teachers in this sample did not describe their role as including responsibility for educating the student with disabilities who was placed in their class. Team members reported that the proximity and availability of the instructional assistants created a readily accessible opportunity for professional staff to avoid assuming responsibility and ownership for the education of students with disabilities placed in general education classrooms.

Different expectations regarding the role of the classroom teacher was a point of conflict within many of the teams. As one related services provider stated, "She (the classroom teacher) doesn't take on direct instruction (of the students with disabilities). In fact, ... she stated at meetings that she doesn't see that as her role. And I disagree with that. I mean she is a teacher."

Although special educators and related services providers were involved in each case, almost universally it was the instructional assistants who were given the responsibility and ownership for educating the students with disabilities. Teachers were observed having limited interactions with the student with disabilities, proportionally less than those with other class members. Involvement by the teachers that did occur most often was limited to greetings, farewells, and occasional praise. Instructional interactions occurred less frequently (e.g., being called on to answer a question in class). A special educator summed up the need for clarification sought by many educational team members when she said, "What should the classroom teacher's role be? Even in our most successful situations we don't have a lot of classroom teachers who are saying, 'I have teaching responsibility for this kid.'" Most teams we observed had not confronted this issue. "We haven't as a team come out and said, 'All right, what is the role of the classroom teacher in teaching this child?'"

Data consistently indicated that it was the instructional assistants, not the professional staff, who were making and implementing virtually all of the day-to-day curricular and instructional decisions. One speech pathologist said, "[We (the team) have talked about this many times. We have our most seriously challenging students with instructional assistants." A special educator explained, "The reality is that the instructional assistants are the teachers. Though I'm not comfortable with them having to make as many instructional decisions." An experienced instructional assistant explained, "I never get that kind of information (about instruction related issues and planning). I just wing it!"

The instructional assistants demonstrated unfettered autonomy in their actions throughout the day as evidenced by entering, leaving, and changing teacher-directed whole class activities whenever they chose with no evidence of consulting the teacher. As one instructional assistant said, "We do not do a lot of what the class does. I do what I think he can do." She justified her role as decision maker by saying, "I am the one that works with him all day long." Instructional assistants reported becoming increasingly comfortable with their role as the primary instructor for the student with disabilities, as one stated, "[We are] the only people who really feel comfortable with Holly."

The instructional assistants in this study reported that they received mostly on-the-job training from other instructional assistants by talking with each other and job shadowing so that patterns of interaction by instructional assistants were passed on. In service training that a small number received typically was conducted in groups that included only other instructional assistants. Ironically, experienced professionals who said things like, "We do not have the training to work with these high needs kids" turned over the education of their most challenging students to instructional assistants, many of whom were high school educated, had no previous classroom experience, and had minimal training. As one special educator acknowledged, from a logical perspective, "It doesn't make sense."

In one site where an instructional assistant was not present, the classroom teacher, with support from special educators and related services providers, successfully assumed the primary role for instructing the student with disabilities. She directed his instructional program, spent time teaching him within groups and individually, used sign language to communicate with him, and included him in all class activities. This teacher stated, "You know the teacher needs to be the one who makes the decisions a lot because she is working with Mark (student with disabilities) and she knows Mark and knows which areas he needs help in." A special educator in this site acknowledged that not every aspect of this student's individualized education program (IEP) requires significant support and that some aspects of the IEP, "left to the regular educator would be just fine." The specialist for the deaf-blind on this team said, "I think a lot of it (the teacher's success with the students with disabilities) is that she has high expectations for Mark. She does not do for him; instead she shows him how to do things. She considers him very much part of the class."

Separation From Classmates

Instructional assistants were regularly observed separating the student with disabilities from the class group. For example, when it was time to go to a special area class (e.g., art, music, physical education) one instructional assistant consistently left class a couple minutes before the rest of the class to wheel the student with disabilities to the specialty classroom.

Even when the students were basically stationary, such as seated on a rug to hear a story, the instructional assistant often physically separated the student with disabilities from the group by positioning him on the fringe of the group (e.g., the farthest away from the teacher). Instructional assistants reported that their positioning of the student allowed them to leave the activity whenever they chose.

Sometimes separation from the class occurred during circumstances where the match between class activity and the student's individual needs appeared highly compatible. For example, Annie entered the classroom during an individual writing time. As the instructional assistant began an adapted writing activity using large chart paper and markers, a second instructional assistant approached her and said, "She can do this writing just as easily in the other room as here." With that prompt, the instructional assistants separated Annie from the class without consultation with, or resistance from, the classroom teacher.

Dependence on Adults

Instructional assistants in close proximity to students with disabilities were observed prompting most every behavior exhibited by the students in this study (e.g., using writing implements, using gestures, following instructions, using materials). There was little evidence of fading prompts to decrease dependence and encourage students to respond to other people (e.g., school staff, peers) and more naturally occurring cues (e.g., the presence of certain toys or school supplies). Alternatively, an instructional assistant who was cognizant of Helen's dependence on her, encouraged her to do things for herself through redirection, especially when the student sought unneeded assistance with tasks such as dressing and grooming.

An example of dependence on adults was observed on the school playground during recess. The student with disabilities was being shadowed on a large wooden play structure by an instructional assistant. The student was capably crossing a wooden bridge where safety was not a concern. The student charged toward the bridge, letting go of her assistant's hand. A few steps onto the bridge she stopped abruptly and quietly turned back toward the instructional assistant who was only a foot behind her. The instructional assistant smiled, saying, "You know me. I stick right with you." The student reached back and took the instructional assistant's hand instead of crossing the short span of the playground bridge on her own. Sometimes the school system's dependence on instructional assistants was so strong that when the instructional assistants were absent, the family was asked to keep the child home from school or the mother was asked to be the substitute instructional assistant.

Impact on Peer Interactions

Data indicated that close proximity of instructional assistants had an impact on interactions between students with disabilities and their classroom peers. As one special educator shared:

> Sometimes I think it inhibits her relationship with her peers because a lot is done for Holly and Holly doesn't have the opportunity to interact with her peers because there is always somebody hovering over her, showing her what to do or doing things for her. I'd like to get the instructional assistant away from Holly a little bit more so that peers will have a chance to get in there and work more with Holly.

A classroom teacher offered her perspectives on how instructional assistants might be used differently.

> I would definitely prefer having a paraprofessional assigned to the classroom and then just as necessary to have her work with a child (with special educational needs) when there is a specific activity, but not exclusively to work with just that child. I think it is important for two reasons. One is that you don't want to give the child any extra stigma that is associated with a special education label. Second is that it is more healthy for the paraprofessional to work with other children so that he or she doesn't get burned out with working with just one child all the time.

Interference with peer interactions did not occur in all cases. Some team members said that if the instructional assistant was well liked by the other children it had a positive impact on the student with disabilities' access to peers. As a physical therapist described, "I have also seen it (proximity of instructional assistants) be very, very positive, in that the instructional assistant is really well liked and has done a lot to establish wonderful friendships for the student."

Conversely, if the instructional assistant was not well liked it had a corresponding negative impact. Sometimes the close proximity students had with instructional assistants led peers to perceive them as a package deal. As one mother cautiously shared, "I don't know if I should say this or not, but a lot of it was that kids didn't like the aide, so they would stay away from Annie for that reason."

When teachers assigned students to student-directed pairs or small groups, instructional assistants were often observed dominating the group's interactions. In some cases, the involvement of the instructional assistant was so omnipresent that children without disabilities simply left the group with the instructional assistant and joined a different group with only classmates, no adults. In other cases when students without disabilities initiated interactions, they were rebuffed by the instructional assistant. Ronny (a student without disabilities) asked the instructional assistant, "Do you want me to help Jamie?" She answered, "No, not yet." Ronny was never asked back to assist his classmate. At other times instructional assistants interrupted initiations made by peers. For example, in a physical education class, Michael went over to Jaime and began to run with him in his wheelchair to participate in the activity. The instructional assistant interrupted this interaction saying to Michael, "If you want to run, I'll push Jaime." After a hesitant pause, Michael reluctantly gave way to the instructional assistant. At times, prolonged close adult proximity adversely affected peer involvement even when the instructional assistant was not present. As one special educator shared:

> We've tried (reducing adult proximity) ... like in the lunchroom. Like putting Maria or any of the other students (with disabilities) in the lunchroom and then backing off a little bit. But I think that it (close adult proximity) has been done for so long, that the peers have stayed away for so long, that they are just kind of hesitant to jump right in and do anything.

When the instructional assistant was not in close proximity to the student with disabilities, peers were more likely to fill the space the instructional assistant had vacated. The following example is typical of what we observed.

> As the instructional assistant leaves momentarily to get some materials, Mallory (student without disabilities) walks over to Elena (student with disabilities). She puts her hand gently on her shoulder and calmly says "easy hands" in response to Elena being a bit rough with her book. Elena turns to look at Mallory and then makes some vocalizations and moves her hands as Mallory talks to her about her book. As the instructional assistant starts to return, Mallory stops talking with Elena and returns to her seat.

Limitations on Receiving Competent Instruction

Observations and interviews indicated that students in this study participated in classroom activities that typically were not planned by trained professional staff. While several team members praised the work of instructional assistants in their "caregiving duties" (e.g., feeding, dressing), they expressed concerns about their role as assistants of instruction.

Many classroom teachers expected capabilities and performance from instructional assistants that were potentially unrealistic. As one teacher explained, "My problem is that I will be teaching a class and my expectations are that the paraprofessional will get the gist of what I am doing and glean some kernel out of it that can be used right then on the spot." Making such on-the-spot decisions requires a depth of instructional knowledge and skill that many paraprofessionals and professionals do not possess.

When instructional assistants are assigned to a task, many of them say they feel compelled to go through the motions of an activity even when it seems apparent to them that their efforts are not being effective. As one instructional assistant explained, "Sometimes it gets discouraging because he is asleep, but I try. I just feel like I'm baby-sitting. I don't feel like I'm doing what I am supposed to be doing." This instructional assistant was observed repeatedly continuing to speak to the student and presenting activity-related objects, even though it was obvious that the student was asleep. In other cases, instructional assistants would both ask and answer questions posed to students with disabilities. "Would you like to paint the turkey?" (after a 1 sec pause with no observable response) "You would!", then the activity would begin.

Loss of Personal Control

When students have significant communication, motor, and/or sensory difficulties, it can be a challenge for students to advocate for themselves, express their preferences, or at times to reject the decisions of the adults who control most aspects of their personal daily functions at school (e.g., eating, toileting, mobility, selection of leisure activities, choice of friends with whom to spend time). A vision specialist put it succinctly when she pointed out the limited opportunities for choices provided to students with disabilities who "can't verbalize and say 'stop talking to me like that' or can't run away." Instructional assistants frequently made such choices for the student under their supervision. In cases where student communication is unclear, we are left to wonder if the decisions are those the student would make. As one parent wondered, "I think it would be intimidating for me if I was a kid. Just being watched over all the time."

The following examples from our observations, presented as questions, highlight the kinds of decisions made every day that represent a loss of personal control by the students:

- Did Mary really want her cheeseburger dipped in applesauce before she ate each bite?
- Did James really need to be excused from the fun activities in the gymnasium early to have his diapers changed?
- Did James really want to stay inside during recess because it was too cold outside?

Loss of Gender Identity by Students With Disabilities

In cases where the instructional assistant and the student were the opposite gender we observed some interactions that suggested the gender of the student with disabilities was secondary to the gender of the instructional assistant. For example, the gender of the instructional assistant superseded that of the student with disabilities in a physical education class. The teacher divided the class into two groups for warm-up activities. The girls were directed to take five laps around the gym and the boys were directed to do jumping-jacks. As the physical education teacher said, "OK. Let's go!", the female instructional assistant grabbed James' wheelchair and began running around the gym with him along with all the other girls. When the activity was switched, she assisted him in moving his arms to partially participate in jumping-jacks, again with the girls.

Interference With Instruction of Other Students

Students without disabilities did not seem to be distracted much by idiosyncratic behaviors of their classmate with disabilities (e.g., coughing, vocalizations, stereotyped body movements) or common classroom sounds and movements (e.g., small group discussions, questions being asked of the teacher, talk among classmates, computers, pencil sharpener being used, doors and drawers being opened and closed). However, in some cases instructional assistant behaviors were observed to cause distraction during large group lessons taught by the teacher. During these times, if the instructional assistant began doing a different activity with the student with disabilities in the midst of the teacher's large group activity (e.g., reading a story, playing a game, using manipulative materials), those students without disabilities closest to the instructional assistant turned their attention away from the teacher and toward the instructional assistant.

Discussion

Although many team members acknowledged that instructional assistants can and do play an important role in educating children with disabilities, our interviews and observations identified a series of concerns regarding their proximity to the students they are assigned to support.... [A]ny generalization to other situations should be approached cautiously, especially considering the modest number of sites, the limited geographic distribution of sites, and their homogeneity in terms of serving students with multiple disabilities in general education classrooms.

... Too often students with disabilities are placed in general education classrooms without clear expectations established among the team members regarding which professional staff will plan, implement, monitor, evaluate, and adjust instruction. This absence of clarity helps create an environment in which the instructional assistant directs a student's educational program and maintains excessive proximity with the student. We believe this occurs not because instructional assistants seize control, but rather because instructional assistants are the people in the most subordinate position in the school hierarchy. When supervisory personnel (e.g., classroom teachers, special educators) engaged in limited planning and implemention of instruction for the student with disabilities, the responsibility fell to the assistants. These observations highlight that some decisions about the use of instructional assistants are not necessarily rational, but rather may be driven by teachers' (a) fear of difference or change, (b) adherence to customary routines, (c) a reluctance to add another substantial task to what many perceive as an already extensive set of responsibilities, or (d) lack of knowledge and/or support for teaching the student with disabilities. Instructional assistants can play a valuable educational role in assisting the teaching faculty, but generally we believe it is inappropriate and inadvisable to have instructional assistants serve in the capacity of "teacher."

Although awareness ... is an important first step in addressing ... potential hazards, teachers and instructional assistants may need specific training in basic instructional methods designed to fade assistance and encourage students to respond to natural cues.... Otherwise adults may inadvertently be strengthening the student's cue and prompt dependence. To some extent, many students are initially dependent on cues and supports from the adults who teach them. This starting point needs to change so that adults are increasingly aware of fading their supports to allow students greater autonomy. While capable learners can often overcome less than stellar teaching approaches, those students with more significant learning difficulties often require more precise planning and instruction in our efforts to help them learn. We believe that this problem is not an issue of placement location, since these same problems can exist in special education classes....We suggest that the classroom involvement of instructional assistants must be compatible within the context of the broader plan for the classroom that is developed and implemented by the classroom team for the benefit of all the students.

Conclusions and Implications for Practice

The findings of this study demonstrate that there are a number of areas of concern regarding the roles of instructional assistants who support the education of students with disabilities in general education settings. The following is a list of considerations for future policy development, school-based practices, training, and research.

- School districts need to rethink their policies on hiring instructional assistants for individual students. We suggest that alternatives be explored that include hiring assistants for the classroom rather than an individual student. This would allow general and special education teachers to distribute instructional assistants' time and job responsibilities more equitably to benefit a variety of students, both with and without disabilities.
- School staff and families need to reach agreement on when students need the close proximity of an adult, when that proximity can be appropriately provided through natural supports such as classmates, and when to appropriately withdraw supports that require close proximity.
- School staff and community members (e.g., classroom teachers, special educators, parents) need awareness training on the effects and potential harm to children caused by excessive adult proximity....
- School teams need to explicitly clarify the role of the classroom teacher as the instructional leader in the classroom including their roles and responsibilities as the teacher for their students with disabilities. It is the classroom teacher's role to direct the activities of the classroom, including the activities of instructional assistants in their charge.
- School staff (e.g., classroom teachers, instructional assistants) should be afforded training in basic instructional procedures that facilitate learning by students with special educational needs in the context of typical

classroom activities. Additionally, training should specifically include approaches related to decreasing dependence and fading prompts often associated with excessive and prolonged proximity of adults.

- Students with disabilities need to be physically, programmatically, and interactionally included in classroom activities that have been planned by a qualified teacher in conjunction with support staff as needed (e.g., special educators, related services providers). Such changes in practice should decrease problems associated with students with disabilities being isolated within the classroom.
- Instructional assistants should be provided with competency-based training that includes ongoing, classroom-based supervision by the teacher.
- Instructional assistants should have opportunities for input into instructional planning based on their knowledge of the student, but the ultimate accountability for planning, implementing, monitoring, and adjusting instruction should rest with the professional staff, just as it does for all other students without disabilities.
- Use of instructional assistants in general education classrooms must increasingly be done in ways that consider the unique educational needs of all students in the class, rather than just those with disabilities.

... [A]ssigning an instructional assistant to a student with special educational needs in a general education class, though intended to be helpful, may sometimes result in problems associated with excessive, prolonged adult proximity. In questioning the current use of instructional assistants, we are not suggesting that instructional assistants not be used or that the field revert to historically ineffective ways of educating students with disabilities (e.g., special education classes, special education schools). We are suggesting that our future policy development, training, and research focus on different configurations of service delivery that provide needed supports in general education classrooms, yet avoid the inherent problems associated with our current practices. Undoubtedly, these service provision variations will necessarily need to be individualized and flexible to account for the diverse variations in students, teachers, schools, and communities across our country. We hope that by raising the issues presented in this study, we can extend the national discussion on practices to support students with varying characteristics in general education classrooms and take corresponding actions that will be educationally credible, financially responsible—helping, not hovering!

Susan Unok Marks, Carl Schrader, and Mark Levine

Paraeducator Experiences in Inclusive Settings

Increasing parental demands to place children in least restrictive environments have resulted in school districts being faced with providing inclusion experiences for students with a range of disabilities. However, the option to place a special education student in an inclusive setting is typically limited by many factors, including the (a) student's academic and social functioning level, (b) presence and severity of challenging behaviors, (c) willingness of the general education classroom teacher, and (d) availability of resources within a particular school. Even so, as the benefits of inclusion, particularly in the social areas, have become highlighted, parents have increasingly asserted that regardless of their child's functioning level, willingness of teachers, or current availability of resources, the best educational environment for their child is the inclusive setting.

A growing number of parents are impatient with waiting for schools to undergo the types of systemic changes necessary for creating inclusion programs.... In other words, although the literature on inclusive practices continues to highlight the limitations of the general education setting in meeting the needs of students with disabilities, particularly for students with challenging behaviors, many parents are not willing to wait for a "right time," a time when all the issues that plague placement in inclusive settings and that are often the focus of heated discussions are completely resolved. From the parents' perspective, a *reasonably good* inclusion program today is preferable to a *perfect* inclusion program tomorrow. These parents appear to concur with Keith Storey, who notes "physical integration is a necessary first step for other forms of integration."

One type of support that general education teachers have identified as essential for placing special education students in their classrooms has been extra classroom support. As a result, many school districts, in an effort to meet both the needs of the teachers and the inclusion students, have hired paraeducators....

From Susan Unok Marks, Carl Schrader, and Mark Levine, "Paraeducator Experiences in Inclusive Settings: Helping, Hovering, or Holding Their Own?" *Exceptional Children*, vol. 65, no. 3 (Spring 1999). Copyright © 1999 by The Council for Exceptional Children. Reprinted by permission. References omitted.

Purpose of the Study

In order to better understand the experiences of paraeducators working with inclusion students, the first author conducted a series of interviews. Our purpose in this article is to highlight the primary themes related to how paraeducators assumed their roles and responsibilities and the dilemmas they faced while providing educational and behavioral supports for inclusion students....

Results

Paraeducators [who were interviewed] assumed a range of job responsibilities, such as providing instruction in academic and social skills; making curricular modifications; managing student behaviors; and developing working relationships with others. What is striking about how paraeducators negotiated their roles and responsibilities is that many of them appeared to assume the primary burden of success for the inclusion students. This involved assuming primary responsibility for both academic and behavioral needs in order to ensure that students would be successful (e.g., would remain in the inclusive setting, would be accepted by the teacher). Paraeducators, however, expressed that it was more appropriate for the classroom teacher to assume these primary responsibilities. Why then did these paraeducators take on so much of the responsibility, which inadvertently downplayed the role of the classroom teacher?...

Not Being a "Bother" to the Teacher

In supporting an inclusion student, paraeducators were very concerned with building a positive working relationship with the teacher to whom they were assigned. As one paraeducator noted, "If I had to look at a single factor that made the largest difference in my job, it's the teacher that I'm placed with." The primacy of this aspect of the job also appeared to perpetuate paraeducators assuming primary responsibility for the inclusion student. This was reflected in how paraeducators attempted to ensure that the teacher was not "burdened" by the inclusion student. In other words, they wanted to ensure that the experience of having an inclusion student would be a positive one for the teacher. Further, most of the paraeducators felt that their own success would be defined by how well the teacher accepted the inclusion student.

Concern for building a positive working relationship with the teacher and concern for ensuring positive teacher responses towards them and the inclusion student resulted in paraeducators assuming primary responsibility for managing student behaviors. For many, this role was viewed as an explicit feature of their job responsibilities. For example, as one paraeducator put it, "My job ... was to make sure the child was calm and safe enough that the person whose job it is to educate him can do that." However, the challenge of managing student behaviors within an inclusive setting created a level of stress and frustration for many of the paraeducators. One paraeducator expressed a sense of responsibility for making sure that the student's behavior did not disrupt the classroom or "disturb the teacher":

> It felt like a lot of pressure [being in the inclusive setting] because I ... didn't want her [the inclusion student] to disturb the others and I didn't want her to disturb the teacher. So I felt responsible for every single little sound she made.

Another paraeducator also expressed the importance of maintaining a sense of control with managing behaviors:

> When I went into this experience, I was expecting a child who just needed academic support and adaptations, and it was really all behavioral ... but [I was] just trying to maintain a calm demeanor around him, when really I was very frustrated and a lot of times, very unsure of what to do.

Even when student behaviors were managed for a period of time, events in a student's life (e.g., home circumstances, medication changes) could result in increased problem behaviors. These "episodes" were at times difficult to manage, and one paraeducator talked about a period of time when his student who was having changes in medication levels, "was having around three tantrums a day, and ... it was so draining." Another paraeducator described a similar period of time as "just riding through that storm."

It is clear that these paraeducators felt the primary responsibility for directly handling almost all of the behaviors that would arise. At times this meant explaining the probable reasons for the challenging behaviors to the teachers in order to help them understand the influence of environmental variables, as well as to support the teacher in not taking challenging behaviors personally. At other times, this meant intervening before the classroom teacher would have to:

> I would address a behavior as it arose, before it got to a point where she'd [the teacher] notice it, and so there wasn't an opportunity for her to set a lot of limits with him, because ... I never let it get to that point.

This paraeducator felt it was important not to involve the teacher in managing the student's behavior. Another paraeducator concurred:

> When he [the student] had control, the teacher ... would usually be the first person to [intervene].... Sometimes she would even have him sit in a chair. That was her way of disciplining him ... and when he was in control of himself, he really did very well in those situations ... And, again, if it was a day when he had no control ... I would usually pull him from that activity right away, and do something else. She didn't know him well enough to know real well if it was a day he had control over what he was doing.

Meeting Students' Immediate Academic Needs

Addressing the immediate and daily academic needs of the inclusion student was an equally challenging role for most of the paraeducators. In fact, more than half of the paraeducators identified this as a primary area of support in their job responsibilities. These responsibilities included designing and making adaptations to the curriculum, and in many ways, functioning as the student's primary teacher. Many of the paraeducators assumed tutoring roles (working with their students, one-on-one) for some part of the school day, particularly if the student was not able to "keep up with what the teacher was teaching." One paraeducator felt the biggest challenge was to help his student "keep up academically." Another described her role as "taking what is being taught and making it appropriate for [the student]."

Paraeducators noted that they felt it was the responsibility of the teacher to manage the curriculum; however, they also expressed that this rarely occurred:

> What happens is that they [teachers] leave it up to the aide to do a lot of the work.... But for the most part, the teachers are the ones to create the curriculum for the child, and modify it. And that takes time.... It usually takes a lot of modifications so the child can participate more in the class.... And it was left for me to initiate, and they would say, "Oh, that sounds like a great idea" ... And I would end up doing it, and trying it.

Another paraeducator expressed that no one seemed to want to take responsibility for creating the student's curriculum, and "it just got to the point where it was just easier to do it than to keep asking people to do it." This same paraeducator noted how one of the teachers had been a special education teacher, but didn't have the time to adapt the curriculum. Others echoed this issue of teachers not having enough time or energy for developing and adapting the curriculum for students with disabilities. Another paraeducator further expressed how the teacher with whom she worked was even apologetic about how little attention and time had been given to curricular adaptations due to being busy with other teaching responsibilities.

One paraeducator also noted how it was up to him to ask for ideas and that teachers were generally open to this; however, paraeducators felt it was up to them to ask for ideas only when he or she felt "at a loss":

> The teachers I've been able to work with have been really open—receptive to everything about the program. I think I can walk up to a teacher and ask them what they're doing in class and then sometimes if I'm just at a loss, they'll give me some ideas on some alterations I can make to the curriculum whether it's simplifying it, or altering it in some way ... but I don't do that very often, probably only about once a month.

For the most part, paraeducators found themselves in situations in which waiting for teachers and other professionals to make curricular and teaching decisions was not feasible. Consequently, faced with the need to provide daily academic activities and to make "on-the-spot" modifications to the classroom activities, paraeducators found themselves assuming primary responsibility for day-to-day educational decisions.

Being the "Hub" and the "Expert"

One interesting subtheme that emerged was how paraeducators were placed in the role of being a "hub," or being the liaison between all the various individuals involved in the inclusion student's school life. As one paraeducator put it, "Frankie is a child with more resources available to him than any child I've ever met." Intricately tied to this role of being the hub was being in a position in which they needed to be able to incorporate a range of suggestions and recommendations made by school team members.

On the other hand, many of the paraeducators felt that their daily close contact with the inclusion student made them an expert on the needs of the student with whom they worked. This feeling of being the expert was reflected in how the paraeducators assumed primary responsibility for managing student behaviors and for the day-to-day academic and teaching roles. For example, one paraeducator noted how the teacher didn't know the student well enough to know if it was a day in which the student "had control over what he was doing ... and I got to know him so well that I could tell pretty quickly in a day what kind of shape he was in and if he had control." Further, most of the paraeducators had received training throughout the year on positive behavioral support strategies, resulting in them actually having more knowledge about behavioral support plans and strategies than the classroom teacher. One paraeducator expressed the dilemma of being an expert, yet being in the position of implementing the various suggestions made by others:

> I felt like ... I was very much the hub, with the spokes coming in.... Sometimes I felt like it was hard to be the liaison, or the hub, the person who was the closest, but with the least to say.... It was just a frustrating situation to be in, as an assistant without the degree that gives me the right to say, "Well, my expertise tells me that this is the case."

Being in their unique position of working closely with the student, their job entailed negotiating, mediating, interpreting, and translating the various suggestions presented to them by various members of the school team. One paraeducator described this process as requiring her to at times "blend" the various orientations and suggestions presented to her. This often proved challenging, particularly when the goals and expectations presented by a range of professionals and parents appeared to conflict.

Paraeducators also talked about their unique position in working with parents of inclusion students. Some found this challenging, while others found the experience rewarding. However, it was also noted that by virtue of their positions, parents often approached the paraeducators for ongoing information as well as making educational suggestions regarding what they wanted their child to learn. For example, one of the paraeducators started developing strategies for teaching the inclusion student how to count money, at the request of the parent. This tendency for parents to communicate through the paraeducator also appeared to contribute to the paraeducator feeling like they were the hub, or the liaison between parents and school personnel and between school service providers as well.

"Representing Inclusion": Advocacy and Feelings About Inclusion

Sometimes being the hub or the expert included representing the student and the idea of inclusion to the rest of the school community. As one paraeducator reflected:

> It really matters so much, the ... personality of the assistant, because you're the one ... you represent him. I represent Chris at work, to the other staff members. (All names are pseudonyms.) I represent the project of full inclusion. And it's not always a popular project; it's not a popular thing to start. And, just how well I get along with the staff members, I think, really mattered.

This sense of responsibility seemed to include the feeling that how well the special education student actually did in the inclusive setting would be a direct reflection on how school personnel would view the paraeducator. Again, the success of the inclusion placement was assumed by many of the paraeducators. Being in a position in which this success appeared to be highly personalized, paraeducators expressed sensitivity to how the school in general responded to the inclusion student as well as the general concept of inclusion. For one student who required significant academic modifications, the paraeducator noted how the responses from the school as a whole had been "mixed."

> What I get from a lot of people is that they don't really see that Cory is intelligent. They see the disability. They don't see beyond it. It's a weekly event that somebody will sit down and say, "Well, you know, how can you expect her to learn to read and write," or "I don't understand why the parents want her to learn to read or write." And it's a lot of education, talking to people about the student, "Well, you know she is very capable, she learns at a slower rate because of her disability, but she is quite capable of functioning as a normal student." With the adaptations, of course.

One paraeducator also noted the "reputation" of the student with whom she worked. To some extent, many of the paraeducators felt that their students were fairly "high profile" in that most students and faculty in a school knew of their students.

> Absolutely everyone knows his name. In the beginning it was hard, because literally, he would be tantrumming in the middle of the hall, he'd be screaming.... I mean, everybody knew he was there. And there were a lot of people who just avoided the situation.... And you know, many people would say to me at the end of the day, "You know, I don't know how you do it." I had one teacher who said to me, "Well at least you're the only person who can see some good in him."

In another case, the paraeducator talked about how the school personnel's perception of the inclusion student actually influenced how they felt about her as a paraeducator:

> Each teacher has their own personality, just like we all do ... and everyone has their opinion of what special ed is ... And some of them have very much different attitudes about what my role is. So, I get the sloughed-off opinions ... it's like what they think of him [the student] gets sloughed off on to me.

Another paraeducator noted that the school personnel did not appear to be supportive of inclusion for her student, which she found surprising since this particular student had been at the same school for most of her 5 years of schooling. This paraeducator described this lack of support by talking about not feeling accepted herself:

> I have never felt very accepted in that school, personally. Or, you know, just the talk I've heard that they didn't agree. And still today, they think that Wendy should be in a special day class and she doesn't belong in a regular classroom.

As can be seen from these quotes, many of the paraeducators found themselves in an advocacy role, one in which it was their responsibility to work towards general acceptance of the inclusion student, or to "represent" the student in a way that would support that acceptance. This responsibility included educating others about the student as well as educating others to the idea of inclusion. Being in a position in which they had a close understanding of the special education student, and oftentimes feeling that they were the only ones in the school who knew the student, resulted in what many of the paraeducators described as a feeling of isolation and loneliness in their daily work. For example, one of the paraeducators noted the importance of positive communication between teachers and the paraeducators, "because sometimes the job can get down and lonely." This theme was also expressed by another paraeducator, who felt she was the only one in the school who truly understood the student's disability (autism):

> I'm on an island, basically; we're alone ... just Paul and me out there. Nobody else knows anything about his disability.... People don't have the experience, the resource teacher didn't have experience, the teacher.... I don't think anybody at my school knows anybody else with autism.

Not having others in the school with whom to share ideas about the particular inclusion student further contributed to this feeling of being on an island:

> [The biggest challenge was] the isolation of the work itself. Being isolated, feeling like an island, as far as in the environment I was working in.... I felt sometimes that, although the kids in the classroom were very supportive, we were sort of on an island.... Even in the special ed environment, you have other aides and other teachers you can discuss things and pass by them.

In a more positive light, one paraeducator described her role as one of "interpreter" for the inclusion student:

> My attention and my care goes to one student; and in the life of that student; I interact with all the adults that he interacts with.... And then to speak to the teachers, to be an advocate for my student, to be in the middle of the adult world and his world makes me a kind of interpreter for my student.

Discussion

... [T]he picture that emerges from interviews with paraeducators is that inclusion students, although generally accepted, are not necessarily included in the overall curriculum planning for the class as a whole. In other words, most of the teachers appeared to act as "hosts." Without the presence of the paraeducator, the educational benefits for the inclusion student would have been extremely minimal. On the other hand, it might be possible that because the paraeducator assumed this role, teachers never really felt the need to make these types of adaptations....

[It] appears that some of the responsibilities, although "accepted" by the teachers and paraeducators, could not be viewed as ideally "acceptable" for supporting inclusive practices. Paraeducators feeling responsible for the success of inclusion students might be viewed as an acceptable role; however, assuming sole responsibility rather than a shared one with the classroom teacher cannot be viewed as acceptable. This shared responsibility, although difficult to create, is the missing ingredient in the inclusive practices reported in this study, resulting in too many of the paraeducators "holding their own." ...

Ongoing Collaborative Meetings for Sharing Expertise Areas

Bringing together all the team members of a special education student's program takes considerable effort and time. Yet, ... it is an extremely important component. Certainly, more collaborative meetings in which the expertise of the teachers (from both special and general education) and the expertise of the paraeducator are utilized needs to be promoted. In this way, paraeducators and teachers can share their expertise: paraeducators on student information and teachers on educational and curricular decision-making strategies. In addition, classroom teachers can begin to develop expertise around the inclusion student, instead of the paraeducator being the sole holder of this knowledge. Paraeducators, in turn, can begin to provide more effective and educationally beneficial learning strategies for the student, rather than making on-the-spot activity decisions which may meet the immediate objective of engaging the student, but may not have sufficient long-term educational benefits.

These ongoing and regular discussions between teachers and paraeducators need to also include defining the teacher's and the paraeducator's roles and responsibilities. As Giangreco et al. also concluded, "school teams need to explicitly clarify the role of the classroom teacher as the instructional leader in the classroom including their roles and responsibilities as the teacher for the students with disabilities." As part of school team discussions, it is important to broach the issue of allowing paraeducators to take some risks, to begin to shift their attention to the class as a whole and to encourage teachers to take a more active role with the inclusion student. Interestingly, paraeducators reported that many of the inclusion students who were close to grade level, regardless of severity of problem behaviors, for the most part were able to be more independent as the year progressed. In other words, as the student's behaviors became increasingly managed, the classroom teacher was gradually able to assume primary responsibility for the student. However, for those students needing instructional adaptations, paraeducators continued to play a prominent role. This would indicate that assuming primary responsibility for providing curricular modifications and adaptations may present more significant and ongoing challenges for classroom teachers.

Including "fading plans" is another important strategy for clarifying the roles and responsibilities of the paraeducators and classroom teachers. Through this process, the goal of having the paraeducator shift attention to the whole classroom rather than just focusing on the inclusion student is made explicit and increases accountability for keeping this general goal at the forefront. For example, beginning with "low-risk" times, we have been successful in gradually increasing the paraeducator's proximity levels from the inclusion student. However, we have found that this process also needs to include natural supports (e.g., teacher reminders, peer supports, written instructions) in order to replace the support levels that were previously provided by the paraeducator.

Training for Paraeducators, Teachers, and Other School Personnel

Further training for paraeducators, teachers, and school personnel is absolutely necessary. Teachers in particular may not feel comfortable with, nor have many of them had training in, positive behavioral support strategies or in curricular modifications for special education students. Providing sufficient release time and opportunities to learn these important strategies will be essential if teachers are to assume greater responsibility for inclusion students with challenging behaviors. If teachers feel they lack this knowledge, they will most likely continue to defer this responsibility to the paraeducator, especially if that paraeducator has specific training in that area. Ironically, in our own practice, we offer training to the paraeducators, but classroom teachers do not typically attend these training sessions due to time constraints. Unfortunately, providing training to paraeducators, although very much needed ..., can increase the possibility that teachers leave the paraeducators to manage on their own.... [S]imply providing consultation and training to paraeducators is not sufficient and may inadvertently perpetuate paraeducators assuming an unbalanced (and in our view, unacceptable) responsibility for inclusion students. Therefore, it is critical that classroom teachers be provided with this training as well. Further, ... it is important for teachers to be provided training on how to supervise paraprofessionals, especially in how to coordinate instructional efforts to better meet the needs of inclusion students.

For the paraeducators, there is a need for training regarding the goals of inclusive practices and their roles in that process. This training needs to include examining what inclusion is and how to work as a team member, including working with and communicating with parents. In other words, we may need to redefine what successful inclusive practices look like, from a vision where inclusion students are simply maintained in general education classrooms and teachers respond in generally positive ways towards the inclusion student, to one in which the inclusion student is supported in his or her membership in the classroom.

Paraeducators will also need ongoing support and supervision by a special educator assigned to overseeing the inclusion student's educational needs. Too often, in our experience, special educators assigned to this role have high caseloads, resulting in extremely limited time for the level of ongoing support that is necessary for daily academic and curricular modifications. Again, in the absence of such resources, paraeducators will likely continue to assume roles that others more qualified should assume.

POSTSCRIPT

Are the Least-Trained Teaching Our Most Needy Children?

According to Giangreco et al., hiring an assistant is viewed as supporting inclusion. Yet that very support seems to isolate, rather than involve, the child. Does an untrained person have the ability to support an educational program?

Marks, Schrader, and Levine state that parents and teachers think that hiring an assistant provides a "good enough" level of inclusion until a more perfect model can be implemented. If teachers are not skilled in inclusive practices or in the supervision of paraprofessionals, how will the high standards of the general curriculum ever reach the child with disabilities?

Litigation has established paraprofessionals as supports that might be necessary for a child to have access to a free and appropriate education (Katsiyannis, Hodge, and Lanford, *Remedial and Special Education*, 2000). The key word here is *supports*. The same legal cases have determined that paraprofessionals who lack appropriate training may not directly provide special education services and may assist only if supervised by certified professionals.

One point of view is that aides need training to be of assistance to teachers (Johnson, Lasater, and Fitzgerald, *Journal of Staff Development*, 1997). Specifically, aides should learn to observe and record student performance using data collection strategies ranging from anecdotal reports to structured records of the frequency, duration, and intensity of target behavior. Skills in behavioral and instructional strategies, such as modeling, shaping, prompting, cuing, reinforcing, questioning, and providing feedback, would help teachers gain information about the response of the inclusion children to educational challenges. The most difficult challenge, helping students become more independent—physically, socially, and academically—requires particular attention. These specialized skills, along with an established support system, will increase the skills of assistants and help both students and teachers focus on instruction.

On the other hand, French (*Teaching Exceptional Children*, 1999) finds that teachers are rarely prepared to share instructional activities and are uncomfortable supervising adults—competencies that should be directly addressed in order to keep the teacher connected with students as more people join the educational team. Educational responsibilities should be shared, not ceded to an assistant. Teacher training needs to incorporate skills as direction-giver, monitor, coach, and support person as well as instructor of students with varied needs.

A third viewpoint argues against assigning paraprofessionals full time to individual students, striving instead for cross-training to decrease both stress and dependency and to rotate tasks (Rea, *Quinlan's Special Education Law Bulletin*, 2001). In addition to building a ready corps of substitutes in case a paraprofessional is absent or leaves the job, such a practice also creates a group of individuals who share concerns and responsibilities rather than bearing them alone. Complementing the option of assigning assistants to classes rather than to students, this strategy provides individual assistance when necessary but is flexible enough to encourage independence and natural supports.

Is it possible that, as educators have tried to include more children, general education teachers have come to believe that the aides know better than they how to teach children with significant disabilities? Is it possible that administrators, parents, and special education teachers assume that general education teachers will know how to use the services of paraprofessionals to assist their teaching? Have paraprofessionals been caught in the middle— without the training but with the responsibility?

On the Internet . . .

Autism Society of America

The mission of the Autism Society of America is to promote lifelong access and opportunity for all individuals within the autism spectrum, and their families, to be fully participating, included members of their community. Education, advocacy at state and federal levels, active public awareness and the promotion of research form the cornerstones of ASA's efforts. This Web site contains a wide range of information regarding autism, treatments and supports for families.

http://www.autism-society.org

Children and Adults with Attention-Deficit/Hyperactivity Disorder

Children and Adults with Attention-Deficit/Hyperactivity Disorder (CHADD), founded in 1987 by families seeking information about this disorder, is now a national organization linked to a variety of activities. The CHADD Web site contains extensive information on ADHD and ADD and is helpful to anyone who wants to learn more about these conditions.

http://www.chadd.org

National Center on Educational Outcomes

The National Center on Educational Outcomes (NCEO), based at the University of Minnesota, is a primary research site for the participation of students with disabilities in large-scale high-stakes testing. This Web site contains current information on the status of testing in all states as well as information on the way in which students with disabilities participate. Resources include numerous NCEO publications.

http://education.umn.edu/nceo

LD OnLine

A service of the Learning Project at WETA (FM) in Washington, D.C., LD OnLine is supported by numerous foundations. Oriented toward parents and children, this Web site provides a range of information, personal stories, homeschooling ideas, and resources for children, parents, and teachers who are interested in learning disabilities.

http://www.ldonline.org

What Works Clearinghouse

The What Works Clearinghouse was established in 2002 by the U.S. Department of Education's Institute of Education Sciences to provide educators, policymakers, researchers, and the public with a central and trusted source of scientific evidence of what works in education.

http://www.w-w-c.org/

PART 3

Issues About Disabilities

*E*arlier *sections of this book focused on global issues regarding the education of children with disabilities. Apart from these issues of law, policy, and practice, exist controversial issues about the reality of particular disabilities and the efficacy of unique methodologies. The fervent desire of parents and educators to help children nurtures the development of approaches which promise success. The challenge of evaluating new ways of thinking will be with us so long as there are children who need extra support in order to learn.*

- Can Brain Scans Unravel the Mystery of Learning Disabilities?

- Is Attention Deficit (Hyperactivity) Disorder Over-Diagnosed?

- Are We Over-Prescribing Medication to Solve our Children's Problems?

- Should Parents Choose Cochlear Implants for Their Deaf Children?

- Are There Scientifically Effective Treatments for Autism?

- Have Schools Gone Too Far in Using Accommodations?

- Should Students with Disabilities Participate in High-Stakes Testing?

ISSUE 14

Can Brain Scans Unravel the Mystery of Learning Disabilities?

YES: Sally E. Shaywitz and Bennett A. Shaywitz, from "Reading Disability and the Brain," *Educational Leadership* (March 2004)

NO: Gerald Coles, from "Danger in the Classroom: 'Brain Glitch' Research and Learning to Read," *Phi Delta Kappan* (January 2004)

ISSUE SUMMARY

YES: Sally E. Shaywitz and Bennett A. Shaywitz, Yale University professors and codirectors of the National Institute of Child Health and Human Development–Yale Center for the Study of Learning and Attention, summarize their recent research findings, suggesting that advances in medicine, together with reading research, can virtually eliminate reading disabilities.

NO: Gerald Coles, an educational psychologist and former member of the Robert Wood Johnson Medical School, University of Medicine and Dentistry of New Jersey, contests the claim that neurological procedures can identify reading disabilities and the methods to help children read.

Specific learning disability: "A disorder in one or more of the basic psychological processes involved in understanding or in using language, spoken or written, that may manifest itself in an imperfect ability to listen, think, speak, read, write, spell, or to do mathematical calculations, including conditions such as perceptual disabilities, brain injury, minimal brain dysfunction, dyslexia, and developmental aphasia. This does not include learning problems that are primarily the result of visual, hearing or motor disabilities, of mental retardation, of emotional disturbance, or of environmental, cultural, or economic disadvantage."

IDEA97

Have you ever met a student who seems to be very capable in many ways— can communicate, compute, and reason well—but who simply cannot read well? Or who is proficient in all academic areas except for the ability to compose a coherent narrative? The puzzle is that the student seems so competent—except in one specific area. Motivation, family support, and good teaching have all been present, but learning in this one area still lags behind success in others.

Curiosity and frustration about this student have been the source of discussion for the last century. In 1963, Samuel Kirk formalized thinking into a condition he termed "learning disabilities." Education has not been the same since.

Since the advent of special education law, educators, parents, and attorneys have argued over the shape and meaning of specific learning disabilities, a set of conditions that seem to be defined mostly by what they are not. The federal definition cited above describes a disability that is most apparent while learning academic subjects and occurs in a child who appears to have the background and capability to learn easily. For much of the twentieth century, researchers sought to identify specific neurological differences hypothesized to be the basis for learning disabilities.

More than half the children receiving special education services has been identified as having a specific learning disability. Most frequently, reading is identified as the primary area of difficulty.

No Child Left Behind (NCLB) sets a goal of having all children learn to read by the end of third grade, emphasizing the use of "effective, research-based reading programs." How do children with learning disabilities fit into this goal?

Sally E. Shaywitz and Bennett A. Shaywitz are prolific researchers in the area of learning. They, along with Reid Lyon, have been instrumental in shaping the reading foundation of NCLB. Shaywitz and Shaywitz believe that learning disabilities exist. In their research, results of functional magnetic resonance imaging (fMRI) identified "glitches" in the brains of struggling readers. They cite evidence that the right type of instruction can eliminate these glitches.

Gerald Coles, a pioneer researcher in the area of learning disabilities, feels that fMRI data do not provide a clear link between brain functioning and reading. He is concerned that the scientific glitz of new technology leads people to think that a glitch exists. By focusing only on brain activity, he fears that critical information might be bypassed about how and why children struggle to learn.

As you read the following selections, decide whether or not you think that advances in medical technology have found the long-sought-for neurological cause of learning disabilities.

**Sally E. Shaywitz and
Bennett A. Shaywitz**

 **YES**

Reading Disability and the Brain

The past decade has witnessed extraordinary progress in our understanding of the nature of reading and reading difficulties. Never before have rigorous science (including neuroscience) and classroom instruction in reading been so closely linked. For the first time, educators can turn to well-designed, scientific studies to determine the most effective ways to teach reading to beginning readers, including those with reading disability (National Reading Panel, 2000).

What does the evidence tell us? Several lines of investigation have found that reading originates in and relies on the brain systems used for spoken language. In addition, accumulating evidence sheds light on the nature of reading disability, including its definition, prevalence, longitudinal course, and probable causes. Although the work is relatively new, we have already made great progress in identifying the neural systems used for reading, identifying a disruption in these systems in struggling readers, and understanding the neural mechanisms associated with the development of fluent reading.

Reading and Spoken Language

Spoken language is instinctive—built into our genes and hardwired in our brains. Learning to read requires us to take advantage of what nature has provided: a biological module for language.

For the object of the reader's attention (print) to gain entry into the language module, a truly extraordinary transformation must occur. The reader must convert the print on the page into a linguistic code: the phonetic code, the only code recognized and accepted by the language system. Unless the reader-to-be can convert the printed characters on the page into the phonetic code, these letters remain just a bunch of lines and circles, totally devoid of meaning. The written symbols have no inherent meaning of their own but stand, rather, as surrogates for the sounds of speech.

To break the code, the first step beginning readers must take involves spoken language. Readers must develop *phonemic awareness*. They must discover that the words they hear come apart into smaller pieces of sound.

On the basis of highly reliable scientific evidence, investigators in the field have now reached a strong consensus: Reading reflects language, and reading disability reflects a deficit within the language system. Results from

Reading Disability and the Brain, an article based upon the book OVERCOMING DYSLEXIA, by Sally E. Shaywitz (NY:Knopf, 2003). Grateful acknowledgement is made to Sally Shaywitz c/o Writers' Representatives LLC. (to whom all rights inquires should be directed) for permission to reprint "Dyslexia and the Brain".

large and well-studied populations with reading disability confirm that in young school-age children and in adolescents, a weakness in accessing the sounds of spoken language represents the most robust and specific correlate of reading disability. Such findings form the foundation for the most successful, evidence-based interventions designed to improve reading (National Reading Panel, 2000).

Understanding Reading Disability

Reading disability, or *developmental dyslexia*, is characterized by an unexpected difficulty in reading in children and adults who otherwise possess the intelligence, motivation, and education necessary for developing accurate and fluent reading. Dyslexia is the most common and most carefully studied of the learning disabilities, affecting 80 percent of all individuals identified as learning disabled and an estimated 5–17 percent of all children and adults in the United States.

Incidence and Distribution of Dyslexia

Recent epidemiological data indicate that like hypertension and obesity, reading ability occurs along a continuum. Reading disability falls on the left side of the bell-shaped curve representing the normal distribution of reading ability.

Dyslexia runs in families: One-fourth to one-half of all children who have a parent with dyslexia also have the disorder, and if dyslexia affects one child in the family, it is likely to affect half of his or her siblings. Recent studies have identified a number of genes involved in dyslexia.

Good evidence, based on surveys of randomly selected populations of children, now indicates that dyslexia affects boys and girls equally. Apparently, the long-held belief that only boys suffer from dyslexia reflected bias in school-identified samples: The more disruptive behavior of boys results in their being referred for evaluation more often, whereas girls who struggle to read are more likely to sit quietly in their seats and thus be overlooked.

Longitudinal studies indicate that dyslexia is a persistent, chronic condition rather than a transient "developmental lag." Children do not outgrow reading difficulties. The evidence-based interventions now available, however, can result in improved reading in virtually all children.

Neurobiological Origins of Dyslexia

For more than a century, physicians and scientists have suspected that dyslexia has neurobiological origins. Until recently, however, they had no way to examine the brain systems that we use while reading. Within the last decade, the dream of scientists, educators, and struggling readers has come true: New advances in technology enable us to view the working brain as it attempts to read.

Perhaps the most convincing evidence for a neurobiological basis of dyslexia comes from the rapidly accumulating and converging data from functional brain imaging investigations. The process of functional brain imaging is quite simple. When we ask an individual to perform a discrete cognitive task, that task places processing demands on specific neural systems in the brain. Through such techniques as functional magnetic resonance imaging (fMRI), we can measure the changes that take place in neural activity in particular brain regions as the brain meets those demands. Because fMRI uses no ionizing radiation and requires no injections, it is noninvasive and safe. We can use it to examine children or adults on multiple occasions.

Using functional brain imaging, scientists around the world have discovered not only the brain basis of reading but also a glitch in the neural circuitry for reading in children and adults who struggle to read. Our studies and those of other investigators have identified three regions involved in reading, all located on the left side of the brain. In the front of the brain, Broca's area (technically the inferior frontal gyrus) is involved in articulation and word analysis. Two areas located in the back of the brain are involved in word analysis (the parieto-temporal region) and in fluent reading (the occipito-temporal region, also referred to as the word form area).

Studies of dyslexic readers document an underactivation of the two systems in the back of the brain together with an overactivation of Broca's area in the front of the brain. The struggling readers appear to be turning to the frontal region, which is responsible for articulating spoken words, to compensate for the fault in the systems in the back of the brain.

Researchers have observed this neurobiological signature of dyslexic readers across cultures and across different languages. The observation of this same pattern in both children and adults supports the view that reading difficulties, including the neural disruption, do not go away with maturity. To prevent failure for students with reading disability, we must identify the disability early and provide effective reading programs to address the students' needs.

The Importance of Fluency

In addition to identifying the neural systems used for reading, research has now revealed which systems the brain uses in two important phases in the acquisition of literacy.

Beginning reading—breaking the code by slowly, analytically sounding out words—calls on areas in the front of the brain (Broca's area) and in the back of the brain (the parieto-temporal region).

But an equally important phase in reading is fluency—rapid, automatic reading that does not require attention or effort. A fluent reader looks at a printed word and instantly knows all the important information about that word. Fluent reading develops as the reader builds brain connections that eventually represent an exact replica of the word—a replica that has integrated the word's pronunciation, spelling, and meaning.

Fluency occurs step-by-step. After systematically learning letters and their sounds, children go on to apply this knowledge to sound out words slowly and analytically. For example, for the word "back," a child may initially represent the word by its initial and final consonants: "b—k." As the child progresses, he begins to fill in the interior vowels, first making some errors—reading "back" as "bock" or "beak," for example—and eventually sounding out the word correctly. Part of the process of becoming a skilled reader is forming successively more detailed and complete representations of familiar words.

After the child has read the word "back" correctly over and over again, his brain has built and reinforced an exact model of the word. He now reads that word fluently—accurately, rapidly, and effortlessly. Fluency pulls us into reading. A student who reads fluently reads for pleasure and for information; a student who is not fluent will probably avoid reading.

In a study involving 144 children, we identified the brain region that makes it possible for skilled readers to read automatically. We found that the more proficiently a child read, the more he or she activated the occipito-temporal region (or word form area) in the back of the brain. Other investigators have observed that this brain region responds to words that are presented rapidly. Once a word is represented in the word form area, the reader recognizes that word instantly and effortlessly. This word form system appears to predominate when a reader has become fluent. As a result of this finding, we now know that development of the word form area in the left side of the brain is a key component in becoming a skilled, fluent reader.

Helping Struggling Readers Become More Fluent

Our study of 144 children also revealed that struggling readers compensate as they get older, developing alternate reading systems in the front of the brain and in the *right* side of the brain—a functioning system, but, alas, not an automatic one. These readers do not develop the critical left-side word form region necessary for rapid, automatic reading. Instead, they call on the alternate secondary pathways. This strategy enables them to read, but much more slowly and with greater effort than their classmates.

This research evidence of a disruption in the normal reading pathways provides a neurobiological target for reading interventions. In a new study, we hypothesized that an evidence-based, phonologically mediated reading intervention would help dyslexic readers develop the fast-paced word form systems serving skilled reading, thus improving their reading accuracy and fluency. Under the supervision of Syracuse University professor Benita Blachman, we provided 2nd and 3rd grade struggling readers daily with 50 minutes of individual tutoring that was systematic and explicit, focusing on helping the students understand the *alphabetic principle*, or how letters and combinations of letters represent the sounds of speech.

Students received eight months (105 hours) of intervention during the school year in addition to their regular classroom reading instruction. The experimental intervention replaced any additional reading help that the students might have received in school. Certified teachers who had taken part in an intensive training program provided the tutoring.

Immediately after the yearlong intervention, students in the experiment made significant gains in reading fluency and demonstrated increased activation in left hemisphere regions, including the inferior frontal gyrus and the parieto-temporal region. One year after the experimental intervention ended, these students were reading accurately and fluently and were activating all three left-side brain regions used by good readers. A control group of struggling readers receiving school-based, primarily nonphonological reading instruction had not activated these reading systems.

These data demonstrate that an intensive, evidence-based reading intervention brings about significant and durable changes in brain organization so that struggling readers' brain activation patterns come to resemble those of typical readers. If we provide intervention at an early age, then we can improve reading fluency and facilitate the development of the neural systems that underlie skilled reading.

Evidence-Based Effective Reading Instruction

In addition to new neurological research on the nature of reading, educators can draw on a body of rigorous, well-designed, scientific studies to guide reading instruction. In 1998, the U.S. Congress mandated the National Reading Panel to develop rigorous scientific criteria for evaluating reading research, apply these criteria to existing reading research, identify the most effective teaching methods, and then make findings accessible for parents and teachers. As a member of the Panel, I can attest to its diligence. After two years of work, the Panel issued its report (2000).

The major findings of the report indicate that in order to read, all children must be taught alphabetics, comprising phonemic awareness and phonics; reading fluency; vocabulary; and strategies for reading comprehension. These elements must be taught systematically, comprehensively, and explicitly; it is inadequate to present the foundational skills of phonemic awareness and phonics incidentally, casually, or fragmentally. Children do not learn how letters represent sounds by osmosis; we must teach them this skill explicitly. Once a child has mastered these foundational skills, he or she must be taught how to read words fluently.

Good evidence now indicates that we can teach reading fluency by means of repeated oral reading with feedback and guidance. Using these methods, we can teach almost every child to read. It is crucial to align all components of a program with one another—for example, to provide so-called decodable booklets that give the student practice in the specific letter-sound linkages we are teaching. The use of decodable booklets enables the repeated practice necessary to build the automatic systems in the word form region that lead to fluent reading.

Neuroscience and Reading Research Agree

We are now in an era of evidence-based education. Objective scientific evidence— provided by brain imaging studies and by the National Reading Panel's rigorous scientific review of the literature—has replaced reliance on philosophy or opinion.

In considering a reading program, educators should ask several key questions:

- Is there scientific evidence that the program is effective?
- Was the program or its methodology reviewed by the National Reading Panel?
- In reading instruction, are phonemic awareness and phonics taught systematically and explicitly?
- How are students taught to approach an unfamiliar word? Do they feel empowered to try to analyze and sound out an unknown word first rather than guess the word from the pictures or context?
- Does the program also include plenty of opportunities for students to practice reading, develop fluency, build vocabulary, develop reading comprehension strategies, write, and listen to and discuss stories?

Children are only 7 or 8 years old once in their lifetime. We cannot risk teaching students with unproven programs. We now have the scientific knowledge to ensure that almost every child can become a successful reader. Awareness of the new scientific knowledge about reading should encourage educators to insist that reading programs used in their schools reflect what we know about the science of reading and about effective reading instruction.

NO

Gerald Coles

Danger in the Classroom: 'Brain Glitch' Research and Learning to Read

Did you know that recent studies of the brain and reading support the reading instruction mandated in George W. Bush's No Child Left Behind (NCLB) legislation? And did you know that this research also supports the legislation he has proposed to dismantle Head Start's comprehensive approach to preschool education? And were you aware that, thanks to this brain research, we now know how children learn to read and which areas of the brain must first be stocked to promote skilled reading? Did you realize that we now have strong brain-based evidence that the best reading instruction is heavily prescriptive, skills-emphasis, building-blocks teaching that starts with small pieces of written language and proceeds to larger ones—and teachers are fortunate because these features are contained in reading programs like Open Court?

You didn't know all that? Good, because none of it is true, although you would never know that if you just listened to the President, the educators and assorted researchers who support his educational agenda, and the media who repeat their assertions.

Over 25 years ago, when I began appraising theories about faulty brain wiring in beginning readers, my criticism of the research then being conducted was limited to ersatz explanations of so-called brain dysfunctions in children called "learning disabled," "reading disabled," or "dyslexic." Contrary to the assertions made then, the research had never shown that the overwhelming number of these children did not have normal brains. Certainly a portion of poor readers had problems that were the result of exposure to such toxins as lead and cadmium, to food additives, and to other environmental influences. But, I argued, there was no evidence that they accounted for more than a small portion of the large numbers of children given these labels and shunted into special education programs.

At some point, thanks to increased, widespread criticism of these "brain-based" explanations, I had thought a change had started toward more informed, measured interpretations. However, my naive thinking has long been gone. Not only are explanations about "brain glitches," to use the term employed by reading researcher Sally Shaywitz, now being applied more forcefully to "dyslexics," but they have also been reworked to explain how all children learn to read, what single method of instruction must be used to teach them, and why the single method mandated in Bush's Reading First, part of the NCLB legislation, is a wise, scientifically based choice. Thus never have these "brain glitch" explanations been more pervasively intrusive for all beginning readers and their teachers in classrooms across the nation....

A new best seller, *Overcoming Dyslexia*, by Sally Shaywitz, who has received considerable NICHD [National Institutes of Child Health and Human Development] funding for her research, claims to present "the advances in brain science" that inform what "at last we know," which are "the specific steps a child or adult must take to build and then reinforce the neural pathways deep within the brain for skilled reading." Shaywitz served on the panel whose findings, she proudly explains to readers, "are now part of the groundbreaking No Child Left Behind Legislation," ...

In this article I will argue that, despite all the unbridled assertions about the wonder of it all, this new "brain glitch " research is theoretically, empirically, and conceptually deficient, as was the deficit-driven work that preceded it by decades ... . More than ever, claims about the research constitute an ideological barrier to a sounder understanding of the connections between brain activity and learning to read. More than ever, this work is a danger in the classroom both because it applies unproven labels to an ever-larger number of children and because it promotes a single kind of instruction that, based on the actual empirical evidence mustered for it, contains no promise for leaving no beginning reader behind. To all of this, add the false and cruel expectations that these claims generate in parents.

To help illustrate my critique, I will use as an example a recent, highly publicized study on reading and brain activity whose co-authors include Reid Lyon, Sally Shaywitz, and several other researchers whose work argues for building-blocks teaching and has been used as evidence for Reading First instruction. (For convenience I call it the Shaywitz/Lyon study).

Is the Brain "Reading"?

Functional magnetic resonance imagery (fMRI) is a valuable diagnostic and investigative technology that can measure blood flow in the brain and thereby provide information about certain kinds of brain activity when someone is performing a task. However, like every technology used in research, its value and the information it produces are never better than the initial theory and concepts that steer its application. Perhaps the biggest misrepresentation in the "brain glitch" research is that the color scans produced by fMRI provide information about "reading." In fact, they provide no such thing, because the "reading" tasks under study are largely a person's performance on simple sound and sound/symbol (phonics) tasks with words and parts of words, rather than performance in reading as conventionally defined, that is, reading and comprehending sentences and paragraphs. (The same misrepresentation appears in claims about "reading" contained in the report of the National Reading Panel, the chief research document cited in the Reading First legislation.)

The puny definition of reading used in this research appears not to concern the investigators, though, because they design their studies on the assumption that these simple tasks involving words and parts of words embrace the core requirements for beginning readers: that is, mastery of phonological awareness (distinguishing and manipulating sounds in words) and sound/symbol relationships. As the Shaywitz/Lyon study explains, there is now "a strong consensus" (that is, a broad unanimity of professional opinion) that phonological awareness is the first building block within the sequence and that reading disability reflects a deficit in this "lower level component" of "the language system." Only after mastering this component can beginning readers effectively continue to master other reading skills.

That's the claim. The reality is that the so-called strong consensus does not exist. I and others have published thorough research reviews that critique—and dismiss—the "lower level component" model and the supposed empirical evidence showing the superior effect of early, direct, and intensive instruction in word sounds on later reading. As I have also argued, this narrow, do-as-you're-told instruction not only pushes aside numerous issues that bear on beginning literacy—such as children's backgrounds, interests, problem-solving approaches, and definitions of "reading" —it also masquerades as a bootstrap policy solution for poor children that takes off the table all other policies required to address the many needs that influence learning success or failure. However, for the advocates of this "strong consensus," especially those linked to the political power pushing these claims, conflicting views are never allowed to ruffle their harmony.

Hence, an experiment, such as those reported in the Shaywitz/Lyon study, can be designed in which subjects do "lower level component" tasks, such as deciding if nonwords rhyme ("Do leat and bete rhyme?") or making judgments requiring both phonological and semantic knowledge ("Are corn and rice in the same category?"), and the researchers can claim that the data generated tell us a great deal about "reading," the reading process, and the best kinds of instruction. The conclusions in this work display no awareness of the self-fulfilling prophecy at play when the research focuses solely on "lower level components" decontextualized from a full appraisal of reading, uses no other model of reading and instruction, and then concludes that these components are the initial and key ones in learning to read.

A Real "Brain Glitch"?

Looking more deeply into the research design of the "brain glitch" studies, we find a problem that dyslexia researchers have long encountered but not overcome when organizing an experiment so that data on brain activity can be meaningfully interpreted: the experiment must start by grouping dyslexics separately from other kinds of poor readers. This distinction is required because even in studies using the fMRI, the data are about brain activity associated with the word-level tasks, not about micro brain damage. Therefore, fMRI differences in brain activity among a group of unsorted poor readers would not provide information about the cause and meaning of the various differences in activity.

To solve the problem, these studies and previous ones employing simpler technologies try first to separate from a group of poor readers those whose problems are assumed to have non-neurological causes, such as emotional, familial, social class, and similar "exclusionary" influences, as they have been called. If these poor readers are excluded, researchers have reasoned, the probability is high that the reading problems of those who remain are caused by a "brain glitch." While this might make sense in theory, in practice it has not worked, because researchers have not created evaluation methods and criteria for separating the two groups of poor readers.

Even worse, for decades, researchers have frequently stated that they have used a thorough process of distinguishing between the two groups, but the assertion has rarely been accompanied by evidence. In the Shaywitz/Lyon study, for example, dyslexics were supposedly identified after the researchers had determined that the subjects' reading problems were not caused by emotional problems or "social, cultural, or economic disadvantage." Yet the researchers, so dedicated to obtaining and reporting a surfeit of brain data, offered not a whit of information on this process of elimination. Presumably, readers of the published study were expected to accept without question the assertion that genuine dyslexics had been identified and that these children could then be compared to "nonimpaired" readers (an odd term, since it refers to normal or average readers but is used in the study to underline a priori the assumption that the dyslexics' brains were impaired).

The need to provide evidence of thorough appraisals of the roots of subjects' reading problems is usually obvious to anyone who has actually taught poor readers and, therefore, knows that there can be numerous contextual causes of poor reading in middle-class children that will not be readily apparent. In my extensive work with children, young adults, and adults with severe reading problems, I have found that causes can be uncovered only after spending considerable time *both* evaluating and teaching a student, with the latter especially necessary. Poor teaching—such as using a one-size-fits-all reading program, insufficient individualized instruction, too much phonics, too little phonics—is just one of the many influences that can produce reading problems in a variety of ways, but those problems will not be apparent without thorough analysis of a person's instructional history and current active reading.

Many unusual family circumstances and stresses can impair a child's early reading progress. A parent losing a job, a family moving to another city in the middle of the first grade, overworked parents, grandparents dying around the time a child began school are all examples of problems I have identified. These experiences hinder reading development by distracting and stressing a child, but they are not overt "emotional" problems. Even when a poor reader comes from a family that appears "normal," only an extensive exploration of the family dynamics can determine whether this appearance might cloak problems that have affected a child's beginning reading.

By not providing criteria and evidence that the "dyslexics" are different from other poor readers, the brain research studies use another self-serving, self-fulfilling prophecy: because the fMRI shows differences in brain activity between "dyslexic" and "nonimpaired" readers, the differences in brain activity must be visual demonstrations of impairment and nonimpairment. How do we know the fMRI data reveal impairment? Because one of the groups was initially identified as impaired. How do we know the group was impaired? Because the group was first identified as impaired and the fMRI data corroborated the impairment. No other explanations can explain the dyslexics' different brain activity. Impaired, for sure! No question about it....

Fixing the "Brain Glitch"

Beyond finding "brain glitches," researchers have reported other good news: building-block skills instruction can remedy the glitch. "An effective reading program" can produce "brain repair," Shaywitz reports. "The brain can be rewired."...

Nearly 20 years ago, Leonide Goldstein and I published a study on differences in brain hemisphere activation in adult beginning readers as they were learning to read. We found that these adults, when they were poor readers or nonreaders, did, indeed, demonstrate brain activation that was different from that found among good readers. However, as their reading improved, through the use of a holistic, comprehensive teaching approach over many months, their brain activation changed toward that commonly found in good readers. We interpreted these data as evidence that new knowledge and competencies were linked to concomitant changes in brain structure and functioning, as one would expect for *all kinds of learning.* There was nothing in the data to suggest that these beginning readers started learning to read with anything other than normal brains that were configured as they were at the beginning of the study because the students had not learned to read; no data suggested that the educational intervention we provided somehow repaired or circumvented dysfunctional brain areas.

To restate a central point for appraising these glitch-fixing interventions: although researchers insist that the training programs they use repair or ameliorate brain hardware or glitches, there is no evidence in any of their studies that this rewiring was different from that which is concomitant with the learning that continues throughout our learning lives. Nor does this so-called repair demonstrate that phonological processing is the *initial* key component in learning to read. The subjects apparently lacked this ability and then learned this ability, and their brain processing changed accordingly. Using modern technology to identify and track brain changes related to changes in reading ability is an extraordinary achievement. Using the achievement for ideological ends is not.

Emotionless "Cognition"

Like the assumed "consensus" on building-blocks instruction, "brain glitch" research assumes that cognition—that is, the process that creates images, concepts, and mental operations—is not a construct but an independent reality that actually describes the brain processes associated with reading. Ignored in this assumption is the ever-growing evidence suggesting that thinking is an inseparable interaction of both cognition and emotion (feelings, desires, enthusiasms, antipathies, etc.)....

Unfortunately, none of this new perspective on the "continuous and interwoven cognitive-emotional fugue,"... has entered the "brain glitch" research. As a result, the question of whether diminished activity in a portion of the brain of someone doing a reading task might be a consequence of an emotional response, in that emotional memories can exert a powerful influence on "thought processes," remains unaddressed. By purging emotions and focusing only on cognition, the "brain glitch" research also purges the alternative: a holistic instructional approach based on the assumption that classrooms are filled with whole children for whom learning is always grounded in the fugue of cognition and affect.

How the Brain Works: Modules?

The interrelationships and interactions missing from the narrow cognitive model of "brain glitch" research lead us to a final concern. A chief premise of this research holds that the brain has specific modules for specialized operations that work in sequence with other modules in learning written language and that foremost of these is at least one module that can process basic sound and sound/symbol skills. This kind of modular model has a certain palpable, visual appeal (not unlike "building-blocks instruction"), but the actual existence of such modules is a theory, not a fact, that has increasingly been questioned. Most likely, the modular model is not one that explains how the brain actually works.

For instance, Merlin Donald, a psychologist who has written extensively on human consciousness, rejects the explanation that modules perform "specialized operations," such as deciphering portions of language. While language areas of the brain, such as those related to aspects of reading, are important in processing particular functions, all are intertwined in extensive networks (a polyphony) of brain areas that are simultaneously and interactively communicating and constructing and reconstructing particular areas within the whole. Yes, the brain has fundamental mechanisms for beginning to learn written language, but it does not begin with a "fixed pattern of connectivity." Instead, the "connectivity pattern is set by experience" with "countless interconnection points, or synapses, which connect neurons to one another in various patterns." In other words, learning and experience create and shape the brain's circuits and how they are used in learning to read; the circuits are not predetermined.

Linguist Philip Lieberman has also criticized modular explanations, calling them "neophrenological theories," that is, theories that "map complex behaviors to localized regions of the brain, on the assumption that a particular part of the brain regulates an aspect of behavior." In these theories, he remarks, the functional organization of the brain is run by "a set of petty bureaucrats each of which controls a behavior." Like Donald, Lieberman proposes that converging behavioral and neurobiological data indicate that human language is composed not of a hierarchical system but of neural networks, including the traditional cortical "language" areas (Broca's and Wernicke's areas), formed through circuits that link populations of neurons in neuroanatomical structures that are distributed throughout the brain. Lieberman stresses, "Although specific operations may be performed in particular parts of the brain, these operations must be integrated into a *network* that regulates an observable aspect of behavior. And so, a particular aspect of behavior usually involves activity in neuroanatomical structures distributed throughout the brain" (emphasis in original)....

The view of a "connectivity pattern" that emerges and is activated as children learn to read contrasts with the model of step-by-step progression from module to module. If the former is an accurate model of brain organization and functioning, it suggests that the connectivity pattern should be the focus of research because only by looking at the overall pattern can researchers begin to determine the functioning and interrelationships of any part and the causal, consequential, or interactive function of that part within the entire pattern.

From the perspective of a connectivity pattern model, not only do the brain areas involved in grasping the sound/symbol correspondence *not* have to be primed first before other areas of the pattern can become effectively operable, the creation and functioning of these areas depends on connections within the entire pattern. And because the pattern is not innately fixed, if instruction were to stimulate certain areas more than others, a particular connectivity pattern would emerge. That specific pattern, however, might not necessarily be the sole one required for reading success and might not be superior to other connectivity patterns. Moreover, a more complex connectivity pattern could be created through richer written language learning. None of this is addressed in the "brain glitch" research.

Conclusion

Philip Lieberman offers a caveat worth emphasizing when appraising "brain glitch" research, learning to read, and the Bush agenda for education: "We must remember that we stand on the threshold of an understanding of how brains really work. The greatest danger perhaps rests in making claims that are not supported by data." Unfortunately, not only have "brain glitch" researchers seldom been guided by such a caveat, they have tended to misconstrue the data and have drawn conclusions that serve to justify unwarranted beliefs, instructional policy, and the politics that have driven the research in the first place....

For research on the brain and reading to become productive, what is needed most is the discarding of fundamental assumptions that have not been validated. Building-blocks instruction has not been proved to be the best way to teach reading. Phonological awareness has not been proved to be the initial, essential component that determines reading success. Thinking does not involve "cognition" alone. The modular organization of the brain is, at best, a disputed theory. Brain activation differences do not necessarily reflect "brain glitches." Dyslexia remains no more a proven malady among a substantial percentage of beginning readers than when Glasgow ophthalmologist James Hinshelwood first discussed it as "congenital word-blindness" at the end of the 19th century.

To make research on the brain and reading work, it must be informed by the complexity of reading acquisition, and it must begin to address such questions as: Will alternative teaching approaches configure brain activity in alternative ways? Will children's differing assumptions about what it means to "read" correspond to differing brain activity and organization? How do different aspects of reading, such as comprehension, syntax, and word analysis, interact in certain reading tasks and what kinds of brain activity do the interactions produce? How does the knowledge children bring to literacy learning affect brain activity?

These and similar questions can begin to contribute to a better understanding of the relationship between brain function and reading acquisition, which in turn can help promote ecological approaches that are grounded in an understanding of the unified interrelationships of brain, active child, and learning environment. They can also begin to help identify genuine brain-related reading impairments. Developing this kind of understanding of integrated interrelationships will require that we eschew views that are either "brain based" or conceive of the brain as an extraneous "black box."

By adding to the current pretensions about the superiority of one brand of "scientifically based" reading instruction, "brain glitch" research remains a danger in the classroom. Unfortunately, because of the political power connected to this sham science and brainless instruction, a mighty effort is required to end that danger.

POSTSCRIPT

Can Brain Scans Unravel the Mystery of Learning Disabilities?

By Christmas of the first grade year, parents and teachers alike begin to worry about children who don't seem to be catching on to the magic of reading—understanding the connection between the sounds we make and their written symbols. Heated disputes about the best way to help struggling readers have existed for hundreds of years.

The latest round of this debate was sounded with the release of the *National Reading Panel Report* (2000). Using a tool called meta-analysis, the National Reading Panel (NRP) reviewed a number of research studies. Based on this analysis, the NRP concluded that most children would learn to read with systematic and intensive instruction, emphasizing phonemics and phonics.

The NRP report generated much controversy, especially from theorists who believe in a more holistic, literature-based method of reading instruction. Researchers argued (and continue to argue) about the studies selected and the studies eliminated from consideration. They argued about the types of students included in the studies and criticized the fact that many of the studies did not seem to include struggling readers. They argued about the definition of reading—is it decoding individual words or gaining meaning from print? The fervor increased when NCLB authors used the NRP's findings to set expectations for the type of research-based instruction schools should be using.

The drive to help all children learn to read easily has generated so much disagreement that it often has been termed "the Reading Wars." A promising method is identified, only to be dashed in a few years in a headline proclaiming that reading researchers failed, yet again, to solve the reading crisis. In an attempt to define common ground, Rona Flippo (2004, 1999, 1998) surveyed "The Experts." Working for over ten years, she learned that 11 prominent researchers with varying philosophies agreed on a number of points. One was that there is no "one best method" of teaching reading. The Experts agreed that it was critical for teachers to match instructional methods to individual children in response to their specific needs, interests, and learning styles.

Shaywitz and Shaywitz use fMRI results to provide evidence that brain "glitches" exist and can be corrected with the right kind of reading instruction. They strongly believe that the type of reading instruction advocated by NCLB can help "virtually" all students learn to read, even those with disabilities. Shaywitz and Shaywitz have great confidence that "teaching matters and good teaching can change the brain."

Coles cautions that demonstrating differences in brain activity is not enough—brains change as they learn. Some students have difficulty reading, he notes, because they have not had sufficient language support or because they might be pre-occupied with troubled lives. According to Coles, the reasons for reading problems are not always simple—neither are the solutions. He is wary that the results of a few studies have been used to further a political agenda that dictates specific reading methodologies for use by all schools.

In the next 10 years, what will we discover about reading and the brain? Will fMRI (or its successor) unlock the mysteries of thinking and learning? Will in-school testing be replaced by visits to the neurologist? Will research identify teaching techniques to match with brain scan patterns? Or will the next set of studies find that the puzzle of reading disability has multiple explanations and solutions?

ISSUE 15

Is Attention Deficit (Hyperactivity) Disorder Overdiagnosed?

YES: Arthur Allen, from "The Trouble With ADHD," *The Washington Post* (March 18, 2001)

NO: Russell A. Barkley, from *Taking Charge of ADHD: The Complete, Authoritative Guide for Parents*, 2d ed. (The Guilford Press, 2000)

ISSUE SUMMARY

YES: Arthur Allen, reporter for *The Washington Post*, believes that attention deficit hyperactivity disorder (ADHD) exists but thinks that too many children are given this diagnosis, masking other conditions (or simply normal behavior) and resulting in the prescribing of drugs that do more harm than good.

NO: Russell A. Barkley, director of psychology and a professor at the University of Massachusetts Medical Center, addresses several current beliefs about ADHD and maintains that ADHD is underdiagnosed and undertreated in today's children.

Attention deficit hyperactivity disorder, or ADHD, describes someone who cannot stop moving, has difficulty concentrating, and is distracted by what happens around him or her. Without the H (hyperactivity), ADD refers to someone who can sit relatively still, but has difficulty concentrating and is likely distracted by internal thoughts. Although ADD and ADHD refer to variations of the same condition, ADHD will be used here to refer to both. Here are the official diagnostic criteria for ADHD:

A. Either (1) or (2):
  8. Six (or more) or the following symptoms of inattention have persisted for at least six months to a degree that is maladaptive and inconsistent with developmental level: often fails to give close attention to details or makes careless mistakes; often has difficulty sustaining attention in tasks or play; often does not seem to listen when spoken to directly; often does not follow through on instruc-

tions and fails to finish chores or duties (not due to oppositional behavior or failure to understand); often has difficulty organizing tasks and activities; often avoids, dislikes, or is reluctant to engage in tasks that require sustained mental effort; often loses things necessary for tasks or activities; often forgetful.

9. Six (or more) of the following symptoms of hyperactivity-impulsivity have persisted for at least six months to a degree that is maladaptive and inconsistent with developmental level: often fidgets with hands or feet or squirms in seat; often leaves seat unacceptably; often runs about or climbs excessively when inappropriate (in adolescents or adults, may feel restless); often has difficulty playing quietly; often talks excessively; often blurts out answers before questions completed; often has difficulty awaiting turn; often interrupts or intrudes on others.

B. Some symptoms present before age 7
C. Present in two or more settings
D. Clear evidence of clinically significant impairment
E. Symptoms are not due to another disorder

—Adapted from *DSM-IV-TR*, 2000

ADHD is one of the most frequently cited medical/behavioral conditions known. Likely, it is the topic of at least one article in at least one of the magazines on the rack at your supermarket's checkout counter. Although a medical condition, ADHD is frequently considered by parents and teachers when a child seems to have difficulty in school.

About 7 percent of children have received a diagnosis of ADHD. The authors of both selections believe that ADHD exists, but they have very different opinions about whether or not this diagnosis is being used appropriately.

Arthur Allen examines the life stories of a number of children—cast in the light of educators, psychologiests, and researchers—to identify how easy it is to apply the ADHD label and prescribe medication to address the "symptoms."

Russel A. Barkley, in a selection from an extensive book that also considers the experiences of children and families, believes that educators and parents are only just beginning to recognize and appropriately treat the challenging problems of the disorder known as ADHD.

As you read the following selections, ask yourself how often you have wondered if you or someone you know has ADHD. Is it possible for us to concentrate fully all the time, or is there a real biological disorder that deserves our attention? Are we leaping too quickly to seize a label—and medical cure?

Arthur Allen  **YES**

The Trouble With ADHD

It's a struggle for Andrew Fraser just to be here.

He is sitting politely in the dining room of a Silver Spring church, where each Thursday morning all 36 students at the tiny Quaker middle school Andrew attends gather for silent meeting. The season is midwinter and the group, described by the school's headmaster as mostly "bright underachievers," is midway between childhood and teenagerdom.... In the opening moments of worship, the room is remarkably quiet.

The silence is finally broken by a teacher who mentions that in this season of short days, ancient cultures treasured light, which explains why winter celebrations center on lavish displays of it. In the Quaker tradition, you pray for someone by "holding him in the light," and the teacher suggests that the students of Thornton Friends Middle School might do that now.

A boy raises his voice to hold his mother and little sister in the light. His father, he says, is leaving the family—"he says he hates me." Soon others chime in, sharing worries about sick grandparents and aggrieved friends.... Andrew, a rail-thin eighth-grader,... announces he is holding in the light a gym teacher who twisted his knee....

Andrew has been struggling to get into the light his whole life. At 6 months he fell off the growth curve; in his toddler years, rough textures and loud sounds vexed him. When he was in second grade, a psychiatrist declared Andrew to have the worst case of "attention deficit disorder" he'd seen in 27 years. Andrew ricocheted and fidgeted through grade school, unable to tolerate more than a few minutes in class. He couldn't bear to write. He left his seat constantly. He got into scuffles all the time.

Home life wasn't much better. The Fraser home, a Rockville rambler with a sunken den, frequently shook with Andrew's tantrums. One morning, when Andrew was in fourth grade, he went after his older sister with a knife. Another, he was so enraged at life that he ripped the folding doors off his closet and threw them into the back yard, where he stomped them into slivers. Most mornings Andrew was a reptile coiled in his room, so unready to face the cruel exposures of the school day that his father had to dress him.

Yet Andrew could be a nice kid—open, friendly, communicative. For that grace his teachers and therapists never entirely gave up on him. "Through it all, Andrew was liked," says his mother, Wendy.

His parents took him to a psychiatrist who diagnosed attention deficit hyperactivity disorder (ADHD) with "co-morbidities"—depression and possible conduct disorder. There were drugs to treat each malady.

... [W]hen he was all of 11 years old, Andrew was on an enormous dose—70 milligrams—of Ritalin for his ADHD, plus two antidepressants, Prozac and Pamelar, and the anti-hypertensive Clonidine, to counter the side effects of Ritalin. To make sure his heart could stand the stimulation of so much Ritalin, Andrew had his blood pressure checked weekly. Yet he seemed as distracted, irritable and unhappy as ever. Sometimes the drugs seemed to be making things worse. His father, Bruce, ... and Wendy... were at wit's end.

"He'd cry. He'd threaten to jump out of the car. It was hard to see how he'd make it in middle school," Wendy recalls.

That summer, she got a call from counselors at a day camp that Andrew was attending. Her son had threatened to run into the street, they said, and was marauding around the place with a branch, intimidating counselors and other kids. Come get him. So they did. But this time, when they took Andrew to his psychiatrist, it was clear they had arrived at a threshold. The psychiatrist suggested putting him on a fifth drug, the antipsychotic Risperdal, whose side effects, the doctor explained, included tics, tremors and the risk of permanent brain damage.

Andrew's parents were floored. "He didn't try to hard-sell us," Bruce recalls, but it dawned on them that ever-stronger behavioral drugs were all the psychiatrist had to offer. And Risperdal was "the last club in his bag."

Children who are hyperactive and distracted, who can't focus on what's in front of them or control their behavior, have always been with us. They entered the medical lexicon in 1902, when a British physician, George Frederic Still, described a group of children with "morbid defects of moral control." Still thought he could detect a child's moral propensities by taking measurements of his skull. Since then, the medical definition of this disorder has certainly undergone many revisions. But in some ways it has come full circle.

... In 1972, Virginia Douglas, a Canadian researcher, characterized it as attention deficit disorder, and her terminology became the accepted way of referring to children like Andrew Fraser. It was part of a turning point in child psychiatry toward defining mental illnesses more on the basis of observable behaviors and less on a patient's life history. This approach located the problem in the child's brain—separated it, in a way, from the child's character. That opened the way for large-scale use of medication to change the behaviors....

The scientists who study ADHD believe these children are predisposed to it by particular patterns of brain chemistry, with most cases having some sort of genetic basis, others possibly the result of environmental factors during pregnancy or after birth.

Because there are no blood-borne proteins that define when a kid has ADHD, no lumps on the head or in it, no physical marks of any kind that clearly distinguish a child with ADHD from anyone else, the diagnosis remains controversial in society at large, even as the number of children—and, increasingly, very young children—who are treated for it is skyrocketing....

Today an estimated 3 million children in this country have been diagnosed with ADHD—including perhaps 200,000 between age 2 and 4. With numbers like these it is not surprising that the diagnosis is controversial or that it has become enmeshed in many of the cultural battles of the past two decades, America's fretful internal argument over the proper way to parent and educate the young.

While scientists struggle to provide a unifying theory of what's different about the brains of children with ADHD, critics charge that it's wrong to view these kids' behavior as pathological in the first place; the fault lies with overcrowded schools, stressed-out parents with little time for the children and a society that wants to dull its rough edges and is intolerant of anything but success. Other, less radical critics of the system still believe that ADHD is severely overdiagnosed in America.

At the heart of the controversy over hyperactive disorder is that most children diagnosed with it get the same treatment: a stimulant....

It wasn't until the 1960s that doctors began regularly treating hyperactive children with methylphenidate—trade name Ritalin. Researchers had long reported that Ritalin at low doses had a paradoxical effect—it was "speed" that slowed children down. Eventually it was recognized that stimulants had the same effect on almost everyone: They improved short-term concentration. It was just that people with ADHD needed more help focusing than the rest of us.

There was a brief backlash against Ritalin in the 1970s, when some studies suggested it might stunt a child's growth, but later research indicated those worries were overblown, and by the early 1990s, when society had generally embraced the idea that many problems could—and should—be dealt with by a pill, Ritalin had taken off again.

Even the biggest proponents of drug therapy agree that drugs work best in combination with behavioral modification and talk therapy. But talk is not cheap in the era of managed health care. And the thing about Ritalin and other stimulants is, they get results. Study after study has shown that low-dose stimulants will improve short-term concentration and reduce impulsivity and fidgetiness in about three-quarters of the kids who get them, as long as they're on them. These kids will often do better in school. They won't anger and alienate friends and teachers as much. That makes their parents saner. As a result of these things, the children often feel better about themselves.

How does Ritalin work? As with much about ADHD, no one is exactly sure, but it is evident that Ritalin increases the availability of dopamine, a chemical that's key to movement and attention and other nervous functions, to certain cells in the brain. By adding to the dopamine pool, the drug seems to speed the flow of impulses through the circuits that help people control the instinct to respond to each and every stimulus. In a way, you could say that Ritalin strengthens willpower.

Or, as Ellen Kingsley, the mother of a 13-year-old who has been on ADHD drugs since age 5, puts it: "It enables him to do the things he wants and needs to do and would not be able to do." Kingsley, ... who ... puts out a magazine about ADD, says her son T.K. would never have made it through school without drug therapy. Like many parents of children with ADHD, Kingsley is impatient with people who don't recognize that kids like hers are deeply impaired and need help. "I could give him all the therapy in the world, but it won't sink in without medication because he can't attend to the task," Kingsley says.

Parents with a morbidly hyperactive or inattentive child, most specialists agree, should be no more reluctant to try Ritalin than to give eyeglasses to a near-sighted child, if Ritalin will calm their child and improve his or her life. But among the millions of parents who have put their children on a permanent ration of behavior-modification drugs, many have undoubtedly had to overcome an initial queasiness and feeling of guilt. Laura and Barney Gault certainly did last fall, when a pediatrician suggested that their son, Sam, might need to be medicated.

"My first thought was denial," recalls Barney, Sam's father. "He's a kid—you aren't going to do this to my son. And then I was a little sad. I was thinking, 'Are we going to alter his personality?'"

It is a dreary winter evening in the [school] cafeteria ..., and Sam's den leader, Jeff Bush, is attempting to get Sam and eight other rambunctious 9- and-10-year-old Webelos to drill for their civics merit badge. The den leader's presentation isn't really pulling in the audience. The boys, a few in their blue uniforms with yellow kerchiefs, most in ordinary kid clothes, are popping up and down in their seats like ducks in a shooting gallery. They all seem to be talking at the same time, except for the kids who are falling off their chairs....

At the far end of the table, quietly fabricating spitballs and loading them into a straw, sits Sam Gault. You wouldn't necessarily know that he's the one with ADHD. He doesn't seem hyper. And he's very focused—not on Jeff Bush, unfortunately, but he's very focused on his spitballs. He fires across the room at his mother, Laura, and narrowly misses.

Laura ... is keeping a close eye on her son.... On the previous Saturday, the den took a field trip to a firehouse. During the tour Sam got bored and started making silly remarks: "Is this an atomic bomb?" he asked about a high-pressure hose. "Is this a nuclear weapon?" Finally the fire chief turned and scolded him. Laura finds such incidents painful and hopes that, eventually, Sam will be embarrassed, too, and change his behavior. "When kids are continually singled out, it just whittles away at their self-esteem," she says.

It was partly concern about self-esteem that led the Gaults to take Sam in for a psychiatric evaluation more than a year ago, when he was 8 and in third grade. Sam was bright and thoughtful and didn't do poorly in school, but he couldn't sit still. Time and again, his second-grade teacher reported that Sam had trouble following through with her instructions. He raised a ruckus in the halls and played the class clown. He literally climbed the walls at times. Sam was an inquisitive, detail-oriented child, but his mind had a way of meandering from the critical to the banal. You could hear it in his speech as he drifted from one topic to the next—teachers, Game Boys, his ADHD—without clearly completing his thoughts on any of them.

Laura Gault had had forebodings before Sam was diagnosed with ADHD. She felt that Sam's ADHD might have had a hereditary connection—Sam's paternal grandfather ... probably had ADHD, though in his era, of course, such a thing was not recognized. Even as an adult, he was impatient and impulsive like Sam, and sometimes he blurted out off-color remarks in mixed company.

And that's partly what bothered Laura about her son—the social improprieties. "I noticed that the other kids would be acting out, but they could stop when an adult said stop," she says. "Sam really couldn't stop. He'd just continue to wiggle."

Kids who wiggle too much stand out in a big classroom, where sheer management is a real challenge. Sam's class had 28 other children.

After Sam was diagnosed with moderate ADHD, the Gaults were urged by their pediatrician to start out with a behavioral modification routine. They got his teacher to provide daily reports on Sam, and rewarded good behavior with trinkets: a sleepover for being especially on-task. But within a couple months it was clear this regimen was not enough to motivate Sam. That's when the Gaults turned to Adderall, ...

"He didn't have the maturity or ability to control his behavior on his own," says Laura. So Sam began taking the drug ..., and his parents waited to see how it would affect him. Tonight, as his den leader winds up the civics session and the games begin, the effects of Adderall have long since worn off, and Sam is lost in his own world. The boys ... divide into teams for sock ball, which is dodge ball using balled-up socks. Everyone runs around, yelling and throwing sock bombs at the kids on the opposing team. Sam wads up a pair of socks to make what he calls a "megabomb."

"Throw it, Sam!" shout two of his friends.

Sam does not respond. He is carefully folding the edges of the sock to make a rounder, more compact megabomb. One quality of Sam's mental architecture, it's plain to see, is a certain perfectionism. For better or worse, Adderall hasn't done anything to change that.

"Come on, throw it, Sam!"

Finally he throws and—whack!—the sock bomb smacks a boy named Chris as he attempts to flee.

Teammates cheer. Sam betrays no emotion but lets out a belch of conquest. "He's very proud of that," Laura says, rolling her eyes.

Notwithstanding that ADHD can be a serious disease, the diagnosis of ADHD in America is an inexact science shaped in large part by the socioeconomic milieu of the kid in the middle of it. All it takes is a look at the diagnostic guide to see that.

The guide divides ADHD into three types: inattentive, hyperactive/impulsive or combined. A hyperactive diagnosis requires that the child exhibit six symptoms from a list that includes fidgeting, frequently leaving classroom seat, interrupting often, excessive climbing and running about, excessive talking, inability to quietly engage in leisure activity, acting "as though driven by a motor." An inattentive diagnosis is for children with symptoms that include failure to listen, failure to follow through, tendency to lose things, etc. It's clear that subjective judgment enters into any diagnosis—almost anyone with a child could imagine him or her meeting the diagnostic criteria, on a bad day at least.

To be sure, the diagnostic guide also requires that to be ADHD, the symptoms must exert a significant impact on the child's life at home and school. But "significant impact" requires a context and that's where the controversy about ADHD begins.

Every November, just after parent-teacher conference days in many schools, Barbara Ingersoll, a leading ADHD diagnostician, ... begins to get calls from parents. Ingersoll, a psychologist, performs assessments of children that parents can use to procure medications, therapy or classroom accommodations—all tools employed to get ADHD children through school with a modicum of success.

"After the parent-teacher conferences, when the honeymoon's over," the parents start seeking assessments, she says. "Wouldn't it be great if we had schools that let them be themselves?" she asks a bit facetiously. "But it ain't going to happen. You can't let them run amok."

Often, it's not the parents but the schools that drive the diagnosis. The principal of an elite ... private school several years ago gave the parents of a 5-year-old kindergartner a gentle bit of advice that was almost an ultimatum. The child, who had a photographic memory of almost anything ever read to him and who could spend hours working on art and science projects, was unable to sit still in the classroom. The school referred him to another D.C. psychologist—not Ingersoll—for an assessment that lasted three hours, cost about $2,500 and resulted in what the parents viewed as a preordained conclusion: Their son had ADHD. "He may need to be on Ritalin," the principal said, "to stay in the school."

The family decided to get a second opinion. A child psychiatrist at Washington's Children's National Medical Center rolled his eyes when he heard about the diagnosis. ADHD was a "garbage can label," he told them, the diagnosis for any kid who was out of the box. Their boy was too young to be diagnosed definitively, he said, and the diagnosis wasn't a trivial matter.

Ritalin could mask an underlying condition, or it could cause serious side effects. The kindergartner had tics, and children with tics sometimes developed full-blown Tourette's syndrome after going on Ritalin.

Deep in their guts it felt wrong to the parents and they worried it would stifle their son's nascent creativity. When he was reassessed at a clinic two years later, the ADHD label turned out to be wrong. The boy was dyslexic. He wouldn't sit still in school, it turned out, because he couldn't make sense of the words put in front of him. In the meantime, the family had switched their child to a public school....

What almost happened to this family captures society's fear of Ritalin, that the drug is being used to convert spirited children into docile sheep. But for most children on medication, the real problem isn't that the "meds" turn them into robots; it's that they rarely work as one would hope. At least half of the children diagnosed with ADHD also suffer from complex mixtures of other problems—learning disabilities, anxiety, depression—that can mandate a complex mixture of other drugs.

Theoretically, you can find a drug to treat each symptom. But the relationship between a behavior and the underlying biological facts isn't cut and dried, particularly in children.

Sometimes, Ingersoll acknowledges, she sees children with mood disorders who've been misdiagnosed as ADHD and put on high doses of stimulant that leave them subdued and distant. "You get better behavior, but it's using medicine as a chemical straitjacket," she says. "You get zombies."

Others wonder if some of the "co-morbidities" described by the psychiatrists are caused by the medicines themselves. "Here's the conundrum—I put you on stimulants because you're running around the classroom too much and you're too impulsive and in people's faces," says Julie Magno Zito, a professor at the University of Maryland School of Pharmacy who tracks the growing tendency to prescribe mind drugs for preschoolers. "About three months later, it looks like the treatment works, and then you go home at night and need medication to go to sleep. Enter Clonidine to help you sleep. Now we've gone from one drug to two. I have to worry about interactions, a wider spectrum of side effects. Then after a couple months it becomes apparent that you cry more easily, you're more sensitive. Now somebody says, 'He needs an antidepressant.' Now you're on three drugs. We could call it co-morbid depression. But to me it's equally possible that it's behavioral medicine toxicity. You probably wouldn't have the insomnia and crying if the other drugs were not on board. You can't just keep treating symptom by symptom."

... Zito and a colleague, Daniel Safer, a child psychiatrist at Johns Hopkins University, made headlines when they published an article in the *Journal of the American Medical Association* that tracked a threefold increase in the use of stimulants, antidepressants and other psychotropic drugs among 2- to 4-year-old Medicaid patients.... The article set off a new round of critical news stories about overuse of psychotropic drugs. And like previous Ritalin scares, the uproar put many physicians and parents who believe the drug can save lives on the defensive.

"When you ask me why I put a child on four drugs, I say look at asthmatics," says Larry Silver, a former NIH [National Institutes of Health] official who now has a large child psychiatry practice in Rockville. "With asthma you have multiple maintenance and emergency drugs, and there's a reason for each of the psychotropic medicines, too."

"The people who tend to criticize the use of these medications," he adds, "are usually in the media, or people who've never had to live with or treat the patients."

For a long time, Andrew Fraser and his parents hewed to this logic and followed the pharmaceutical trail wherever their psychiatrist advised them it led. They spent thousands of dollars and hundreds of hours in therapy and classes and doctor's appointments for Andrew. But when the psychiatrist suggested Risperdal, with its terrible potential side effects, it was a step too far.

"We've got to try something else," Bruce Fraser told his wife.

And so they stepped out of the mainstream and into the ... office of Peter Breggin, who provided an unexpected answer to the problem of their son.

"Andrew," Breggin said, looking at the thin, ... boy ... sitting in front of him, "they say you're mentally ill, my friend. But actually you're a brat."

Peter Breggin, whose office is within mortar distance of the National Institute of Mental Health, is the bete noire of psychiatrists. He has written several books attacking the misdiagnosing and overmedicating of America's children. Some view him as his profession's prickly conscience, but his point of view, that there is no such thing as ADHD, is a fringe one among psychiatrists. Many of them believe that his crusading ways have done more harm than good by driving parents away from treatments that could help sick kids. Yet at least a few parents with difficult children view him as a savior who gives voice to their doubts and worries.

Breggin ... believes that ADHD is essentially a "bunch of behaviors that make it difficult to teach kids in a big classroom. That's all it is! You wouldn't have a parent coming in and saying, 'Joey squirms in his seat.' What parent would claim that was an illness? It's the teacher saying, 'You're out of control, take some Ritalin.'"

Most of the worst symptoms of ADHD, he believes, are caused by the drugs that are used to treat it. "Once psychiatry went in the direction of drugs, it basically lost its knowledge and skills," he says. "If you look at the leading psychiatric journals today, there's nothing about family therapy, child development, how to handle an out-of-control kid. It's all about drugs. They act as if children don't need parents, they need drugs! Quite literally! We've abandoned our kids."

Breggin is the medical consultant in ... class action lawsuits ... on behalf of children medicated with Ritalin. The lawsuits, filed ... by some of the same lawyers involved in anti-tobacco litigation, accuse[d] Novartis Pharmaceutical Corp., the maker of Ritalin, the American Psychiatric Association, and CHADD [Children and Adults with Attention-Deficit/Hyperactivity Disorder], an advocacy group for people with ADHD, of conspiring to poison America's children....

"Breggin's effect has been to make families wary of medical treatment," says Laurence Greenhill, a Columbia University child psychiatrist who is leading a clinical trial of Ritalin for preschoolers, which he hopes will provide a means of testing Breggin's theory that Ritalin itself causes brain changes that scientists attribute to ADHD. "He feels that the kids don't get enough tender loving care, they aren't hugged enough. But he doesn't believe in evidence-based medicine and that's the standard now."

The Frasers had had enough of evidence-based medicine when they first stepped into Breggin's office ..., and they instantly took to him and his message. Breggin told them that "in the overload of daily issues we'd failed to pay attention to teaching basic human dignity," Bruce recalls. "Breggin saw a lack of attention had been paid to the basic nurturing of a child. I didn't take umbrage. It sounded reasonable."

... Breggin took Andrew off the medications, one by one. In family and individual therapy,... he told the Frasers that Andrew had to learn to act civilized. He could learn to check his impulses, to pay attention, to show respect. Willpower was his to grasp. Wendy and Bruce had to love him tough and tender. The Frasers were happy to toss out the biological psychiatry, with its talk of titration and syndromes and EEG patterns. Ceremoniously, in the presence of his parents, Andrew flushed the leftover pills down the toilet: Out with impersonal chemicals! Human beings rule!

But Andrew did not immediately improve. He struggled through a year at a public middle school ... then a year in a ... special ed program. Finally, this fall, Andrew began something new—Thornton Friends. The small Quaker school ... was created expressly for kids with promise who had trouble sitting still or paying attention, kids who got teased or harassed in traditional schools, kids who were a little different—but reachable. Thornton Friends stressed individual growth and community feeling. "We want to help people understand themselves and find a style that works for them," says the headmaster, Michael DeHart.

Roughly one-third of the kids in Thornton's middle school are on psychotropic medications of some kind, DeHart says. He agrees with Breggin, who has written positively about Thornton, that the surge in prescription drug use in children reflects our society's anxiety to produce kids who fit expectations, and its inability to create schools that handle their needs. But he also believes—unlike Breggin—that drugs sometimes are necessary. "It's clear to us that some kids, in order to make it work here, need to be on medication. That's where we kind of part ways with Peter."

When Andrew arrived at Thornton, the administrators were up to the challenge of educating a drug-free Andrew. But it wasn't a lovefest. In his first three months Andrew showed little patience and a lot of anger. In the middle of English once, he'd gotten up and yelled that he hated poetry.

"I'm not going to say Andrew needs to be medicated, and I'm not going to say he doesn't," says Jonathan Meisel, the principal of the middle school. "There have been times when it's been very difficult for him. He's very easily distracted. Does that mean it's not worth continuing to try being off them? I'm not sure. Ultimately, is this the right place for him to be as a student, medication aside? We don't know."

Sitting on the couch in Meisel's office, ... Andrew says he is embarrassed to tell old friends he goes to this school. "I hate it here," he says matter-of-factly. "A lot of kids here have a lot of problems. They feel like they don't fit in. They are like really big dorks."

At the same time, Andrew, now 13, knows he never wants to take medication again. He hated himself on drugs: "Nothing seemed fun; everything seemed boring." His goal is to get back to public school, which he knows will be impossible unless he shapes up. "I don't want to, but I think I'll end up here," he says. "I'm going to try to make do with what I've got."

Do Andrew and Sam do what they do because of flaws in the wiring of brain circuits that inhibit inappropriate action, or is the apparent difference in their brains more in the nature of an evolutionary mismatch with modern life, an alternate state of readiness that represents a holdover from prehistoric times when extremely alert, impulsive people presumably had advantages in the struggle to survive? These are two of the untestable hypotheses of pop psychology concerning ADHD.

This much is clear: Our brains evolved with a great deal of variation. If children's height was as variable as the size of their brains, some would be giants stooping to get in the classroom door each morning while others would barely be tall enough to reach their computer keyboards.

That fact poses one of the formidable challenges for researchers such as Xavier Castellanos, a doctor who has been studying ADHD for a decade in the child psychiatry branch of the National Institute of Mental Health.... "Some kids' brains are twice the volume of those of other kids, with both completely normal and healthy," he says. "There's a wide range in brain volume that we don't understand."

For the past several years, Castellanos has been studying the brains of ADHD children as they appear in magnetic resonance imagery (MRI). He's doing the measurements to see if size can tell us something about the seat of abnormality. The current theory is that ADHD may derive from abnormal neural circuits linking the frontal lobes, the deep brain structures called the basal ganglia, and the cerebellum.

But Castellanos ..., is the first to admit how few facts have been established. "The problem with neuroscience at this point is that everything in the brain seems to be related to everything else," he says. "It's like you're attempting to make out which notes of a symphony come from the different instruments, but you are listening from the hall through the wall with a stethoscope."

Castellanos and others have found that the brains of children with carefully diagnosed ADHD are approximately 4 percent smaller, on average, than those of healthy children. Some parts of the brains of ADHD children can be particularly small—the posterior-inferior vermis, a tiny segment of the cerebellum, for instance, is 10 to 15 percent smaller, on average. Castellanos doesn't want to make too much of that—or too little. For the record, he doesn't know what that teaspoon-size region of the brain does.

But he was extremely excited when a study ... found that in macaque monkeys the posterior-inferior vermis was packed with dopamine receptors. That's interesting to Castellanos because an inadequate supply of dopamine is believed to hamper attention and self-control. So the smallness of the posterior-inferior vermis in ADHD kids might mean a shortage of the right neural circuitry.

The smaller the brain size in these children, the worse the ADHD symptoms tend to be. But there's an awful lot of variation, Castellanos says. Two-thirds of the brains of ADHD children are indistinguishable, in size, from those of healthy kids. If you're a skeptic, you say size has nothing to do with it.

Similar caveats cover the genetic work on ADHD so far. "My favorite nightmare is there are going to turn out to be 300 or 500 genes, each of which contributes a couple percent of risk here and there," Castellanos says. The leading candidate gene for ADHD is a variant of the gene known as DRD4. This variant apparently causes a receptor on certain brain cells to have trouble sucking dopamine out of brain synapses. That presumably slows the feedback messages in the brain that inhibit impulses. But you can't call it a defective gene because it turns out fully 30 percent of the U.S. population has it, and not all of those people have been diagnosed with ADHD. And not everyone with ADHD has that particular DRD4 gene variant....

At least two drug companies are said to be working on DRD4-related drugs that could be used to improve the brain circuitry of ADHD patients. But Jim Swanson, one of the UC-Irvine professors involved with the study, has an intriguing hypothesis that the ADHD patients with the suspect DRD4 variant might be the subgroup that benefits most from behavioral modification strategies—rather than medication.

Because it was treatment, rather than diagnosis, that was the most contentious element of the ADHD debate, the National Institute of Mental Health set out to settle the issue of how best to treat ADHD by funding a six-site, 14-month study comparing Ritalin with behavioral modification and combined therapy. The researchers who designed the study included Ritalin advocates ... and behavioral modification proponents....

... The study found that, overall, combined therapy worked best, but drugs alone were significantly more effective than behavioral modification therapy alone.

Swanson was surprised. "We thought intensive behavior modification would meet or beat the medication effects, and it didn't," he says. "We have to face the facts."

But there was another way of looking at the study. More than one-third of the ... kids in the study who were treated with behavioral techniques alone improved their ADHD symptoms. Which means, in Swanson's words, "If there are 3 million kids medicated in the United States, maybe 1 million of them could have a good response to non-drug therapy."

And that would be a good thing. Because the drugs have side effects, and they don't work perfectly, and there will always be parents who, for a variety of reasons, refuse to give their kids mind-altering chemicals.

Before she started him out on Adderall ..., Laura Gault wrote a letter to Sam that explained his disorder and compared the drug to the glasses a near-sighted kid would have to wear. She wanted him to have something to look at in case he started to worry about being called ADHD.

Sam tried to avoid telling friends at school that he had the condition; one reason his parents chose to give him Adderall was that it was long-acting. A single dose, it was hoped, would get him through the entire school day. Kids on Ritalin, which the body metabolizes faster, often have to see the school nurse at lunchtime to get a booster dose—and Sam felt that would be embarrassing.

In the first month on the drug, Sam lost four pounds, and he was a skinny boy to begin with. "I was very concerned about that," Laura recalls. "You can tell a child to eat, but you can't make them eat."

"But," she says with a shrug, "it did help with his behavior." Sam no longer seemed compelled to pester his neighbors in class. He could walk from room to room without climbing the walls or rattling a pen along the lockers.

But the tiny blue ... pill he takes at breakfast wears off by 2 p.m., and from that point Sam's teachers and parents use their wits and wisdom to keep Sam on track. One evening a week, Sam attends a group therapy session with other children with ADHD who need help learning how to act appropriately in social settings. He says he doesn't like it, but he clearly tunes in—you can tell by his recall of some details.

"If you see two people having a conversation there are six things you do," he recites. "First, you stand near them. Then you move closer, and smile. Then you see if they smile back. If they do, then you smile again. Then if you know something about what they're talking about, you join in the conversation, but maybe just a small comment at first."

Laura doesn't give Sam the medication on weekends or evenings, mainly because she worries about his weight. Too, she doesn't want him to be on medication forever. "Our goal is eventually to get him off," she says. "From what I've read, a lot of boys, once they go through puberty can ... not outgrow it exactly, but the hyperactivity can be less.

"In the meantime I want him to learn how to cope."

For now coping begins with the pills, which clearly have an effect. Sam forgot to take his medication the first day back at school after winter break this year—and the teacher noticed right away. He couldn't sit still and his attention wandered. Which got Laura thinking again about the dosage. "I've been kind of waiting to see if there's a need to increase it," she says.

Before Thornton Friends' two-week winter break, Jonathan Meisel had written up a contract for Andrew. It was a one-page list of do's and don'ts, and it essentially stipulated that if Andrew's behavior didn't improve, he was out of the school.

One thing the contract required was more frequent therapy, and so Andrew began seeing Breggin weekly, instead of every few months. But the new system also made a concession: Instead of writing by hand, which was torture for Andrew as it is for many ADHD kids, he was allowed to bring a laptop to school so he could type his notes.

All in all, it was a challenge.

The family drove to South Carolina to visit Bruce's parents for part of the school vacation. The trip went smoothly. One evening, back in town but before he returned to school, Andrew joined his father and a family friend in a sort of woodshed behind the friend's house. While the adults drank cognac and smoked cigars, they talked with Andrew about his future. "You could just tell how excited he was to be treated as an adult," Bruce says, "and at the end my friend said, 'This is a good kid. He doesn't need to be in special education.'"

Recently, Andrew has begun to feel he has a goal in life. He downloads music from the Internet and burns CDs for his friends, earning a little money that way. He's been thinking he'd like to take a mail-order computer course. "That's what I'd like to do when I'm older," he says, "become a computer programmer."

In written evaluations submitted at the end of the third week of the new trimester, all of Andrew's teachers had noted a remarkable turnaround. "Andrew has developed some qualities in the science classroom since holiday break that I have not usually seen," one teacher wrote, "—improved attentiveness to discussion and explanation, more thoughtful questioning and answering, and decreased distractions with other students...."

His parents are keeping their fingers crossed.

"It took a lot of people—his teachers and friends and therapists and family and him—to get this far," Wendy says. "We feel like he's turned a corner."

NO

Russell A. Barkley

What Is Attention-Deficit/ Hyperactivity Disorder?

Attention-deficit/hyperactivity disorder, or ADHD, is a developmental disorder of self-control. It consists of problems with attention span, impulse control, and activity level. But, as you will discover here, it is much more. These problems are reflected in impairment in a child's will or capacity to control her own behavior relative to the passage of time—to keep future goals and consequences in mind. It is not, as other books will tell you, just a matter of being inattentive and overactive. It is not just a temporary state that will be outgrown, a trying but normal phase of childhood. It is not caused by parental failure to discipline or control the child, and it is not a sign of some sort of inherent "badness" in the child.

ADHD is real—a real disorder, a real problem, and often a real obstacle. It can be heartbreaking and nerve-wracking.

"Why Don't They Do Something About That Kid?"

It's easy to see why many people find it hard to view ADHD as a disability like blindness, deafness, cerebral palsy, or other physical disabilities. Children with ADHD look normal. There is no outward sign that something is physically wrong within their central nervous system or brain. Yet I believe it is an imperfection in the brain that causes the constant motion and other behavior that people find so intolerable in a child who has ADHD.

By now you may be familiar with the way others react to ADHD behavior: At first many adults attempt to overlook the child's interruptions, blurted remarks, and violation of rules. With repeated encounters, however, they try to exert more control over the child. When the child still fails to respond, the vast majority decide that the child is willfully and intentionally disruptive. Ultimately most will come to one conclusion, albeit a false one: The child's problems result from how the child is being raised. The child needs more discipline, more structure, more limit setting. The parents are ignorant, careless, permissive, amoral, antisocial, unloving, or, in contemporary parlance, "dysfunctional."

"So, Why Don't They Do Something About That Kid?"

Of course the parents often are doing something. But when they explain that the child has been diagnosed as having ADHD, judgmental outsiders typically react with skepticism. They see the label as simply an excuse by the parents to avoid the responsibility of child rearing and an attempt to make the child yet another type of helpless victim unaccountable for his actions. This hypocritical response—viewing the child's behavior so negatively, while at the same time labeling the child as "just normal"—leaves outsiders free to continue blaming the parents.

Even the less censorious reaction of considering ADHD behavior as a stage to be outgrown is not so benign in the long run. Many adults, including professionals, counsel the parents not to worry. "Just hang in there," they advise, "and by adolescence the child will have outgrown it." This is certainly true in some milder forms of ADHD: In perhaps half or more of these very mild cases, the behaviors are likely to be within the normal range by adulthood. If your preschool child has more serious problems with ADHD symptoms, however, such advice is small comfort. Being advised to "hang in there" for 7 to 10 years is hardly consoling. Worse, it is often grossly mistaken, harmful advice. The life of a child whose ADHD is left unrecognized and untreated is likely to be filled with failure and underachievement. Up to 30–50% of these children may be retained in a grade at least once. As many as 35% may fail to complete high school altogether. For half of such children, social relationships are seriously impaired, and for more than 60%, seriously defiant behavior leads to misunderstanding and resentment by siblings, frequent scolding and punishment, and a greater potential for delinquency and substance abuse later on. Failure by the adults in a child's life to recognize and treat ADHD can leave that child with an unremitting sense of failure in all arenas of life.

"Isn't ADHD Overdiagnosed? Aren't Most Children Inattentive, Active, and Impulsive?"

Imagine the toll on society when, conservatively estimated, 3–7%, or more than 2 million school-age children, have ADHD. This means that at least one or even two children with ADHD are in every classroom throughout the United States. It also means that ADHD is one of the most common childhood disorders of which professionals are aware. Finally, it means that all of us know someone with the disorder, whether we can identify it by name or not.

The costs of ADHD to society are staggering, not only in lost productivity and underemployment but also in reeducation. And what of the costs to society in antisocial behavior, crime, and substance abuse? More than 20% of children with ADHD have set serious fires in their communities, more than 30% have engaged in theft, more than 40% drift into early tobacco and alcohol use, and more than 25% are expelled from high school because of serious misconduct. Recently the effects of ADHD on driving have also been studied. Within their first two years of independent driving, adolescents with a diagnosis of ADHD have nearly four times as many auto accidents, are more likely to cause bodily injury in such accidents, and have three times as many citations for speeding as young drivers without ADHD.

Recognition of these consequences has spawned a huge effort to understand ADHD. Besides ... thousands of scientific papers ..., more than 50 textbooks have been devoted to the subject, with again as many books written for parents and teachers. Countless newspaper stories have addressed ADHD over the course of the 100 years that clinical science has recognized the disorder as a serious problem. Many local parents' support associations have sprung up, most notably Children and Adults with Attention Deficit Disorder (CHADD), which has grown into a national organization of more than 50,000 members. At least five professional organizations include a number of scientific presentations on the subject in their convention programs each year. ... All this is hardly what you would expect if the disorder were not "real," as some critics have claimed.

Fact Versus Fiction

...[V]arious unsubstantiated claims about the legitimacy of the disorder we call ADHD have been making the media rounds [recently]. Trying to sort through these, in addition to facing the skepticism of friends, family, and teachers, can make it difficult for parents to accept a diagnosis of ADHD and move forward into productive treatment of their child. Here is what we know to date:

Fiction: ADHD is not real, because there is no evidence that it is associated with or is the result of a clear-cut disease or brain damage.

Fact: Many legitimate disorders exist without any evident underlying disease or pathology. ADHD is among them.

Disorders for which there is no evidence of brain damage or disease include the vast majority of cases of mental retardation (various brain-scanning methods reveal no obvious disease or damage in children with down's syndrome, for example), childhood autism, reading disabilities, language disorders, bipolar disorders, major depression, and psychosis, as well as medical disorders involving early-stage Alzheimer's disease, the initial onset of multiple sclerosis, and many of the epilepsies. Many disorders arise due to problems in the way the brain has developed or the way it is functioning at the level of nerve cells. Some of these are genetic disorders, in which the condition arises from an error in development rather than from a destructive process or an invading organism. The fact that we do not yet know the precise causes of many of these disorders at the level of the molecules in the brain does not mean they are not legitimate. A disorder ... is defined as a "harmful dysfunction," not by the existence of pathological causes.

As for ADHD, the evidence is quickly mounting that we are dealing in most cases with a disorder in brain development or brain functioning that originates in genetics. Although most cases of ADHD appear to arise from ... genetic effects and difficulties with brain development and functioning, ADHD can certainly arise from direct damage to or diseases of the brain as well. Fetal alcohol syndrome is known to create a high risk for ADHD in children with that syndrome, and so is prematurity of birth in which small brain hemorrhages may have occurred during delivery. And it is well known that children suffering significant trauma to the frontal part of the brain are likely to develop symptoms of ADHD as a consequence. All of this indicates to scientists that any process that disrupts the normal development or functioning of the frontal part of the brain and its connections to the striatum is likely to result in ADHD. It just so happens that most cases are not due to such damage, but seem to arise from problems in the development of critical brain regions or in their normal functioning. Someday soon we will understand the nature of those problems with greater precision. But for now, the lack of such a precise understanding does not mean that the disorder is not valid or real. If the demonstration of damage or disease were the critical test for diagnosis, then the vast majority of mental disorders, nearly all developmental disabilities, and many medical conditions would have to be considered invalid. Countless people suffering from very real problems would go untreated, and their problems would be unexplored.

Fiction: If ADHD were real, there would be a lab test to detect it.

Fact: There is no medical test for any currently known "real" mental disorder.

Just as we cannot identify any disease or brain damage for ADHD, we cannot give children a test to detect it. Neither is there a test for schizophrenia, alcoholism, Tourette's syndrome, anxiety disorders, or any of the other well-established mental disorders, or for many widespread medical disorders such as arthritis. Yet they are all very real in being harmful dysfunctions.

Fiction: ADHD must be an American fabrication, since it is diagnosed only in the United States.

Fact: Recent studies conducted in numerous foreign countries show that all cultures and ethnic groups have children with ADHD.

Japan has identified up to 7% of children as having the disorder, China up to 6–8%, and New Zealand up to 7%. Other countries may not refer to ADHD by this term, they may not know as much about its causes or treatment, and (depending on the countries' level of development) they may not even recognize is yet as a legitimate disorder. But there is no question that ADHD is a legitimate disorder and is found worldwide.

Remember, the United States is among the few leaders, if not the leader, in the amount of scientific research conducted on childhood mental disorders. It is therefore highly likely that the United States at times comes to recognize disorders and develop treatments for them long before other countries do.

Fiction: Because the rate of diagnosis of ADHD and the prescription of stimulants to treat it have risen markedly in the last decade or two, ADHD is now widely overdiagnosed.

Fact: As the National Institute of Mental Health (NIMH) Consensus Conference on ADHD concluded in late 1998, underdiagnosis and undertreatment of ADHD remain big problems in the United States today.

Several studies indicate that fewer than half of all children who have ADHD are diagnosed or properly treated for the disorder, and that only one-half of these are treated with medication. The greatest problems for our children continue to be that a large percentage of those with legitimate disorders in need of treatment are not being referred, diagnosed, or properly treated, and that services across the United States for children with ADHD are inconsistent, erratic, and often well below what is considered the standard of care for the disorder. So evidence for proclamations that we are overdiagnosing ADHD in the United States and overusing stimulants for its management lack credible scientific evidence.

One possible reason for the rise in diagnosis and stimulant treatment of ADHD is that the prevalence of the disorder has actually increased. However, we do not have a lot of research that has measured the rates of children's mental disorders across multiple generations. The little research we do have indicates that ADHD has not been on the rise over the last two generations of children, but that a few other disorders may be, such as oppositional defiant disorder …. Mainly what I think we have been witnessing is an increase in the recognition of the disorder by the general population, and therefore an increase in the number of children being referred and diagnosed with the disorder. Tremendous strides have been made to educate the American public about ADHD in the last 20 years. Thanks to a substantial upsurge in research on the disorder, to the various parent advocacy groups raising the level of public and political awareness about ADHD (such as CHADD and ADDA [Attention Deficit Disorder Association] …, to increased professional education on the disorder, and to the recognition of ADHD as a legitimate disability in the Individuals with Disabilities in Education Act and the Americans with Disabilities Act, more children with this disorder are getting proper diagnosis and management. But again, we still have a long way to go. A recent study by Dr. Peter Jensen and colleagues at the NIMH found that as many as half or more of children with the disorder in five major regions of the United States that were studied had not been diagnosed or were not receiving appropriate treatment.

The same scenario seems to have been occurring more recently in other countries, such as Australia, Great Britain, and the Scandinavian countries, where greater efforts are under way to educate the public and professional communities about the disorder. The result has been a marked increase in the number of children being referred for professiona help, properly diagnosed, and possibly being treated with stimulant medications, among other treatments, So I have to think that most of the increase in diagnosis in the United States is due to greater awareness about the disorder.

In conclusion, a number of facts suggest the we do not have widespread overdiagnosis or overmedication with stimulants, despite the marked rise in both in the United States over the last 10 to 20 years. That is not to say that there may not be some locales within the United States where more children than expected are being diagnosed or where more medication than would be prudent is being prescribed. But these appear to be very local problems and do not indicate a national scandal.

A Question of Perspective

Intense interest in demystifying ADHD has instigated voluminous research....
[The] research done by the time [my] book was first published in 1995 led me
to a new view of ADHD—a view that has been reinforced by studies undertaken in the last five years. I see ADHD as a developmental disorder of the
ability to regulate behavior with an eye toward the future. I believe the disorder stems from underactivity in an area of the brain that, as it matures, provides ever-greater means of behavioral inhibition, self-organization, self-
regulation, and foresight. Relatively hidden from view in a child's moment-to-
moment behavior, the behavioral deformity this underactivity causes is perni-
cious, insidious, and disastrous in its impact on a person's ability to manage
the ciritical day-to-day affairs through which human beings prepare for the
future, both near and far.

The fact that its daily impact is subtle but its consequences for the child's
adaptive functioning are severe has led to many changes in the labels and concepts applied to the disorder over the last century. It explains why clinical science, in its attempts to pin down the nature of the problem, has moved from
vague, unfocused notions of defective moral control 100 years ago to sharper,
more specific concepts of hyperactivity, inattention, and impulsivity in
recent decades. This evolution of our knowledge from the very general to the
very specific has taken us leaps forward in understanding the abnormalities of
children with ADHD, but it has caused us to lose our perspective on how
those behaviors affect the social adaptation of these children over long periods of time.

Now, however, clinical science is stepping back from its microscope on
the social moments of children with ADHD and once again peering through
its telescope at longer-term social development. We are beginning to understand how these "atoms" of momentary ADHD behavior come to form "molecules" of daily life, how these daily "molecules" form the larger "compounds"
of weekly and monthly social existence, and how these social "compounds"
form the larger stages or structures of a life played out over many years. As a
result, we see that ADHD is not just the hyperactivity or distractibility of the
moment or the inability to get the day's work done, but a relative impairment
in how behavior is organized and directed toward the tomorrows of life.

This larger, longer view of ADHD clarifies why those with the disorder
struggle in their adaptation to the demands of social life and so often fail to
reach the goals and futures that they have tried to set for themselves or that
others demand of them. If we remember that the behavior of those with
ADHD is focused on the moment, we won't judge their actions so harshly. No
one would understand half of what we "normal" adults do if these actions
were judged solely by their immediate consequences. Many of the actions we
take have been planned with the future in mind. Likewise, we don't understand—and are quick to criticize—the behavior of those with ADHD because
we are expecting them to act with foresight when they have always focused
instead on the moment. We find it difficult to tolerate the way those with
ADHD behave, the decisions they make, and their complaining about the neg-

ative consequences that befall them because we, who do not have the disorder, can see where it is all leading and use that vision to determine our current behavior while they cannot. Only now is clinical science coming to understand this very important feature of ADHD.

POSTSCRIPT

Is Attention Deficit (Hyperactivity) Disorder Overdiagnosed?

Allen considers whether or not ADHD reflects an "inexact science," affected by a busy and demanding society that has little tolerance for individual variation. While all treatments have their place, he wonders if adults are overlooking natural variations, seeking a "magic pill" to achieve conformity and compliance.

Barkley, on the other hand, feels that medical science is just beginning to develop the tools to help us understand how to assist all individuals reach their potential and function effectively in a demanding society. He holds that the dissemination of voluminous research on ADHD is leading a more informed set of parents and teachers to identify a disorder that can be effectively addressed.

An International Consensus Statement on ADHD (2002), signed by a consortium of over 80 international researchers, reports that there is much agreement about ADHD, beginning with it existence. The researchers attest that ADHD exists internationally and can lead to "devastating problems." Most significantly, the consortium asserts that "less than half of those with the disorder are receiving treatment." The consortium urges the media to resist distracting people by publishing "propaganda" questioning the reality or extent of ADHD.

Extensive information on ADHD is provided by Children and Adults with Attention-Deficit/Hyperactivity Disorder (CHADD), which maintains a very active Web site http://www.chadd.org, containing numerous fact sheets, legislative updates, instructional and behavioral management strategies, and a newsletter, in addition to links to related sites.

Examining "Interesting Kids Saddled with Alienating Labels," Thomas Armstrong (2001), a prolific writer, believes that we are ignoring the natural range of difference in the human population, seeking instead to attach pathological labels (and putative cures) to normal—and desirable—individual variation. Armstrong challenges adults to embrace the differences in children, seeing the possibilities rather than seeking the diagnostic label of a disorder.

Several other authors (among them Peter Breggin and Lawrence Diller) have written popular books questioning the reality and growth of interest in ADHD and the wisdom of using medication so freely with children.

In 2003 the National Institute of Mental Health reprinted its informational booklet *Attention Deficit Hyperactivity Disorder*, which reviews research data that supports a genetic basis for ADHD. Cautioning that ADHD-like behaviors can result from underachievement in school, attention lapses due to epileptic seizures, hearing problems due to ear infections, or disruptive or unresponsive behavior caused by anxiety or depression, the authors emphasize the critical need for accurate, careful analysis of the events in a child's life as opposed to a quick assumption that ADHD is present.

Real or not, the existence of ADHD is firmly established in our society. Information about the behavior of ADHD children and treatments is readily available. The scientific community has not identified a specific cause or universally effective treatments, and few believe that ADHD can be cured. Standard treatments include medication, behavioral supports, and counseling. A combination of these is usually found to achieve the most significant and long-lasting change.

Healthy caution is advisable. Many circumstances impact the behavior of children and adults alike. Medication is an important tool to use—when it is needed. Counseling and guidance from a caring adult help the most children (diagnosed with ADHD or not). Deciding whether or not a problem exists—and what to do about it—is the challenge for all of us.

Has society lost the ability to tolerate anything other than total compliance and predictability—especially from little boys? Or is it just now becoming known that there are powerful biomedical conditions that affect our ability to attend, learn, and work? Are people running to the diagnosis of ADHD (and medication) to make life easier or are they just beginning to understand its prevalence and implications?

ISSUE 16

Are We Over-Prescribing Medication to Solve Our Children's Problems?

YES: **Lawrence H. Diller,** from "The Run on Ritalin: Attention Deficit Disorder and Stimulant Treatment in the 1990s," *Hastings Center Report* (March/April 1996)

NO: **Larry S. Goldman, Myron Genel, Rebecca Bezman, and Priscilla Slanetz,** from "Diagnosis and Treatment of Attention-Deficit/Hyperactivity Disorder in Children and Adolescents," *JAMA, The Journal of the American Medical Association* (April 8, 1998)

ISSUE SUMMARY

YES: Lawrence H. Diller, a pediatrician and family therapist, believes that the use of stimulants has risen to epidemic proportions, occasioned by competitive social pressures for ever more effective functioning in school and at work.

NO: Larry Goldman, Myron Genel, Rebecca Bezman and Priscilla Slanetz, after reviewing twenty years of medical literature regarding the diagnosis of ADHD and the use of stimulants, conclude that the condition is not being overdiagnosed or misdiagnosed and that medications are not being over-prescribed or over-used.

In a 1996 issue, *Newsweek* (March 18) asked whether Ritalin was a miracle cure or a dangerous drug; a 2000 article (April 24) responded that "Stimulants are still the most effective treatment for ADHD: The challenge is to use them wisely." In a 1998 cover story, *Time* (November 30) addressed "The Age of Ritalin," including a discussion on Prozac; by 2000 (March 20), its Families section included "When pills make sense: Some parents turn too quickly to mood-altering drugs. But often medication is the right choice."

Every class contains children who rely on medication. It might be inhalers for asthma or epipens in case of bee sting. Most likely there will be at least one child who takes some sort of medication for either issues of attention or depression. Or both.

An entire new field—pediatric psychopharmacoepidemiology—the study of the prevalence and patterns of psychiatric medication use among children—has developed, along with *The Journal of Child and Adolescent Psychopharmacology*. Although this field—and daily practice—covers much more than Ritalin, most of the questions around the use of medications and children focus on the drugs designed to treat Attention Deficit Hyperactivity Disorder.

Russell A. Barkley (*ADHD: A Handbook for Diagnosis and Treatment*, 1998), cites research showing that 70 to 80% of children diagnosed with ADHD will require medication. Most respond to one of three stimulants, but some rely on anti-depressants and a small minority need anti-hypertensives.

Lawrence Diller, author of *Running on Ritalin*, is shocked by the 500% increase in the prescribed use of Ritalin in the mid-90s. He believes medication is an easy and fast answer for parents whose schedules do not permit them to spend time with their children; doctors whose managed care responsibilities limit the amount of time they can spend with patients; and educators, whose underfunded schools do not provide the resources to spend time with children, and society, which demands faster, better performance from everyone.

Goldman, Genel, Bezman and Slanetz, authors of an extensive study and report for the American Medical Association, acknowledge the increase in use of medication, but ascribe this rise to a shift in diagnostic criteria and recognition that a useful intervention has been identified and is being used appropriately.

If a child has difficulty seeing the blackboard (more often now the whiteboard), it is easy to check to see if there are difficulties in visual acuity. If a child can't see the board, glasses might help. The prescription written by a doctor is filled and learning can move forward.

When a child's behavior and/or learning raises questions for parents and/or teachers, educational testing used to be the way to learn about the child's learning style and capabilities. More and more frequently, the questions about behavior and/or learning revolve around whether medication can help.

Medication is different than glasses. There are few side effects to wearing glasses. There might be many connected with medication. And yet both seem to be very effective if appropriately used.

As you read these articles, ask yourself whether you would choose medication for yourself or your child in order to improve concentration or moderate behavior. Are the benefits and the long term costs worth the risks? Or are the risks minimal, considering the overall improvement in quality of life?

Lawrence H. Diller  **YES**

The Run on Ritalin

Stimulants were first reported as a pharmacologic treatment for children's behavioral problems in 1937. Methylphenidate, a derivative of piperidine, was synthesized in the 1940s and marketed as Ritalin in the 1960s. It is structurally related to the older drug still used for the treatment of hyperactivity, d-amphetamine. Their pharmacological actions are essentially the same.

Stimulant treatment for children became more common in the 1960s when its short-term benefits for what was then called hyperactivity were documented in controlled trials. In 1970 it was estimated that 150,000 children were taking stimulant medication in the U.S.

A furor over stimulants began in 1970. The reaction stemmed from an article in the popular press charging that 10 percent of the children in the Omaha school district in Nebraska were being medicated with Ritalin. While ultimately shown to contain inaccuracies, the article spurred other reports of "mind control" over children and led to congressional hearings about stimulants that same year. Numerous articles in newspapers and magazines and one book attacked Ritalin and the "myth" of the hyperactive child. Subsequently it was found that some of the criticism appeared to be led by supporters of the Scientology movement, who have consistently challenged mainstream psychiatry's use of psychoactive medications. Yet the negative publicity struck a nerve with the general public, which by the mid-1970s made it quite difficult to convince parents and teachers in many communities to attempt a trial of Ritalin.

The DEA [Drug Enforcement Agency] began monitoring the amounts of methlyphenidate and amphetamine produced in this country in 1971. Both became Schedule II controlled drugs partly in response to an epidemic of methylphenidate abuse occurring in Sweden and the illegal use of stimulants in this country. Estimates on the number of children using stimulants have varied widely. In 1980 it was estimated that from 270,000 to 541,000 elementary school children were receiving stimulants. In 1987 a national estimate of 750,000 children was made. Both estimates were guesses extrapolated from local surveys.

More precise than national estimates of children taking stimulants are the records of production quotas maintained by the DEA that show a steady output of approximately 1,700 kilograms of legal methylphenidate through the 1980s followed by a sharp increase in production in 1991. From 1990 through May 1995, the annual U.S. production of methylphenidate has increased by 500 percent to 10,410 kilograms, "an increase rarely seen for any other Schedule II Controlled Substance," according to the DEA. A national survey of physician's diagnoses and practices based upon data collected in 1993 found that of the 1.8 million persons receiving medication for Attention Deficit-Hyperactivity Disorder, 1.3 million were taking methylphenidate. A comparison of 1993 Ritalin production with the latest figures available for 1995 suggests that 2.6 million people currently are taking Ritalin, the vast majority of whom are children ages five through twelve.

Who is taking all of this Ritalin, and why? To get at the answers to these questions, we need to look at changes in professional and lay attitudes regarding psychoactive drugs, the brain, and children's behavior. Six hypotheses are suggested to explain the sudden increase in the demand for this drug.

Changes in Diagnostic Criteria

As more children's behavior is viewed as abnormal, more treatment is offered. The American Psychiatric Association distinguishes deviancy from normalcy in its *Diagnostic and Statistical Manual of Mental Disorders (DSM)*. With the introduction of the *DSM III* in 1980, mainstream psychiatry officially changed its view from a diagnosis of hyperactivity, highlighting physical movement, to one where problems with attention, Attention Deficit Disorder, were of primary concern. This change reflected research that suggested the primary problem for children was one of focus and distractibility. Hyperactivity, as a reflection of motoric impulsivity, was still important but not critical to the diagnosis. Thus, one could meet the criteria for ADD without being overly motorically active at all. The name of the condition was changed again in *DSM III-R* to Attention Deficit-Hyperactivity Disorder, and in *DSM-IV* separate subtypes of inattention and hyperactivity/impulsivity were restored.

There have been additional interpretative changes to the diagnosis. One need not demonstrate symptoms in every situation. Rather one need only display symptoms in at least two environments. Similarly one may concentrate satisfactorily at a number of tasks, perhaps even overfocus, yet still meet criteria for diagnosis if concentration and focus are problems for important tasks....

The changes in diagnostic criteria and interpretation have greatly broadened the group of children *and adults* who might qualify for the diagnosis. The line between children with "normal" variations of temperament, lively or spontaneous children who are sensitive to stimuli, and those who have a "disorder" has become increasingly blurred. The sine qua non for the diagnosis of hyperactivity in the mid-1970s was a demonstration of motoric overactivity and/or distractibility in nearly all settings including the doctor's office. Some children who may have benefited from identification and treatment were undoubtedly missed under these criteria, but this is less likely today. Now children who sit quietly and perform well in social situations or in one-on-one psychometric testing can still be candidates for the diagnosis and treatment of ADHD if their parents or teachers report poor performance in completing tasks at school or at home.

Prior to *DSM III*, etiologic factors were important in the diagnosis of psychiatric disorders. Since 1980 diagnosis has been descriptive, based primarily on observed behavior and self-report. While the multiaxial codings of the *DSM III* presumably account for medical factors and social stressors on the patient, less emphasis is placed on psychosocial influences, such as family, school, or work environments. In addition, the ascendancy of biological psychiatry, with its emphasis on the genetic and neurochemical factors directing behavior, implicitly diminishes the significance of development, learning disabilities, emotional status, family interaction, classroom size, and other environmental factors that may be relevant. Meeting ADHD criteria, which strictly speaking involves demonstrating a group of behaviors, has come to mean "having" ADHD, a neurological condition, such as Pervasive Developmental Disorder or Tourette Syndrome. Research purported to support a biological basis for ADHD, a brain scan of the cerebral cortex, or a survey of family epidemiology, cannot conclusively distinguish between biological or environmental etiologies.

Environmental factors can be seen either as contributing to the etiology or maintaining the symptomatic behavior. Indeed, a strongly stated case for neurological factors has been useful to counterbalance beliefs that such behaviors were attributable to lazy children and disorganized adults. However, if the symptoms of ADHD are to be viewed within the biopsychosocial model, calling ADHD a neurological disorder can mislead some into discounting psychosocial factors as unimportant.

The "Lean and Mean" '90s

As professional viewpoints have changed, so too have societal pressures and public attitudes toward attention and behavior problems in children and adults. Over the past two decades the pressure on children to perform has increased while support needed to help maximize performance has declined. Twenty-five years ago three- and four-year-old children were not expected to know the alphabet and numbers. Community programs like Head Start and television shows such as Sesame Street, while benefiting millions, have also led to expectations that children can learn at an earlier age. Yet over the concurrent past twenty years poverty rates for children, as a measure of their general well-being, have increased from 15 percent to 20 percent nationwide and children comprise 40 percent of all those who live in poverty.

More families are requiring two incomes to maintain their standard of living, and the increasing number of women in the workforce has led to large-scale preschool enrollment of children, requiring that younger children adhere to a more organized and less flexible social structure. Many children adapt easily to preschool and thrive in that group environment. Yet some children are not developmentally or socially ready for preacademic learning and a more demanding social structure. These children, had they stayed at home, would not be exposed to community scrutiny or come to the attention of teachers and physicians at an early age. At age three or four their behavior may qualify them for an ADHD diagnosis.

At the elementary school level, funding pressures on school systems have led to increased classroom sizes and higher student-to-teacher ratios. Also, more stringent criteria exist to qualify for special education services, which are often inadequately funded.

Similar conditions exist for high school and college students, especially in public education. The pressure to do well academically is immense. Inexorable pressures have developed to maintain a high grade point average in order to gain entry into a "good" college or graduate school.... Increasing attention through the use of medication may be seen as just another method to improve performance and results....

Pressures on Physicians and Educators

Physicians are also under pressure. Even before the managed care era, the time and economic constraints on the primary care physician were great. When presented with a potentially complex child behavioral problem, the physician may be attracted to the option of prescribing a medication rather than addressing the thornier and more time-consuming issues of emotions, family relationships, or school environment. Even with genuine concern for a multimodal evaluation and treatment plan, often little else is done on the primary care level.

Specialists, such as behavioral-developmental pediatricians and child psychiatrists, should be capable of spending more time and lending greater expertise to the resolution of the intricacies of the child, family, and school situation. These specialists are concerned, however, that the cost-containment measures of managed care will increasingly permit referrals only when medication is being considered for the child.

Increasing pupil-teacher ratios and diminishing special education services also have an effect. These conditions make it "easier" to medicate a child than to work with a dysfunctional family, decrease the size of the classroom, or augment funding for special education services. Because stimulants "work" more quickly, they are more attractive not only to families and physicians, but to managed care companies and financially strapped educational systems. It is unlikely that either would insist on medication in lieu of counseling or special education services, but neither would protest if medication allowed the child to function better without either service.

The Disability Issue

Society increasingly has interpreted performance problems as disease, which then become defined as a disability. People with defined disabilities cannot legally face discrimination and are entitled to the benefits of special services. The increasing numbers of children and adults who meet the broader ADHD criteria are beginning to have an impact in the classroom and workplace. Parents find the only way to get extra help for their children is to have them labeled with a disorder. The Individuals with Disabilities Education Act of 1990 and recent interpretations of Section 504 of the 1973 Rehabilitation Act have become broad and potent legal tools for families of children with ADHD seeking special services from their school districts....

Categorizing ADHD as a disability has created other dilemmas. Typically someone with a disability is provided special circumstances or allowances for optimal performance, for example, more time provided in a college entrance examination.... In the workplace more and more employers are being asked to make changes for their workers who are affected with ADHD. It is only a matter of time until an employer balks and a suit is filed. The trend is being followed closely by the business community....

The Culture of Prozac

Prozac (fluoxetine), the first of the serotonin reuptake inhibitors, went on the market in 1988. With its low side-effect profile compared to the earlier generation of antidepressants, it widened the range of individuals who might tolerate a psychotropic drug for depression and led to widespread popular debate on the subject. Peter Kramer's best-selling book, *Listening to Prozac*, reflected and further encouraged popular interest in the use of psychiatric medication to enhance mood and performance. The overall prevalence of antidepressant use in certain communities has quadrupled in a ten-year period. It has become much more acceptable to take a psychotropic medication. This new atmosphere has also increased acceptance of stimulant use for behavioral problems in children and attentional problems in adults.

The Role of Mass Media

The effects of mass media on the practice of medicine and concerns of patients are well documented. As TV news, talk shows, and print journalism have highlighted the use of psychotropic medication to cope with one's problems, a corresponding public interest in Ritalin and ADHD has developed. Personal and affecting testimonies of dramatic improvements after using Ritalin have been reported on national television broadcasts and many syndicated talk shows.... Prominent local and national news weeklies have made ADHD their cover stories.

In both the professional and lay media ADHD is routinely referred to as a neurological disorder. While most experts agree that generic-biochemical factors influence behavior to some degree, the general public tends to transform this view into a biological determinism in which only heredity and brain chemistry determine behavior rather than in interactions with the environment. This interpretation may be comforting to some perplexed and worried parents who feel responsible for their children's difficulties and help overburdened teachers gain assistance in teaching children with this "disability." Psychotherapeutic strategies can help "externalize" the disease as separate from the child. Yet when behavior is regarded as stemming from biological pathology, interventions like stimulant medication become more easily justified and emphasized, while others become less valued. Indeed,

ADHD has become the somewhat dubious leading self-diagnosis as the "bio-logical cause ... for job failure, divorce, poor motivation, lack of success, and chronic mild depression."

Cosmetic Ritalin

"Cosmetic psychopharmacology," as Kramer puts it, is the elective use of med-ically prescribed drugs to enhance mood or improve behavior. Currently, it is considered medically and ethically justifiable to prescribe stimulants only when behavior meets criteria for a medical or psychiatric disorder. It is not known how much Ritalin currently is being prescribed for those on the indis-tinct line between "disease" and the general struggle for success. It is known, however, that Ritalin improves the focus and performance of those who do not meet ADHD criteria (normal, nonreferred children) and that the drug is pre-scribed for such use.

There remains no definitive "test" for ADHD. The ambiguities of the ADHD diagnosis were highlighted in a study on stimulant medication and primary care. Over one quarter of children diagnosed with ADHD by their physician failed to meet criteria for the diagnosis when the cases were com-pared to structured psychiatric interviews with the parents. The number of children who failed to meet criteria increased to half when compared to struc-tured interviews with the children's teachers. While the overall number of children medicated was not seen as high by the investigators, they noted the nonspecificity of the behavioral symptoms in the children that responded to stimulants. Thus, the ADHD diagnosis was seen as a diagnostic cover, albeit inaccurate, for the use of stimulants in a range of behavioral and performance problems in children.

Questioning Ritalin

Stimulants can be used in an effective and sensible way, especially when other modalities of treatment for attentional problems are addressed concurrently. Undoubtedly many parents of children with ADHD and adults with ADHD feel Ritalin has been of immense benefit to their children or themselves. How-ever, important questions remain unanswered and a pending request to decrease DEA controls on methylphenidate production and physician prescrip-tion practices makes them all the more urgent.

Ritalin's reemergence as a popular "fix" overlooks adverse side effects, a dearth of long-term studies, and a host of other ethical questions concerning unwitting coercion, fairness, informed consent, and potentially inadequate treatment of patients. Larger societal questions also should be asked: Should society use a biological fix to address problems that have roots in social and environmental factors? If it consistently does, how might society be affected?

If elective treatments are to warrant consideration, their side effects must be minimal. The short- and long-term physical side effects of Ritalin are gen-erally considered minor on the basis of fifteen- to twenty-year follow-up studies involving children who took stimulants for several years up until early adolescence. The effects of continuous Ritalin use through adolescence and into adulthood have not, as yet, been studied. The drug's immediate side effects, brief appetite suppression and possible insomnia, are generally well tolerated by children. Some reports suggest Ritalin unmasks the tics of Tourette Syndrome, but this remains controversial. Long-term growth suppression has been attributed to Ritalin, but this effect can be minimized through the scheduling of drug "holidays."

Although one reason for the much greater use of Ritalin compared to amphetamine for ADHD has been the erroneous belief that it has less abuse potential, there exists a possibility of abusing Ritalin. The Swedish experience of the late 1960s and very recent examples of Ritalin abuse by teenagers in this country belie this myth of safety. However, there is little evidence of physical addiction to or abuse of Ritalin when used *appropriately* for ADHD. Despite the possibilities of abuse, Ritalin appears relatively safe from a strictly physical standpoint.

Evaluation of the emotional and psychological consequences of Ritalin use is more complex. There is still a strong cultural belief that it is better to cope by using one's inherent resources and interacting with people than by resorting to medication. This 'pharmacological Calvinism' may lead to feelings of inadequacy in the child who takes the drug, despite the physician's and family's view that Ritalin is necessary or benign. Teenagers, particularly sensitive about their identity, are especially vulnerable to issues of competence and biological integrity. These beliefs can be overcome, but remain a potential downside.

While physical addiction doesn't occur when Ritalin is used as prescribed for ADHD, psychological dependence is possible for the child, the family, the adolescent or adult. When queried, children attributed most of their success in a "vigilance" assignment to their own efforts rather than medication. It is family members and teachers who more often notice the child performing suboptimally and ask, "Did you take your pill today?" The question expresses an underlying message to the child about the drug's important contribution to performance and behavior, and ultimately, this message may undermine the child's confidence. This sense of dependency is highlighted when the medication is used "as necessary," in event-driven dosing, for example, when studying for an exam or attending a weekend family gathering. It is even possible that event-driven dosing may promote or exacerbate the often disorganized ADHD lifestyle by allowing the procrastinating individual to "catch up" at the last minute. The teenager and adult may also be tempted to stretch the normal wake-sleep cycle in order to achieve even greater performance, which could ultimately lead to an abuse pattern. The long-term consequences of self-administered stimulants by teenagers and adults for ADHD have not been studied to determine the likelihood of such a pattern developing. Thus, while achievements made under the influence of stimulants can enhance a sense of competence, self-esteem, and independence, the specter of psychological dependence, altered self-image, and potential abuse remains, especially in a society that paradoxically continues to be somewhat critical of psychotropic drugs while demanding greater performance.

Ritalin should be questioned further because no long-term studies prove its efficacy. Numerous reports show the stimulants to be of value in short-term memory and performance. In long-term studies benefits to children formally classified under the hyperactivity diagnosis have not been demonstrated. For children with ADHD without hyperactivity or for teenagers and adults there are *no* long-term studies of Ritalin's efficacy.

Long-term controlled studies are difficult to run and fund, and one can question the ethics of withholding a potentially effective treatment until there is more definitive proof of benefit. However, a single study in which children received Ritalin along with child-family counseling and special education services is the *only* research demonstrating long-term improvements. Most child behavior experts advocate a multimodal approach to treatment despite the lack of definitive evidence of improvement. In actual practice, though, the follow through for behavioral recommendations is poor. The multimodal model of treatment is also suggested for adults. Yet, here too, the emphasis in professional and lay articles is on the pharmacological interventions.

The increasing availability and use of Ritalin to enhance performance also raise questions of subtle coercion and fairness. As more children and adults use Ritalin to work more efficiently at school or in the office, will those who are also struggling to perform feel pressured to consider medication? Will there be an impetus to keep up with others, to compete for the good grade, bonus, or job promotion by whatever means necessary, medication or otherwise? Moreover, is it fair to use the same performance criteria for those who use Ritalin as for those who do not? In athletic competition, stimulants remain banned precisely because of fairness issues. Yet, recently, the case has been made that athletes with ADHD be allowed to compete while taking Ritalin because of their "handicap." Somehow viewing behavior as neurologically based makes it more acceptable to use medication.

Because many Ritalin users are children, issues concerning informed consent also arise. Although the treatment of undesired nonpathological conditions in adult medicine is not uncommon (for example, plastic surgery, topical minoxidil for baldness, estrogens for menopause, treatment for infertility, and contraceptives), elective therapies for children have been more controversial because it is the parents, not the children, who decide upon treatment. For example, growth hormone for constitutional short stature has been hotly debated. Who decides for whom in these cases? And how high should the standard be?

One last question concerns the tendency for genetic contributions and neurochemical influences on behavior to be understood deterministically by society, such as the media and the courts. Such an interpretation can have the effect of eclipsing other treatment options. Even "good" psychopharmacology decreases the need to scrutinize the child's social environment and may permit a poor situation to continue or grow worse. Should dysfunctional family patterns and overcrowded classrooms be tolerated just because Ritalin improves the child's behavior? An effort is underway to determine which combination of treatments is most effective. The National Institutes of Mental

Health has funded a multisite ADHD study involving several thousand children, with the goal of comparing treatment efficacies with a variety of approaches and combinations. Yet in the absence of confirmed, effective long-term treatment for ADHD and the general recommendations for a multimodal approach, will medication-only treatment produce persistent problems later in a child's life?

Furthermore, this bioreductionistic interpretation of the neurobiological components of ADHD behavior attributes less power to free will and individual choice. Thus, the popular viewpoint of maladaptive behavior as disease conflicts with another historically strong cultural perspective: accountability and responsibility. This clash of views is likely to be resolved ultimately in the civil and criminal court systems and by the economic imperatives of the workplace. It is worth noting how recent court decisions on recovered memory of child sexual abuse are influencing psychiatric technique and practice and the frequency of diagnosis of multiple personality disorder. Similar court guidelines are likely to emerge for those on the borderline of an ADHD diagnosis.

Responses to the Epidemic

The main response to date over the epidemic of ADHD and the use of stimulants in America has been further efforts at informing professionals and the public about the "new" ADHD (without hyperactivity). For many physicians, psychologists, and educators, the identification of potential ADHD and consequent stimulant treatment are meeting an important need of the community. Further education about the benefits of diagnosis and stimulants is the present goal. Academic medicine remains primarily focused on substantiating a biological substrate for ADHD. A notable exception is a recent study on the effects of family stressors in the development of ADHD.

However, another view of ADHD diagnosis and the rise in stimulant use is far more sobering. As suggested earlier, the ADHD/stimulant phenomenon may reflect how the demands on children and families have increased as the social network supporting them has declined. The rise in the use of stimulants is alarming and signals an urgent need for American society to reevaluate its priorities.

On a clinical level, physicians treating children and adults may be locked into a "social trap." Though it may make sense to medicate individuals so they can function more effectively and competently within a certain environment, do doctors unwittingly permit and support a long-term collective negative outcome for the society? Are they unintentionally promoting an antihumanistic, competitive environment that demands performance at any cost? Should they more aggressively promote a general redistribution of society's resources to children and families? Some say there is no choice but to offer medication; it is not up to physicians to address society's ills. Peter Kramer in *Listening to Prozac* seems rather sanguine about a society that copes with newer, safer, improved psychopharmacologic agents. Whether individually beneficial or societally dangerous it behooves the physician to at least raise these questions about ADHD and stimulants with parents, teachers, and colleagues.

NO

Larry S. Goldman et al.

Diagnosis and Treatment of Attention-Deficit/Hyperactivity Disorder in Children and Adolescents

Attention-deficit/hyperactivity disorder (ADHD) is a common neuropsychiatric syndrome with onset in childhood, most commonly becoming apparent (and thus coming to medical attention) during the first few years of grade school. ADHD may be associated with a number of comorbid psychiatric conditions as well as with impaired academic performance and with both patient and family emotional distress. While it was previously thought that the disorder remitted before or during adolescence, it has become well established that many patients will have an illness course that persists well into adulthood. Pharmacological treatment, particularly with stimulant medication, is the most-studied aspect of management, although other forms of treatment (eg, behavior therapy, parent training) are important parts of good clinical care.

Despite an enormous body of research into this disorder, various aspects of ADHD have generated controversy over the years. Three features of ADHD in particular seem to have contributed to the controversy: (1) like most mental disorders, its diagnostic criteria involve patient history and behavioral assessment without the availability of laboratory or radiologic confirmation; (2) like many chronic illnesses of childhood, it has an early onset and extended course, thus requiring at times treatment of children and adolescents over many years; and (3) its treatment often includes stimulant medications that have abuse or diversion potential.

Debate has centered on the appropriate assessment and "labeling" of children: there have been allegations that the diagnosis is merely applied to control children who exhibit unwanted behaviors in the classroom or elsewhere and that medication is simply used to control such behavior. Along similar lines, concerns have been expressed about whether thorough enough evaluations are being performed by physicians prior to prescribing medication. Apart from diagnostic issues, concerns have been raised about young children taking medications for lengthy periods of time. In addition, some critics have complained that overemphasis on psychopharmacological treatment has led to neglect of other treatment modalities or served as a distraction from family problems or school shortcomings. It should be stressed that

From Larry S. Goldman, Myron Genel, Rebecca J. Bezman, and Priscilla J. Slanetz, "Diagnosis and Treatment of Attention-Deficit/Hyperactivity Disorder in Children and Adolescents," *JAMA, The Journal of the American Medical Association*, vol. 279, no. 14 (April 8, 1998). Copyright © 1998 by The American Medical Association. Reprinted by permission. References omitted.

these issues have been raised polemically or theoretically, rather than on the basis of particular scientific findings.

Another concern has been raised by the dramatic increase in methylphenidate (Ritalin) hydrochloride production and use in the United States in the past decade. This has raised questions about whether there has been a true increase in the prevalence of ADHD in this time period; a change in diagnostic criteria affecting practice; improved physician recognition of the disorder; a broadened spectrum of indications for use of stimulants; and an increase in stimulant abuse, diversion, and prescription for profit.

Debate over ADHD within the research and medical communities has been mild and mostly concerned with nuances in the diagnostic and treatment paradigms. By contrast, highly inflammatory public relations campaigns and pitched legal battles have been waged (particularly by groups such as the Church of Scientology) that seek to label the whole idea of ADHD as an illness a "myth" and to brand the use of stimulants in children as a form of "mind control." These efforts, which have been widely reported in the news media, have created a climate of fear among physicians, parents, and educators and have sown anxiety and confusion among the general public. It is thus most important to separate legitimate concerns raised by scientific studies from abstract, distorted, or mendacious information from other sources.

There are 6 main questions that underlie this professional and public concern and that this report will address by reviewing the pertinent research:

1. Is there an agreed-on set of diagnostic criteria for ADHD that reflects sufficient reliability and validity so as to delineate a clinically meaningful syndrome?
2. What is the epidemiology of ADHD, and how can the apparent disparities in prevalence in different populations be explained?
3. What is the course of the illness, and what are the adverse consequences of the illness that would justify treatment?
4. What constitutes optimal treatment for ADHD, and how do stimulants fit into it?
5. What are the adverse consequences of using stimulants, and in particular, what is known about the risks of abuse and diversion?
6. Are children being appropriately assessed and treated in clinical settings to ensure that diagnostic criteria are being used appropriately; ie, is there evidence of underdiagnosis, overdiagnosis, or misdiagnosis? ...

Diagnosis of ADHD

... The *DSM-IV* [*Diagnostic and Statistical Manual of Mental Disorders*, Fourth Edition] criteria emphasize several factors:

The symptoms specified in the criteria must be present for at least 6 months, ensuring that persistent rather than transient symptoms will be included.

The symptoms must be "maladaptive and inconsistent with developmental level." This ensures that the symptoms are of sufficient severity to cause problems and that the child's age and neurodevelopment are considered in evaluating symptoms.

The symptoms must be present across 2 or more settings, ie, school problems alone do not meet criteria for the diagnosis.

The symptoms are not better explained by another disorder, such as mood disorder, psychosis, or pervasive developmental disorder (autism).

Taken as a whole, these criteria require an illness pattern that is enduring and has led to impairment. To make this diagnosis appropriately, the clinician must be familiar with normal development and behavior, gather information from several sources to evaluate the child's symptoms in different settings, and construct an appropriate differential diagnosis for the presenting complaints. This helps, for example, to distinguish children with ADHD from unaffected children whose parents or teachers are mislabeling normal behavior as pathological. The diagnostic criteria as used by appropriate examiners demonstrate high interrater reliability of individual items and of overall diagnosis.

A number of other psychiatric, medical, and neurologic disorders (eg, traumatic brain injury, epilepsy, depression) can lead to disturbances in attention and/or activity level. Thus, the diagnosis of "primary" ADHD is made when there is no evidence from the history, physical examination, or laboratory findings of another condition producing the clinical picture.

... [T]he overall approach to diagnosis may involve (1) a comprehensive interview with the child's adult caregivers; (2) a mental status examination of the child; (3) a medical evaluation for general health and neurologic status; (4) a cognitive assessment of ability and achievement; (5) use of ADHD-focused parent and teacher rating scales; and (6) school reports and other adjunctive evaluations if necessary (speech, language assessment, etc) depending on clinical findings. An evaluation can be performed by a clinician with the skills and knowledge to carry out those components....

Even with the use of carefully applied diagnostic criteria, there remains the issue of the validity of ADHD as a discrete condition. With regard to unitary etiology, many medical conditions (eg, heart failure, seizures) are syndromes representing a final common presentation of a number of pathophysiological disturbances. Thus, the absence of a single cause would be a weak argument against the validity of ADHD as a discrete syndrome. The familial, genetic, neuroanatomical, and neurophysiological studies are mounting evidence to date for postdictive validity. Findings with regard to concurrent validity are mixed: there is clearly a great deal of overlap between ADHD and a number of learning conditions and conduct disorder, among other conditions. The strongest evidence of validity has been for course prediction and treatment response. Overall, ADHD is one of the best-researched disorders in medicine, and the overall data on its validity are far more compelling than for any medical conditions.

Epidemiology of ADHD

A number of studies have examined the prevalence of ADHD in various populations. The patient sample used is critical because of variations in different settings: at least 10% of behavior problems seen in general pediatrics settings are due to ADHD, while children with ADHD make up to 50% of some child psychiatric populations. In general, most ADHD patients in the United States are cared for by pediatricians and family practitioners, while child psychiatrists, neurologists, and behavioral pediatricians tend to see refractory patients and those with significant comorbidity. Community studies have yielded prevalences between 1.7% and 16%, depending on the population and the diagnostic methods....

These results suggest that across fairly diverse populations (geographically, racially, socioeconomically) there exists a sizable percentage of school-aged children with ADHD. The evolution of criteria from *DSM-III* to *DSM-IV*, although based on a progressively larger empirical base, has broadened the case definition, so that more children appear to be affected. This is largely a function of the increased emphasis on attentional problems as opposed to a more narrow focus on hyperactivity in earlier diagnostic sets. As a result, girls have been diagnosed as having ADHD more frequently than they were in the past.

Illness Course and Comorbidity of ADHD

Longer-term follow-up studies of children with ADHD as well as "lookback" studies of symptomatic adults who can be retrospectively diagnosed as having had childhood ADHD show that there is symptomatic persistence into adulthood in many cases. On average, symptoms diminish by about 50% every 5 years between the ages of 10 and 25 years. Hyperactivity itself declines more quickly than impulsivity or inattentiveness.

A number of psychiatric conditions co-occur with ADHD. Between 10% and 20% of children with ADHD in both community and clinical samples have mood disorders, 20% have conduct disorders, and up to 40% may have oppositional defiant disorder. Bipolar disorder is being increasingly recognized. Only about 7% of those with ADHD have tics or Tourette syndrome, but 60% of those with Tourette syndrome have ADHD, raising questions about common etiologic mechanisms. Learning disorders (especially reading disorder) and subnormal intelligence also are increased in the total population of those with ADHD and vice versa. Overall, perhaps as many as 65% of children with ADHD will have 1 or more comorbid conditions, although their presence will not be recognized without appropriate questioning and evaluation. In general, when ADHD is untreated there is a gradual accumulation of adverse processes and events that increase the risk of serious psychopathology later in life. Whether this can be reversed by long-term treatment remains unknown.

The relationship between substance use disorders and ADHD is complex. Children with ADHD who do not have comorbid conditions have a risk of substance use disorders that is no different from children without ADHD up to the age of about 14 years. The risk of developing substance use disorders in those with ADHD is increased in adolescents, and the risk ratio increases further in adulthood, regardless of whether there is comorbidity. Persistence of ADHD symptoms and family history of both ADHD and substance use disorders are risk factors for their development. Highly potent risk factors are the presence of comorbid conduct disorder or bipolar disorder. There is debate about whether long-term treatment of ADHD may decrease the risk of subsequent development of substance use disorders....

Treatment of ADHD

Methylphenidate, created in 1955, now accounts for more than 90% of the stimulant use in ADHD in the United States. A racemic mixture of amphetamines (Adderall), dextroamphetamine sulfate (Dexedrine and others), and pemoline (Cylert) are also used. Methylphenidate is strongly favored by US physicians, perhaps because the overuse of amphetamines for treatment of obesity and their misuse in the 1960s gave that class of drugs a reputation as more problematic than methylphenidate.

There have been more than 170 studies involving more than 6000 school-aged children using stimulant medication for ADHD. The response rate for any single stimulant drug in ADHD is approximately 70%, and up to 90% of children will respond to at least 1 stimulant without major adverse events if drug titration is done carefully. A "response" in this context means a statistically or clinically significant reduction in hyperactivity or increase in attention as rated by parents, teachers, and/or research raters. There have been only about a half-dozen studies in adolescents.

Medications have been unequivocally shown (ie, by double-blind, placebo-controlled studies) to reduce core symptoms of hyperactivity, impulsivity, and inattentiveness. They improve classroom behavior and academic performance; diminish oppositional and aggressive behaviors; promote increased interaction with teachers, family, and others; and increase participation in leisure time activities. Finally, stimulants have demonstrated improvement in irritability, anxiety, and nail biting. A recent meta-analysis found that the effect of stimulants on behavior and cognition may be severalfold greater than the effects on academic achievement.

Contrary to earlier assertions, the response to stimulant medications in those with ADHD is not "paradoxical": the direction of changes in behavioral measures in those with ADHD, those with conditions other than ADHD (eg, learning disabilities, depression), and normal controls is the same. Thus, a favorable response to stimulants does not confirm a diagnosis of ADHD (nor, of course, does a nonresponse refute the diagnosis). A nonspecific performance-enhancing effect may mask other problems and delay use of other interventions.

In addition to their value in childhood and adult ADHD, methylphenidate and other stimulants may play a role in the treatment of other medical conditions, including narcolepsy, as a short-term treatment for depression in the medically ill, as potentiating agents with conventional antidepressants for major depressive disorder, as potentiating agents with opiates for pain control, and to reduce apathy in dementia and some other brain diseases. The number of patients receiving these drugs for these indications probably represents no more than a small percentage of all stimulant use in the United States.

For patients with ADHD who are intolerant of or unresponsive to stimulants, a number of other drugs have proven useful in clinical practice, including tricyclic antidepressants and bupropion hydrochloride, a newer antidepressant that blocks the reuptake of norepinephrine and dopamine. Serotonin-specific reuptake inhibitors have not been effective to date. Centrally acting α-blocking drugs (clonidine, guanfacine hydrochloride) have been helpful in some children, but data are still limited. Subsets of children seem to have some response to lithium carbonate. Neuroleptic medication is occasionally effective, but the risk of tardive dyskinesia makes this a problematic long-term approach. By contrast, some 20 studies have refuted the efficacy of dietary manipulations (eg, the Feingold diet) in ADHD.

It is important to emphasize that pharmacotherapy alone, while highly effective for short-term symptomatic improvement, has not yet been shown to improve the long-term outcome for any domain of functioning (classroom behavior, learning, impulsivity, etc). This may be a function of several factors: most studies have been carried out only for a short term, there may have been inadequate dosage titration to maximize the number of responders, and dose-response relationships may be different for different domains.

... [A] careful review of all review studies of stimulant use in children in 1993 ... found overwhelming evidence for temporary improvement of core symptoms (hyperactivity, inattention, and impulsivity) as well as the associated features of defiance, aggression, and negative social skills. On the other hand, changes that point toward longer-term improvement (eg, in academic outcome, antisocial behavior, or arrest rate) were not found, and only small effects were observed on learning and achievement.

Children should be reevaluated periodically while not taking medications to see if the medications are still appropriate and necessary.

Multimodal therapy, ie, integrating pharmacotherapy with a number of environmental, educational, psychotherapeutic, and school-based approaches, is a tailored approach that seems intuitively powerful, matching the child's particular problems to selections from a menu of focused treatment interventions. In a few studies, multimodal therapy has affected long-term results, although how applicable these findings are beyond research settings remains unclear. While three quarters of treatment review articles assert that multimodal therapy is superior to medication or psychosocial interventions separately, there is in fact little empirical evidence to support such a conclusion.

Nonmedication approaches include parent education; parent management training (contingency management in individual or group setting; this technique decreases disruptive behavior, increases parents' self-confidence, and decreases family stress); classroom environmental manipulations (special class, seating in class, etc); contingency management and daily report cards by teacher; individual psychotherapy for depression, anxiety, and low self-esteem; impulse and social skills control training; support groups such as Children and Adults With Attention Deficit Disorder and Attention Deficit Disorder Association for families; and summer treatment programs.

Some experts feel that stimulants alone may be adequate for cases of ADHD without comorbidity, but that additional treatments are necessary where there are co-occurring conditions. Behavioral therapy has not proved effective alone, although it has been when combined with pharmacotherapy. Since psychosocial treatments may be labor intensive and expensive, it is important to establish when and which treatments are indicated. A large multisite study is currently being carried out by the National Institute of Mental Health to clarify the role of multimodal treatment: carefully evaluated children will be randomized to receive standard community care, medication alone, psychosocial treatments alone, or multimodal therapy (medication and psychosocial treatments together).

A number of textbooks and many review articles are available to practitioners. The Academy of Child and Adolescent Psychiatry's practice parameters have recently been released. A recent American Academy of Pediatrics position paper emphasizes the need for careful evaluation and monitoring of children with ADHD, and it stresses that drugs be used as part of an overall care plan.

Adverse Effects of Stimulants

Adverse effects from stimulants are generally mild, short lived, and responsive to dosing or timing adjustments. The most common effects are insomnia, decreased appetite, stomach ache, headache, and jitteriness. Some children will exhibit motor tics while on stimulants: whether this reflects a true drug effect or an "unmasking" of a latent tic disorder is unknown. A small percentage of children experience cognitive impairment that responds to dosage reduction or drug cessation. Rare cases of psychosis have occurred. Pemoline has been infrequently associated with hepatic toxic effects, so periodic monitoring of liver enzymes is necessary.

Concerns had been raised about the effects of chronic stimulant ingestion on growth and development. It is unclear whether children's heights are affected by long-term use of these medications.

A great deal of concern has been raised by the DEA [Drug Enforcement Agency] and others about the potential for abuse or diversion of stimulant medication: production (and use) of methylphenidate in the United States has risen from less than 2000 kg in 1986 to 9000 kg in 1995, with a tripling between 1990 and 1995 alone. By contrast, amphetamine production rose from 400 to 1000 kg in the same period. More than 90% of US-produced methylphenidate is used in the United States.

The reasoning for the concern about possible overproduction of methylphenidate has been expressed as follows: Stimulants at times are abused by adolescents and adults; those with ADHD are at increased risk of developing a substance use disorder; methylphenidate and other stimulants may either become the drug abused by those with ADHD, or they may serve as a "gateway" to other drug use; and even if they do not abuse their medication themselves, children and adolescents with access to stimulants will be under pressure to divert their medication to those who will.

There is little disagreement that stimulants as a class have marked abuse potential, and their misuse can have severe adverse medical and social consequences. However, stimulants differ in their ability to induce euphoria and thus liability to abuse. Almost all of the reports of abuse of methylphenidate itself have been of polysubstance-abusing adults who have tried to solubilize the tablets and inject them (with disastrous results from talc granulomatosis in some cases). This last problem in particular led Sweden to withdraw methylphenidate from the market in that country entirely in 1968.

It is clear that there is a fair amount of use of stimulants by adolescents. The annual school survey of drug use conducted by the University of Michigan has shown an increase from 6.2% to 9.9% of eighth-graders reporting nonmedical stimulant use in the preceding year between 1991 and 1994. However, lifetime nonmedical methylphenidate use has remained essentially constant around 1% during the same period. Sixty percent of students who used any stimulants reported using them fewer than 6 times in their lifetime, and 80%, fewer than 20 times. Only 4% reported any injection use of stimulants. Thus, while nonmedical stimulant use may be somewhat more common among adolescents in recent years, little use is of methylphenidate itself, and the pattern of use for the vast majority appears to be experimental and not of the type (regular, heavy, injecting, etc) likely to lead to serious adverse consequences.

Drug Abuse Warning Network data on emergency department visit monitoring show a 6-fold increase between 1990 and 1995 in mentions of methylphenidate. A "mention" simply indicates that the patient listed the drug as one taken: it is not necessarily the drug leading to the emergency department visit, nor is there any medical confirmation. The rate of cocaine mentions, by contrast, is 40 to 50 times higher. The methylphenidate cases are overwhelmingly young women, not the population (ie, male adolescents) felt to be at highest risk for abusing prescription methylphenidate. The DEA has had reports of thefts of methylphenidate, street sales, drug rings, illegal importation from outside the United States, and illegal sales by health professionals. There have also been reports of theft of school supplies of methylphenidate.

On the other hand, abuse of methylphenidate by patients with ADHD or their family members has been reported rarely. Only 2 cases of methylphenidate abuse by adolescents with ADHD have been described, and only 2 cases of methylphenidate abuse by parents of children taking it for ADHD have been reported. While there is no way to know how many cases may have been unrecognized or unreported, such a minimal published experience is quite remarkable in light of the population exposed....

Current Practice

It is clear from the discussion of diagnostic assessment that ADHD simply cannot be diagnosed in a typical 15-minute primary care office visit.... Few data exist on actual practice habits in terms of what diagnostic criteria (if any) are used by clinicians, how they are applied, or exactly what a minimally satisfactory level of investigation entails.

A national survey of physicians found that 5.3% of elementary school children in pediatrics practices were diagnosed as having ADHD, and 4.2%

were diagnosed by family practitioners. When explicit *DSM-III-R* [*Diagnostic and Statistical Manual*, Revised Third Edition] criteria were used, however, only 72% of those assigned a diagnosis of ADHD by their physicians would have received the diagnosis based on a structured interview. Only 53% of the physician diagnoses included teachers' reports. Eighty-eight percent of the physician-diagnosed children were prescribed methylphenidate, and 85% of the parents reported that the medication was helpful. Only 22% of the parents reported treatment with behavioral modification, and in 70% of those cases that modality was recommended by someone other than the treating physician. Eleven percent received counseling from the physician, and no parents queried judged it effective. The authors of this survey drew attention to the mismatch between physician diagnosis from a single source, often an unreliable one, and the use of stimulant medication. They also stressed the low rates of use of nonpharmacological treatment by their physician sample....

There is evidence to suggest that stimulants in ADHD populations are simply being used more broadly, for longer periods, and without interruptions in recent years than was done previously. Overall, there has been a 2.5-fold increase in the prevalence of child and adolescent methylphenidate treatment from 1990 to 1995, so that some 2.8% of US youth between the ages of 5 and 18 years were taking this medication in mid 1995. A recent national study found no evidence of overdiagnosis of ADHD or overprescription of methylphenidate.

... [F]rom 1990 to 1993 the number of patients diagnosed as having ADHD increased from 900,000 to 2 million, and the number of outpatient visits for the condition rose from 1.7 million to 4.2 million. The percentage of patients given methylphenidate remained around 70%. Thus, the amount of methylphenidate produced per 1 million patients increased from 1.98 g to 2.53 g, a 27% increase.

There are several important clinical reasons for the increased diagnosis and stimulant treatment of ADHD. These include increased public and physician awareness and acceptance of the condition; acceptance of a broader case definition as appropriate; greater knowledge of the illness course, justifying lengthier treatment (eg, of adolescents); fewer interruptions in treatment because of diminished concerns about growth retardation; and increased treatment of adults.

Finally, with regard to cross-national data, there is some consensus that most non-US clinicians are more likely to rely on older, more stringent diagnostic criteria, reserve the diagnosis for only the most obvious or severe cases, or even be reluctant to diagnose ADHD at all. Physicians from countries with strong psychoanalytic traditions may be particularly reluctant to use discrete diagnostic criteria at all. Physicians in the United Kingdom, for example, tend to use a *DSM-II* approach, so they place more emphasis on hyperactivity and therefore diagnose ADHD far less frequently than their US counterparts. When physicians in the United Kingdom are instructed in applying US criteria, however, they diagnose ADHD as often as their US counterparts do in US children. Thus, the apparent discrepancy is more a matter of case recognition than actual prevalence. Canadian physicians, who tend to use later *DSM* criteria, diagnose and treat children at rates similar to those seen in the United States.

Conclusions

1. ADHD is a childhood neuropsychiatric syndrome that has been studied thoroughly over the past 40 years. Available diagnostic criteria for ADHD are based on extensive empirical research and, if applied appropriately, lead to the diagnosis of a syndrome with high interrater reliability, good face validity, and high predictability of course and medication responsiveness. ADHD is one of the best-researched disorders in medicine, and the overall data on its validity are far more compelling than for most mental disorders and even for many medical conditions. Nonetheless, the pathophysiology of ADHD remains unknown, although a number of neurophysiological theories are under investigation. ADHD demonstrates a very high heritability.

2. The diagnostic criteria for ADHD are designed to be used by a clinician familiar with childhood development and behavioral disorders. Application of the diagnostic criteria requires time and effort to obtain a careful history from parents, teachers, and the child. As with almost all mental disorders, there is as yet no confirmatory genetic, radiologic, biochemical, neurophysiological, or neuropsychological test for ADHD, but such examinations may be helpful at times in evaluating presenting complaints suggestive of ADHD.

3. ADHD is associated with significant potential comorbidity and functional impairment, and its presence at any age increases the risk of behavioral and emotional problems at subsequent stages of life. It is thus a chronic illness with persistence common into adolescence and beyond.

4. Epidemiologic studies using standardized diagnostic criteria suggest that 3% to 6% of the school-aged population may have ADHD. A few studies have suggested a somewhat lower prevalence, but others, particularly those using newer, broader criteria, yield prevalences well above 6%. These studies have been conducted in a number of different countries and encompass a range of racial and socioeconomic backgrounds in the populations examined.

5. The percentage of US youth being treated for ADHD is at most at the lower end of this prevalence range. More cases of ADHD are being recognized and treated, and the duration of treatment is increasing. However, ADHD is also diagnosed inappropriately at times because of failure to do a thorough enough evaluation or to use established diagnostic criteria.

6. Pharmacotherapy, particularly stimulants, has been extensively studied. Medication alone generally provides significant short-term symptomatic and academic improvement, but response to stimulant medication is not specific to ADHD, and it is currently unknown whether long-term outcomes will be altered. The risk-benefit ratio of stimulant treatment in ADHD must be evaluated and monitored on an ongoing basis in each case, but in general is highly favorable.

7. Optimal treatment of ADHD involves an individualized plan based on any comorbidity as well as child and family preferences. This treatment generally will include pharmacotherapy (usually with stimulant medication) along with adjunctive psychoeducation, behavioral therapy, environmental changes, and, at times, supportive psychotherapy of the child, the family, or both. Non-

pharmacological treatment modalities are well accepted by parents and probably significantly underused in primary care settings.

8. There should be documentation in the medical record showing evidence that appropriate diagnostic criteria for ADHD have been met, that common comorbid conditions have been assessed, that there is a clear treatment
plan, and that there is appropriate follow-up, including medication monitoring for efficacy, adverse effects, and ongoing need.

9. There is little evidence to suggest that stimulant abuse or diversion is
currently a major problem, particularly among those with ADHD, although
recent trends suggest that this could increase with the expanding production
and use of stimulants. Clinicians need to be mindful of the risk of abuse and
diversion: in addition to keeping careful records of medication prescribed,
they may consider alternatives to stimulant use in patients at high risk (eg,
patient or family members with substance use disorders or bipolar or conduct
disorder co-occurrent in the patient).

POSTSCRIPT

Are We Over-Prescribing Medication to Solve Our Children's Problems?

The arguments around the use of medication are very powerful. Both articles believe drugs can be the right answer to a problem. They disagree on whether society is using the medications to create new problems.

Diller challenges the medical profession to break free of the "social trap" of using medication to support societal demands. He sees the consequence of continuing along the current path a life where much about human behavior becomes attributable to a disability, out of the individual 's control, except for the ingestion of a magic pill.

A darker view is predicated by Peter Breggin, the author of *Talking Back to Ritalin* (1998), *Talking Back to Prozac* (1995). In addition to doubting the existence of many of the "disabilities" that are being identified, Breggin views children as the new market for drug companies who have saturated adult need. He warns that many of the prescribed drugs have not been adequately tested on children, but also cautions against the "cloak of acceptability" that might come with FDA approval. He worries that we may be heading toward a time when more children use these prescribed drugs than tobacco.

Sydney Walker, (*The Hyperactivity Hoax: How to Stop Drugging Your Child and Find Real Medical Help,* 1998), suggests that, for today's system of managed care, a prescription for Ritalin is faster and easier than finding the real cause for concerning behavior. Time on Ritalin (or similar medications) is time away from real treatment for a range of causes from "medical disorders, lifestyle problems or just plain bad behavior."

Supporting the idea that people turn too quickly to Ritalin, Thomas Armstrong 's book, *ADD/ADHD Alternatives in the Classroom* (1999) offers a range of interventions, of which Ritalin may be one.

The National Institute of Mental Health (NIMH) ADHD Handbook (1996) cautions that medications do not cure ADHD; they only temporarily control symptoms. Although 90% of individuals respond positively, drugs alone do not increase knowledge or skill on their own.

Golden et.al. found little research evidence that behavioral interventions alone—or in combination with medication—are better than medication alone, despite what many articles may say. They do not however, suggest that drug therapy continue forever, once begun, urging doctors, families and educators to investigate effective environmental interventions as well.

Cautioning against a backlash that could eliminate valid medical interventions, Forness, Kavale and Crenshaw (*Reclaiming Children and Youth*, 1999) believe research that stimulant drugs are very effective and should be, for valid cases of ADHD, the primary treatment, supported with psychosocial therapies.

In *ADHD and the Nature of Self Control* (1997), Russell A. Barkley reflects on the debate about the use of medication. He reasons that if ADHD (or any other behavior) is the result of the conditions of a child 's life, then the use of drugs is a scandal. If, however, the source of the behavior is biological in nature, then the use of medication is rational, ethical and humane.

Patricia Dalton, writing in *The Washington Post* (September 17, 2000), warns readers not to react to media hype against medications by running away from a treatment that has shown positive results for many individuals.

Until we read the results of the NIMH study contrasting various modes of treatment, each of us must face the questions on our own. Is society finding it easy to turn to medications to solve our problems and those of our children or is cutting edge science identifying a new tool to help us all? Will all learning and behavior problems someday be addressed with a pill? Is that wise? If we don't use the medicines available, are we preventing children from having access to positive treatment? If we do use the medicines available, are we preventing children from taking responsibility for their own, normal lives?

ISSUE 17

Should Parents Choose Cochlear Implants for Their Deaf Children?

YES: Thomas Balkany, Annelle V. Hodges, and Kenneth W. Goodman, from "Cochlear Implants for Young Children: Ethical Issues," in Warren Estabrooks, ed., *Cochlear Implants for Kids* (Alexander Graham Bell Association for the Deaf and Hard of Hearing, 1998)

NO: National Association of the Deaf, from "NAD Position Statement on Cochlear Implants," http://www.nad.org/infocenter/newsroom/positions/CochlearImplants.html (October 6, 2000)

ISSUE SUMMARY

YES: Thomas Balkany, Annelle V. Hodges, and Kenneth W. Goodman, of the University of Miami, argue that the Deaf community actively works to dissuade families from choosing cochlear implants for their children, preferring to have the decision made by Deaf individuals as a way to perpetuate the existence of a separate culture. The authors maintain that parents must decide whether or not their children receive cochlear implants, based on each child's best interest.

NO: The National Association of the Deaf (NAD), an education and advocacy organization committed to supporting the deaf and the hard of hearing, uses its updated position paper on cochlear implants to express concern that medical professionals will dissuade parents from considering the positive benefits of the Deaf community and choose, instead, a medical procedure that is not yet proven.

When a hearing family learns that their child is deaf, a sense of loss descends. They feel troubled, guilty, and desperate to "make things better." Teams of medical professionals and therapists arrive with interventions, remediation regimens, and hearing aids. The goal is to make the hearing problem go away—to "fix" the disability.

What would you do if your child was profoundly deaf and you thought a medical procedure could make hearing possible? Many parents jump at this chance when they learn of cochlear implants, a technology that, when it works correctly, can help people hear environmental sounds and conversation well enough for learning to occur. Who would not jump at the opportunity to help their child communicate more efficiently and learn through speech?

In reality, a lot of parents cringe instead of jump when they consider that their child, who can be fluent in American Sign Language (ASL), will lose his or her natural signed language and be unable to communicate and share the culture of her or his Deaf parents (capital "D" intended in reference to the culture of the Deaf). The cringing can become downright fear when they learn that this "medical miracle" might result in facial paralysis and no change in the child's hearing status. Families who belong to the Deaf community do not see themselves as disabled. The birth of a deaf child is greeted with joy and happiness—a celebration of a child with whom the family can freely communicate and share cultural values and traditions.

Cochlear implants replace a damaged cochlea (middle ear) with battery-powered technology to electronically stimulate the nerves that convey sound. Surgically inserted behind the ear, the device is connected to an external microphone and speech processor.

Implants, which were first approved for use in 1985, have caused a huge controversy between medical professionals and the Deaf community. Parents—especially those who are hearing and give birth to children who are deaf—find themselves in the middle of this debate. The choices they make—and the way their choices are made—pose a challenge to which schools must react.

In the following selection, Thomas Balkany, Annelle V. Hodges, and Kenneth W. Goodman examine the influences that parents face when deliberating cochlear implant surgery for their children and conclude that excessive force is being exerted by the Deaf community to influence parents away from a promising technological development. Although they acknowledge the value of Deaf culture, Balkany et al. maintain that parents should not be pressured by those whose agenda is to continue a way of life that they fear is threatened by technology.

In the second selection, the National Association of the Deaf asserts that the pressure comes from another direction and cautions parents not to be enchanted by a technology that has not been medically proven until they are advised by members of the Deaf community, who can speak for the quality of life without implants.

As you read these selections, consider the difficult choice for parents and the resultant educational impact. On whom should parents rely the most—doctors and therapists who are optimistic about the latest technology or Deaf individuals who live a rich life without hearing? Is a cochlear implant a safe choice for a child? Does it improve the child's educational chances? Does it result in isolation from the Deaf community?

Thomas Blakany, Annelle V. Hodges, and Kenneth W. Goodman

 **YES**

Cochlear Implants for Young Children: Ethical Issues

Ethics is the study of such concepts as goodness, duty, rightness, and obligation. In bioethics, these concepts are applied to practical problems raised in health care and biomedical research. Many of these problems arise along with the testing and adoption of new medical technologies. The second half of the 20th century has seen an extraordinary array of new and evolving technologies, ranging from organ transplantation and gene manipulation to life support systems and electronic medical records. This [selection] considers ethical controversy surrounding another technological development: cochlear implants for children, and is based in part on the authors' previous work in this area (Balkany, Hodges & Goodman, 1996).

Cochlear implants (CIs) represent an emerging technology that has the potential to change fundamentally the way people live. From the medical point of view, the CI is a safe and effective treatment for a severe disability—profound deafness. From the point of view of Deaf culture, however, it is unnecessary technology that is demeaning to deaf people's way of life (Lane, 1993). In the opinion of some Deaf activists, anything that prevents deafness or restores hearing to children who are deaf threatens Deaf society (Lane, 1993; Pollard, 1987). As a result of this perceived threat, there have been organized attempts to suppress CIs through the 1990s (Balkany, 1993).

It is essential to appreciate that Deaf society is dependent for perpetuation of itself on children who are deaf whose parents have normal hearing. Since 90 percent of children who are deaf are born to two hearing parents and 97 percent to at least one hearing parent, it is widely thought that if parents were given a safe and effective option to provide hearing to their child, many would choose to do so. If a large number of children who are deaf did not enter Deaf society, that society could be essentially changed. And because medical technology affects society, conflicts of an ethical nature may occur.

Members of mainstream society, or even the blind (who share with the deaf the inability to utilize one of humankind's dominant senses, but may not otherwise be similar), may have difficulties understanding opposition to providing a child who is deaf with the ability to hear. However, many in the Deaf community see their way of life as emotionally fulfilling, promising, and independent without hearing (Balkany, 1993; Balkany & Hodges, 1995; Balkany, 1995). Some Deaf leaders also claim that the deaf are an oppressed linguistic minority and that any intervention to provide hearing to children who are deaf is inherently racist (Lane, 1993).

In the case of cochlear implants for children, the elements of conflict may be framed as issues that concern honesty, autonomy, beneficence, the best interests of the child, the needs of a linguistic minority to perpetuate itself, the cost of deafness to society, and acceptance of diversity.

Truthfulness

It is inherent that CI teams recommending implantation truthfully provide full information to parents as part of the process of obtaining informed consent. This includes not only describing the risks and benefits of the operation, but also ensuring that parents understand the limitations of the technology, the requirement for auditory (re)habilitation, as well as the options of joining Deaf society, communicating in American Sign Language (ASL), and avoiding "treatment" of deafness entirely.

Deaf culture is rich and diverse, and its members are bonded by ASL as well as by social and political organizations (Balkany, 1993; Lane, Hoffmeister, & Bahan, 1996). Deaf people attend parties, date, marry, have families, and raise children. In short, there are many positive aspects of life in the Deaf community, and they are best described to parents by a member of Deaf society.

Just as CI teams do with CIs, Deaf society proponents have an inherent responsibility to describe fully the positive as well as the negative aspects of life in Deaf society and to state their reasons for opposition to restoration of hearing. As in the informed-consent process for surgery, this discussion needs to be truthful and complete, allowing parents the autonomy to decide for themselves whether their child should receive a CI. Unfortunately, many members of Deaf society have been misinformed about CIs. One reason this has occurred is that the average graduate of a Deaf residential high school reads at a third- to fourth-grade level (Dolnick, 1993; Conrad, 1979) and is thus incapable of accessing moderately sophisticated published information in the lay media. Since there is no written form of ASL, many in the Deaf community rely on informal sources of information such as newsletters and storytellers at Deaf clubs. Deaf leaders and educators who, to a substantial degree, control this information, have misled the Deaf community in a highly successful effort to generate opposition to CIs (Balkany, 1995).

Examples of the misleading, pejorative picture of CIs painted by Deaf leaders include articles in Deaf culture newsletters:

"I would be remiss not to equate cochlear implants with genocide." (Silver, 1992)

"There is absolutely no question that our government has a hidden agenda for deaf children much akin to Nazi experiments on Holocaust victims." (Silver, 1992)

"Using deaf children as 'lab rats' and medical guinea pigs is profoundly disturbing." (Roots, 1994)

Much more distressing, however, are inventions by respected colleagues designed to sway public opinion. Dr. Yerker Andersson, Professor and Chairman, Department of Deaf Studies at Gallaudet University and Emeritus President of the World Federation of the Deaf, published an article in the *World Federation of the Deaf News* in which he reported (without supporting reference) a surgeon who was "eager to use his skills on 17 Deaf individuals." According to Prof. Andersson, "Three died due to complications and one became mentally ill. The rest were failures" (Andersson, 1994). In fact, no deaths or cases of mental illness have been caused by CIs, and after hundreds of scientific papers and years of study, the U.S. Federal Drug Administration, medical oversight organizations, and even insurance carriers have concluded that CIs are safe and effective (Balkany, 1993). To say simply that Andersson was incorrect is to underestimate his scholarly abilities.

It is generally considered unethical to mislead people purposefully in order to persuade them to a point of view. The ethical principle violated by Andersson and others is autonomy as it relates to self-determination. People are deprived of their right to decide for themselves when they have been purposefully misled.

It is not surprising that, as a result of widespread misinformation, there is widespread misunderstanding. Many people who are deaf fervently believe that CIs are often fatal or severely damaging to children and they are therefore opposed to them.

The following are representative verbatim quotations from the future leaders of the Deaf community, college students at Gallaudet:

"I read few articles about how cochlear implant. For deaf people died from cochlear implant. It was explained about how cochlear implant affected to brain damage."

"I feel that cochlear implants are wrong because it makes the recipient a robot with wires sticking out of their head."

"I may not aware of cochlear implant much but I do have a strong against it" (letters to the William House Cochlear Implant Study Group, a committee of the American Academy of Otolaryngology—Head and Neck Surgery, 1993; author's files).

Internal Inconsistency and Conflict of Interest

Other examples of failure to respect the value of truthfulness are seen in Deaf leaders' advocacy of mutually contradictory positions. For example, it is claimed that deafness is not a disability and, at the same time, that people who are deaf are entitled to disability benefits amounting to billions of dollars per year. Another is that CIs do not work and also that they work so well as to eliminate deafness (genocide). Consciously supporting both sides of mutually exclusive arguments in order to influence public opinion is not considered ethical behavior. Deaf advocates must decide whether to tell parents that the deaf or hard of hearing are independent or that the majority require disability (and other entitlement) benefits. They must decide whether it is ethical to say to parents that CIs don't work and to politicians that CIs work so well that they are genocidal.

Deaf activists who believe that their way of life is threatened by CIs may find themselves in conflict of interest. Barbara White, writing as an Associate Professor at Gallaudet [University], succinctly reveals this conflict of interest: " ... the future of the deaf community is at stake. An entire subculture of America will no longer exist" (letters to the William House Cochlear Implant Study Group, a committee of the American Academy of Otolaryngology—Head and Neck Surgery, 1993; author's files). (Ear surgeons may be at similar risk for conflict of interest. It is estimated that CI surgery, however, constitutes less than one-tenth of one percent of the operations performed by otologists. A CI program, rather than generating income, actually costs a great deal to sustain by cost shifting and philanthropy.)

This potential conflict of interest among members of the Deaf community may operate to the disadvantage of individual children who are deaf. Australian physician Henley Harrison wrote, "The motive in opposing cochlear implants in children is self-interest rather than the children's welfare ... it is the welfare of the children that should be borne in mind, not some other group" (Harrison 1991).

Ethical standards hold that Deaf advocates should reveal such conflicts of interest to parents who are considering the merits of life in Deaf society for their children. As a three-generation member of the Deaf community warns, "Parents should cast a cautious eye towards anyone wanting to sacrifice a deaf child towards preserving a culture" (Bertling, 1994).

In short, representatives of the Deaf community who wish to influence parents and the public must begin truthfully to reveal both the advantages and the disadvantages of life in Deaf society. Only in this way can parents make an informed decision regarding the best interests of their child.

Is Deafness a Disability?

Examination of the position that deafness constitutes neither a handicap nor a disability, but only an oppressed linguistic minority (Lane et al., 1996) is a central issue in the discourse about CIs for children. Deaf leaders surely understand that if deafness is not a disability, people who are deaf or hard of hearing must give up billions of dollars in public assistance that is intended for the disabled. In writing from the ethical perspective, Englehardt (1986) defines disability as the failure to achieve an expected state of function. Boorse (1975) more precisely defines disability as occurring (a) when a specific function is impaired, (b) there is reduced ability below typical efficiency, or (c) a limitation of functional ability occurs with reference to the patient's age or gender group.

It is clear that, in addition to its cultural definition, deafness fits the functional definition of a disability; but how does it compare with other disabilities? According to a California Department of Rehabilitation survey published in 1993, in which clients with all types of disabilities filled out self-assessment forms, deafness was associated with the lowest educational level, the lowest family income, the lowest percentage working, the lowest percentage in professional/technical jobs, and the poorest self-assessment of well-being (Harris, Anderson, & Novak, 1995). This study suggests that deafness is not only a disability, but that it may be among the most disabling of disabilities.

To deny that deafness is a disability, Deaf leaders must also deny its cost to society: $377,000 per child in K-12 residential Deaf school education (estimated $121.8 billion for educating all people who are deaf or hard of hearing at residential schools), $2.5 billion per year in lost workforce productivity, and more than $2 billion annually for the cost of equal access, Social Security Disability Income, Medicare, and other entitlements of the disabled (National Institutes of Health, 1992). As Tom Bertling, a third-generation member of Deaf culture, notes in his book, *A Child Sacrificed*, "Virtually every aspect of the deaf community is dependent on government support for the disabled" (Bertling, 1994).

Perhaps the greatest monetary cost to society of the disability of deafness is in education. It is estimated that the cost of kindergarten through 12th-grade education in Rhode Island is about $9,000 per hearing child. For children who are deaf who are mainstreamed in public schools, the cost jumps to $44,000 per child. If the same deaf students attend residential schools for the Deaf, the cost becomes $429,000 per child (Johnson, Mauk, Takeawa, Simon, et al., 1993).

At this high cost, what are the outcomes of current methods of, and approaches to, educating students who are deaf or hard of hearing? The average reading level of an adult who is deaf is at third or fourth grade (National Institutes of Health, 1992); further, when students who are deaf or hard of hearing finish high school, three of four cannot read a newspaper (Dolnick, 1993). In large part because of this low educational outcome, the deaf are too often unemployed or underemployed, resulting in a cost to society of $2.5 billion per year in lost wages (National Institutes of Health, 1992).

The Deaf community is well aware of the rights of the disabled under the Americans with Disabilities Act. As an example, a woman who was deaf sued a Maryland volunteer fire department because she was not selected to be a fire fighter (Strom, 1994). She was presumably unable to hear sirens, alarms, calls for help, or instructions for emergency action, and she could not express her own needs or instructions with sign language while holding a fire hose or climbing a ladder.

A controversial risk of deafness that is rarely discussed with parents is the prevalence of psychological disorders. Although the relationship has been confirmed by hundreds of independent investigators and scientific papers, the data on morbidity have been attributed by Deaf leaders both to poor parenting and to culturally/linguistically biased testing (Lane, 1993). Debate over the value of such data notwithstanding, ethical representatives of Deaf society must decide whether it is appropriate to discuss these studies with parents whom they are counseling about life in Deaf culture.

Another area that remains obscured from parents is much more difficult to approach delicately. Tom Bertling, in his second book, *No Dignity for Joshua* (1997), describes in painful detail the ongoing problem with the physical, emotional, and sexual abuse that occurs, especially to the very young children, in residential Deaf schools. He feels that abuse is widespread, owing to a combination of low salaries paid to the nonprofessional members of the staff at state-run Deaf schools, a tendency among the Deaf community to conceal internal affairs, quasi-acceptance of such behavior within Deaf culture, and difficult communication between parents and their children who use ASL. Bertling's experiences are supported by scientific studies of over 480 abused children by Sullivan and colleagues (Sullivan, Brookhouser, Scanlan, Knutson, et al., 1991) showing a high incidence of sexual abuse in residential Deaf schools. On the basis of this awareness, several states are interceding to provide better supervision, especially for children who are deaf under the age of five years. (Bertling, 1994). Although similar problems may also occur at any residential school where poorly trained staff are underpaid, Deaf advocates must decide whether the ethical principle of truthfulness requires that parents be made aware of possible problems of sexual and other abuse at residential Deaf schools.

Deaf Leaders vs. Parents

Deaf activities hold conferences on the unseemly topic, "Who Owns the Deaf Child?" (Barringer, 1993). Their answer is that children who are deaf or hard of hearing are de facto members of the Deaf community and that hearing parents are obliged to "give up the child" (a phrase used by the Deaf) to be acculturated by Deaf society (Dolnick, 1993).

By this, Deaf activists mean that the usual values taught in families, including morals, ethics, religion, love, security, self-esteem, as well as language, should be taught by culturally Deaf adults who are not part of the child's family (Lane, 1993). This is process is termed *horizontal acculturation* (as opposed to *vertical acculturation,* in which these values are taught by parent to child, generation after generation). They claim that horizontal acculturation is best accomplished by removing the child from the home and placing him or her in a residential Deaf school (Lane, 1993).

Dr. Marina McIntire, director of ASL programs at Northeastern University, notes, "It has been argued that hearing parents have 'the right' to raise youngsters who are linguistically and culturally like themselves. We disagree" (letters to the William House Cochlear Implant Study Group, a committee of the American Academy of Otolaryngology–Head and Neck Surgery, 1993; author's files). Roz Rosen, president of the U.S. National Association of the Deaf in 1992, concurs: "Hearing parents are not qualified to decide about implants" (Coffey, 1992). In his book, *The Mask of Benevolence*, Dr. Harlan Lane states that parents cannot make decisions for their own child who is deaf because they don't "really know the patient" and are in a "conflict of interest with their own child." Lane has previously taken the position that a culturally Deaf adult who is not related to the child should be empowered to override the child's parents and make the decision as to whether a child should receive a CI (Lane, 1993).

This proposed intrusion into the American family is in direct conflict with Public Laws 94-142 and 99-4457, which ensure that children who are deaf are educated in the least restrictive environment (i.e., most like nonhandicapped children). These laws empower families of deaf children, and are directly opposed to horizontal acculturation (Gearhart, Wright, 1979; Katz, Marthis, & Merril, 1978).

Important Questions

Thus, two important questions arise regarding CIs for children: (1) Who should decide for the child? and (2) According to what standards should the decision be made?

The courts, as well as legal scholars and ethicists, concur that the rights and concerns of self-interest groups should be strictly excluded from decisions concerning the well-being of individual children (Buchanan & Brock, 1989). Interference from outside groups deprives families of their right to privacy. As Buchanan and Brock (1989) state in their book, *Deciding for Others: The Ethics of Surrogate Decision Making*, "the family must have great freedom from oversight, control and intrusion to make important decisions about the welfare of its children. Society should be reluctant to intercede in a family's decision." Parents exercise free informed consent on behalf of their children. "Others do not have the right to intervene in their ... actions" (Englehardt, 1986).

In addition, "There must be a clear locus of authority or decision making will lack coherence, continuity and accountability" (Buchanan & Brock, 1989). Only the child's parents, or in their absence, a legal guardian who has authority for all aspects of the child's life, can provide such continuity and accountability. The suggestion that a culturally Deaf individual be appointed to decide whether a child should or should not receive a CI (or, for that matter, any other medical treatment or procedure) would violate the principle of a clear locus of authority because that individual would not have authority or responsibility for any aspect of the child's life.

However, parental rights to make health care decisions for children, while broad, are not unlimited. For instance, a decision to forgo treatment for a disability or other treatable disorder might appropriately be regarded as neglect. Nontheless, the exercise of a parent's judgment is rarely constrained, and only in extreme cases of neglect is parental judgment overridden.

Parents must bear the consequences and are financially responsible for decisions made about their children. Thus, only parents can decide for the child. But according to what principles should the choice be made?

Autonomy and Beneficence

Buchanan and Brock (1989) identify two underlying ethical values in making decisions for others: respect for self-determination (autonomy) and concern for well-being (beneficence).

In foreseeing the desire of special-interest groups such as Deaf society for influence, Engelhardt (1986) states, "This principle of autonomy provides moral grounding for public policies aimed at defending the innocent." In exercising autonomy for their children, parents act within the rights of their children, which include freedom of choice, respect for the individual, and free, informed consent to make decisions on behalf of their child. Engelhardt (1986) defines free choices, as "being unrestrained by prior commitments or justified authority, and being free from coercion."

Associated with the right to self-determination is the right to privacy. When Deaf activists attempt to impose their wishes on parents of deaf children and suggest that parents are in conflict of interest with their own children, that they are not aware of their own children's best interests, and that only culturally Deaf adults should be allowed to act as proxy decision makers on behalf of the deaf child (Lane, 1993), they ignore the family's right to privacy and self-determination and, in doing so, trample the family's autonomy.

The ethical value of beneficence also guides parents. In simplest terms, it involves a prudent effort to do good and avoid evil (Englehardt, 1986). Advocates of Deaf culture who claim that making CIs available to children who are deaf is tantamount to "genocide" for Deaf culture are more concerned with doing good and avoiding evil to their culture than honoring the value of beneficence as it applies to the child.

Beneficence also applies to the child's "right to an open future" (Buchanan & Brock, 1989). Children have clear interest in maintaining and developing functional abilities. The ability to hear not only has communicative value but also provides auditory enjoyment and is important to safety. Children who are deaf or hard of hearing also have an "opportunity interest" regarding preservation of opportunity for their future education, employment, and interpersonal relationships. Educational and employment expectations for culturally Deaf persons are unfortunately lower than those for hearing people (Balkany & Hodges, 1995; Dolnick, 1993). Since 99.8 percent of the population of the United States cannot communicate in ASL (Padden, 1987), opportunities for personal relationships (teachers, bus drivers, neighbors, friends) are highly restricted by primary or sole communication in ASL. Conversely, entering the hearing world may increase opportunity for education, employment, and personal relationships.

Standards for Making Surrogate Decisions

In addition to the two ethical values mentioned, there are three well-established standards for making surrogate decisions: advance directive, substituted judgment, and best interest. If an advance directive has been established by the patient, such as a living will or a specific nomination of surrogate, it should be meticulously followed. If none is available, a family member should make decisions on the basis of substituted judgment (using knowledge of the person, the surrogate does what he or she believes the person would do under the circumstances, if the person were competent). Neither of these first two standards applies to children. The third guiding standard, which does apply to children, is that of best interest. It is the parents' responsibility to make decisions according to their understanding of what is in the best interest of their child.

Diversity

A possible solution to the ethical conflict between the child's best interest and the needs of Deaf society to perpetuate itself lies in the well-established principle of social diversity. Efforts by Deaf leaders to keep the Deaf community pure, however, systematically exclude people who may be slightly different, for example, children who are deaf or hard of hearing and who have CIs. This demand for cultural purity, and the attendant exclusionary behavior, is generally not tolerated in advanced societies.

Diversity is a valued strength of modern society that requires open-mindedness and fairness. Whereas Deaf leaders rightfully insist that mainstream society accept Deaf persons, Deaf society itself systematically excludes children who are deaf or hard of hearing and who use CIs. As Bienvenue and Colonomos state, " ... implanted children can never be fully accepted within the Deaf community" (letters to the William House Cochlear Implant Study Group, a committee of the American Academy of Otolalryngology–Head and Neck Surgery, 1993; author's files). Lane (1993) agrees that if CI patients "turn to the deaf community for support, they experience discrimination." Donnel Ashmore states that "if a child shows 'signs of hearism' this will result in a hostile, silent reprimand" (Lane, 1993).

CI recipients in elementary schools have recently been taught a new sign for CIs by adult interpreters for the Deaf: the sign for "snake bite" made behind the ear. Such stigmatization is typical of societies that attempt to keep their ranks "pure" and avoid diversity.

Deaf advocates who oppose the diversity that children with CIs might bring seem to ignore the fact that the Deaf community is already diverse—socially, economically, educationally, and politically. Welcoming children who are deaf or hard of hearing and who are "different" (because they can use the CI to help them communicate) to be part of their community may enlarge and strengthen Deaf society.

Changing With the Times

Two recent strategic shifts in position have been notable in opposition to CIs: (a) in view of data showing remarkable hearing and language acquisition by children with CIs, some leaders have stopped emphasizing that CIs don't work and have begun to promote the notion that even if CIs restored hearing perfectly, they would be unacceptable (Lane, 1993); and (b) many Deaf leaders have retreated from their arguments that a representative of Deaf culture must decide whether a child receives a CI. They now agree that parents must be allowed that choice (Lane et al., 1996). It is hoped that others will follow this logic.

Another recent position adopted by some Deaf leaders is that cochlear implant professionals are in violation of United Nations conventions proscribing limitation of the growth of linguistic minorities. It would follow that since CIs work, they would limit the growth of the Deaf community (a linguistic minority): therefore, CIs are forbidden by the United Nations. This line of reasoning clearly establishes that these leaders are more concerned with the needs of their culture than with the best interests of deaf children.

In summary, the term deafness describes both an important, respected way of life and a disability. The ethical standard of truthfulness requires that representatives of Deaf society inform parents of both the positive and the negative qualities of life in Deaf society and that CI teams do the same regarding CIs.

The ethical values of autonomy and beneficence and the need for a single locus of authority in raising children determine that parents decide whether their child should receive a CI. The guiding standard for such a surrogate decision is best interest. Thus, parents must determine what is in the best interest of their child. The need of Deaf society to perpetuate itself has no bearing on that decision, although parents should consider the opinions and experiences of truthful Deaf adults.

The Deaf community should demand the same acceptance of diversity from itself that it does from mainstream society. There must be room for all who wish to join. Deaf society's goal of ethnic purity and its exercise of discriminatory exclusion of deaf children who have CIs countervail the norms of ethical behavior and weaken its moral position.

References

Andersson, Y. (1994). Do we want cochlear implants? *World Federation of the Deaf News, 1,* 3-4.

Balkany, T. (1993). A brief perspective on cochlear implants. *New England Journal of Medicine, 328,* 281-282.

Balkany, T. (1995). The rescuers, cochlear implants: Habilitation or genocide? *Advances in Otorhinolarynology, 50,* 4-8.

Balkany, T., & Hodges, A.V. (1995). Misleading the deaf community about cochlear implantation in children. *Annals of Otolaryngology, 104* (Suppl. 116), 148-149.

Balkany, T. Hodges, A.V., & Goodman, K.W. (1996). Ethics of cochlear implantation in young children. *Archives of Otolaryngology—Head & Neck Surgery, 114,* 748-755.

Barringer, F. (1993, May 16). Pride in a soundless world. *New York Times* (pp. 1, 14).

Bertling, T. (1994). *A child sacrificed to the deaf culture.* Wilsonville, OR: Kodiak Media Group.

Bertling, T. (1997). *No dignity for Joshua.* Wilsonville, OR; Kodiak Media Group.

Boorse, C. (1975). On the distinction between disease and illnesses. *Philosophy and Public Affairs, 5,* 61.

Buchanan, A.E., & Brock, D.W. (1989). *Deciding for others. The ethics of surrogate decision making.* Cambridge, MA: Cambridge University Press.

Coffey, R. (1992). Caitlin's story on "60 Minutes." *The Biocultural Center News, 53,* 3.

Conrad, R. (1979). *The deaf school child: Language and cognitive function.* New York: Harper & Row.

Dolnick, E. (1993, September). Deafness as culture. *The Atlantic Monthly*, 37-53.

Englehardt, H.T. (1986). *The foundation of bioethics*. New York: Oxford University Press.

Gearhart, B.R. & Wright, W.S. (1979). *Organizations and administration of educational programs for exceptional children*. Springfield, IL: Charles C. Thomas.

Harris J.P., Anderson, J.P., and Novak R. (1995). An outcome study of cochlear implants in deaf patients. *Archives of Otolaryngology—Head & Neck Surgery, 121*, 398-404.

Harrison, H.C. (1991). Deafness in children. *Medical Journal of Australia, 154*, 11.

Johnson, J.L., Mauk, G.W., Takekawa, K.M., Simon, P.R., et al. (1993). Implementing a statewide system of services for infants with hearing disabilities. *Seminars in Hearing, 14*, 105-118.

Katz, L., Marthis, S.L., & Merril, E.C. (1978). *The deaf child in the public schools*. Danville, IL: Interstate Printers.

Lane, H., (1993). *The mask of benevolence*. New York: Vintage Books.

Lane, H. Hoffmeister, R., & Bahan, B. (1996). *A journey into the deaf world*. San Diego, CA: Dawn Sign Press.

National Institutes of Health Consensus Statement. (1992). *Early identification of hearing impairment in infants and young children, 11* (1), 1-12.

Padden, C.A. (1987). American Sign Language. In *Gallaudet encyclopedia of deaf people and deafness* (Vol. 3, pp. 43-53). Washington, DC: Gallaudet University Press.

Pollard, R.Q. (1987). Cross cultural ethics in the conduct of deafness research. *Rehabilitation Psychology, 37*, 87-99.

Roots, J. (1994). Deaf Canadian fighting back. *World Federation of the Deaf News,* 2-3.

Silver, A. (1992). Cochlear implant: Surefire prescription for long-term disaster. *TBC News, 53*, 4-5.

Strom, K.E., (1994, February). Disability regulations review. *Hearing Review*, 12-14.

Sullivan, P.M., Brookhouser, P.E., Scanlan, J.M., Knutson, J.F., et al. (1991). Patterns of physical and sexual abuse of communicatively handicapped children. *Annals of Otology, Rhinology & Laryngology, 100*, 188-194.

 **National Association of the Deaf**

NAD Position Statement on Cochlear Implants

The NAD [National Association of the Deaf] recognizes that diversity within the deaf community itself, and within the deaf experience, has not been acknowledged or explained very clearly in the public forum. Deafness is diverse in its origin and history, in the adaptive responses made to it, and in the choices that deaf adults and parents of deaf children continue to make about the ever-increasing range of communication and assistive technology options. Diversity requires mutual respect for individual and/or group differences and choices. The NAD welcomes all individuals regardless of race, religion, ethnic background, socioeconomic status, cultural orientation, mode of communication, preferred language use, hearing status, educational background, and use of technologies. The NAD also welcomes deaf, hard of hearing and hearing family members, educators, and other professionals serving deaf and hard of hearing children and adults.

The NAD subscribes to the wellness model upon which the physical and psychosocial integrity of deaf children and adults is based. The general public needs information about the lives of the vast majority of deaf and hard of hearing individuals who have achieved optimal adjustments in all phases of life, have well-integrated and healthy personalities, and have attained self-actualizing levels of functioning, all with or without the benefits of hearing aids, cochlear implants, and other assistive devices.

The NAD recognizes all technological advancements with the potential to foster, enhance, and improve the quality of life of all deaf and hard of hearing persons. During the past three decades, technological developments such as closed captioning, email and the Internet, two-way pagers, text telephones, telecommunications relay services, video interpreting services, visual alerting devices, vibro-tactile devices, hearing aids, amplification devices, audio loop and listening systems have had an important role in leveling the playing field. The role of the cochlear implant in this regard is evolving and will certainly change in the future. Cochlear implants are not appropriate for all deaf and hard of hearing children and adults. Cochlear implantation is a technology that represents a tool to be used in some forms of communication, and not a cure for deafness. Cochlear implants provide sensitive hearing, but do not, by themselves, impart the ability to understand spoken language through listening alone. In addition, they do not guarantee the development of cognition or reduce the benefit of emphasis on parallel visual language and literacy development.

The NAD recognizes the rights of parents to make informed choices for their deaf and hard of hearing children, respects their choice to use cochlear implants and all other assistive devices, and strongly supports the development of the whole child and of language and literacy. Parents have the right to know about and understand the various options available, including all factors that might impact development. While there are some successes with implants, success stories should not be over-generalized to every individual.

Rationale

The focus of the 2000 NAD position statement on cochlear implants is on preserving and promoting the psychosocial integrity of deaf and hard of hearing children and adults. The adverse effects of inflammatory statements about the deaf population of this country must be addressed. Many within the medical profession continue to view deafness essentially as a disability and an abnormality and believe that deaf and hard of hearing individuals need to be "fixed" by cochlear implants. This pathological view must be challenged and corrected by greater exposure to and interaction with well-adjusted and successful deaf and hard of hearing individuals.

The media often describe deafness in a negative light, portraying deaf and hard of hearing children and adults as handicapped and second-class citizens in need of being "fixed" with cochlear implants. There is little or no portrayal of successful, well adjusted deaf and hard of hearing children and adults without implants. A major reason implantation and oral language training have been pursued so aggressively by the media, the medical profession, and parents is not simply because of the hoped-for benefits that come with being able to hear in a predominantly hearing society but more because of the perceived burdens associated with being deaf.

Because cochlear implant technology continues to evolve, to receive mainstream acceptance, and to be acknowledged as part of today's reality, it is urgent to be aware of and responsive to the historical treatment of deaf persons. This perspective makes it possible to provide more realistic guidelines for parents of deaf and hard of hearing children and for pre-lingually and post-lingually deafened adults.

Wellness Model

Many deaf and hard of hearing people straddle the "deaf and hearing worlds" and function successfully in both. There are many people with implants who use sign language and continue to be active members of the deaf community and who ascribe to deaf culture and heritage. There are many deaf and hard of hearing individuals, with and without implants, who are high-achieving professionals, talented in every imaginable career field. They, too, are successfully effective parents, raising well-adjusted deaf, hard of hearing and hearing children. As citizens, they continue to make contributions to improve the quality of life for society at large. Deaf and hard of hearing individuals throughout the ages have demonstrated psychological strength and social skills when surviving and overcoming society's misconceptions, prejudices, and discriminatory attitudes and behaviors, thus attesting to their resilience, intelligence, and integrity.

Given the general lack of awareness about the reality of the wellness model, the NAD strongly urges physicians, audiologists, and allied professionals to refer parents to qualified experts in deafness and to other appropriate resources so that parents can make fully informed decisions—that is, decisions that incorporate far more than just the medical-surgical. Such decisions involve language preferences and usage, educational placement and training opportunities, psychological and social development, and the use of technological devices and aids.

The Cochlear Implant

The most basic aspect of the cochlear implant is to help the user perceive sound, i.e., the sensation of sound that is transmitted past the damaged cochlea to the brain. In this strictly sensorineural manner, the implant works: the sensation of sound is delivered to the brain. The stated goal of the implant is for it to function as a tool to enable deaf children to develop language based on spoken communication.

Cochlear implants do not eliminate deafness. An implant is not a "cure" and an implanted individual is still deaf. Cochlear implants may destroy what remaining hearing an individual may have. Therefore, if the deaf or hard of hearing child or adult later prefers to use an external hearing aid, that choice may be removed.

Unlike post-lingually deafened children or adults who have had prior experience with sound comprehension, a pre-lingually deafened child or adult does not have the auditory foundation that makes learning a spoken language easy. The situation for those progressively deafened or suddenly deafened later in life is different. Although the implant's signals to the brain are less refined than those provided by an intact cochlea, an individual who is accustomed to receiving signals about sound can fill in certain gaps from memory. While the implant may work quite well for post-lingually deafened individuals, this result just cannot be generalized to pre-lingually deafened children for whom spoken language development is an arduous process, requiring long-term commitment by parents, educators, and support service providers, with no guarantee that the desired goal will be achieved.

Parents

Parents face challenges when their child is born deaf or becomes deaf. At least ninety percent of deaf and hard of hearing children are born to hearing parents who usually want their children to be like themselves, to understand sound, to use their voices and verbally express their thoughts through spoken language, and to hear the voices and spoken language of those around them.

However, language and communication are not the same as speech, nor should the ability to speak and/or hear be equated with intelligence, a sense of well-being and lifelong success. Communication and cognition are vital ingredients of every child's development, regardless of the mode in which it is expressed, i.e., visual or auditory.

Despite the pathological view of deafness held by many within the medical profession, parents would benefit by seeking out opportunities to meet and get to know successful deaf and hard of hearing children and adults who are fluent in sign language and English, both with and without implants. The NAD encourages parents and deaf adults to research other options besides implantation. If implantation is the option of choice, parents should obtain all information about the surgical procedure, surgical risks, post-surgical auditory and speech training requirements, and potential benefits and limitations so as to make informed decisions.

Cochlear implant surgery is a beginning, not an end. The surgery decision represents the beginning of a process that involves a long-term, and likely, life-long commitment to auditory training, rehabilitation, acquisition of spoken and visual language skills, follow-up, and possibly additional surgeries. Whatever choices parents make, the primary goal should be to focus on the "whole child " and early language development/literacy and cognitive development. The absence of visual language opportunities can result in developmental delays that can be extremely difficult to reverse. Since the first six years are critical for language acquisition and usage, concurrent acquisition of visual and written language skills should be stressed.

Further improvements to cochlear implant technology and greater experience with educating and supporting pre-lingually deafened children and adults may later result in better outcomes for both of these populations than are achieved at present. In the meantime, though, parents of deaf and hard of hearing children need to be aware that a decision to forego implantation for their children does not condemn their children to a world of meaningless silence. Regardless of whether or not a deaf or hard of hearing child receives an implant, the child will function within both the hearing and the deaf communities. For these reasons, parents of pre-lingually deaf children presently have a reasonable basis upon which to decline implantation for their child. Parents must feel comfortable with their decision, whether they choose implantation or not.

Once parents have arrived at a decision, they want their decision to be validated. They seek reassurances often solely from within the medical and professional hearing health care community. This is a serious and major concern to the NAD. By releasing this position statement, the NAD seeks to alert, educate, and inform parents about deafness and the deaf community.

Recommendations

The NAD hereby makes the following recommendations for action:

Professional Training

Medical professionals have historically been the first point of contact for parents of deaf children. Their expertise is valuable but is primarily limited only to their medical areas of expertise. They should not be viewed as, nor should they function as, experts with regard to larger issues such as the educational, psychological, social, and linguistic needs of the deaf child. Medical professionals may be experts regarding the mysteries of the inner ear, but they are not experts regarding the inner lives of deaf children and adults. Psychological, social, educational, cultural and communication aspects of deafness, including the wellness model, must be a significant part of every medical school curriculum, especially within the specialty of otolaryngology. In-service training programs should be implemented for all interdisciplinary staff at cochlear implant centers that would include guidance and counseling methods with parents of deaf children and adults considering cochlear implants. These training programs should be conducted by professional counselors who are trained, qualified, and competent to work and communicate with deaf and hard of hearing children and adults and their families.

Early Assessment of Hearing Aid Benefit

It is widely understood and accepted that a trial period of hearing aid use is necessary prior to cochlear implantation. Advanced digital hearing aids should be explored. The NAD encourages that this effort be earnest and of appropriate duration for adequate assessment by objective testing and skilled observation of behaviors and communication skills. This assessment is complicated by the child's lack of prior auditory experience, and inability to communicate what s/he is hearing. The length of this trial period will vary with the individual. Further research by the medical and educational communities regarding objective hearing assessment and hearing aid trials is strongly encouraged.

Cochlear Implant Team

Candidacy assessment and surgery must be performed in a medical setting that has a close working relationship with a team of professionals that will provide ongoing long-term support to implant recipients. To be a responsible implant center, caution must be taken when describing the potential benefits of implantation, including risks, limitations, and long-term implications. Parents of deaf children and adults must be assisted in developing realistic and appropriate expectations. Critical to both pediatric and adult cochlear implantation and the long-range medical, audiological, psychological, social, emotional, educational, and vocational adjustment is access to implant centers fully complemented by an interdisciplinary staff, including rehabilitation specialists, psychologists and counselors. Implant center personnel must also work with and involve deafness professionals in education and in the helping professions. It takes a coordinated team of specialists, parents, educators and counselors to raise an implanted child and to support an implanted adult over an extended period of time. The implant team is also morally obligated to recognize when the implant experience has been unsuccessful and provide alternate strategies for language training.

Habilitation

An essential component of the cochlear implant process is habilitation. Parents and professionals must make a long-term commitment to integrating listening strategies throughout the child's day at home and at school. It is important to recognize that a newly implanted child is unable to understand spoken language through listening alone. Therefore parents and professionals should continue to use sign language to ensure age-appropriate psychological, social, cognitive, and language development.

Insurance Coverage

The NAD recommends that medical insurance carriers also provide fair and equitable coverage for hearing aid devices and associated support services.

Media

Reporters, journalists, anchors and directors of newspapers, television networks and film are encouraged to research and prepare their material more carefully and without bias. There is a serious need for a more balanced approach to fact-finding and reporting.

Research

Longitudinal research is critically needed, including a more thorough analysis of those for whom the implant is not working. Future research should involve highly controlled, manufacturer-independent and unbiased research on the long-term outcomes of childhood implants on auditory and communicative development, academic and intellectual development and achievement, psychological, social and emotional adjustment, and interpersonal relationship functioning. Comparative research on children without implants receiving parallel support services should also be conducted, especially those for whom sign language is the primary form of communication. Research findings relative to children with and without cochlear implants in educated lay terms must be made available and disseminated to deaf individuals, to parents of implanted children, to those in the helping professions, and to those contemplating implants.

Parents

The NAD knows that parents love and care deeply about their deaf children. Since the decision to perform implant surgery on the deaf child is made for the child, it is necessary for parents to become educated about cochlear implants—the potential benefits, the risks, and all the issues that they entail. During this critical education process, parents have both the need and the right to receive unbiased information about the pros and cons of cochlear implants and related matters. The NAD knows that parents want to make informed decisions. Parents also would benefit by opportunities to interact with successful deaf and hard of hearing adults, as well as with parents of deaf and hard of hearing children.

Deafness is irreversible. Even with the implant and increased sound perception, the child is still deaf. Cochlear implants are not a cure for deafness. The most serious parental responsibility from the very beginning is total commitment to, and involvement with, their child's overall development and well-being. Throughout the developmental years, the deaf child—implanted or not, mainstreamed or not—should receive education in deaf studies, including deaf heritage, history of deafness and deaf people, particularly stories and accounts of deaf people who have succeeded in many areas of life.

Support Services

Parents must understand that, after suitability testing and the decision-making process, the actual surgical procedure is just the beginning—a prelude to a lifetime proposition for the child and years of commitment by the parents. Implanted children are still deaf and will continue to require educational, psychological, audiological assessment, auditory and speech training, and language support services for a long period of time. Services for families and children should be provided in a manner that is consistent with standards set by the Individuals with Disabilities Education Act (IDEA), with focus on the whole child and the family. It is imperative that psychological support be available, including counseling services. Such services are to be available throughout the child's developmental years, often until adulthood.

Visual Environment

The NAD has always and continues to support and endorse innovative educational programming for deaf children, implanted or not. Such programming should actively support the auditory and speech skills of children in a dynamic and interactive visual environment that utilizes sign language and English. In closing, the NAD asserts that diversity in communication modes and cultures is our inherent strength, and that mutual respect and cooperation between deaf, hard of hearing, and hearing individuals ultimately benefit us all.

POSTSCRIPT

Should Parents Choose Cochlear Implants for Their Deaf Children?

Approximately 95 percent of deaf individuals are born with little or no hearing and are referred to as *prelingually deaf*. People who lose their hearing —through accident, illness, or aging—after they have acquired language are referred to as *postlingually deaf*.

The NAD and Balkany, Hodges, and Goodman agree on many points. They agree that individuals who had hearing during the critical period for learning language benefit more from cochlear implants than do those who are prelingually deaf. They also acknowledge that parents are under pressure, they agree on the sources of the pressure, and they all hold that the ultimate choice made by the parents should be accepted and valued. The two sides diverge when they weigh the merits and motivations of those who try to influence parental choice. There is much support for each point of view.

Linda Benton (*Hearing Loss*, 1997) speaks of her personal decision as an adult to undergo cochlear implant surgery despite the objections of her family. Melissa Chaikof, in the Cochlear Implant Association publication *Contact* (2000), relates the experiences of a deaf family of four who are all using implants now. Although each story acknowledges the difficulty of their medical and cultural choices as well as the competing influences brought to bear by various groups, all report satisfaction with the results of their surgeries.

Acknowledging that their views might change if implants are perfected and additional research certifies their efficacy, Harlan Lane, Robert Hoffmeister, and Ben Bahan (*A Journey Into the Deaf-World*) caution that the unnecessary surgical risks of cochlear implants are significant. Identifying the clash of cultures, they contend that Deaf individuals see no reason to operate on a healthy child, and they say that the opinions of those in the Deaf culture should have equal (if not superior) weight to those of hearing parents who are uninformed about the options that are open to their children.

Shelli Delost and Sarah Lashley (http://www.drury.edu/ess/irconf/DelostLashley.html) recognize that hearing parents have the best interests of their children in mind, but they hold that these parents focus too much on their own experiences and that only consultation and guidance by Deaf individuals will help them see the potential within their deaf children.

The complexities of cochlear implant decisions are portrayed strongly in the film *Sound and Fury*, which received a 2001 Academy Award nomination for Best Documentary Feature. Following an extended family through deliberations over whether or not to provide implants for two deaf children, this film has sparked much controversy as well as an online discussion (http://www.thirteen.org/soundandfury/cochlear/debate.html) between the executive directors of the National Association of the Deaf and the Alexander Graham Bell Association, which advocates the use of implants for suitable candidates.

IDEA97 places decision-making power in the hands of the parents for educational programs. The NAD is concerned that parents will listen exclusively to doctors and therapists. Balkany, Hodges, and Goodman are concerned that parents will be swayed by Deaf individuals with a personal interest.

Child-rearing decisions are never easy. Decisions about surgery are always full of tension and doubt. The cochlear implant choice illustrates the intersection of medicine, culture, and education, an encounter that is increasing in frequency as technology affects disabilities.

It is clear that many questions are yet to be answered. Until they are, should parents take the advice of medical strangers and risk surgery for the possibility of verbal communication or trust the opinions of cultural strangers that their child will flourish with a language and in a culture other than the one of her or his parents? Whom should parents trust? And what is the appropriate educational response—rehabilitative medical therapies or enrollment in separate schools for the Deaf?

ISSUE 18

Are There Scientifically Effective Treatments for Autism?

YES: James B. Adams, Stephen M. Edelson, Temple Grandin, and Bernard Rimland, from "Advice for Parents of Young Autistic Children," Autism Research Institute http://www.autism.org (Spring 2004)

NO: Committee on Educational Interventions for Children With Autism, Division of Behavioral and Social Sciences and Education, National Research Council, from "Educating Children with Autism" (National Academy Press, 2001)

ISSUE SUMMARY

YES: James B. Adams, a professor at Arizona State University; Stephen M. Edelson, director of the Center for the Study of Autism; Temple Grandin, an associate professor at Colorado State University; and Bernard Rimland, director of the Autism Research Institute (ARI), recommend to parents of young children with autism an array of effective treatment options, many of them biomedically based.

NO: The Committee on Educational Interventions for Children with Autism, chaired by Catherine Lord, director of the University of Michigan's Autism and Communication Disorders Center, summarizes its examination of research studies of educational treatments for children with autism, finding little consistent evidence to support the efficacy claims made by proponents.

In 1943, Leo Kanner described a puzzling type of young child who seemed to prefer isolation from others and "aloneness." Such children did not respond readily to the smiles and games of adults. They did not react with anticipation when a caretaker reached out to pick them up, and they seemed to ignore other people. Kanner identified a combination of social isolation, significant delays in language development, and a tendency to engage in repetitive behavior and resist change. He called this group of behaviors *infantile autism*.

Early in the recognition of this disorder, Bruno Bettleheim and other psychoanalytically oriented psychologists, posited that this condition stemmed from cold, unloving "refrigerator mothers" who did not provide the child with warm and responsive parenting. This theory was disproven by other researchers who found no difference between parents of children with autism and those with typical children. In fact, parents of children with autism often had other children who developed with no difficulty.

Autism is referred to as a spectrum disorder, spanning a range of severity. Among the subtypes identified are pervasive developmental disorder (not otherwise specified), childhood disintegrative disorder, and Rett's Syndrome. Individuals who exhibit the characteristics to a lesser degree are identified as having Asperger's Syndrome, sometimes called high-functioning autism.

For the first 30 years, autism occurred two to five times per 10,000 births. Since the mid-1980s, however, prevalence figures have skyrocketed. Experts now say from ten to twelve children out of every 10,000 are given this diagnosis. In response to powerful lobbying, IDEA97 identified autism as a distinct disability category, separate from emotional disturbance.

Some say these exploding numbers are due to more refined diagnostic knowledge and practice. Others assert that something environmental must be behind these increases. Regardless of cause, experts agree that this is a serious disability, which can have disastrous consequences. Strong educational programming is essential to helping these children achieve a productive life.

Reaching agreement on what constitutes good educational programming is another matter entirely. An incredible abundance of Web sites address autism and its causes and cures. Testimonial books speak powerfully about children who have been "cured" of autism by a specific method, medical treatment, or diet. Some programs cost well over $60,000 per year per child.

Adams and his colleagues all have personal and professional connections with this field. A number of the coauthors are parents of children with autism. Temple Grandin is an adult diagnosed with autism. Offering advice to parents of young children with autism, the authors review a number of methodologies that they believe are helpful and supported by research.

At the request of the federal Office of Special Education Programs, the Committee on Educational Interventions for Children with Autism was charged with integrating information from existing research, theory, and policy. This group concludes that no one method has been substantiated as irrefutably effective for children with autism.

As you read the following selections, consider that almost every method speaks to the urgency of beginning services early—sometimes before two years of age. Parents, reeling from their child's diagnosis often feel compelled to make a rapid choice rather than lose crucial learning time. Educators want to respond to parents but also use research-based methods. How can each group make informed decisions? What happens when they disagree?

James B. Adams, Stephen M. Edelson,
Temple Grandin, and Bernard Rimland  **YES**

Advice for Parents of
Young Autistic Children

INTRODUCTION

This paper is geared toward parents of newly diagnosed autistic children and parents of young autistic children who are not acquainted with many of the basic issues of autism. Our discussion is based on a large body of scientific research. Because of limited time and space, detailed explanations and references are not included.

Receiving a diagnosis of autism can be devastating to some parents, but for others it can be a relief to have a label for their child's symptoms. Many parents can be overwhelmed by fear and grief for the loss of the future they had hoped for their child. No one expects to have a child with a developmental disability. A diagnosis of autism can be very upsetting. Joining parent support groups may help. However, these strong emotions also motivate parents to find effective help for their children. The diagnosis is important because it can open the doors to many services, and help parents learn about treatments that have benefited similar children.

The most important point we want to make is that autistic individuals have the potential to grow and improve. Contrary to what you may hear from outmoded professionals or read in outmoded books, *autism is treatable*. It is important to find effective services, treatments and education for autistic children as soon as possible. The earlier these children receive appropriate treatment, the better their prognosis. Their progress through life will likely be slower than others, but they can still live happy and productive lives.

What Is Autism?

Autism is a developmental disability that typically involves delays and impairment in social skills, language, and behavior. Autism is a spectrum disorder, meaning that it affects people differently. Some children may have speech, whereas others may have little or no speech. Less severe cases may be diagnosed with Pervasive Developmental Disorder (PDD) or with Asperger's Syndrome (these children typically have normal speech, but they have many "autistic" social and behavioral problems).

Left untreated, many autistic children will not develop effective social skills and may not learn to talk or behave appropriately. Very few individuals recover completely from autism without any intervention. *The good news is that there are a wide variety of treatment options which can be very helpful.* Some treatments may lead to great improvement, whereas other treatments may have little or no effect. No treatment helps everyone. A variety of effective treatment options will be discussed below.

Onset of Autism: Early Onset vs. Regression

Autism develops sometime during pregnancy and the first three years of life. Some parents report that their child seemed different at birth. These children are referred to as early-onset autism. Other parents report that their child seemed to develop normally and then had a major regression resulting in autism, usually around 12-24 months. These children are referred as late-onset or regressive autism. Some researchers argue that the regression is not real or the autism was simply unnoticed by the child's parents. However, many parents report that their children were completely normal (e.g., speech, behavior, social) until sometime between 1 and 2 years of age. The possible causative role of vaccinations, many of which were added to the vaccination schedule in the 1980's, is a matter of considerable controversy at present ...

Prior to 1990, approximately two-thirds of autistic children were autistic from birth and one-third regressed sometime after age one year. Starting in the 1980's, the trend has reversed—fewer than one-third are now autistic from birth and two-thirds become autistic in their second year. The following results are based on the responses to ARI's [Autism Research Institute's] E-2 checklist, which has been completed by thousands of autism families. These results suggest that something happened, such as increased exposure to an environmental insult, possibly vaccine damage, between ages 1 and 2 years.

Several brain autopsy studies have indicated that brain damage occurred sometime during the first trimester of pregnancy, but many of these studies involved individuals who were born prior to 1990. Thus, these findings may not apply to what appears to be the new population of regressive autism.

Speech Development

One of the most common questions parents ask is: Will my child develop speech?

An analysis of ARI's data involving 30,145 cases indicated that 9% never develop speech. Of those who develop speech, 43% begin to talk by the end of their first year, 35% begin to talk sometime between their first and second year, and 22% begin to talk in their third year and after. A smaller, more recent survey conducted by the first author found that only 12% were totally non-verbal by age 5. So, with appropriate interventions, there is reason to hope that children with autism can learn to talk, at least to some extent.

There are several ways to help autistic children learn to talk, including:

- Teaching speech with sign language; it is easy for parents to learn a few simple signs and use them when talking to their child. This is referred to as 'simultaneous communication' or 'signed speech.' Research suggests that the use of sign language increases the chance of children learning spoken language.
- Teaching with the Picture Exchange Communication System (PECS), which involves pointing to a set of pictures or symbols on a board. As with sign language, it can also be effective in teaching speech.
- Applied Behavior Analysis: described in more detail later
- Encouraging child to sing with a videotape or audiotape
- Vestibular stimulation, such as swinging on a swing, while teaching speech
- Several nutritional/biomedical approaches have been associated with dramatic improvements in speech production including dimethylglycine (DMG), vitamin B6 with magnesium, and the gluten-/casein-free diet. (To be discussed further below.)

Genetics of Autism

Genetics appear to play an important role in causing some cases of autism. Several studies have shown that when one identical twin has autism, the other co-twin often has autism. In contrast, when one fraternal twin has autism, the co-twin is rarely autistic. Studies trying to identify specific genes associated with autism have been inconclusive. Currently, it appears that 20 or more genes may be associated with autism. This is in contrast to other disorders, such as Fragile X or Rett's syndrome, in which single genes have been identified.

A large number of studies have found that autistic individuals often have compromised immune systems. In fact, autism is sometimes described as an autoimmune system disorder. One working hypothesis of autism is that the child's immune system is compromised genetically and/or environmentally (e.g., exposure to chemicals). This may predispose the child to autism. Then, exposure to an (additional) environmental insult may lead to autism (e.g., the MMR vaccine) or mercury-containing vaccine preservatives (i.e., thimerosal).

If parents have a child with autism, there is an increased likelihood, estimated at 5% to 8%, that their future children will also develop autism. Many studies have identified cognitive disabilities, which sometimes go undetected, in siblings of autistic children. Siblings should be evaluated for possible developmental delays and learning disabilities, such as dyslexia.

Possible Environmental Causes of Autism

Although genetics play an important role in autism, environmental factors are also involved. There is no general consensus on what those environmental factors are at this point in time. Since the word "autism" is only a label for people who have a certain set of symptoms, there are likely to be a number of factors that could cause those symptoms. Some of the suspected environmental causes for which there is some scientific evidence include:

- Childhood vaccinations: The increasing number of vaccines given to young children might compromise their immune system. Many parents report their child was normal until vaccinations.
- MMR Vaccine: Evidence of measles virus have been detected in the gut, spinal fluid and blood. Also, the incidence of autism began rising significantly when the MMR was introduced in the US (1978) and in the United Kingdom (1988).
- Thimerosal (a mercury-based preservative) in childhood vaccines. The number of vaccines given to children has risen over the last two decades, and most of those vaccines contained thimerosal, which is 50% mercury. The symptoms of mercury poisoning in children are very similar to the symptoms of autism.
- Excessive use of oral antibiotics: can cause gut problems, such as yeast/bacterial overgrowth, and prevents mercury excretion
- Maternal exposure to mercury (e.g., consumption of seafood high in mercury, mercury dental fillings, thimerosal in RhoGam shots)
- Lack of essential minerals: zinc, magnesium, iodine, lithium, and potassium may be especially important
- Pesticides and other environmental toxins
- Other unknown environmental factors

Prevalence of Autism

There has been a rapid increase in the number of children diagnosed with autism. The most accurate statistics on the prevalence of autism come from California, which has an accurate and systematic centralized reporting system of all diagnoses of autism. The California data show that autism is rising rapidly, from 1 per 2,500 in 1970 to 1 per 285 in 1999. Similar results have been reported for other states by the US Department of Education. Whereas autism once accounted for 3% of all developmental disabilities, in California it now accounts for 45% of all new developmental disabilities. Other countries report similar increases.

We do not know why there has been a dramatic increase in autism over the past 15 years, but there are several reasonable hypotheses. Since there is more than one cause of autism, there may be more than one reason for the increase. A small portion of the increase of autism where speech is delayed may be due to improved diagnosis and awareness, but the report from California reveals that this only explains a minute part of the increase. However, the increase in the milder variant called Asperger's Syndrome may be due to increased diagnosis. In Asperger's Syndrome, there is no significant speech delay and early childhood behavior is much more normal. The major reason for the increase is certainly due to environmental factors, not genetics, since there is no such thing as a 'genetic epidemic.' Some *possible* environmental factors were discussed in the previous section, and an increased occurrence of one or several of those factors probably accounts for the rapid increase in autism...

What is the Difference Between Asperger's Syndrome and Autism?

Asperger syndrome is usually considered a subtype of high-functioning autism. Most of the individuals with Asperger syndrome are described as "social but awkward." That is, they want to have friends, but they do not have the social skills to begin and/or maintain a friendship. While high-functioning autistic individuals may also be "social but awkward," they are typically less interested in having friends. In addition, high-functioning autistic individuals are often delayed in developing speech/language. Those with Asperger syndrome tend not to have speech/language delays, but their speech is usually described as peculiar, such as being stilted and perseverating on unusual topics.

Medical Testing and Treatments

A small but growing number of physicians (many of whom are themselves parents of autistic children) are involved in trying safe and innovative methods for treating the underlying biomedical basis of autism—the Defeat Autism Now! (DAN!) program. Parents and physicians can learn about this approach by ... visiting the Autism Research Institute's Web site (www.AutismResearchInstitute.com).

Routine medical tests are usually performed by traditional pediatricians, but they rarely reveal problems in autism that can be treated. Genetic testing for Fragile X syndrome can help identify one possible cause, and this testing is typically recommended when there is mental retardation in the family history. Many physicians do not conduct extensive medical testing for autism, because they believe, incorrectly, that the only useful medical treatments are psychiatric medications to reduce seizures and behavioral problems.

Some of the major interventions suggested by DAN! practitioners include:

- Nutritional supplements, including certain vitamins, minerals, amino acids, and essential fatty acids
- Special diets totally free of gluten (from wheat, barley, rye, and possibly oats) and free of dairy (milk, ice-cream, yogurt, etc.)
- Testing for hidden food allergies, and avoidance of allergenic foods
- Treatment of intestinal bacterial/yeast overgrowth
- Detoxification of heavy metals

Psychiatric Medications

The various topics covered in this overview paper for parents of young autistic children represent, for the most part, a consensus of the views, based on research and personal experience, of all four authors. However, the authors differ in their opinions on the role of psychoactive drugs should play ....

Grandin has a relatively accepting position on the use of psychiatric medications in older autistic children and adults. She feels that it is worthwhile to consider drugs as a viable and useful treatment. Rimland and Edelson, on the other hand, are strongly opposed to the use of drugs except as a possible last resort,...—[t]hey feel the risks are great and consistently outweigh the benefits. Adams has an intermediate view ....

Educational/Behavioral Approaches

Educational/behavioral therapies are often effective in children with autism, with Applied Behavioral Analysis (ABA) usually being the most effective. These methods can and should be used together with biomedical interventions, as together they offer the best chance for improvement.

Parents, siblings, and friends may play an important role in assisting the development of children with autism. Typical pre-school children learn primarily by play, and the importance of play in teaching language and social skills cannot be overemphasized. Ideally, many of the techniques used in ABA, sensory integration, and other therapies can be extended throughout the day by family and friends.

Applied Behavior Analysis: Many different behavioral interventions have been developed for children with autism, and they mostly fall under the category of Applied Behavioral Analysis (ABA). This approach generally involves therapists who work intensely, one-on-one with a child for 20 to 40 hours/week. Children are taught skills in a simple step-by-step manner, such as teaching colors one at a time. The sessions usually begin with formal, structured drills, such as learning to point to a color when its name is given; and then, after some time, there is a shift towards generalizing skills to other situations and environments.

A study published by Dr. Ivar Lovaas at UCLA in 1987 involved two years of intensive, 40-hour/week behavioral intervention by trained graduate students working with 19 young autistic children ranging from 35 to 41 months of age. Almost half of the children improved so much that they were indistinguishable from typical children, and these children went on to lead fairly normal lives. Of the other half, most had significant improvements, but a few did not improve much.

ABA programs are most effective when started early, (before age 5 years), but they can also be helpful to older children. They are especially effective in teaching non-verbal children how to talk.

There is general agreement that:

- behavioral interventions involving one-on-one interactions are usually beneficial, sometimes with very positive results
- the interventions are most beneficial with the youngest children, but older children can benefit
- the interventions should involve a substantial amount of time each week, between 20–40 hours depending on whether the child is in school
- prompting as much as necessary to achieve a high level of success, with a gradual fading of prompts
- proper training of therapists and ongoing supervision

- regular team meetings to maintain consistency between therapists and check for problems
- most importantly, keeping the sessions fun for the children is necessary to maintain their interest and motivation

Parents are encouraged to obtain training in ABA, so that they provide it themselves and possibly hire other people to assist. Qualified behavior consultants are often available, and there are often workshops on how to provide ABA therapy.

Sensory Integration   Many autistic individuals have sensory problems, which can range from mild to severe. These problems involve either hypersensitivity or hyposensitivity to stimulation. Sensory integration focuses primarily on three senses—vestibular (i.e., motion, balance), tactile (i.e., touch), and proprioception (e.g., joints, ligaments). Many techniques are used to stimulate these senses in order to normalize them.

Speech Therapy   This may be beneficial to many autistic children, but often only 1–2 hours/week is available, so it probably has only modest benefit unless integrated with other home and school programs. As mentioned earlier, sign language and PECS may also be very helpful in developing speech. Speech therapists should work on helping the child to hear hard consonant sounds such as the "c" in cup. It is often helpful if the therapist stretches out and enunciates the consonant sounds.

Occupational Therapy   Can be beneficial for the sensory needs of these children, who often have hypo- and/or hyper-sensitivities to sound, sight, smell, touch, and taste. May include sensory integration (above).

Physical Therapy   Often children with autism have limited gross and fine motor skills, so physical therapy can be helpful. May also include sensory integration (above).

Auditory Interventions   There are several types of auditory interventions. The only one with significant scientific backing is Berard Auditory Integration Training (called Berard AIT or AIT) which involves listening to processed music for a total of 10 hours (two half-hour sessions per day, over a period of 10 to 12 days). There are many studies supporting its effectiveness. Research has shown that AIT improves auditory processing, decreases or eliminates sound sensitivity, and reduces behavioral problems in some autistic children.

Other auditory interventions include the Tomatis approach, the Listening Program, and the SAMONAS method. There is limited amount of empirical evidence to support their efficacy. Information about these programs can be obtained from the Society for Auditory Intervention Techniques' website (www.sait.org).

Computer-based auditory interventions have also received some empirical support. They include Earobics (www.cogconcepts.com) and Fast For-

Word (www.fastforword.com). These programs have been shown to help children who have delays in language and have difficulty discriminating speech sounds. Earobics is less much expensive (less than $100) but appears to be less powerful than the Fast ForWord program (usually over $1,000). Some families use the Earobics program first and then later use Fast ForWord.

Computer Software   There are many educational programs available for typical children, and some of those may be of benefit for autistic children. There is also some computer software designed specifically for children with developmental disabilities. One major provider is Laureate (www.llsys.com).

Vision Training and Irlen Lenses   Many autistic individuals have difficulty attending to their visual environment and/or perceiving themselves in relation to their surroundings. These problems have been associated with a short attention span, being easily distracted, excessive eye movements, difficulty scanning or tracking movements, inability to catch a ball, being cautious when walking up or down stairs, bumping into furniture, and even toe walking). A one- to two-year vision training program involving ambient prism lenses and performing visual-motor exercises can reduce or eliminate many of these problems. See www.AutisticVision.com. More information on vision training can be found on Internet Web site of the College of Optometrists in Vision Development (www.pavevision.org).

Another visual/perceptual program involves wearing Irlen lenses. Irlen lenses are colored (tinted) lenses. Individuals who benefit from these lenses are often hypersensitive to certain types of lighting, such as florescent lights and bright sunlight; hypersensitive to certain colors or color contrasts; and/or have difficulty reading printed text. Irlen lenses can reduce one's sensitivity to these lighting and color problems as well as improve reading skills and increase attention span. See www.Irlen.com.

Relationship Development Intervention (RDI)   This is a new method for teaching children how to develop relationships, first with their parents and later with their peers. It directly addresses a core issue in autism, namely the development of social skills and friendships. See www.connectionscenter.com.

Preparing for the Future

Temple Grandin: "As a person with autism I want to emphasize the importance of developing the child's talents. Skills are often uneven in autism, and a child may be good at one thing and poor at another. I had talents in drawing, and these talents later developed into a career in designing cattle handling systems for major beef companies. Too often there is too much emphasis on the deficits and not enough emphasis on the talents. Abilities in children with autism will vary greatly, and many individuals will function at a lower level than me. However, developing talents and improving skills will benefit all. If a child becomes fixated on trains, then use the great motivation of that fixation to motivate learning other skills. For example, use a book about trains to teach reading, use calculating the speed of a train to teach math, and encourage an interest in history by studying the history of the railroads."

Developing Friendships

Although young children with autism may seem to prefer to be by themselves, one of the most important issues for older children and adults is the development of friendships with peers. It can take a great deal of time and effort for them to develop the social skills needed to be able to interact successfully with other children, but it is important to start early. In addition, bullying in middle and high school can be a major problem for students with autism, and the development of friendships is one of the best ways to prevent this problem.

Friendships can be encouraged informally by inviting other children to the home to play. In school, recess can be a valuable time for teachers to encourage play with other children. Furthermore, time can be set aside in school for formal "play time" between children with autism and volunteer peers— typical children usually think that play time is much more fun than regular school, and it can help develop lasting friendships. This is probably one of the most important issues to include in a student's Individualized Education Program (IEP, or education plan for the child). Children with autism often develop friendships through shared interests, such as computers, school clubs, model airplanes, etc. Encourage activities that the autistic individual can share with others.

School Programs

For children younger than 3 years old, there are early intervention programs. For children over 3 years of age, there are pre-school and school programs available. Parents should contact their local school district for information on their local programs. In some cases a separate program for special-needs children may be best, but for higher-functioning children integration into a regular school setting may be more appropriate, provided that there is enough support (a part- or full-time aide, or other accommodations as needed). It is important that parents work with their child's teacher on an Individual Education Plan (IEP), which outlines in great detail the child's educational program. Additionally, meeting with the child's classmates and/or their parents can be helpful in encouraging other students to interact positively with the autistic child.

In some states, home therapy programs (such as ABA and speech therapy) may be funded by the school district, rather than through the state. However, it may take considerable effort to convince the school district to provide those services. Check with your local ASA chapter and other parents about how services are usually provided in your state ....

Long-Term Prognosis

Today, most adults with autism are either living at home with their parents or living in a group home. Some higher-functioning people live in a supported-living situation, with modest assistance, and a very few are able to live independently. Some are able to work, either in volunteer work, sheltered work-shops, or private employment, but many do not. Adults with PDD/NOS (not otherwise specified) and Asperger's generally are more likely to live independently, and they are more likely to work. Unfortunately, they often have difficulty finding and then maintaining a job. The major reason for chronic unemployment is not a lack of job skills, but rather due to their limited social skills. Thus, it is important to encourage appropriate social skills early on, so they are able to live and work independently as much as possible.

Some of the most successful people on the autism spectrum who have good jobs have developed expertise in a specialized skill that often people value. If a person makes him-/herself very good at something, this can help make up for some difficulties with social skills. Good fields for higher functioning people on the spectrum are architectural drafting, computer programming, language translator, special educator, librarian and scientist. It is likely that some brilliant scientists and musicians have a mild form of Asperger's Syndrome (Ledgin, 2002). The individuals who are most successful often have mentor teachers either in high school, college or at a place of employment. Mentors can help channel interests into careers. Untreated sensory oversensitivity can severely limit a person's ability to tolerate a work-place environment. Eliminating fluorescent lights will often help, but untreated sound sensitivity has caused some individuals on the spectrum to quit good jobs because ringing telephones hurt their ears. Sensory sensitivities can be reduced by auditory integration training, diets, Irlen lenses, conventional psychiatric medications and vitamin supplementation. Magnesium often helps hypersensitive hearing.

It should also be pointed out that the educational, therapy, and biomedical options available today are much better than in past decades, and they should be much better in the future. However, it is often up to parents to find those services, determine which are the most appropriate for their child, and ensure that they are properly implemented. *Parents are a child's most powerful advocates and teachers.* With the right mix of interventions, most children with autism will be able to improve. As we learn more, children with autism will have a better chance to lead happy and fulfilling lives.

Educating Children with Autism

Conclusions and Recommendations

This [selection] summarizes the committee's conclusions about the state of the science in early intervention for children with autistic spectrum disorders and its recommendations for future intervention strategies, programs, policy, and research. The [selection] is organized around seven key areas pertaining to educational interventions for young children with autistic spectrum disorders: how the disorders are diagnosed and assessed and how prevalent they are; the effect on and role of families; appropriate goals for educational services; characteristics of effective interventions and educational programs; public policy approaches to ensuring access to appropriate education; the preparation of educational personnel; and needs for future research.

Diagnosis, Assessment, and Prevalence

Conclusions

Autism is a developmental disorder of neurobiologic origin that is defined on the basis of behavioral and developmental features. Autism is best characterized as a spectrum of disorders that vary in severity of symptoms, age of onset, and association with other disorders (e.g., mental retardation, specific language delay, epilepsy). The manifestations of autism vary considerably across children and within an individual child over time. There is no single behavior that is always typical of autism and no behavior that would automatically exclude an individual child from a diagnosis of autism, even though there are strong and consistent commonalities, especially relative to social deficits.

The large constellation of behaviors that define autistic spectrum disorders—generally representing deficits in social interaction, verbal and nonverbal communication, and restricted patterns of interest or behaviors—are clearly and reliably identifiable in very young children to experienced clinicians and educators. However, distinctions among classical autism and atypical autism, pervasive developmental disorder-not otherwise specified (PDD-NOS), and Asperger's disorder can be arbitrary and are often associated with the presence or severity of handicaps, such as mental retardation and severe language impairment.

Identifying narrow categories within autism is necessary for some research purposes; however, the clinical or educational benefit to subclassifying autistic spectrum disorders purely by diagnosis is debated. In contrast, individual differences in language development, verbal and nonverbal communication, sensory or motor skills, adaptive behavior, and cognitive abilities have significant effects on behavioral presentation and outcome, and, consequently, have specific implications for educational goals and strategies. Thus, the most important considerations in programming have to do with the strengths and weaknesses of the individual child, the age at diagnosis, and early intervention.

With adequate time and training, the diagnosis of autistic spectrum disorders can be made reliably in 2-year-olds by professionals experienced in the diagnostic assessment of young children with autistic spectrum disorders. Many families report becoming concerned about their children's behavior and expressing this concern, usually to health professionals, even before this time. Research is under way to develop reliable methods of identification for even younger ages. Children with autistic spectrum disorders, like children with vision or hearing problems, require early identification and diagnosis to equip them with the skills (e.g., imitation, communication) to benefit from educational services, with some evidence that earlier initiation of specific services for autistic spectrum disorders is associated with greater response to treatment. Thus, well meaning attempts not to label children with formal diagnoses can deprive children of specialized services. There are clear reasons for early identification of children, even as young as two years of age, within the autism spectrum.

Epidemiological studies and service-based reports indicate that the prevalence of autistic spectrum disorders has increased in the last 10 years, in part due to better identification and broader categorization by educators, physicians, and other professionals. There is little doubt that more children are being identified as requiring specific educational interventions for autistic spectrum disorders. This has implications for the provision of services at many levels. Analysis of data from the Office of Special Education Programs, gathered for school-age children since the autism category was recognized in 1991, would support investigation of whether the dramatic increases in the numbers of children served with autistic spectrum disorders are offset by commensurate decreases in other categories in which children with autistic spectrum disorders might have previously been misclassified or whether these dramatic increases have come about for other reasons.

Although children with autistic spectrum disorders share some characteristics with children who have other developmental disorders and may benefit from many of the same educational techniques, they offer unique challenges to families, teachers, and others who work with them. Their deficits in nonverbal and verbal communication require intense effort and skill even in the teaching of basic information. The unique difficulties in social interaction (e.g., in joint attention) may require more individual guidance than for other children in order to attract and sustain their children's attention. Moreover, ordinary social exchanges between peers do not usually occur without deliberate planning and ongoing structuring by the adults in the child's environment. The absence of typical friendships and peer relationships affects children's motivation systems and the meaning of experiences. Appropriate social interactions may be some of the most difficult and important lessons a child with autistic spectrum disorders will learn.

In addition, the frequency of behavior problems, such as tantrums and self-stimulatory and aggressive behavior, is high. The need for systematic selection of rewards for many children with autistic spectrum disorders, whose motivation or interests can be limited, requires creativity and continued effort from teachers and parents to maximize the child's potential. Although general principles of learning and behavior analysis apply to autistic spectrum disorders, familiarity with the specific nature of the disorder should contribute to analysis of the contexts (e.g., communicative and social) of behaviors for individual children and result in more effective programming. For example, conducting a functional assessment that considers contexts, and then replacing problem behaviors with more appropriate ways to communicate can be an effective method for reducing problem behaviors ....

Role of Families

Conclusions

Having a child with an autistic spectrum disorder is a challenge for any family. Involvement of families in the education of young children with autistic spectrum disorders can occur at multiple levels, including advocacy, parents as participating partners in and agents of education or behavior change, and family-centered consideration of the needs and strengths of the family as a unit. Nearly all empirically supported treatments reviewed by the committee included a parent component, and most research programs used a parent-training approach. More information is needed about the benefits of a family-centered orientation or combined family-centered and formalized parent training in helping parents.

It is well established that parents can learn and successfully apply skills to changing the behavior of their children with autistic spectrum disorders, though little is known about the effects of cultural differences, such as race, ethnicity, and social class, nor about the interactions among family factors, child characteristics, and features of educational intervention. For most families, having a child with an autistic spectrum disorder creates added stress. Parents' use of effective teaching methods can have a significant effect on that stress, as can support from within the family and the community. Parents need access to balanced information about autistic spectrum disorders and the range of appropriate services and technologies in order to carry out their responsibilities. They also need timely information about assessments, educational plans, and the available resources for their children. This information needs to be conveyed to them in a meaningful way that gives them time to prepare to fulfill their roles and responsibilities.

In the last ten years the widespread availability of the Internet and media attention to autistic spectrum disorders have increased parents' knowledge but often conveyed perspectives that were not balanced nor well-supported scientifically. Of crucial importance is the question of how to make information available to parents and to ensure their active role in advocacy for their children's education ....

Goals for Educational Services

Conclusions

At the root of questions about the most appropriate educational interventions lie differences in assumptions about what is possible and what is important to give students with autistic spectrum disorders through education. The appropriate goals for educational services are the same as those for other children: personal independence and social responsibility. These goals imply continuous progress in social and cognitive abilities, verbal and nonverbal communication skills, adaptive skills, amelioration or behavioral difficulties, and generalization of abilities across multiple environments. In some cases, reports have suggested that particular treatments can foster permanent "recovery". However, as with other developmental disabilities, the core deficits of autistic spectrum disorders have generally been found to persist, to some degree, in most individuals.

Research concerning outcomes can be characterized by whether the goal of intervention is broadly defined (e.g., "recovery" or "best outcome") or more specifically defined (e.g., increasing vocabulary or peer-directed social behavior); whether the design involves reporting results in terms of group or individual changes; and whether the goals are short term (i.e., to be achieved in a few weeks or months) or longer term (i.e., over years). A large body of single-subject research has demonstrated substantial progress in individual responses to specific intervention techniques in relatively short periods of times (e.g., several months) in many specific areas, including gains in social skills, language acquisition, nonverbal communication, and reductions in challenging behaviors. Studies over longer periods of time have documented joint attention, symbolic play, early language skills, and imitation as core deficits and hallmarks of the disorder that are predictive of longer term outcome in the domains of language, adaptive behaviors, and academic skills.

Many treatment studies report postintervention placement as an outcome measure. While successful participation in regular classrooms is an important goal for some children with autistic spectrum disorders, the usefulness of placement in regular education classes as an outcome measure is limited, because placement may be related to many variable other than the characteristics of the child (e.g., prevailing trends in inclusion, availability of other services). The most commonly reported outcome measure in group treatment studies of children with autistic spectrum disorders has been changes in IQ scores, which also have many limitations.

Studies have reported substantial changes in large numbers of children in intervention studies and longitudinal studies in which children received a variety of interventions. Even in the treatment studies that have shown the strongest gains, children's outcomes are variable, with some children making substantial progress and others showing very slow gains. The needs and strengths of young children with autistic spectrum disorders are very hetero-geneous. Although there is evidence that many interventions lead to improve-ments and that some children shift in specific diagnosis along the autism spectrum during the preschool years, there does not appear to be a simple relationship between any particular intervention and "recovery" from autis-tic spectrum disorders. Thus, while substantial evidence exists that treatments can reach short-term specific goals in many areas, gaps remain in addressing larger questions of the relationships between particular techniques, child characteristics, and outcomes ....

Characteristics of Effective Interventions

Conclusions

In general, there is consistent agreement across comprehensive intervention programs about a number of features, though practical and, sometimes, ethi-cal considerations have made well-controlled studies with random assignment very difficult to conduct without direct evaluation. Characteristics of the most appropriate intervention for a given child must be tied to that child's and family's needs. However, without direct evaluation, it is difficult to know which features are of greatest importance in a program. Across primarily pre-school programs, there is a very strong consensus that the following features are critical:

- Entry into intervention programs as soon as an autism spectrum diag-nosis is seriously considered;
- Active engagement in intensive instructional programming for a mini-mum of the equivalent of a full school day, 5 days (at least 25 hours) a week, with full year programming varied according to the child's choronological age and developmental level;
- Repeated, planned teaching opportunities generally organized around rel-atively brief periods of time for the youngest children (e.g., 15–20 minute intervals), including sufficient amounts of adult attention in one-to-one and very small group instruction to meet individualized goals;
- Inclusion of a family component, including parent training;
- Low student/teacher ratios (no more than two young children with autistic spectrum disorders per adult in the classroom); and
- Mechanisms for ongoing program evaluation and assessments of indi-vidual children's progress, with results translated into adjustments in programming.

Curricula across different programs differ in a number of ways. They include the ways in which goals are prioritized, affecting the relative time spent on verbal and nonverbal communication, social activities, behavioral, academic, motor, and other domains. Strategies from various programs repre-sent a range of techniques, including discrete trials, incidental teaching, struc-tured teaching, "floor time", and individualized modifications of the environment, including schedules. Some programs adopt a unilateral use of one set of procedures, and others use a combination of approaches. Programs also differ in the relative amount of time spent in homes, centers, or schools, when children are considered ready for inclusion into regular classrooms, how the role of peers as intervention agents is supported, and in the use of distraction-free or natural environments. Programs also differ in the credentials that are required of direct support and supervisory staff and the formal and informal roles of collateral staff, such as speech language pathologists and occupational therapists.

Overall, many of the programs are more similar than different in terms of levels of organization, staffing, ongoing monitoring, and the use of certain techniques, such as discrete trials, incidental learning, and structured teaching. However, there are real differences in philosophy and practice that provide a range of alternatives for parents and school systems considering various approaches. The key to any child's educational program lies in the objectives specified in the IEP and the ways they are addressed. Much more important than the name of the program attended is how the environment and educational strategies allow implementation of the goals for a child and family. Thus, effective services will and should vary considerably across individual children, depending on a child's age, cognitive and language levels, behavioral needs, and family priorities ....

Public Policies

Conclusions

The Individuals with Disabilities Education Act (IDEA) contains the necessary provisions for ensuring rights to appropriate education for children with autistic spectrum disorders. However, the implementation and specification of these services are variable. Early intervention for young children with autistic spectrum disorders is expensive, and most local schools need financial help from the state and federal programs to provide appropriate services.

The large number of court cases is a symptom of the tension between families and school systems. Case law has yielded an inconsistent pattern of findings that vary according to the characteristics of the individual cases. The number of challenges to decision-making for programming within school systems reflects parents' concerns about the adequacy of knowledge and the expertise of school systems in determining their children's education and implementing appropriate techniques.

The treatment of autistic spectrum disorders often involves many disciplines and agencies. This confuses lines of financial and intellectual responsibility and complicates assessment and educational planning. When communication between families and school systems goes awry, it can directly affect children's programming and the energy and financial resources that are put into education rather than litigation. Support systems are not generally adequate in undergirding local service delivery programs and maximizing the usefulness of different disciplines and agencies, and transitions between service delivery agencies are often problematic.

A number of states have successful models for providing services to children with autism, and mechanisms are becoming increasingly efficient and flexible in some states. In most cases, existing agencies at state and federal levels can develop appropriate programs without restructuring—with the possible addition of special task forces or committees designed to deal with issues particular to children with autistic spectrum disorders ....

Personnel Preparation

Conclusions

The nature of autistic spectrum disorders and other disabilities that frequently accompany them has significant implications for approaches to education and intervention at school, in the home, and in the community. Approaches that emphasize the use of specific "packages" of materials and methods associated with comprehensive intervention programs may understate the multiple immediate and long-term needs of children for behavior support and for instruction across areas.

Teachers are faced with a huge task. They must be familiar with theory and research concerning best practices for children with autistic spectrum disorders, including methods of applied behavior analysis, naturalistic learning, assistive technology, socialization, communication, inclusion, adaptation of the environment, language interventions, assessment, and the effective use of data collection systems. Specific problems in generalization and maintenance of behaviors also affect the need for training in methods of teaching children with autistic spectrum disorders. The wide range of IQ scores and verbal skills associated with autistic spectrum disorders, from profound mental retardation and severe language impairments to superior intelligence, intensify the need for personnel training. To enable teachers to adequately work with parents and with other professionals to set appropriate goals, teachers need familiarity with the course of autistic spectrum disorders and the range of possible outcomes.

Teachers learn according to the same principles as their students. Multiple exposures, opportunities to practice, and active involvement in learning are all important aspects of learning for teachers, as well as students. Many states and community organizations have invested substantial funds in teacher preparation through workshops and large-audience lectures by well-known speakers. While such presentations can stimulate enthusiasm, they do not substitute for ongoing consultation and hands-on opportunities to observe and practice skills working with children with autistic spectrum disorders.

Personnel preparation remains one of the weakest elements of effective programming for children with autistic spectrum disorders and their families. Ways of building on the knowledge of teachers as they acquire experience with children with autistic spectrum disorders, and ways of keeping skilled personnel within the field, are critical. This is particularly true given recent trends for dependence on relatively inexperienced assistants for in-home programs. Providing knowledge about autistic spectrum disorders to special education and regular education administrators, as well as to specialized providers with major roles in early intervention (e.g., speech language pathologists) will be critical in effecting change that is proactive. Findings concerning change in educational and other opportunities suggest that administrative attitudes and support are critical in improving schools ....

Needed Research

Conclusions

There are several distinct and substantial bodies of research relevant to young children with autistic spectrum disorders. One body identifies neurological, behavioral, and developmental characteristics. Another body of research addresses diagnostic practices and related issues of prevalence. Another has examined the effects of comprehensive early treatment programs on the immediate and long-term outcomes of children and their families. These treatment studies tended to use some form of group experimental design. An additional body of research has addressed individual instructional or intervention approaches, with many studies in this literature using single-subject experimental methodology. Altogether, a large research base exists, but with relatively little integration across bodies of literature. Highly knowledgeable researchers in one area of autistic spectrum disorders may have minimal information from other perspectives, even about studies with direct bearing on their findings.

Most researchers have not used randomized group comparison designs because of the practical and ethical difficulties in randomly assigning children and families to treatment groups. In addition, there have been significant controversies over the type of control or contrast group to use and the conditions necessary for demonstrating effectiveness. Although a number of comprehensive programs have provided data on their effectiveness, and, in some cases, claims have been made that certain treatments are superior to others, there have been virtually no comparisons of different comprehensive interventions of equal intensity.

Across several of the bodies of literature, the children and families who have participated in studies are often inadequately described. Standardized diagnoses, descriptions of ethnicity, the social class, and associated features of the children (such as mental retardation and language level) are often not specified. Fidelity of treatment implementation has not been consistently assessed. Generalization, particularly across settings, and maintenance of treatment effects are not always measured. Though there is little evidence concerning the effectiveness of discipline-specific therapies, there is substantial research supporting the effectiveness of many specific therapeutic techniques.

POSTSCRIPT

Are There Scientifically Effective Treatments for Autism?

T he authors on the two sides of this issue agree on several points: Autism is a serious disorder; left alone, its consequences could be disastrous; intensive, early intervention is critical; and there are many methods from which to choose.

There are critical areas of disagreement, however. Adams and his colleagues believe strongly in a biomedical cause for autism. Our environment is hurting children they say. While educational interventions are important, they advocate medical treatment as well.

The Committee on Educational Interventions for Children with Autism holds that the increased numbers of children diagnosed with autism are due to changes in diagnostic practices. As the field learns about autism, more children are given this diagnosis instead of another. Noting the wide range of characteristics in this group, the Committee says that much more systematic research is needed to find the best educational interventions.

Weighing both points of view about the increasing numbers, Goode (*The New York Times*, 2004) observes that if the increase is due to environmental problems, numbers are likely to continue to rise unless something changes. If diagnostic knowledge is behind the increase, she posits that "rates should level off as the number of previously overlooked children diminishes."

In the meantime, educators and parents need to decide what education is best. Attorneys may play the largest role in resolving disagreements through administrative hearings (Drasgow, Yell, and Robinson, *Remedial and Special Education*, 2001).

One of the most hotly debated treatments is Applied Behavioral Analysis (ABA). An intensive therapy based on the work of Lovaas and colleagues, ABA methods require many daily hours of 1:1 work, reinforcing children for increasingly complex behaviors. This approach begins with an emphasis on eye contact and basic attention and moves on to academic and social interactions. Supporters proclaim that ABA has "cured" their child of autism. Detractors claim that existing research studies are flawed and that learned behavior does not generalize to new settings. Could parental reports of improvement be flawed? Do research design problems override the observation of parents? Or do small changes delude everyone into overestimating progress?

Equally heated is the debate about whether or not autism stems from vaccines. U.S. Representative Dan Burton, chair of the Subcommittee of Human Rights and Wellness and grandfather of a child with autism, is convinced that the mercury used to preserve vaccines leads to autism. In a recent subcommittee hearing updating federal initiatives in this area, Burton claims to have convened over 20 hearings on this topic (Committee on Government Reform, 2004). Speakers at the May 2004 hearing included researchers reporting intravenous treatments to remove mercury from the bloodstream. Within the very same month, a report of the Immunization Safety Review Committee (National Academy of Sciences, 2004) "rejected the causal relationship between MMR [measles, mumps, rubella] vaccine and autism." Given conflicting views, should parents have their children vaccinated?

The conflict between the passionate parental search for a real "cure" and the need for scientific support is poignantly described in "A Father's Fight" (Bernstein, *Health*, 2004). The M.I.N.D. Institute is one of the largest research and treatment centers devoted to autism. This is a unique collaboration, funded by a group of fathers who want their children cured of autism and staffed by researchers committed to the scientific method. Dedicated to the same goal but driven by different forces, the article describes the institute as a place nurtured by "creative tension." Will this unique collaboration result in solid answers? Will they come soon enough for the children?

How do schools select effective programs? How do parents decide if their school's proposed program is effective? The evidence is clear but often contradictory. If each child is unique, how can research prove the worth of any method? Should schools follow the lead of parents excited by a promising method unsubstantiated by research? Or should they adhere to more established methods of treatment? Can ethics and approved research protocols coexist? How would you decide for a student? Would you decide differently if it were your own child?

ISSUE 19

Have Schools Gone Too Far in Using Accommodations?

YES: James M. Kauffman, Kathleen McGee, and Michele Brigham, from "Enabling or Disabling? Observations on Changes in Special Education," *Phi Delta Kappan* (April 2004)

NO: MaryAnn Byrnes, from "Accommodations for Students with Disabilities: Removing Barriers to Learning," *National Association of Secondary School Principals' Bulletin* (2000)

ISSUE SUMMARY

YES: James M. Kauffman, a faculty member at the University of Virginia, along with Kathleen McGee and Michele Brigham, both special education teachers, maintains that special education has pursued its goal of normalization to an extreme. The emphasis has shifted from increasing competence to perpetuating disabilities through the unwise use of accommodations.

NO: MaryAnn Byrnes, a University of Massachusetts–Boston faculty member, former special education administrator, and editor of this *Taking Sides*, argues that relevant accommodations are necessary to ensure that people with disabilities have a fair chance to demonstrate what they know and can do.

Have you ever used a curb-cut to ease the passage of your bike or a stroller? Have you pushed the automatic door opener button when your arms were full? Did you know that the now-ubiquitous food processor was designed to meet the cooking needs of a one-handed person?

All of the above are accommodations. Originally designed to make the world more accessible for people with disabilities, they often make life easier for the rest of society. Federal laws require that reasonable accommodations like these be provided so that people with disabilities have fair and equal access to normal life activities.

Think about Braille texts and ramps in school. About amplification systems that expand the range of hearing aides in classrooms. Are they reasonable and acceptable accommodations to make school more accessible for children who have sensory or motoric disabilities? Most people would say they are.

Now think about scribes to transfer the words of a student into print. Or extended time for assignments and exams. Or permitting some students to submit a video or taped project instead of a written report. These are accommodations as well—for people who have difficulty writing or processing material quickly or sustaining attention. Do you accept them as easily? Many people pause here, wondering if these cross the line into making school a little too easy. Are these unreasonable?

Accommodations in school are adjustments to setting, timing, presentation mode and/or response mode that allow students with disabilities to demonstrate what they know and can do. Their purpose is to make the task accessible. They are not intended to change the nature of a task, make it easier or ensure that a student passes.

The issue of accommodations achieved controversial status with the advent of high stakes testing and school accountability that includes students with disabilities. Federal laws require that schools provide appropriate accommodations to students with disabilities so they can participate fully in educational and assessment activities.

The argument is whether these accommodations are fair, just and reasonable or whether they go beyond leveling the playing field to create a whole new game that is just not fair to everyone else, including the students with disabilities.

Kauffman, McGee and Brigham feel that accommodations have gone too far. Citing a number of powerful examples, they make the case that accommodations are being used too indiscriminately. Bowing to threats from parents and their lawyers, educators extend accommodations which attempt to disguise a disability. In doing so, they abandon the commitment to hold students to high standards and responsibility.

Byrnes asks educators and parents to be thoughtful about the use of accommodations, choosing them to remove a barrier to learning. In her view, accommodations are to be selected carefully and matched with learning challenges so that students' disabilities don't stand in the way of acquiring knowledge and competence.

As you read these articles, ask yourself what you have seen, read, or heard about accommodations in schools. Do you think they help or hinder? Do educators and parents want to create opportunities or give excuses? In this era of high stakes, are people tempted to give the benefit of the doubt, extending accommodations in the cause of raising scores and granting diplomas? If so, does this create a climate of learned helplessness? Will students feel entitled rather than responsible?

James M. Kauffman, Kathleen McGee, and Michele Brigham

Enabling or Disabling? Observations on Changes in Special Education

Schools need demanding and distinctive special education that is clearly focused on instruction and habilitation. Abandoning such a conception of special education is a prescription for disaster. But special education has increasingly been losing its way in the single-minded pursuit of full inclusion.

Once, special education's purpose was to bring the performance of students with disabilities closer to that of their nondisabled peers in regular classrooms, to move as many students as possible into the mainstream with appropriate support. For students not in regular education, the goal was to move them toward a more typical setting in a cascade of placement options. But as any good thing can be overdone and ruined by the pursuit of extremes, we see special education suffering from the extremes of inclusion and accommodation.

Aiming for as much normalization as possible gave special education a clear purpose. Some disabilities were seen as easier to remediate than others. Most speech and language disorders, for example, were considered eminently remediable. Other disabilities, such as mental retardation and many physical disabilities, were assumed to be permanent or long-term and so less remediable, but movement *toward* the mainstream and increasing independence from special educators were clear goals.

The emphasis in special education has shifted away from normalization, independence, and competence. The result has been students' dependence on whatever special programs, modifications, and accommodations are possible, particularly in general education settings. The goal seems to have become the *appearance* of normalization without the *expectation* of competence.

Many parents and students seem to want more services as they learn what is available. Some have lost sight of the goal of limiting accommodations in order to challenge students to achieve more independence. At the same time, many special education advocates want all services to be available in mainstream settings, with little or no acknowledgment that the services are atypical. Although teachers, administrators, and guidance counselors are often willing and able to make accommodations, doing so is not always in students' best long-term interests. It gives students with disabilities what anthropologist Robert Edgerton called a cloak—a pretense, a cover, which actually fools no one—rather than actual competence.

In this article, we discuss how changes in attitudes toward disability and special education, placement, and accommodations can perpetuate disability. We also explore the problems of ignoring or perpetuating disability rather than helping students lead fuller, more independent lives. Two examples illustrate how we believe good intentions can go awry—how attempts to accommodate students with disabilities can undermine achievement.

"But he needs resource...." Thomas, a high school sophomore identified as emotionally disturbed, was assigned to a resource class created to help students who had problems with organization or needed extra help with academic skills. One of the requirements in the class was for students to keep a daily planner in which they entered all assignments; they shared their planner with the resource teacher at the beginning of class and discussed what academic subjects would be worked on during that period .

Thomas consistently refused to keep a planner or do any work in resource (he slept instead). So a meeting was set up with the assistant principal, the guidance counselor, Thomas, and the resource teacher. As the meeting was about to begin, the principal announced that he would not stay because Thomas felt intimidated by so many adults. After listening to Thomas' complaints, the guidance counselor decided that Thomas would not have to keep a planner or show it to the resource teacher and that the resource teacher should not talk to him unless Thomas addressed her first. In short, Thomas would not be required to do any work in the class! When the resource teacher suggested that, under those circumstances, Thomas should perhaps be placed in a study hall, because telling the parents that he was in a resource class would be a misrepresentation, the counselor replied, "But he *needs* the resource class."

"He's too bright...." Bob, a high school freshman with Asperger's Syndrome, was scheduled for three honors classes and two Advanced Placement classes. Bob's IEP included a two-page list of accommodations. In spite of his having achieved A's and B's, with just a single C in math, his mother did not feel that his teachers were accommodating him appropriately. Almost every evening, she emailed his teachers and his case manager to request more information or more help for Bob, and she angrily phoned his guidance counselor if she didn't receive a reply by the end of the first hour of the next school day.

A meeting was scheduled with the IEP team. When the accommodations were reviewed, Bob's mother agreed that all of them were being made. However, she explained that Bob had been removed from all outside social activities because he spent all night, every night, working on homework. The accommodation she demanded was that Bob have *no* homework assignments. The autism specialist agreed that this was a reasonable accommodation for a child with Asperger's Syndrome.

The teachers of the honors classes explained that the homework in their classes, which involved elaboration and extension of concepts, was even more essential than the homework assigned in AP classes. In AP classes, by contrast, homework consisted primarily of practice of concepts learned in class. The honors teachers explained that they had carefully broken their long assignments into segments, each having a separate due date before the final project, and they gave illustrations of their expectations. The director of special education explained the legal definition of accommodations (the mother said she'd never before heard that accommodations could not change the nature of the curriculum). The director also suggested that, instead of Bob's sacrificing his social life, perhaps it would be more appropriate for him to take standard classes. What Bob's mother was asking, he concluded, was not legal. She grew angry, but she did agree to give the team a "little more time" to serve Bob appropriately. She said she would "be back with her claws and broomstick" if anyone ever suggested that he be moved from honors classes without being given the no homework accommodation. "He's too bright to take anything less than honors classes, and if you people would provide this simple accommodation, he would do just fine," she argued. In the end, she got her way.

Attitudes Toward Disability and Special Education

Not that many decades ago, a disability was considered a misfortune—not something to be ashamed of but a generally undesirable, unwelcome condition to be overcome to the greatest extent possible. Ability was considered more desirable than disability, and anything—whether a device or a service—that helped people with disabilities to do what those without disabilities could do was considered generally valuable, desirable, and worth the effort, cost, and possible stigma associated with using it.

The disability rights movement arose in response to the widespread negative attitudes toward disabilities, and it had a number of desirable outcomes. It helped overcome some of the discrimination against people with disabilities. And overcoming such bias and unfairness in everyday life is a great accomplishment. But the movement has also had some unintended negative consequences. One of these is the outright denial of disability in some cases, illustrated by the contention that disability exists only in attitudes or as a function of the social power to coerce.

The argument that disability is merely a "social construction" is particularly vicious in its effects on social justice. Even if we assume that disabilities are socially constructed, what should that mean? Should we assume that socially constructed phenomena are not "real," are not important, or should be discredited? If so, then consider that dignity, civil rights, childhood, social justice, and nearly every other phenomenon that we hold dear are social constructions. Many social constructions are not merely near and dear to us, they are real and useful in benevolent societies. The important question is whether the idea of disability is useful in helping people attain dignity or whether it is more useful to assume that disabilities are not real (i.e., that, like social justice, civil rights, and other social constructions, they are fabrications that can be ignored when convenient). The denial of disability is sometimes expressed as an aversion to labels, so that we are cautioned not to communicate openly and clearly about disabilities but to rely on euphemisms. But this approach is counterproductive. When we are able only to whisper or mime the undesirable difference called disability, then we inadvertently increase its stigma and thwart prevention efforts.

The specious argument that "normal" does not exist—because abilities of every kind are varied and because the point at which normal becomes abnormal is arbitrary—leads to the conclusion that no one actually has a disability or, alternatively, that everyone has a disability. Then, some argue, either no one or everyone is due an accommodation so that no one or everyone is identified as disabled. This unwillingness to draw a line defining something (such as disability, poverty, or childhood) is based either on ignorance regarding the nature of continuous distributions or on a rejection of the unavoidably arbitrary decisions necessary to provide special services to those who need them and, in so doing, to foster social justice.

Another unintended negative consequence of the disability rights movement is that, for some people, disability has become either something that does not matter or something to love, to take pride in, to flaunt, to adopt as a positive aspect of one's identity, or to cherish as something desirable or as a badge of honor. When disability makes no difference to us one way or the other, then we are not going to work to attenuate it, much less prevent it. At best, we will try to accommodate it. When we view disability as a desirable difference, then we are very likely to try to make it more pronounced, not to ameliorate it.

Several decades ago, special education was seen as a good thing—a helpful way of responding to disability, not something everyone needed or should have, but a useful and necessary response to the atypical needs of students with disabilities. This is why the Education for All Handicapped Children Act (now the Individuals with Disabilities Education Act) was written. But in the minds of many people, special education has been transformed from something helpful to something awful.

The full-inclusion movement did have some desirable outcomes. It helped overcome some of the unnecessary removal of students with disabilities from general education. However, the movement also has had some unintended negative consequences. One of these is that special education has come to be viewed in very negative terms, to be seen as a second-class and discriminatory system that does more harm than good. Rather than being seen as helpful, as a way of creating opportunity, special education is often portrayed as a means of shunting students into dead-end programs and killing opportunity.

Another unintended negative consequence of full inclusion is that general education is now seen by many as the *only* place where fair and equitable treatment is possible and where the opportunity to learn is extended to all equally. The argument has become that special education is good only as long as it is invisible (or nearly so), an indistinguishable part of a general education system that accommodates all students, regardless of their abilities or disabilities. Usually, this is described as a "unified" (as opposed to "separate") system of education. Special education is thus something to be avoided altogether or attenuated to the greatest extent possible, regardless of a student's inability to perform in a general setting. When special education is seen as discriminatory, unfair, an opportunity-killing system, or, as one writer put it, "the gold-plated garbage can of American schooling," then it is understandable that people will loathe it. But this way of looking at special education is like seeing the recognition and treatment of cancer as the cause of the problem.

The reversal in attitudes toward disability and special education—disability from undesirable to inconsequential, special education from desirable to awful—has clouded the picture of what special education is and what it should do for students with disabilities. Little wonder that special education stands accused of failure, that calls for its demise have become vociferous, and that contemporary practices are often more disabling than enabling. An unfortunate outcome of the changing attitudes toward disability and special education is that the benefit of special education is now sometimes seen as freedom from expectations of performance. It is as if we believed that, if a student has to endure the stigma of special education, then the compensation should include an exemption from work.

Placement Issues

Placing all students, regardless of their abilities, in regular classes has exacerbated the tendency to see disability as something existing only in people's minds. It fosters the impression that students are fitting in when they are not able to perform at anywhere near the normal level. It perpetuates disabilities; it does not compensate for them.

Administrators and guidance counselors sometimes place students in programs for which they do not qualify, even as graduation requirements are increasing and tests are mandated. Often, these students' *testing* is modified although their *curriculum* is not. The students may then feel that they have beaten the system. They are taught that the system is unfair and that the only way to win is by gaming it. Hard work and individual responsibility for one's education are often overlooked—or at least undervalued.

Students who consistently fail in a particular curriculum must be given the opportunity to deal with the natural consequences of that fact as a means of learning individual responsibility. For example, social promotion in elementary and middle school teaches students that they really don't have to be able to do the work to pass. Students who have been conditioned to rely on social promotion do not believe that the cycle will end until it does so—usually very abruptly in high school. Suddenly, no one passes them on, and no one gives them undeserved credit. Many of these students do not graduate in four years. Some never recover, while others find themselves forced to deal with a very distasteful situation.

No one wants to see a student fail, but to alter any standard without good reason is to set that same student up for failure later in life. Passing along a student with disabilities in regular classes, pretending that he or she is performing at the same level as most of the class or that it doesn't really matter (arguing that the student has a legal "right" to be in the class) is another prescription for disappointment and failure in later life. Indeed, this failure often comes in college or on the job.

Some people with disabilities do need assistance. Others do not. Consider Deborah Groeber, who struggled through degenerative deafness and blindness. The Office of Affirmative Action at the University of Pennsylvania offered to intercede at the Wharton School, but Groeber knew that she had more influence if she spoke for herself. Today, she is a lawyer with three Ivy League degrees. But not every student with disabilities can do or should be expected to do what Groeber did. Our concern is that too many students with disabilities are given encouragement based on pretense when they could do much more with appropriate special education.

Types of Accommodations

Two popular modifications in IEPs are allowing for the use of calculators and granting extended time on tests and assignments. Calculators can be a great asset, but they should be used when calculating complex problems or when doing word problems. Indiscriminate use of a calculator renders many math tests invalid, as they become a contest to see if buttons can be pushed successfully and in the correct order, rather than an evaluation of ability to do arithmetic or use mathematical knowledge.

Extended time on assignments and tests can also be a useful modification, but it can easily be misused or abused. Extended time on tests should mean *continuous* time so that a test is not studied for first and taken later. Sometimes a test must be broken into smaller segments that can be completed independently. However, this could put students with disabilities at a disadvantage, as one part of a test might help with remembering another part. Extensions on assignments need to be evaluated each time they are given, not simply handed out automatically because they are written into an IEP. If a student is clearly working hard, then extensions may be appropriate. If a student has not even been attempting assignments, then more time might be an avoidance tactic. Sometimes extended time means that assignments pile up and the student gets further and further behind. The result can then be overwhelming stress and the inability to comprehend discussions because many concepts must be acquired in sequence (e.g., in math, science, history, and foreign languages).

Reading tests and quizzes aloud to students can be beneficial for many, but great caution is required. Some students and teachers want to do more than simply read a test. Reading a test aloud means simply reading the printed words on the page *without* inflections that can reveal correct answers and without explaining vocabulary. Changing a test to open-notes or open-book, without the knowledge and consent of the classroom teacher, breaches good-faith test proctoring. It also teaches students dependence rather than independence and accomplishment. Similarly, scribing for a student can be beneficial for those who truly need it, but the teacher must be careful not to add details and to write only what the student dictates, including any run-on sentences or fragments. After scribing, if the assignment is not a test, the teacher should edit and correct the paper with the student, as she might do with any written work. But this must take place *after* the scribing.

How Misguided Accommodations Can Be Disabling

"Saving" a child from his or her own negative behavior reinforces that behavior and makes it a self-fulfilling prophecy. Well-intentioned guidance counselors often feel more responsibility for their students' success or failure than the students themselves feel. Sometimes students are not held accountable for their effort or work. They seem not to understand that true independence comes from *what* you know, not *whom* you know. Students who are consistently enabled and not challenged are never given the opportunity to become independent. Ann Bancroft, the polar explorer and dyslexic, claims that, although school was a torment, it was disability that forged her iron will. Stephen Cannell's fear for other dyslexics is that they will quit trying rather than struggle and learn to compensate for their disability.

Most parents want to help their children. However, some parents confuse making life *easier* with making life *better* for their children. Too often, parents feel that protecting their child from the rigors of academic demands is in his or her best interest. They may protect their child by insisting on curricular modifications and accommodations in assignments, time, and testing. But children learn by doing, and not allowing them to do something because they might fail is denying them the opportunity to succeed. These students eventually believe that they are not capable of doing what typical students can do, even if they are. Sometimes it is difficult for teachers to discern what a student actually can do and what a parent has done until an in-class assignment is given or a test is taken. At that point, it is often too late for the teacher to do much remediation. The teacher may erroneously conclude that the student is simply a poor test-taker.

In reality, the student may have been "protected" from learning, which will eventually catch up with him or her. Unfortunately, students may not face reality until they take a college entrance exam, go away to college, or apply for a job. Students who "get through" high school in programs of this type often go on to flunk out of college. Unfortunately, the parents of these students frequently blame the college for the student's failure, criticizing the postsecondary institution for not doing enough to help. Instead, they should be upset both with the secondary institution for not preparing the child adequately for the tasks to come and with themselves for their own overprotection.

The Benefits of Demands

Many successful adults with disabilities sound common themes when asked about their ability to succeed in the face of a disability. Tom Gray, a Rhodes Scholar who has a severe learning disability, claims that having to deal with the hardest experiences gave him the greatest strength. Stephen Cannell believes that, if he had known there was a reason beyond his control to explain his low achievement, he might not have worked as hard as he did. Today, he knows he has a learning disability, but he is also an Emmy Award-winning television writer and producer. Paul Orlalea, the dyslexic founder of Kinko's, believes God gave him an advantage in the challenge presented by his disability and that others should work with their strengths. Charles Schwab, the learning-disabled founder of Charles Schwab, Inc., cites his ability to think differently and to make creative leaps that more sequential thinkers don't make as chief reasons for his success. Fannie Flagg, the learning-disabled author, concurs and insists that learning disabilities become a blessing *only if you can overcome them*. Not every student with a disability can be a star performer, of course, but all should be expected to achieve all that they can.

Two decades ago, special educators thought it was their job to assess a student's achievement, to understand what the student wanted to do and what an average peer could do, and then to develop plans to bridge the gap, if possible. Most special educators wanted to see that each student had the tools and knowledge to succeed as independently as possible. Helping students enter the typical world was the mark of success for special educators.

The full-inclusion movement now insists that *every* student will benefit from placement in the mainstream. However, some of the modifications and accommodations now being demanded are so radical that we are doing an injustice to the entire education system. Special education must not be associated in any way with "dumbing down" the curriculum for students presumed to be at a given grade level, whether disabled or not.

Counselors and administrators who want to enable students must focus the discussion on realistic goals and plans for each student. An objective, in-depth discussion and evaluation must take place to determine how far along the continuum of successfully completing these goals the student has moved. If the student is making adequate progress independently, or with minimal help, special education services might not be necessary. If assistance is required to make adequate progress on realistic goals, then special education may be needed. Every modification and every accommodation should be held to the same standard: whether it will help the student attain these goals—*not* whether it will make life easier for the student. Knowing where a student is aiming can help a team guide that student toward success.

And the student must be part of this planning. A student who claims to want to be a brain surgeon but refuses to take science courses needs a reality check. If a student is unwilling to attempt to reach intermediate goals or does not succeed in meeting them, then special education cannot "save" that student. At that point, the team must help the student revisit his or her goals. Goals should be explained in terms of the amount of work required to complete them, not whether or not the teacher or parent feels they are attainable. When goals are presented in this way, students can often make informed decisions regarding their attainability and desirability. Troy Brown, a university dean and politician who has both a doctorate and a learning disability, studied at home with his mother. He estimates that it took him more than twice as long as the average person to complete assignments. Every night, he would go to bed with stacks of books and read until he fell asleep, because he had a dream of attending college.

General educators and special educators need to encourage all students to be responsible and independent and to set realistic expectations for themselves. Then teachers must help students to meet these expectations in a more and more independent manner. Special educators do not serve students well when they enable students with disabilities to become increasingly dependent on their parents, counselors, administrators, or teachers—or even when they fail to increase students' independence and competence.

Where We Stand

We want to make it clear that we think disabilities are real and that they make doing certain things either impossible or very difficult for the people who have them. We cannot expect people with disabilities to be "just like everyone else" in what they can do...

In our view, students with disabilities *do* have specific shortcomings and *do* need the services of specially trained professionals to achieve their potential. They *do* sometimes need altered curricula or adaptations to make their learning possible. If students with disabilities were just like "regular" students, then there would be no need whatever for special education. But the school experiences of students with disabilities obviously will not be—*cannot* be—just like those of students without disabilities. We sell students with disabilities short when we pretend that they are no different from typical students. We make the same error when we pretend that they must *not* be expected to put forth extra effort if they are to learn to do some things—or learn to do something in a different way. We sell them short when we pretend that they have competencies that they do not have or pretend that the competencies we expect of most students are not important for them.

Like general education, special education must push students to become all they can be. Special education must countenance neither the pretense of learning nor the avoidance of reasonable demands.

Accommodations for Students with Disabilities: Removing Barriers to Learning

Think about taking a driver's test without wearing glasses (if you do, that is). Not fair, you say; you need the glasses to see. You have just identified an accommodation that you need. Wearing glasses does not make a bad driver better or make driving easier; rather, wearing glasses makes driving possible. Glasses are so much a part of our lives that we do not even consider that they remove a barrier caused by a disability.

Secondary school teachers encounter students every day on an Individualized Education Plan (IEP) or 504 Plan, both of which address programs for students with disabilities. Most likely, the person charged with monitoring this plan has indicated that particular students need changes in teaching style, assignments, or testing strategies.

It is usually easy to understand the need for glasses or wheelchairs or hearing aids. These sound like changes the student must make. Other adjustments, modifications, or accommodations on these plans, such as extended time, may not be as clear.

What Is an Accommodation?

An accommodation is an adjustment, to an activity or setting, that removes a barrier presented by a disability so a person can have access equal to that of a person without a disability. An accommodation does not guarantee success or a specific level of performance. It should, however, provide the opportunity for a person with a disability to participate in a situation or activity.

Think of that pair of glasses, or the time you broke your leg and could not drive. Think of how your life was affected by these conditions. Your competence did not change. Your ability to think and work did not change. Your ability to interact with (have access to) the reading material may be very limited without your glasses. Your ability to get to (have access to) work or the grocery store may be very limited without someone to transport you. The support provided by the glasses—or the driver—made it possible for you to use your abilities without the barrier presented by less than perfect vision or limited mobility.

The accommodations in IEPs or 504 Plans serve the same purpose. They identify ways to remove the barrier presented by a person's disability.

Why Do We Need to Provide Accommodations?

Accommodations are required under Section 504 of the Federal Rehabilitation Act of 1974 as well as the Americans with Disabilities Act. Both these federal laws prohibit discrimination against individuals who have a disability. Situations that limit access have been determined to be discriminatory.

Accommodations must be provided not just by teachers to students, but by employees for workers and governments for citizens. Curbs have been cut to provide access. Doors have been widened and door handles altered to provide access to people for whom the old designs posed a barrier. Employers provide computer adaptations or other adjustments in work schedules and circumstances.

For employers and schools, individuals with disabilities may have a document called a 504 Plan, which details the types of accommodations that are required. Students who have a 504 Plan will not require special education services, just changes to the environment or instructional situation.

Students who have a disability and require special education services in addition to accommodations will have this information contained in an IEP, which also details the types of direct services that need to be provided and the goals of these services. Accommodations will be listed within this IEP.

With the recent changes in IDEA '97, the federal law governing special education, you will be addressing accommodations that must be made so a student with a disability can participate in large-scale districtwide or statewide assessment systems as well as classwork and school life.

Who Needs Accommodations?

According to Section 504, an individual with a disability is any person who has "a physical or mental impairment that limits one or more major life activities." IDEA '97, the federal special education law, lists the following disabilities: autism, deaf-blindness, deafness, hearing impairment, mental retardation, multiple disabilities, orthopedic impairment, other health impairment, serious emotional disturbance, specific learning disability, speech or language impairment, traumatic brain injury, and visual impairment.

Some conditions are covered by Section 504, but not special education. These can include attention deficit disorder—ADD, (also attention deficit hyperactivity disorder—ADHD); chronic medical conditions (such as cancer, Tourette Syndrome, asthma, or epilepsy); communicable diseases; some temporary medical conditions; physical impairments; and disorders of emotion or behavior. To qualify, there must be a demonstrated and substantial limitation of a major life activity.

Students (or adults) who have disabilities may require accommodations to have equal access to education. Not every student with a disability will require accommodations, and not every student with a disability requires the same accommodation all the time.

Think of Jim, a student who has limited mobility in his hands, affecting his ability to write. This disability will present a barrier in a class that requires the student to take notes quickly or write long essays in class. In a class that does not require either of these activities, no barrier may be present. Equal access is possible without accommodation. The student can learn and demonstrate what he knows and can do unaffected by his disability.

What Kind of Accommodations Are There?

Just as there is no limit to the range of disabilities, there is no limit to the range of accommodations. The point is to understand disability and determine if it presents a barrier to equal access. If so, decide whether an accommodation can be identified to remove the barrier—and make sure the accommodation is implemented.

Think of the student described above. The limited mobility in Jim's hands presents a barrier in a class that requires rapid note taking or the writing of long essays in class. There are several accommodations that can result in equal access. Jim might tape the lesson and take notes later. These notes could be written or dictated into a computer. Essays could be composed verbally at a computer workstation or dictated into a tape recorder or to a scribe. A computer might be adapted so typing becomes an effective way to record information on paper. In yet another type of accommodation, essays could be replaced by oral reports.

Are There Some Accommodations That Should Not Be Used?

Like many difficult questions, the answer depends on the context. An accommodation should not alter the essential purpose of the assignment. If the skill you want to measure is the ability to make multiple rapid hand movements, then there is probably no accommodation that is appropriate. Jim will not do well because of his disability. Alternately, if the purpose of a task is to see if someone has perfect vision without glasses, using those glasses is not an appropriate accommodation. If the purpose is to see if you can read, the glasses become a reasonable accommodation.

Who Decides about Accommodations?

The team that writes IEPs and 504 Plans reviews the disability and determines what accommodations, if any, are necessary. These are then written into the EIP or 504 Plan.

Once more, return to Jim. As you consider the requirements of your class, think of the most appropriate way to remove the barrier that is presented by the limited mobility Jim has in his hands.

If We Use Accommodations, How Will the Student Ever Be Prepared for Independent Life in College or the World of Work?

Some people are concerned that the supports provided in school will result in the student being unable to work productively when he or she leaves school.

As a matter of fact, Section 504 applies to colleges and employers as well. Colleges offer support centers and provide accommodations upon documentation that a disability exists. Employers are required to provide reasonable accommodations to any person who is otherwise qualified to fulfill the elements of the job.

If companies remove barriers at the workplace, educators should be willing and able to take barriers out of the school activities that prepare a student for the workplace. Teachers can help a student identify the type of accommodation that will be the least cumbersome for everyone, and those that will permit the student to be most independent.

Don't Accommodations Just Make School Easier?

That depends on how you view the world. Does wearing glasses make driving easier? Not really—for a person with limited vision, wearing glasses makes driving *possible*. With or without glasses, you need to be able to drive to pass the test. The same is true of an academic accommodation; whether or not the accommodation is provided, the students still must demonstrate that they know required material.

Think about the important elements of your class: Is it more important that Jim take notes in class or understand the material? Is it more important that Jim demonstrate good handwriting or the ability to communicate thoughts in print? Often, when you identify the main purpose of your assignments and consider the skills and abilities of a student, you will see that an accommodation lets you determine more clearly what a student knows, understands, and can do.

Does a Student Need to Follow the IEP Accommodations in All Classes?

The IEP or 504 Plan needs to address any area in which the student's disability affects life in school. Sometimes this means in all classes, but not always. For example, a student who was blind would need to use Braille in all classes dealing with written material. Jim, our student with limited mobility in his hands, might not require accommodations in world languages or physical education.

Can We Make Accommodations without Having Students on an IEP?

Many accommodations are just different ways of teaching or testing. You should be able to have this freedom in your classes. In some cases, the way in which a class is taught makes accommodations unnecessary. Accommodations change the situation, not the content of the instruction. However, accommodations on standardized tests must be connected to IEP's or 504 Plans.

May Teachers Give Different Assignments on the Same Content as a Way to Meet the Needs of Different Learning Styles without Lowering Standards?

Absolutely. The point is to remove the barrier of the disability; this is one way to accomplish that. Some teachers find they tap student knowledge best in active projects; others find that written work is best. Many secondary schools are using portfolios or performance activities to document student learning.

These assessment activities can be very compelling and they do tap different methods of expression. A student like Jim, for example, might communicate depth of understanding and analysis to a social studies debate that might be difficult to capture in an on-demand written test. A student with a disability in the area of speech or language might find barriers in the performance activities that do not exist on a paper-and-pencil task.

What if Accommodations Are Not Implemented?

Since accommodations allow equal access, refusing to provide them can be viewed as discrimination. Individuals who knowingly refuse to implement accommodations make themselves personally liable for legal suit.

This sounds serious, and it is serious. Once the accommodations are found to be necessary, everyone must implement them in situations where the student's disability poses a barrier that prevents equal access.

If no barrier exists in your class, the accommodation is not necessary. No one has the option, however, of deciding not to implement a necessary accommodation. Telling students they could not wear glasses or use a hearing aid is unthinkable. Just as inappropriate is a decision not to allow Jim to use accommodations to remove the barrier posed by his disability, even though it means making some changes to your own work.

Questions About Specific Accommodations

Now that the issues underlying accommodations have been addressed, it is time to talk about frequently-encountered accommodations that raise questions and concern. All these questions have come from secondary school faculty members in a variety of school systems.

Why Is It Fair to Read Material Aloud to Some Students?

Some students have a learning disability that makes it difficult for them to decode print. They can understand the concepts; they can comprehend the material when they hear it; they can reason through the material. They just can't turn print into meaning. If the task is to determine if the student can read, you already know they will have difficulty. If the task is to determine if the student has content knowledge, reading material aloud removes the barrier of the learning disability. Reading material aloud to a student who does not understand the material will not result in a higher grade.

Why Is It Fair to Give Some Students Extra Time on Tests?

Some students have motor difficulties that make writing an enormous challenge. They may not be able to form the letters correctly. They may not be able to monitor their thoughts while they work on the physical act of writing. They understand the material, and they know what they want to respond; it just takes longer to write the answer. If the task is to determine how quickly the student can respond, you already know they will have difficulty. If the task is to determine if the student has the knowledge, providing extra time removes the barrier of the motor disability. Providing extra time to a student who does not understand the material will not result in a higher grade.

Why Is It Fair to Permit Some Students to Respond Orally to Tests?

Think about the example above. For some students, responding orally would be a comparable accommodation. In this case, allowing an oral response will not result in a higher grade if the student does not know the material.

The Bottom Line

It all comes down to deciding what is important. Think about your assignment and expectations. Think about the disability. If the disability provides a barrier, the accommodation removes it. The accommodation does not release a student from participating or demonstrating knowledge—it allows the student to be able to participate and demonstrate knowledge. And isn't that what school is all about?

POSTSCRIPT

Have Schools Gone Too Far in Using Accommodations?

Truth be told, all the authors really answer YES to this issue's question. Their differences hinge on the meaning of "enable." Consider the following definitions: "a: to provide with the means or opportunity; b: to make possible, practical, or easy" (*Merriam-Webster Online Dictionary*).

Kauffman and colleagues use the second definition. Just as the popular press talks about how people can "enable' someone to be co-dependent or addicted, they feel special education randomly tosses about accommodations to make life "easy" for students. Byrnes would apply the first definition, saying that judicious use of accommodations provides students with an opportunity to learn.

This shading of meaning disguises a basic commonality in the articles. Both agree that accommodations are necessary and can be an important educational tool. Two questions are at the heart of the debate. When should accommodations be provided? Which accommodations should be provided?

Horn and Tynan (Fordham Foundation, 2001) agree with Kauffman and colleagues that accommodations are used too widely. They believe accommodations made sense early on when the intention was to ensure that students with significant sensory or motor disabilities had access to a Free and Appropriate Public Education. Now, they say, their use has been broadened to create a "lifetime of dependence" often at taxpayers' expense.

Writing in *Education Week's* 2004 Quality Counts edition focusing on the state of special education in a standards based environment, Olson observes that states differ widely in their definition of acceptable accommodations. She references the continuing challenge of deciding whether a particular accommodation helps or give an unfair advantage. The difficulty of selecting appropriate accommodations makes it easy to identify too many, too few, or incorrect options.

Extending the significant work of the National Center on Educational Outcomes, Bolt and Thurlow (*Remedial & Special Education*, 2004), emphasize the need to provide appropriate accommodations to ensure students with disabilities are included in the curriculum and assessment changes of education reform. Educators must determine which accommodations enhance access without changing demands.

Some say that anyone would do better if they had more time; a reader; a computer. The evidence seems to say that is not so. To be appropriate, an accommodation must confer a "differential boost." It must result in a gain for students with disabilities, without enhancing the scores of typical learners. This would show that students could demonstrate knowledge, once the impact of a disability were removed. Reviewing research on the differential impact of the most commonly allowed accommodations, including extended time, Bolt and Thurlow (2004) uncovered mixed results. Some had very little impact. Elliott & Marquart (*Exceptional Children,* 2004) found that extended time on math tests did not provide an advantage to students with disabilities. It did, however, help everyone feel more relaxed and provided them more time to check the accuracy of their responses.

The point, say Fuchs and Fuchs (*The School Administrator,* 1999), is to choose accommodations that result in valid, rather than optimal, performance. It is not always easy to make this determination. Students and disabilities are different. Task demands differ. The Fuchs have developed the Dynamic Assessment of Testing Accommodations (DATA) to help educators determine which accommodations are most appropriate to choose. While this evidence-based method holds much promise, it requires a substantial investment of time.

Because this field is so new, research evidence is not comprehensive. Because students differ dramatically, research is difficult to conduct. Would you want your child in the control group? Because stakes can be so high for students and schools, correct decisions are critical. How can we all be sure we make the right choices as we continue to provide meaningful education?

ISSUE 20

Should Students With Disabilities Participate in High-Stakes Testing?

YES: Martha L. Thurlow and David R. Johnson, from "High-Stakes Testing of Students With Disabilities," *Journal of Teacher Education* (September/October 2000)

NO: Pixie J. Holbrook, from "When Bad Things Happen to Good Children: A Special Educator's View of MCAS," *Phi Delta Kappan* (June 2001)

ISSUE SUMMARY

YES: Martha L. Thurlow, director of the National Center on Educational Outcomes, and David R. Johnson, director of the Institute on Community Integration, both at the University of Minnesota, assert that high-stakes testing may hold many benefits for students with disabilities, especially if the tests are carefully designed and implemented.

NO: Pixie J. Holbrook, a special education teacher and consultant, maintains that high-stakes testing marks children with disabilities as worthless failures, ignores their accomplishments and positive attributes, and seriously limits their range of possibilities in adult life.

$\mathbf{F}$ind a state that has instituted new tests to measure educational progress and you will find controversy. Add the element of including all students with disabilities and the emotional pitch increases dramatically.

Historically, most students with disabilities have been excluded from formal districtwide and national tests. Sometimes people assumed that these children would not do well and acted to spare them stress. At other times schools were concerned that participation of students with disabilities would reduce overall test scores. In order to maximize results, some districts worked to classify low-performing students into special education so their scores would not be counted. Once a student's scores did not count, less attention was paid to the curriculum content of that child's education. Special education and general education often pursued very different goals.

IDEA97 changed the playing field with its mandate that schools be held accountable for the academic performance of all students—even those with significant disabilities. Parents and educators now choose from a number of participation options. The majority of students with disabilities can take the tests along with other students. Other students with disabilities use accommodations that remove the barriers of their disabilities—like Braille for students who are blind. For the very small number of students who cannot demonstrate what they know and can do with accommodations, an alternate test option is possible. Whatever the choice, the school and district—and sometimes the student—are held accountable for test results.

In all states, these tests are used for accountability purposes. In some cases the stakes are highest for districts, each of which is held responsible for student performance. In these states, penalties exist for schools not achieving to expectations, but there are no direct consequences for individual students. In other states, the stakes are highest for individual students. The Test must be passed in order to be promoted or graduate.

In the following selection, Martha L. Thurlow and David R. Johnson assert that strong opportunities exist for students with disabilities in this new world of high-stakes testing. If your score counts, you will count. Furthermore, schools will care more about curriculum and instruction for students with disabilities. And higher expectations will lead to greater gains. Thurlow and Johnson urge teachers and administrators to be actively involved in constructing and implementing tests which are truly fair to students and to schools.

In the second selection, Pixie J. Holbrook shares the struggles of her students, who are trying hard to jump the hurdles posed by a statewide test that is based on high-level academic skills that must be passed before a high school diploma is granted. She knows that her students—and her own son—are able to develop skills that will serve them well as adults in the working world, but she agonizes over the possibility that their spirits will be crushed as they pursue a goal that is unattainable—and irrelevant.

As you read these selections, consider these questions: Is it fair to include students with disabilities in high-stakes testing when it is already known that they are doing poorly in school? Can high stakes testing be designed and implemented to be fairer to all students? Would the "average" score be more reachable if the results of all children were included? Will the confidence of students with disabilities be destroyed by high-stakes tests, or will they—and their schools—rise to the challenge set for their peers? Who is accountable in your state? What happens when standards are not met?

Martha L. Thurlow and
David R. Johnson

 **YES**

High-Stakes Testing of Students With Disabilities

High-stakes testing is becoming a common component of educational reform. When the stakes are high for students, there is always concern about the potential for unintended consequences, such as increased rates of students dropping out of school. There are increased concerns when students have disabilities. Despite the apparent potential for unintended consequences, there are also intended effects to be considered—benefits to students and others....

Testing students with disabilities is not something new. These students take a series of individualized assessments when their eligibility for special education services is first under consideration. After that, they may be given additional tests to measure their progress toward the goals listed on their Individualized Education Plans (IEPs). Every 3 years, they are again administered a wide range of assessments designed to determine whether they are still eligible for services. These kinds of assessments have been in place for 25 years, since the enactment of Public Law 94-142, the Education of All Handicapped Children Act.

What is new is the requirement that students with disabilities participate in assessments that in many places were developed for students not receiving special education services. These tests include the state and district tests used to document how students are performing. Sometimes these tests are norm referenced, providing comparisons of children across the nation, and sometimes they are standards based or criterion referenced, providing comparisons with specific standards.... [S]tates must document the number of students participating in the tests, report on their performance, and develop alternate assessments for students unable to participate in existing state or district tests. Guidelines must be developed to assist in deciding which students take state and district assessments and which take an alternate assessment. Performance reports are to be made available to the public with the same frequency and in the same detail as reports that are provided to the public for students without disabilities.

IDEA 97 [Individuals with Disabilities Education Act Amendment of 1997] added these new requirements for several reasons. Researchers had documented that when students are excluded from state or district assessments, several unintended consequences occur. In addition to concerns about inappropriate referrals to special education and increased rates of retention in grades prior to those tested, there are concerns about the focus of instruction for students not included in assessments. Teachers had reported how their students with disabilities were sent on field trips on the day of district-wide testing; parents told of receiving phone calls from the school principal suggesting that their son or daughter stay home on the day of testing to avoid a testing process that would be much too stressful for their child. These students, however, missed important experiences and instruction that other students received, simply because they were not taking the test. Eventually, excluded students suffered in many ways because expectations for them were lowered, and their access to the general education curriculum and to the benefits of standards-based reform was limited. Requirements to include students with disabilities in state and district assessments and to report on their performance recognize that students with disabilities benefit from being held to high standards, from having access to the general education curriculum, and from being part of the student body for which educators are held accountable for teaching.

Including students with disabilities in state and district assessments has always been done to some extent. Typically, however, only those students who could take the test in the same way that everyone else took the test (i.e., under standard administration conditions) were included in the assessments....

What It Takes for Students With Disabilities to Participate in Assessment Systems

Beginning from the assumption that it is beneficial for students with disabilities to participate in state and district assessments, and also beginning from the need to comply with federal law, it is important to ask what is required for these students to take state and district assessments in a way that best reflects what they have learned—what they know and can do. These are three basic considerations: (a) purpose of the assessment, (b) accommodations, and (c) alternate assessments.

Purpose. Most of the initial discussion about the need for students with disabilities to participate in assessments occurred without considering the different purposes of state or district assessments. Initial concern was that schools were not being held accountable for teaching these students. Little thought was given to the assessments that were used for student accountability—to determine whether students were promoted from one grade to the next or whether they received a diploma. High-stakes testing that has consequences for students with disabilities, however, becomes a tricky issue because of the students' disabilities, which may interfere with learning and with the student being able to actually demonstrate what she or he knows and can do.

Accommodations. It is generally recognized that providing accommodations increases the participation of students with disabilities in assessments. Yet, controversy surrounds for use of accommodation, especially certain accommodations. This is evident in court cases about the use of scribes and word processors as well as new cases involving the use of spell checkers and readers. States and districts often have complex policies about the use of accommodations, and these policies often differ from one place to the next.

Despite the controversy, it is generally recognized that accommodations are an important aspect of the assessment of students with disabilities, just as they are for instruction. Examples of accommodations used during assessments are extended testing time, marking answers in the test booklet rather than on a separate sheet, being tested individually, and having directions repeated. There is much variability in the nature of accommodations, from setting and timing changes to changes in how the test is presented or how the student responds. There is also variability in how easy it is to provide accommodations to students. The logistics of providing accommodations is a concern with which schools are now dealing, sometimes with more resistance than necessary.

Alternate assessments.   Alternate assessments are new in most states and districts. They are measures for students unable to take state or district assessments, usually less than 2% of the total student population (about 20% of students with disabilities). Most states are in the process of developing these assessments. Surveys indicate that states are taking a variety of approaches to alternate assessment procedures, from versions of paper-and-pencil tests to checklists to portfolios. In some places, alternate assessments are a way for some students to show that they have met the graduation requirement.

Including Students With Disabilities in Assessments With High Stakes for Students

The consequences of educational accountability systems for schools and educators are much better understood than are those for students. The consequences of high-stakes systems for students with disabilities are much less understood. Tests should be considered as high stakes for students with disabilities when the results are used to make critical decisions about the individual's access to education opportunity, grade-level retention or promotion, graduation from high school, or receipt of a standard diploma versus an alternative diploma (e.g., special education diploma, certificate of completion). The decisions all have immediate and long-range implications for the student. The use of exit exams to determine whether a student earns a high school diploma, for example, has lifelong consequences and directly affects an individual's economic self-sufficiency and well-being as an adult.

Access to Educational Opportunity

For students with disabilities and for others who experience difficulties on these tests, there is a variety of possible system responses. Test results, either favorable or unfavorable, are designed to have an effect on the content in focus as a curriculum, instructional strategies, intervention strategies to improve the learning of all students, professional development support for teachers and administrators, the use of assessment results, and the use and nature of test preparation materials. These and other examples are the intended consequences of using student test scores as an index of system performance. Information on student test scores can be used to revisit and modify the curriculum, instructional approaches, and strategies and to identify the skills teachers and administrators may need to address critical areas where students' scores are found to be poor.

There are, however, several unintended consequences for students, including students with disabilities who perform poorly on state and local tests. Observable consequences may include (a) increased referrals to special education for services, (b) lowered expectations of students as learners, (c) narrowing of the curriculum and instruction to focus on the specific learning outcomes assessed in state tests, (d) teaching to tests, (e) using test preparation materials that are closely linked to the assessment without making changes to the curriculum, (f) limiting the range of program options students can participate in because of intensified efforts to concentrate on areas of weakness identified by testing, and (g) the overall impact test scores have on judging whether a student will graduate from school with a standard education diploma. Although these consequences certainly affect all students, students with disabilities in particular are significantly affected by high-stakes testing programs.

These and other consequences potentially limit access to educational opportunities. A primary concern is that scores on high-stakes tests will be used to place students with disabilities in low-track classes, where they learn less than they are capable of learning. Research shows that when students with disabilities are placed in low-track classes, they do not catch up with their peers in other tracks. For students with disabilities, the IEP team, with general education involvement, should strive to maintain high standards and expectations for students, to provide meaningful access to the general education curriculum through appropriate accommodations and support systems, and to actively engage general education and special education teachers in collaborative instructional arrangements to support students in meeting state standards.

Retention and Social Promotion

State tests also become high stakes when they are used for grade-level retention and promotion decisions. Increasingly, states are requiring that schools and school districts use state test scores to determine whether students should be promoted to the next grade level.... Retention has been referred to as a kind of academic *redshirting*, that is, the act of keeping students back a grade to improve test scores. Retaining students could be viewed as an appropriate intervention; however, there is little research evidence to suggest that this is the case. Persuasive evidence indicates that repeating a grade does not improve the achievement of students with disabilities overall.

A second concern is based on documented increases in the dropout rate for students who have been retained. Dropping out of school is one of the most serious and pervasive problems facing special education programs nationally, yet very limited data are presently available on dropout rates among youth with disabilities. The last congressionally mandated study of the secondary school experiences of students with disabilities found that nearly 40% had left school by dropping out.

Graduation Requirements and Diploma Options

Some states have attached high-stakes exit exams to graduation since the late 1960s and early 1970s. Requirements that states set for graduation can range from Carnegie unit requirements (a certain number of class credits earned in specific areas) to the successful passing of minimum competency tests, high school exit exams, and/or a series of benchmark exams. States may also require almost any combination of these. Diversity in graduation requirements is complicated further by an increasingly diverse set of possible graduation diploma options. The standard high school diploma is not the only exit document available to students, including students with disabilities, at high school completion. Among the array of diploma options are special education diplomas, certificates of completion, occupational diplomas, and others. There is a critical need to better understand the implications of state graduation requirements because of findings that students with disabilities experience significant negative outcomes when they fail to earn a high school or equivalent diploma. There are also data to suggest that more stringent graduation requirements may be related to higher rates of dropping out of school among students with disabilities compared with the dropout rates of their counterparts without disabilities.

Currently, 16 states have had their exams in place long enough to affect the graduating class of 2000. Approximately 9 other states have developed graduation exams that students in future graduating classes will have to pass to receive a standard diploma. Additional states have legislated exams that are now being developed; add to these numerous local exams to determine whether students will receive diplomas. The states with active graduation exams have diploma options that reflect the array of diplomas and certificates and the criteria for earning them....

As with other students, those with disabilities are allowed multiple opportunities to take exit exams. States with graduation exams generally have more diploma options available to students overall. Many states also offer students with disabilities additional flexibility in meeting standard diploma requirements. For example, most states with only course credit requirements for graduation allow their students with disabilities to meet requirements by taking modified coursework or completing IEPs or by having IEP teams or districts decide the requirements. More than half the states that require both credits and exams to earn a standard diploma allow changes in requirements for students with disabilities.

Implications for Teachers and Teacher Educators

As more and more states and school districts implement performance standards and tests in an effort to improve educational accountability, they are faced with several critical questions. Many of these questions apply to all students, yet there are several that specifically address the experiences of students with disabilities.... For example, how do we ensure that results on state tests do not unnecessarily limit educational experiences and opportunities? What steps must be taken to ensure that states carefully align current grade-level retention and promotion policies with newly emerging state tests and related performance standards? What do schools need to consider about using state test scores to retain or promote students with disabilities? What is the role and importance of accommodations in supporting student participation in these and other exams? Is the standard diploma the only option that should be available to students, or should there be some type of diploma for students who do not pass the test but who meet other criteria? If more than one type of diploma is available, what specific requirements should be aligned with each diploma option? These are difficult and complex questions. Exploring the answers to them produces several suggestions for including students with disabilities in high-stakes assessments.

Maintain high expectations for students with disabilities. For students with disabilities, the IEP team should serve as the focal point for discussions about student participation in state testing and standards-based accountability systems. The IEP must indicate whether the student is to participate in the assessment and the nature and scope of accommodations that might be required by the student.... The IEP team must work to ensure that high expectations for learning and achievement are maintained for students with disabilities. If students experience difficulties in passing state tests, efforts must be undertaken to ensure that they remain on a full curriculum track, with learning expectations that guide the instruction of general education students.... General education teachers, in collaboration with special education personnel, must determine the strategies, accommodations, and overall supports needed to ensure that students meet high standards and have access to the full range of curricular options available to other students. Difficulties in test performance should not result in lower expectations, narrowing of curricular options, or displacement of the student from the general education curriculum....

Accommodating the test situation.   IEP team members need to think about the link between assessment accommodations and instructional accommodations. It is important that assessment accommodations are familiar to students and that they be used prior to test administration....

Nonapproved accommodations.   There are several accommodations that are considered to change the construct tested, such as reading a reading test to a student, and therefore are not approved for use. Nonapproved accommodations are needed for some students to be able to take the test. For example, students who are blind and have not learned Braille are essentially denied access to the test if it is not read to them regardless of whether the test's content is mathematics, reading, or some other content area. This same situation occurs for students with significant reading disabilities and other conditions as well. Denying access to the assessment because of the effects of a disability, especially when the assessment provides access to a benefit (such as a diploma), raises many concerns. Simply denying diplomas or providing certificates of attendance for these students does not seem to be reasonable because it can be argued that they have met standards and simply are not being allowed to appropriately show their mastery of them. One approach is to have a special request process, through which students needing nonapproved accommodations could request permission to use them, with the reason for needing each accommodation documented. For these students, test performance might be just one part of a larger body of evidence required for meeting graduation requirements.

A phase-in approach to testing.   Historically, students with disabilities either have been excluded from the general education curriculum or have received a watered-down version of it, although there are examples in which students have indeed had the same exposure and opportunities that other students have had to master the general education curriculum.... As a result, questions can be raised about whether it is appropriate to expect that today's ninth-grade students have had equal access to the general education curriculum and standards. Because of questions about opportunity to learn, educators might want to ask for an extended phase-in of the requirements for students with disabilities. For example, those students now in elementary school would be the first required to meet state graduation requirements.

Providing retesting opportunities.   How retesting interacts with disability issues should be considered. Retesting must be available to students with disabilities just as often as it is to other students. This means that special editions of the test are needed and that accommodations need to be provided during retesting. IEP teams need to determine whether to request additional accommodations with each retake, thereby recognizing the possibility that the accommodations are needed even though the student may have hoped not to use them. Changing rules about test format, administration procedures, or accommodations for retesting must be addressed.

Available appeals and waiver processes.   It is important that teachers and those who train them know whether any procedures are available for students to appeal a poor test score or to obtain a waiver from taking a test. An appeals process that ensures consideration of individual student needs or a process for requesting a waiver from testing may reduce the number of problems students encounter. However, it is important for these students to still be held to high standards. Alternative ways for them to show that they have met high standards should be pursued.

Teacher Educators Influencing Policies on Inclusive Diploma Options and Graduation Policies

It is critical for teacher educators to know about the existing policies that affect students, which in turn affect teachers. Beyond that, it is important for teacher educators to speak up about policies that are implemented or that are being considered. More than half the states do not yet have graduation exams, but most are thinking seriously about adding them. It is a good time to get involved in discussions about these exams. Many states that have graduation exams are rethinking some of their policies. Knowing what is being thought about and adding input to the discussion are equally important. There are several points that might be considered in relation to graduation requirements and graduation exams for students with disabilities.

Recognize that not all students demonstrate high knowledge and skills in the same way.   Just as this calls for alternative testing practices, it also can mean that there should be other avenues to diplomas, such as an appeals process. Only 1% to 2% of the total student enrollment (i.e., students with severe disabilities) should require alternate tests or special accommodations to participate in testing programs at any level.

Clarify the implications of different diploma options for continued special education services.   It is important for parents and educators to know that if a child graduates from high school with a standard high school diploma, the student is no longer entitled to special education services. Special and general education teachers should carefully work with students and families to consider what it actually means to receive a standard high school diploma. In some cases, it may be advisable to delay formal receipt of a standard high school diploma until the conditions (goals and objectives) of the student's IEP have been fully met, including all transition service requirements outlined in IDEA 97. A pressing concern is to ensure that the agreed-on goals and objectives in the student's IEP have been fulfilled by the educational agency and that students have been connected with the adult services needed to support postschool education, employment, and independent living needs.

Consider the views of others about diploma options and policies.   Postsecondary education representatives need to determine whether they will accept an alternative diploma as part of their admission requirements. The question is whether graduating from high school with a special education diploma or other certificate of completion grants students who earn them access to postsecondary education programs. High schools and postsecondary programs should thoroughly discuss the meaning and rigor of these alternative diplomas and agree on their use for postsecondary education admissions. This issue is not the same as concerns about the meaning of grade point averages or class ranks earned by students (regardless of disability) who have taken easier classes or programs of study.

Employers need to be consulted and informed about the types of diplomas students receive on graduation. Although it is unfair to generalize on the motivations of employers, it is fair to say that employers are interested in hiring the most qualified individuals they can. If members of the business community are not engaged in discussions about plans to use an array of alternative diplomas, employers may view these alternative diplomas as a convenient screening mechanism for new employees. Students who hold a standard high school diploma might thereby be viewed as more desirable candidates for employment than those with an alternative, or "lesser," diploma....

Conclusions

The consequences of high-stakes testing for students with disabilities, particularly of tests used to determine graduation status or type of diploma, last well beyond the time a student is in school. Participation in postsecondary education programs, employment and future earnings, civic participation, and the individual's overall social and emotional well-being are affected by the credential they receive in high school and carry forward into adulthood. A substantial body of research has documented the negative consequences of dropping out of school, yet limited research has been conducted on the consequences of receiving less than a standard high school diploma.

There may indeed be high-stakes consequences related to granting students an alternative diploma rather than the standard high school diploma. Some educators and policy makers have expressed concern that the current diploma and graduation requirements may give students with disabilities an unfair advantage over students without disabilities who may be held to higher standards. Alternatively, receiving less than a standard high school diploma may limit an individual's future opportunities to access postsecondary education and employment.

These issues, coupled with the possibility of lower expectations, off-target teaching, and denial of responsibility for students with disabilities, form an unfortunate set of unintended consequences that surface when addressing the participation of students with disabilities in educational accountability systems. Balancing these against a desire to be fair to students and not to harm them creates significant challenges for states and districts today. Teachers must take a major role in raising and addressing the tough questions as high stakes affect students' educational opportunities, retention or promotion, and graduation from high school.

When Bad Things Happen to Good Children

Sarah is in fourth grade. She's the daughter of two professional parents and has an older brother, whom she lovingly describes as a "pain in the neck." Every time she writes an entry in her journal, she's eager to include one of her brother's adventures. Her teacher has taught her to start each entry with a line that grabs the reader's attention. "My, what a week this has been!" or "You're not going to believe what my brother did this time!" Sarah loves to write, always filling a page or two with ease. She's bright and clever, eager and creative. Her words are engaging and her stories pull you in.

But Sarah can't read her own writing, and I can't either. She brings her weekly journal to my special education resource room each Thursday, and together we labor over the confusion of half words and reversed letters. The sentences are literally endless, with that one capital and maybe that final period. In the middle are wonderful ideas, but we can't figure out where they start and end. Little by little, word by word, Sarah and I piece together the writing. She says, "Oh yes, I remember, that's the word uncle. My uncle had a flat tire." And I ask, "Sarah, could that be the word *shaking*? Was your dog shaking?"

The story takes form, but Sarah's luster is fading. She knows her failings. She knows that, as hard as she tries, she can't spell or read like other students. She knows that, as fast as these stories emerge, she can't reread them. Ideas start and stop in her mind, but she can't find them on her paper. Sarah has a learning disability that affects all that she does during the school day. Social studies, science, and math all require reading and writing, which Sarah labors over daily. School is a struggle from beginning to end, but Sarah perseveres with the support of her family and teachers.

Sarah has been tested, and her intellectual potential is above average. Through a series of subtests that involve verbal and nonverbal tasks, it's discovered that Sarah has the learning potential of students her age and older. However, on certain tasks that involve the perception of visual information, her brain confuses the images. It's particularly evident when she encounters symbols. When asked to reproduce those skewed images in writing, her brain once again confuses the message. Her coordination is weak, and the letters are labored and poorly formed. Her writing is a series of words with omitted, misordered, or illegible letters. In terms that we can relate to, Sarah reads, spells, and writes like a student at the end of first grade. She has the interests, experiences, and enthusiasm of a 10-year-old, but her work in school is that of a 7-year-old.

When Sarah was in kindergarten, her ability to master readiness skills was strong. She was well socialized and had good background information from an enriched home life and some preschool experience. Her parents and teachers were prepared for her to experience school success in all ways. However, by the middle of first grade, Sarah's progress was slowing. As the demands of decoding the symbols for letters and numbers increased, Sarah was not moving forward. Her peers were already building an automatic sight vocabulary and were playing with the phonic units of reading and spelling. All this eluded Sarah. She was struggling with the basic deciphering of the very *direction* of the symbol or with associating a cluster of visual information (letters) with its meaning as a word.

By the end of first grade, it was recommended that Sarah get the help of a remedial reading teacher. Thanks to the enthusiasm of this teacher, Sarah was able to maintain her love of stories and writing. Second grade brought little change, and Sarah's official referral for a complete evaluation came at the end of that year. By third grade Sarah was placed in special education, and in fourth grade, with daily services by a trained professional, she made a substantial leap in reading, going from preprimer (early first grade) to the mid-second-grade level.

Days in school can be very long for Sarah, but weekends bring relief. She is a fine athlete and excels at soccer. Her weekends are filled with cheering crowds and team hugs. There are sleepovers and dinners with grandparents. She has pets, a new clarinet, and a Diskman. She's a friend to many and is well liked by her peers and teachers. Back at school, her classmates chose her to be a peer mediator, an esteemed role that many students aspire to. Sarah will certainly succeed in that role, too. She's an average, healthy, middle-class, suburban girl. The only thing that separates her from thousands of other 10-year-old girls is a learning disability.

Our board of education says that we have to assess all students. We need to track their progress and be certain that we have set our expectations high. We need to help all students access the curriculum, and we need to support them and recognize their achievement. I want nothing less for Sarah. I test her individually at the beginning and end of every year. I want to see how I have helped her, and I share the results with her so that she too can mark her progress. We enjoy seeing how she has changed, comparing her two spelling tests and giggling over how she read that same word back in September. These tools help me create an individual program for Sarah. Her needs are unique, but this kind of assessment, coupled with my training and experience, allows me to select the appropriate techniques and materials that will ensure her progress.

Sarah took the MCAS (Massachusetts Comprehensive Assessment System) test this spring. It was her first time taking it and my second time giving it. I have opposed this one-dimensional, trivia-laden test since its inception. But I have an obligation as a professional to administer this test to my special-needs students. I had already separated out the two children who qualified for the "alternate" assessment. The state allows me to choose between 1% and 3% of my students for this option. It is like being in a Biblical story. Whom shall I sacrifice? I sent those two bewildered but grateful students to the library for 15 hours over two weeks to work with learning packets and play educational games under the supervision of our paraprofessionals. The other two special education teachers in my building had done the same.

My two students joined several others, who grew increasingly irritated by the change in their schedule and unfamiliar activity. "Why can't we come back to your class?" they asked me each day. "Because the governor wants to know how all the children in Massachusetts are doing," I replied, offering my best explanation. One was grateful; the other, insulted. "Thanks for getting me out of that one," exclaimed one. "Sure. I'm not smart enough!" said the other. It hurt no matter what I did.

As a special-needs student who did not qualify for the alternative assessment, Sarah is entitled to certain "allowable accommodations" for the MCAS that were determined at her team meeting. I can help Sarah in several ways. I can administer the test in a small-group setting in my resource room. I can read all directions until I'm certain she understands. I can read all parts of the test to her, "except for the English Language Arts test," I kept repeating to myself. This makes absolutely no sense. None at all.

Now they are really losing me. How is this "accommodation" fair to a disabled reader? She must pass the reading section of the MCAS for graduation; yet by 10th grade, Sarah will still be a highly disabled reader. Does anyone imagine that she will be *un*disabled by 10th grade and so able to read 10th grade material? Do blind people suddenly see in 10th grade in order to take the MCAS without using Braille? Sarah has a reading disability, but I can make no adjustments to the reading section of the MCAS. I can read all the other sections, but not that one. Yet, ultimately, all the Sarahs in Massachusetts must pass that one in particular for graduation.

❧❦❧

I came to the testing session with a positive attitude. I can do this, I told myself. I'll make this as productive a day as I can for my students. Correction. I mean as productive a two weeks as I can. I'm upbeat, and this will spread to my students, I reassure myself.

With the help of the other two special education teachers and our paraprofessionals, we have arranged a complicated schedule in order to administer the test with the proper accommodations for individual test-takers. Some will have the allowable sections read to them, some we will scribe for, and several just need the directions clarified. But because of the special reading and scribing arrangements, we have to do this one-on-one. How can we write for more than one student at a time? For our students who are not in grade 4, substitutes have been hired, and we have provided materials and activities so that their programs will be as little disrupted as possible. Perhaps I am making this sound easy, but any teacher would shudder at what this entails. It is instructional time used unwisely, it's an additional expense for substitutes, and it's a great deal of extra work for us. We resent this, but we are trying to be professional, and, above all, we are trying to ensure that all our students are comfortable and using their time productively.

Sarah is my student, and we will spend about two hours a day together for the next several days, working through the test. The subtests are untimed, which is both a blessing and a curse. There will be no pressure to rush for Sarah, who processes everything slowly. But by the same token, she is a perfectionist and is likely to need a great deal of time to select her answers or develop her ideas for the open-response questions. There are three sessions for English/language arts, two for math, two each for science and history. The "long essay" had been done the week before.

Sarah is smiling, cautious but ready to work. Her parents and regular classroom teacher have prepped her well. She is a shy girl who is wary of making mistakes. It's a condition she is used to, and she compensates for it with a fixed smile and a feigned positive attitude. Her face is quite flushed as we begin.

The first reading selection is manageable, and she chooses to read silently. She can independently answer the comprehension questions, though I can see that there are many errors. The second exercise takes 45 minutes, the equivalent of a daily reading lesson together. Sarah's face reddens when she sees the next page, and deep sighs are audible. The next selection is a poem, and I estimate that she can read perhaps one out of four words. She reads silently and answers all the questions wrong. We can't fool Sarah anymore. She knows she doesn't know. And she knows that I know she doesn't know. This is so very humiliating.

Her eyes are wet now, but she's silent and stoic. I check in, and she reassures me she's fine. She appears to be on the verge of weeping, but she will not be deterred. I cannot help her in any way; I can only sit nearby and return a false smile. I can offer a break, nothing more. Later, I calculated the reading level of this selection. Sarah reads like a second-grader, and the poem is at the high end of the fifth- grade scale. Her eyes are now just scanning the paragraphs. I know she has stopped reading and is just glancing and gazing. It's meaningless, and it hurts. Yet she attempts to answer every question.

It is now 2½ hours, and my anger is growing. This is immoral and has become intolerable. This is professionally irresponsible. And it's only the first day.

That night my desire for dinner is gone, and I unload my frustrations on my understanding husband, long into the evening and night. How can I meet my professional obligations to my administrators and to the intent of the assessment, while meeting my obligations to nurture and support the development of these special young people? My priority is always the children. Maybe I should tell Sarah, "Just skip them. You tried, and this test is just too hard. Forget it. You tried." But this is not the way I teach. I would never approach a lesson with my students in this way. I always want them to give it their all. To compromise my values as a teacher hurts deeply.

Finally, I resolve to try a new plan, after discussing it with Sarah the next day. Having seen the next session of reading and noting that the reading levels are even higher, I commit to not having her experience a higher level of defeat and frustration. Sarah is paler today, and there are dark circles under her eyes for the first time. I know she will work another long day without complaint. We decide to skip all the sections except one. Together we select the easiest one, and she agrees to read it aloud to me. In this way she and I can be certain that she has really read the passage, rather than breezed over the text, pretending to read. Sarah is a conscientious student and tells me that she's worried what "they" will say if she doesn't read everything. I reassure her that "they" will like it if she does well on just this one.

Her reading is halting and labored. She struggles with words like *medium, altogether,* and *participate.* I can't help her, though her eyes seem to plead for my help. She pushes on, and her comprehension of the passage slips away. She is just going through a meaningless exercise. Sarah cannot read critical words, and she has no understanding of what she has just read. The multiple-choice questions follow. She reads them aloud and takes cautious guesses. The selections are random, and she gets only one out of eight correct.

Sarah has an organic, physiological disability, and the blind are being asked to see. Learning disabilities are invisible, and the board of education is requiring this reading-disabled young lady to read at grade level—in fact, above grade level. Does this make any sense to anyone?

I value this child, I support her struggle, and I am dedicated to her special form of education. But I participated in hurting Sarah. I took away a piece of her pride, her joys, and her dreams. I forced her to face the fact that she is less than normal and that she will be judged as such. She'll receive a letter in the early fall, just before the excitement of a new school year, that will state definitively that she is a "failure." It will arrive in her home mailbox, and like other children her age, she'll enjoy the anticipation of the daily mail and will open the letter that is addressed "To the Parents of Sarah B." She can't read the long sustained text, but she can read a graph. And the graph will show that small black bar at the bottom that designates "failing." Members of the board of education, how dare you do this to all these fine children? Or to 10? Or to one? How dare you!

·◄❦►·

I am sorry to say that I know this firsthand. Our disabled and complex son took the MCAS three years ago as an eighth-grader and boycotted it in his 10th-grade year. He was not about to be subjected to that experience ever again. It was not for a political statement as much as for the necessity of acting as responsible parents that we told the school to make other provisions for our son. He was not to take that test. However, three years ago, we knew less than we do now, and we allowed him to take the MCAS with our daily support and encouragement. His teacher fed him donuts and soft drinks to help secure his and his friends' compliance. Seven learning-disabled boys, reading at the third-grade level, took the eighth-grade MCAS and played along. Each day, our son would arrive home telling us he couldn't answer any of the questions. "I can't do any of it, Mom," I can still hear him say.

My son loves to walk our long rural driveway and deliver our mail to us each day. He can read "To the Parents of ...", and the day the letter arrived, he knew it was the MCAS results. It was too late for me to stop him. He scanned the text and read the graph. He threw an angry glare at me and tossed the wadded letter across the room. "I told you I was stupid!" he yelled. My heart broke, broke in pieces. How dare they do that to our son! After his years of holding his fragile self-esteem intact, of walking through that school door one more time and facing yet another day of being less able than everyone, the state board of education informs him that he's a failure.

Sarah is only one of my 24 students. That's a reasonable amount of students to attend to, but what the state board is asking of them is not reasonable. Sarah is privileged with intelligence and a healthy home. Not so for Mandy, who has cerebral palsy and mild retardation and who would not qualify for the alternative assessment. Not so for Cynthia, who isn't sure whether her mom will be home each night and who chews the skin off the tips of her fingers and has to have every direction repeated. She, too, won't qualify for the alternative assessment. How about D.C., whose dad is in prison and whose mom is a heroin addict? He lives with his mom in the local shelter, and as a third-grader he enjoyed shocking us by imitating a needle plunging into his arm. He reads three grade levels lower than his agemates, but still he has to take the MCAS. Paul is autistic and spins in his chair repeating TV commercials when he's stressed. He's very bright and reads years above his age level—but with no comprehension of what he just encountered. Sorry, he doesn't qualify for the alternative either.

And there are many more. They live in condos, raised ranches, tenements, and converted chicken coops. They play in city parks, cornfields, groomed soccer fields, and back alleys. They are your neighbors and your nieces—perhaps your own child. They are developmentally delayed, have attention deficits, are autistic, abused, and neglected. They have compulsive disorders, expressive language delays, and are scared about their fragile lives. Do I need to go on? Please make me stop because this is just the beginning, and their faces parade before me. And none of this makes any sense.

My disabled fourth-graders cannot take the MCAS in its present form. They still cannot read. There is a critical point in students' education when they go from learning to read to reading to learn. This typically takes place in the third or fourth grades. My students have not yet made that transition. For my fourth-graders, the present MCAS is a ridiculous waste of time, emotion, and self-esteem. By eighth grade, these same students may have made the basic reading transition, but their understandings will still be far behind those of their peers, and their progress will be at a decidedly slower pace. By eighth grade, the average disabled reader is probably reading at the third-grade level. By 10th grade, if their motivation can be sustained, they might achieve seventh or eighth-grade levels in reading. These children have a disability. Their brains don't work in the same way as yours and mine. More services will help, and we should always expect a little more for each of them. But let us be realistic: the disability won't go away, just as blindness, deafness, or cerebral palsy won't vanish.

However, with seventh- or eighth-grade reading skills, they can function in the world of work in many capacities. Remember, they are disabled readers—not disabled *people*. A specific learning disability is often accompanied by average or above-average intelligence and a host of strengths in such areas as spatial relationships, social perception, problem solving, fine motor coordination and dexterity, mechanical ability, aesthetic senses, and empathy and compassion. (The MCAS does not assess these skills for any student.) Reading is only one aspect of their abilities, only one tool for learning, only one portion of a developed human being. Young people with disabilities can graduate with the motivation to continue to learn on the job and from travel, television, discussions, cinema, and their family members and friends. They will be providing services in the fields of day care and hospitality and in medical reception and computer repair. They can be our police force, design our gardens, process our banking, and make the music we listen to. The possibilities are vast. But without a diploma and without self-esteem, none of these things will happen.

Are there any solutions? Yes, many. I would *not* recommend exemptions from such accountability measures as MCAS for disabled children. I am committed to equal access to public education. All students must be assessed, disabled and nondisabled. But changes in the current MCAS must be made.

Many teachers, parents, and advocates for disabled students have the answers. Just ask us. For starters, we could stop using the word "failure." Such language is powerful, but it is not productive. For standardized testing, let's use the Iowa Tests of Basic Skills, a shorter and easier test that is nationally normed. Revise the present MCAS, making it easier, and lower those inflated readability levels. Base this new MCAS on agreed-upon frameworks, and eliminate social studies and science. End the use of the single paper-and-pencil task as a determinant for graduation. Use broader, more diverse, and more authentic assessment techniques such as portfolios and videotaping. Assess students' multiple intelligences by means of projects, public speaking, or science fairs. Expand the criteria for the alternative assessment to include 80% of the disabled students, not just 1% to 3%. Maybe we should even try this broader view of assessment for *all students*. Now there's an idea!

On several occasions, I have been asked to ponder this question: Does the disabled student deserve the same diploma that the valedictorian receives? My response is, yes! The world of work will determine what the value of the diploma is. And the disabled student doesn't necessarily want the job that the valedictorian wants, and the valedictorian doesn't necessarily want the job that my disabled son seeks. However, without a diploma our son will not be able to be a landscaper—grooming people's lawns, paving their walkways, and advising them on proper fertilizer or drainage stone. The valedictorian has options for higher education in a four-year college and even for graduate-level work. The disabled student can enter the work force with basic knowledge and perhaps additional vocational skills from one of our state's fine technical high schools. That disabled student can continue his or her education at work or in a two or four-year college, with the support and understanding of peers, educational institutions, and employers.

If children are marked as "failures" at age 10, again at 14, and again at 16, their motivation will die, and they will spiral downward. They will be robbed of an education and marked forever as failures who have no worth. Surely, this is not what our state board of education intended. We must stop MCAS in its present form, before more harm is done.

Postcript.   In early September 2000, I sent this article to the then lieutenant governor of Massachusetts, Jane Swift. She immediately contacted me and came to my school to meet with me and my students. We had a lengthy discussion about what it is to be learning disabled and about the effects of the MCAS on these young learners. In addition to this meeting, hundreds of parents and educators across Massachusetts have voiced their opposition to the current MCAS.

As of spring [2001], the state allows a new set of "nonstandard accommodations." A teacher can now read the reading sections of the test to the student, and the student can dictate the "long essay" to the teacher to write down. The state tells us that if a student passes the 10th-grade MCAS with these "nonstandard accommodations," he or she will receive a diploma. I recognize this as an important step for disabled students but look forward to other critical revisions of the test.

POSTSCRIPT

Should Students With Disabilities Participate in High-Stakes Testing?

The furor over high-stakes testing is voiced on many fronts. Writer-lecturer Alfie Kohn regularly decries the unfairness of standardized testing, which he feels forces students into molds and plays a cruel game of rewards and punishments. Senator Paul Wellstone sees high-stakes tests as harsh punishment for all children, especially for those who live in poverty or have disabilities. He has proposed an amendment to the Elementary and Secondary Education Act Reauthorization, which would prohibit using the results of one single standardized test for high-stakes decisions.

Local legislators feel that high-stakes testing is essential to validate the impact of the billions of dollars spent on education reform and to guarantee that high school diplomas are meaningful. Federal legislators believe that participation of all students is essential to ensure that students with disabilities are not shunted aside and relegated to substandard educational programs.

A small number of legal suits have shed interesting light. In *Brookhart v. Illinois State Board of Education* (1983), the court ruled that students with disabilities could be held to the state standard of needing to pass a minimum competency test for graduation. However, the 18-month notice provided by Illinois was deemed to be too short to make up for the length of time that the students had not had access to the general curriculum.

The state of Oregon settled a class action suit brought by parents whose children with learning disabilities were not permitted to utilize accommodations that were a regular part of their educational program to take the test. The parents argued that without the accommodations, their children were unable to show what they know and can do. The state maintained that the accommodations compromised the test. However, the settlement agreement permitted the use of many of the accommodations that were used daily as part of the students' educational program.

Most students with disabilities do require some accommodations. Many teachers believe that these are fair ways for a student to participate. The National Center for Educational Outcomes (http://www.education.umn.edu/nceo), directed by Thurlow, conducts extensive studies of the appropriate use of accommodations, as well as nationwide practices with regards to the inclusion of students with disabilities in standardized testing. In *Testing Students With Disabilities: Practical Strategies for Complying With District and State Requirements* (1998), Thurlow, Elliott, and Ysseldyke provide a school-oriented guide to effective participation of students with disabilities on standardized tests.

Holbrook fears for her students' self-esteem and long-term future. She sees their potential sacrificed to standards that are too high for anyone to reach. Yet, at the close of her selection, she sees hope in the possibility of increased use of alternate assessments to show what students know and can do. This option, usually portfolio based, could permit some students to demonstrate grade level competence and earn their diploma.

What will happen to individual students who do not meet the individual expectations of high-stakes testing? Will they drop out of school in large numbers as soon as they see the bar as unattainably high? Will costs for special education skyrocket as those with disabilities stay in school, accessing their right to remain until they receive a diploma or turn 22?

How will employers and colleges react to applicants who have met local school requirements but have no diploma because they have not passed "The Test"? Will doors slam shut, or will individual characteristics be more important than test scores? Have IDEA97 and No Child Left Behind (NCLB) created an opportunity for all students to count or a demand that will have disastrous consequences, eliminating options for the very students they were designed to support?

Contributors to This Volume

EDITOR

MARYANN BYRNES is a practitioner and an academic in the field of special education. She is a member of the faculty of the Graduate School of Education at the University of Massachusetts–Boston, serving jointly in the teacher education and special education programs. Dr. Byrnes consults with schools and districts on issues of assessment, focusing on the effective participation of all students. Her other school-based activities include long-term consultation for system change, curriculum alignment, and staff development, as well as program and budget evaluation. She has taught at elementary, middle, high school, and graduate school levels, and is a past president of the Massachusetts Association of Administrators of Special Education (ASE). Dr. Byrnes earned her B.A. at the University of Chicago, her M.Ed. in learning disabilities at Northwestern University, and her Ed.D. in learning theory at Rutgers University. She has written numerous articles on standards-based instruction and assessment as well as special education finance.

STAFF

Larry Loeppke   Managing Editor
Jill Peter   Senior Developmental Editor
Nichole Altman   Developmental Editor
Lori Church   Permissions Coordinator
Beth Kundert   Production Manager
Jane Mohr   Project Manager
Kari Voss   Lead Typesetter
Craig Purcell   eContent Coordinator
Charles Vitelli   Cover Designer

AUTHORS

JAMES B. ADAMS is a father of a young girl with autism, diagnosed in 1994, and that is what led him to eventually shift much of his research emphasis to autism, focusing on biological causes and treatments. He is currently a Full Professor in the Department of Chemical and Materials Engineering at Arizona State University. He created and teaches a course on Heavy Metal Toxicity, focused on lead and mercury toxicity.

ARTHUR ALLEN is a Washington-area writer whose work appears in *The Washington Post* magazine, the *New Republic* and *Salon.com.*

LEWIS M. ANDREWS is Executive Director of the Yankee Institute for Public Policy Inc. at Trinity College, a Connecticut research and educational institute.

BEN BAHAN is a professor in and chair of the Department of Deaf Studies, with a joint appointment in the Department of ASL, Linguistics, and Interpretation, at Gallaudet University in Washington, D.C. The recipient of the President's Distinguished Faculty Award for 2001, he is also vice president of DawnSignPress in San Diego, California, and co-investigator for the American Sign Language Linguistic Research Project. He earned his Ph.D. in applied linguistics from Boston University in 1996, and he is coauthor of *The Syntax of American Sign Language: Functional Categories and Hierarchical Structure* (MIT Press, 2000).

RICHARD A. BAKER, JR., is a middle school teacher at Hurst Middle School in the St. Charles Parish Public Schools.

THOMAS BALKANY is the Hotchkiss Professor in and vice chairman of the Department of Otolaryngology in the University of Miami School of Medicine. Board certified by the American Board of Otolaryngology, he earned his M.D. from the University of Miami in 1972. His interests include otology, neurotology, and cochlear implants, and he is coeditor, with Nigel R. T. Pashley, of *Clinical Pediatric Otolaryngology* (Mosby, 1986).

DR. RUSSELL BARKLEY is the Director of Psychology and Professor of Psychiatry and Neurology at the University of Massachusetts Medical Center, and has written 14 books and more than 150 scientific articles related to the nature, assessment and treatment of AD/HD. As the leading expert on the subject, he speaks eloquently and passionately about the need to recognize the complexities of the disorder and to treat it properly.

SHELDON BERMAN is superintendent of the Hudson Public Schools in Massachusetts. He is on the board of directors of the Compact for Learning and Citizenship, and he is a founder and former president of Educators for Social Responsibility. He is the author of numerous articles and the book *Children's Social Consciousness and the Development of Social Responsibility* (New York Press, 1997).

TOM BERTLING is an author who has been hearing-impaired since age five. Among his books are *No Dignity for Joshua: More Vital Insight Into Deaf Children, Deaf Education, and Deaf Culture* (Kodiak Media Group, 1997) and *An Intellectual Look at American Sign Language: Clear Thinking on*

American Sign Language, English and Deaf Education (Kodiak Media Group, 2001), which he edited.

FREDERICK J. BRIGHAM is an assistant professor of special education in the Department of Curriculum, Instruction, and Special Education at the Curry School of Education of the University of Virginia. He has also taught at Dickinson State College and served as director of special education for the West River Special Education Unit in Dickinson, North Dakota. He earned his M.Ed. from Bowling Green State University in 1983 and his Ph.D. from Purdue University in 1992.

PAUL D. CALALUCE, JR., is the principal of Humiston School and director of Pupil Personnel Services for the Cheshire Public Schools in Cheshire, Connecticut.

GARY M. CHESLEY is the superintendent of the Bethel Public Schools in Bethel, Connecticut.

CHRISTOPHER T. CROSS is a Senior Fellow at the Center for Education Policy and a Distinguished Senior Fellow at the Education Commission of the States. During his 32 years in Washington, D.C., he served in both the executive and legislative branches, as an assistant secretary at the U.S. Department of Education, the Republican staff director of the House Committee on Education and Labor, and a deputy assistant secretary in the old Department of Health, Education and Welfare.

SCOT DANFORTH is an assistant professor in the Department of Behavioral Studies at the University of Missouri–St. Louis. He has also taught at the University of South Florida, and he is cofounder of the Disability Studies in Education Special Interest Group of the American Educational Research Association. He earned his M.Ed. from the University of North Carolina, Chapel Hill, in 1987 and his Ph.D. from the University of South Florida in 1994. He is coauthor, with Joseph R. Boyle, of *Cases in Special Education*, 2d ed. (McGraw-Hill, 2001) and *Cases in Behavior Management* (Merrill, 2000).

LAWRENCE H. DILLER practices behavioral pediatrics in Walnut Creek, California. He is an assistant clinical professor at the University of California and the author of *Running on Ritalin: A Physician Reflects on Children, Society, and Performance in a Pill* (Bantam, 1998).

STEPHEN EDELSON, M.D., has practiced medicine for more than 20 years. As an autoimmune specialist and founder of the Edelson Center for Environmental and Preventative Medicine in Atlanta, he has successfully treated thousands of patients using innovative and effective alternative therapies. Dr. Edelson lives and works in Atlanta, Georgia.

ALAN GARTNER is a professor of educational psychology and dean of research in the Graduate School and University Center at the City University of New York. He has published a number of books, including *Inclusion and School Reform: Transforming America's Classrooms*, coauthored with Dorothy Kerzner Lipsky (P. H. Brookes, 1997).

MICHAEL F. GIANGRECO is a research associate professor in the Center of Disability and Community Inclusion at the University of Vermont. His professional interests focus on how to plan, adapt, coordinate, implement, and evaluate educational programs and services for students with disabilities who are included in general education classrooms. He is the author of *Ants in His Pants: Absurdities and Realities of Special Education* (Peytral, 1998) and *Vermont Interdependent Services Team Approach: A Guide to Coordinating Educational Support Services* (P. H. Brookes, 1996).

LARRY S. GOLDMAN is an associate professor of clinical psychiatry at the University of Chicago in Chicago, Illinois. He is also a member of the Council on Scientific Affairs of the American Medical Association.

KENNETH W. GOODMAN is founder of the Forum for Bioethics and Philosophy at the University of Miami, where he is currently director of the Bioethics Program. He also holds appointments in the university's Department of Medicine, Department of Philosophy, School of Nursing, and Department of Epidemiology and Public Health. He has written extensively about science, medicine, and science policy, and he is coauthor, with James G. Anderson, of *Ethics and Information Technology: A Case-Based Approach to a Health Care System in Transition* (Springer, 2002).

DANIEL P. HALLAHAN is a professor of education in and chair of the Department of Curriculum, Instruction, and Special Education at the University of Virginia in Charlottesville, Virginia. He earned his Ph.D. in a combined program in education and psychology from the University of Michigan in 1971, and received the Council for Exceptional Children Research Award in 2000. Among his many publications is *Exceptional Learners: Introduction to Special Education,* 8th ed., coauthored with J. M. Kauffman (Allyn & Bacon, 2000).

FREDERICK M. HESS is an assistant professor of education and government at the University of Virginia in Charlottesville, Virginia. He is the author of *Spinning Wheels: The Politics of Urban School Reform* (Brookings Institution Press, 1999) and *Bringing the Social Sciences Alive* (Allyn & Bacon, 1999).

ANNELLE V. HODGES is an associate professor and chief of audiology in the Department of Otolaryngology at the University of Miami School of Medicine. Her clinical interests include cochlear implants, deaf education, and audiology, and her current research focuses on objective methods of setting cochlear implants in infants and small children. She earned her Ph.D. from the University of Virginia.

ROBERT HOFFMEISTER is an associate professor of education and director of the Center for the Study of Communication and Deafness at the Boston University School of Education. His research has focused on the acquisition of American Sign Language (ASL) by Deaf children, Deaf people as a bilingual/bicultural minority group, and other areas related to the Deaf culture. He holds an M.Ed. from the University of Arizona and a Ph.D. from the University of Minnesota.

PIXIE J. HOLBROOK is a special education teacher for the Northampton Public Schools in Massachusetts and a private consultant. She has worked in public and private education in Connecticut and Massachusetts for 30 years, teaching and advocating for children with special needs in urban, suburban, and rural settings.

KAY S. HYMOWITZ is a senior fellow at the Manhattan Institute and a contributing editor of *City Journal*. She writes extensively on education and childhood in America. Ms. Hymowitz has also written for many major publications including *The New York Times, The Washington Post, The Wall Street Journal, The New Republic, New York Newsday, The Public Interest, Commentary, Dissent,* and *Tikkun*. A native of Philadelphia, Hymowitz received a B.A. magna cum laude with honors in English and American literature from Brandeis University, an M.A. in English literature from Tufts University, and a Masters of Philosophy from Columbia University. Before becoming a full-time freelance writer, she taught English literature and composition at Brooklyn College and Parsons School of Design.

JERRY JESNESS is a special education teacher at Las Yescas Elementary School in Los Fresnos, Texas. His extensive writings on many aspects of education have appeared in such publications as *Principal, Reason,* and *Teacher*.

K. FORBIS JORDAN is a professor emeritus in the Department of Educational Leadership and Policy Studies at Arizona State University. He is coauthor, with L. Dean Webb and Arlene Metha, of *Foundation of American Education*, 3rd ed. (Prentice Hall PTR, 1999).

TERESA S. JORDAN is an associate professor in and chair of the Department of Educational Leadership at the University of Las Vegas, where she has been teaching since 1990. She has also served as director of research and evaluation in a large Arizona school district and as head of a private consulting firm that provided staff development and special education support services to public school systems, private school administrators, speech-language pathologists, and special education early childhood teachers. Her policy and research expertise is in public school finance, particularly funding for special-needs youth, state-level educational accountability systems, and school improvement programs. She holds an M.S. in communication disorders and a Ph.D. in educational leadership and policy studies from Arizona State University.

JAMES M. KAUFFMAN is the Charles S. Robb Professor of Education at the University of Virginia in Charlottesville, Virginia, where he also serves as director of the doctoral program in special education. His primary areas of interest in special education are emotional and behavioral disorders and learning disabilities. He is coeditor of *Behavioral Disorders*, the journal of the Council for Children with Behavioral Disorders, and he is coprincipal investigator of the Center of Minority Research in Special Education (COMRISE). Among his many publications are *Characteristics of Emotional and Behavioral Disorders of Children and Youth*, 7th ed. (Prentice Hall PTR, 2000) and *The Least Restrictive Environment: Its Origins and Interpretations*

416   CONTRIBUTORS

in Special Education, coauthored with Jean B. Crockett (Lawrence Erlbaum, 1999). He received his M.Ed. in teaching in the elementary school from Washburn University in 1966 and his Ed.D. in special education from the University of Kansas in 1969.

REX KNOWLES is a retired college professor living in Claremont, California.

TRUDY KNOWLES is an associate professor of education at Westfield State College in Westfield, Massachusetts, where she helps coordinate the middle-level education program. She is actively involved in the education of young adolescents through her work in local schools, the Commonwealth of Massachusetts Middle-Level Educators, the New England League of Middle Schools, and the National Middle School Association. She is coauthor, with David F. Brown, of *What Every Middle School Teacher Should Know* (Heinemann, 2000).

HARLAN LANE is the University Distinguished Professor in the Department of Psychology at Northeastern University in Boston, Massachusetts, where he specializes in speech, language, deafness, and Deaf culture, and a research affiliate in the Research Laboratory of Electronics at the Massachusetts Institute of Technology. He has also taught at Université de Paris VII, Harvard Medical School, and the University of California, San Diego. He earned his M.A. from Columbia University in 1958 and his Ph.D. from Harvard University in 1960. His publications include *The Mask of Benevolence: Disabling the Deaf Community*, exp. ed. (DawnSignPress, 1999) and *When the Mind Hears: A History of the Deaf* (DIANE, 1998).

MARK LEVINE works in the Behavioral Counseling and Research Center of the California Department of Education and is on the board roster of the California Association for Behavior Analysis, a statewide organization that represents and promotes the interests of the behavior analysis profession.

DOROTHY KERZNER LIPSKY is director of the National Center on Educational Restructuring and Inclusion at the City University of New York. She is the author of *Inclusion and School Reform: Transforming America's Classrooms* (Paul H. Brookes, 1997).

DANIEL J. LOSEN is a research associate with The Civil Rights Project at Harvard University and the principal investigator for the Conference on Minority Issues in Special Education. He is presently developing research and policy fact sheets for members of Congress on the topics of Dropouts and Title I of the Elementary and Secondary School Act. Before becoming an attorney, he taught in public schools for nearly 10 years, including work as a founder of an alternative public school.

SUSAN UNOK MARKS, a project staff member of SRI International, is currently on the advisory panel for the Special Education Elementary Longitudinal Study (SEELS), a project funded by the Office of Special Education Programs. She is coauthor, with Russell M. Gersten and Scott K. Baker, of *Teaching English-Language Learners With Learning Difficulties: Guiding Principles and Examples for Research-Based Practice* (Council for Exceptional Children, 1999).

BARBARA MINER is managing editor of the Milwaukee-based newspaper *Rethinking Schools* and has two children in the Milwaukee Public Schools. She recently co-edited the book *Failing Our Kids: Why the Testing Craze Won't Fix Our Schools.*

NATIONAL ASSOCIATION OF THE DEAF (NAD) is a private, nonprofit organization that works to safeguard the accessibility and civil rights of 28 million deaf and hard of hearing Americans in education, employment, health care, and telecommunications. Headquartered in Silver Spring, Maryland, the NAD's programs and activities include grassroots advocacy and empowerment, captioned media, the certification of American Sign Language professionals, legal assistance, policy development and research, and youth leadership development.

NATIONAL COUNCIL ON DISABILITY (NCD) is an independent federal agency that makes recommendations to the president and Congress on issues affecting 54 million Americans with disabilities. The NCD is composed of 15 members appointed by the president and confirmed by the Senate. The NCD's overall purpose is to promote policies, programs, practices, and procedures that guarantee equal opportunity for all individuals with disabilities, regardless of the nature or severity of the disability, and to empower individuals with disabilities to achieve economic self-sufficiency, independent living, and inclusion and integration into all aspects of society.

GARY ORFIELD is a professor at the Harvard Graduate School of Education and Director of its Project on School Desegregation. His report, "The Growth of Segregation in American Schools: Changing Patterns of Separation and Poverty since 1968" was recently issued to the National School Board Association.

BERNARD RIMLAND is a research psychologist (Ph.D.) and a Director of the Autism Research Institute, which he founded in 1967. He is also the founder of the Autism Society of America (1965), and the editor of the *Autism Research Review International.* His book, *Infantile Autism: The Syndrome and Its Implication for a Neural Theory of Behavior* (1964) is widely credited with changing the field of psychiatry from its claim that autism is an emotional illness, caused by destructive mothers, to its current recognition that autism is a biological disorder.

CARL SCHRADER works in the Behavioral Counseling and Research Center of the California Department of Education.

SUSAN SHAPIRO-BARNARD is a lecturer in education at the University of New Hampshire in Durham, New Hampshire. She is also affiliated with the university's Institute on Disability, for which she has coauthored a number of booklets and manuals.

JEFFREY R. SPRAGUE is codirector of the Institute on Violence and Destructive Behavior at the University of Oregon. He is a nationally recognized researcher on school-based violence prevention, severe behavior disorders, functional behavioral assessment, positive behavioral support, and school safety.

JOHN PAUL STEVENS is an associate justice of the U.S. Supreme Court. He worked in law firms in Chicago, Illinois, for 20 years before being nominated by President Richard Nixon to the U.S. Court of Appeals in 1970. He served in that capacity until he was nominated to the Supreme Court by President Gerald Ford in 1975.

JAMES A. TAYLOR, Sr., J.D., Ph.D., retired from St. Charles Parish Public School District, Louisiana, as Director of Middle Schools and teaches at Dillard University.

CLARENCE THOMAS is an associate justice of the U.S. Supreme Court. A former judge on the U.S. Court of Appeals for the District of Columbia, he was nominated by President George Bush to the Supreme Court in 1991. He received his J.D. from the Yale University School of Law in 1974.

MARTHA L. THURLOW is director of the National Center on Educational Outcomes, where she addresses the implications of contemporary U.S. policy and practice for students with disabilities. She has conducted research involving special education for the past 25 years in a variety of areas, including assessment and decision making, learning disabilities, early childhood education, and integration of students with disabilities in general education settings. She has authored or coauthored numerous books, including *Improving Test Performance of Students With Disabilities: On District and State Assessments,* coauthored with Judy L. Elliott (Corwin Press, 2000), and she has published more than 200 articles and reports. In 1995 she assumed the position of coeditor of *Exceptional Children,* the research journal of the Council for Exceptional Children.

HILL M. WALKER is a professor in and codirector of the Institute on Violence and Destructive Behavior at the University of Oregon and director of the Center on Human Development. He is an international leader in the assessment and treatment of antisocial behavior. Among his publications is *Making Schools Safer and Violence Free: Critical Issues, Solutions and Recommended Practices,* coauthored with Michael H. Epstein (PRO-ED, 2001).

CAROLYN A. WEINER is president of Syndactics, Inc., in Phoenix, Arizona. She is coauthor, with Judith M. Creighton and Teresa S. Lyons, of *K-TALK: Kindergarten Teacher-Administered Language Kit* (Communication Skill Builders, 1989).

Index